AMERICAN STUDIES – A MONOGRAPH SERIES
Volume 226

Edited on behalf
of the German Association
for American Studies by
REINHARD R. DOERRIES
GERHARD HOFFMANN
ALFRED HORNUNG

SEBASTIAN HOEPFNER

Jewish Organizations in Transatlantic Perspective

Patterns of Contemporary Jewish Politics
in Germany and the United States

Universitätsverlag
WINTER
Heidelberg

Bibliografische Information der Deutschen Nationalbibliothek
Die Deutsche Nationalbibliothek verzeichnet diese Publikation
in der Deutschen Nationalbibliografie;
detaillierte bibliografische Daten sind im Internet
über *http://dnb.d-nb.de* abrufbar.

Zugl.: Passau, Univ., Diss., 2012

ISBN 978-3-8253-6073-3

Dieses Werk einschließlich aller seiner Teile ist urheberrechtlich geschützt.
Jede Verwertung außerhalb der engen Grenzen des Urheberrechtsgesetzes
ist ohne Zustimmung des Verlages unzulässig und strafbar. Das gilt insbesondere für Vervielfältigungen, Übersetzungen, Mikroverfilmungen und
die Einspeicherung und Verarbeitung in elektronischen Systemen.

© 2012 Universitätsverlag Winter GmbH Heidelberg
Imprimé en Allemagne · Printed in Germany
Druck: Memminger MedienCentrum, 87700 Memmingen

Gedruckt auf umweltfreundlichem, chlorfrei gebleichtem
und alterungsbeständigem Papier

Den Verlag erreichen Sie im Internet unter:
www.winter-verlag.de

Contents

List of Abbreviations ix
List of Tables xi
Note on Citation xii
Acknowledgements xiv

PART ONE: THE INTELLECTUAL TERRAIN   1

1 Introduction: Jews, Jewish Organizations and "Jewish Politics"   1

2 Methodology and Empirical Evidence   5
   2.1   Interviews   5
   2.2   Archival Collections   7

3 Plan of the Dissertation   9

4 Review of the Literature   11
   4.1   Jewish Organizations in Horizontal and Vertical
         Perspectives   13
       4.1.1   Horizontal Perspective: the Polity   14
       4.1.2   Vertical Perspective: Politics and Policy   16
   4.2   Summary   23

5 Theoretical Background   25
   5.1   Jewish Political Studies and Perspectives for Analysis   25
       5.1.1   Origins of the Field   25
       5.1.2   Perspectives for Analysis: Functional, Historical,
              Differential   27
   5.2   The Politics of Jewish Organizations: a Political Science
         Perspective   31
       5.2.1   Politics, Power, and Political Science   31
       5.2.2   Horizontal and Vertical Relationships of Power   34
   5.3   Summary   44

PART TWO: JEWISH ORGANIZATIONS IN THE UNITED STATES — 47

1. Postwar Trends in American Jewry — 49
   1.1 From Integrationism to Survivalism — 50
   1.2 A Divided Community — 54
   1.3 "Political Judaism" and Israel Advocacy in the United States — 59

2. Society-Centered Politics in the United States: Fragmentation and Competition — 65
   2.1 Interest Group System and Current Trends — 65
   2.2 Governmental System and the Practice of Interest Mediation — 68

3. Political Implications for Jewish Organizations: a Pattern of Self-Governance — 71
   3.1 Communal Organization — 71
   3.2 The Issue of Duplication — 72
   3.3 Consensus and Marginalization — 75

4. Typologies of American Jewish Organizations — 79
   4.1 Overview and General Typologies — 79
   4.2 A Process-Oriented Typology of Jewish Political Organizations — 81

5. Modern Jewish Politics — 85
   5.1 The "Big Three" Jewish Defense Organizations — 85
     5.1.1 The American Jewish Committee — 86
     5.1.2 The Anti-Defamation League — 100
     5.1.3 The American Jewish Congress — 111
   5.2 Umbrellas — 121
     5.2.1 The Jewish Council for Public Affairs — 122
     5.2.2 The Conference of Presidents of Major American Jewish Organizations — 137
     5.2.3 The Conference on Jewish Material Claims Against Germany — 155
   5.3 Summary — 181

6. New Jewish Politics — 185

6.1	American Israel Public Affairs Committee		185
	6.1.1 Founding History and Internal Structure		185
	6.1.2 Political Style: Horizontal and Vertical Politics		190
	6.1.3 Summary		221
6.2	J Street		222
	6.2.1 Founding History and Internal Structure		222
	6.2.2 Political Style: Horizontal and Vertical Politics		227
6.3	Summary		240

7 Summary 243

PART THREE: THE CENTRAL COUNCIL OF JEWS IN GERMANY 245

1 Postwar Trends in German Jewry 247
  1.1 Overview of German Jewry Today 247
  1.2 Jewish Immigration to Germany After 1989 250
  1.3 Comparison with German Jewry After 1945 255

2 State-Centered Politics in Germany: Partnership and Dependency 259
  2.1 Institutional Factors: Neo-Corporatism and *Einheitsgemeinden* 259
  2.2 Non-Institutional Factors: Issues and Financial Support 262

3 An Imperfect "Special Relationship" 265
  3.1 *Wiedergutmachung* and Re-Nazification 265
  3.2 Bitburg Controversy and Börneplatz Scandal 267
  3.3 Public Opinion and the "Special Relationship" 271

4 The Political Style of the Central Council of Jews in Germany 277
  4.1 Founding History and Internal Structure 278
  4.2 Modesty and Self-Restraint 283
  4.3 "A Group of Exotic People" 288
  4.4 "Loyalty" and Patriotism 292
  4.5 Personal Politics: Portraits of the Presidents of the Central Council 297
    4.5.1 Heinz Galinski 298
    4.5.2 Herbert Lewin 301

4.5.3		Werner Nachmann	303
4.5.4		Ignatz Bubis	305
4.5.5		Paul Spiegel	308
4.5.6		Charlotte Knobloch	309
4.5.7		Dieter Graumann	312

5 Why the State Always Wins 315
   5.1   "Establishmentization" 315
   5.2   Instrumentalization and Alibi Politics 318
   5.3   "Exculpatory Witnesses" – German Unification and the
        Central Council 322

6 Summary 331

PART FOUR: CONCLUSIONS AND PERSPECTIVES FOR
                RESEARCH 333

List of Author Interviews and Conversations 343
Archival Collections 346
Bibliography 348

List of Abbreviations

ACJ	American Council for Judaism
ACLU	American Civil Liberties Union
ADL	Anti-Defamation League
AFSI	Americans for a Safe Israel
AIPAC	American Israel Public Affairs Committee
AJC	American Jewish Committee
AJCongress	American Jewish Congress
API	Americans for Progressive Israel
APN	Americans for Peace Now
AZC	American Zionist Council
BEG	Bundesentschädigungsgesetz
BMF	Bundesministerium der Finanzen
CDU	Christlich Demokratische Union Deutschlands
CEEF	Central Eastern and European Fund
CIPAC	Christians' Israel Public Action Campaign
CJH	Center for Jewish History
CJP	Combined Jewish Philanthropies
COH	Center for Oral History
CRC	Community Relations Council
CRIF	Conseil Représentatif des Institutions juives de France
CSU	Christlich-Soziale Union in Bayern
CUFI	Christians United for Israel
C.V.	Centralverein deutscher Staatsbürger jüdischen Glaubens
D-	Democrat (followed by abbreviation of home state)
DPs	displaced persons
EVZ	Stiftung "Erinnerung, Verantwortung und Zukunft"
FDP	Freie Demokratische Partei
FSU	former Soviet Union
GDP	Gross Domestic Product
GDR	German Democratic Republic
GOP	Grand Old Party, Republican Party

H.R.	designation for bills introduced in U.S. House of Representatives
JCC	Conference on Jewish Material Claims Against Germany
JCPA	Jewish Council for Public Affairs
JCRC	Jewish Community Relations Council
JDL	Jewish Defense League
Jg.	Jahrgang (year)
JLC	Jewish Labor Committee
JPL	Jewish Peace Lobby
JTA	Jewish Telegraphic Agency
LBI	Leo Baeck Institute
n/a	not applicable
NCRAC	National Community Relations Advisory Council
NJA	New Jewish Agenda
NJCRAC	National Jewish Community Relations Advisory Council
NJDC	National Jewish Democratic Council
NPR	National Public Radio
Nr.	Nummer (number)
NYPL	The New York Public Library
OU	Union of Orthodox Jewish Congregations of America
PAC	political action committee
PLO	Palestine Liberation Organization
R-	Republican (followed by abbreviation of home state)
RJC	Republican Jewish Coalition
SFVV	Stiftung Flucht, Vertreibung, Versöhnung
SPD	Sozialdemokratische Partei Deutschlands
UJC	United Jewish Communities
UPJ	Union progressiver Juden in Deutschland
USCJ	United Synagogue of Conservative Judaism
WINEP	Washington Institute for Near East Policy
WIZO	Women's International Zionist Organization
WRV	Weimarer Reichsverfassung
ZOA	Zionist Organization of America
ZWST	Zentralwohlfahrtsstelle der Juden in Deutschland

List of Tables

Table 1:	Overview of American Jewish Organizations, General Typology	79
Table 2:	Comparison of "Big Three" Jewish Defense Organizations, Main Features	121
Table 3:	Comparison of Largest American Jewish Umbrellas, Main Features	181
Table 4:	Reasons for Close U.S.-Israeli Relations, Survey of Public Opinion	205
Table 5:	Comparison of AIPAC and J Street, Main Features	241
Table 6:	Geographical Distribution of Jews in Germany, Affiliated Members	249
Table 7:	Jewish Population in Germany, 1871-1989	254
Table 8:	Growth of Jewish Communities in Germany From 1990 to 2008, Affiliated Members	255
Table 9:	Central Council of Jews in Germany, Main Features, in 2010	297
Table 10:	Chairmen/Presidents of the Central Council of Jews in Germany, Terms of Office	298

Note on Citation

Since this dissertation relies on a variety of sources, both primary and secondary, choices had to be made in terms of a coherent citation method. Primary sources such as annual reports, pamphlets, internal memoranda or correspondences are quoted in full at every single entry, including the library call number where applicable, e.g. Conference on Jewish Material Claims Against Germany, *2007 Annual Report with 2008 Highlights* (New York: Claims Conference, 2008), or: Morris J. Amitay, Memorandum to I. L. Kenen, September 12, 1974, CJH Archives P-680, #3-32. In order to facilitate the retrieval of archival sources such as periodicals or other material stored on microfilms, these documents are cited as they appear in their original form and in which they are usually referred to on library call slips, e.g. Heinz Galinski, "Neutralität hat Grenzen", *Allgemeine jüdische Wochenzeitung*, 28. Jg. Nr. 46, November 16, 1973, or: Robert S. Rifkind and David A. Harris, Letter to Members, January 28, 1998, AJC Blaustein Library.

The author interviews conducted for this dissertation are cited in full and then abbreviated at every subsequent entry, e.g. Interview with Charlotte Knobloch, President, Zentralrat der Juden in Deutschland, September 1, 2009, Munich, and henceforth: Knobloch (2009 Interview). Recordings (if applicable) and transcripts of the interviews are available upon request from the author. Interviews cited from oral history collections were quoted according to the respective guidelines of the New York Public Library and the Columbia University Center for Oral History, e.g. Interview with Gary Rubin, November 12, 1990, The New York Public Library-American Jewish Committee Oral History Collection, Dorot Jewish Division, The New York Public Library, Astor, Lenox and Tilden Foundations, 135-136, or: Reminiscences of Isaiah L. Kenen (June 2, 1975), Ethnic Groups and American Foreign Policy Project, page 2 in the Columbia University Center for Oral History Collection. Permission to cite, quote or reproduce is generally required (and was granted) by Columbia University.

The bibliography comprises secondary sources such as monographs, theses, book chapters, and encyclopedia and scholarly articles. Scholarly articles in journals are cited by author, title, volume, number, date of publication, and relevant page(s), e.g. Daniel J. Elazar, "Jewish Political Studies", *Modern Judaism* 11:1 (February 1991), 67-90. Newspaper and magazine articles are cited in footnotes only, with the date of publication, and marked as online sources where applicable, e.g. Michael Massing, "The Storm over the Israel Lobby", *The New York Review of Books* (online), June 8, 2006. All other online sources are quoted with the entire URL and date of access.

All Hebrew terms are transcribed according to the system set forth by the *Encyclopaedia Judaica*, which may occasionally entail differences from the German spelling, e.g. Chaim Yahil instead of Chaim Yachil in German.

All translations from the German are my own unless otherwise specified. Of course, I bear full responsibility for all the mistakes and possible mistranslations.

Acknowledgements

Writing a dissertation is a rare privilege indeed. As these lines are written, nearly 800 million adults worldwide are still deprived of basic literacy skills, according to a recent study by the United Nations Educational, Scientific and Cultural Organization – a fact that makes me all the more appreciative of the contributions of the individuals and institutions that have chosen to support my work over the past few years.

To begin with, I would like to thank the Bavarian American Academy and the Harvard Club of Munich, whose generosity allowed me to spend a semester at Harvard University. I am particularly indebted to Professor Dr. Dr. h.c. Karl Kaiser, a political scientist specializing in transatlantic relations and international affairs, for kindly inviting me to Harvard as well as for the many helpful hints in the initial stages of this project. Likewise, I have benefited greatly from an extended stay in New York, one of the world's most vibrant centers of Jewish life, where I had the opportunity to pursue my research at Columbia University's Institute for Israel and Jewish Studies. I am most thankful to Professor Dr. Jeremy Dauber, a scholar of Yiddish language, literature, and culture, who not only made this stay possible, but who also offered me the chance to fully participate in the scholarly exchange at the Institute.

I further extend my deep gratitude to the Studienstiftung des deutschen Volkes (German National Academic Foundation) for its outstanding and generous support throughout this project. As a Leo Baeck Fellow, I had the good fortune to receive valuable feedback as well as some provocative comments in the graduate seminars held in Sussex and Berlin. Central ideas of this dissertation were also discussed at the Annual Graduate Conference in Political Science, International Relations and Public Policy at the Hebrew University of Jerusalem, which provided an equally propitious forum for debate.

Of course, this study could neither have materialized without the support of the many representatives of Jewish organizations in Germany and the United States who took the time to grant me lengthy interviews despite tight schedules and provided me with a firsthand view of their organizations. Various experts in the field, conversations with whom are referenced in the annex of this dissertation, have shared with me their thoughts on the topic. I thank all of them for their interest and dedication.

Nothing is more valuable in academia than independence and freedom of research. This is why I owe a special debt to my thesis advisors at the University of Passau, Professor Dr. Winand Gellner, a political scientist who specializes in German and American politics, and Professor Dr. Karsten Fitz, an Americanist with an interest in the study of minority cultures. I thank both of them for encouraging me to pursue this interdisciplinary project to a large part outside of Germany, and thus beyond their immediate supervision, as well as for granting me the necessary academic freedom to complete it. Moreover, I would like to express my gratitude to the Bavarian State Ministry of Sciences, Research and the Arts for supporting the publication of this dissertation with a grant from the Oskar Karl Forster Foundation.

Last but not least, this book is dedicated to my parents.

Part One: The Intellectual Terrain

The first part of this dissertation on "Jewish Organizations in Transatlantic Perspective: Patterns of Contemporary Jewish Politics in Germany and the United States" is intended to introduce the subject and delineate its scope. Following a note on methodology and the gathered empirical evidence, it proceeds with a plan of the dissertation before turning to a review of the literature. In addition, it develops a theoretical framework suggesting various axes for analysis as well as a political science approach to the study of Jewish organizations, which can then be applied empirically in the subsequent chapters.

1 Introduction: Jews, Jewish Organizations and "Jewish Politics"

From Max Liebermann to Marc Chagall, from Felix Mendelssohn to Arnold Schoenberg, from Heinrich Heine to Philip Roth – much has been made, and perhaps justifiably so, of the Jewishness of these outstanding artists and the manifold ways in which it may have influenced their works. Accordingly, we have grown accustomed to an array of expressions that carry the related epithet – be it Jewish culture, Jewish art, Jewish literature or Jewish humor, to name but a few of the most prominent examples. The usage of these terms is well-established, and rarely warrants adverse comments or further scrutiny; like many other terms, they have become part of our everyday language. At the same time, however, to draw a similar parallel with regard to the Jewish political experience is far less self-evident. The evocative question whether there is such a thing that can arguably be qualified as "Jewish politics" is one that yet remains to be addressed and examined in a systematic fashion; and while it is a question that promises to generate spirited scholarly debate in both political science and the field of Jewish studies, it also serves as the impetus and overarching interest of the present dissertation.[1]

This is a study of the most important contemporary Jewish political organizations in Germany and the United States. Its main theoretical and empirical ambition is to describe and explain, by means of a contrastive analysis, how Jewish organizations operate in what shall be termed a state-centered and a society-centered model of politics. At the most basic level, it argues that the underlying institutional logic of the polity has a decisive impact on the politics of these organizations; that Jewish organizations evince substantial differences in terms of their mission, operations, and political styles, both across and within the countries here under review; and that the term Jewish politics, though generally to be used with great caution, can still be fruitfully applied to certain, limited cases.

In order to allow for systematic comparison, this analysis centers on the horizontal and vertical politics of Jewish organizations. While the latter refers to the interaction between Jewish organizations and the state, the former is concerned with the issue of cooperation and conflict between Jewish organizations themselves as well as with their coalitional behavior towards non-Jewish interest groups. As part of our study, we will also briefly cover the founding histories and internal structure of the organizations in question and give a concise overview of the respective decision-making processes, finances, membership, and issue priorities.

A few remarks on what this dissertation is not about may likewise be in order. For starters, it is important to reiterate that our focus is exclusively on major Jewish political organizations. The vast number of synagogues, educational and cultural institutions, or Jewish philanthropic organizations, all of which contribute significantly to the vibrancy of Jewish life especially in the United States, had therefore to be omitted, as were Jewish political organizations that only play a marginal role in both countries. In the American case, we will review various individual and umbrella organizations: the American Jewish Committee, the Anti-Defamation League, the American Jewish Congress, the American Israel

---

[1] This is especially true in light of the abundant academic literature on ethnic and religious politics, which has included research areas such as Latino politics, Black politics, or the politics of the Christian Right, among others. See chapter 4, review of the literature, in the first part of this dissertation.

Public Affairs Committee, and J Street, as well as the Jewish Council for Public Affairs, the Conference of Presidents of Major American Jewish Organizations, and the Conference on Jewish Material Claims Against Germany. In the German case, we focus on the Central Council of Jews in Germany, the country's single most important Jewish (umbrella) organization.

Nor are Jewish organizations located within the larger debate on the influence of an alleged "Israel lobby". While the notion of such a unified network is by itself questionable (and, as we shall see, empirically invalid), it also includes a variety of actors other than Jewish organizations that lie beyond the scope of our investigation. Rather than subscribe to the convenient mode of collectivist thinking, then, the kind of analysis proposed here takes a decidedly disaggregated view of Jewish organizations.

It should also be said that it is not our intention to provide a historical account of the politics of Jewish organizations. Though extensive use is made of archival sources and oral history collections, this study does not trace the political activities of Jewish organizations in chronological order or over a fixed period of time. Special attention is however devoted to the Central Council's role during a decisive moment in German history: the fall of the Berlin Wall and the unfolding process of German unification.

The present study furthermore hopes to offer fresh insights through the adoption of a transatlantic perspective as opposed to a comparison of two random countries. The selection of cases – Jewish organizations in the U.S. and in the Federal Republic – is made in light of the demographic and political significance of the respective Jewish communities. Both are exceptional in their own way: while American Jewry is rivaled in numbers only by the state of Israel, the German Jewish community is now the fastest-growing of the world. To inquire about Jewish life and organizations in post-Holocaust Germany also seems a particularly worthwhile endeavor; in the United States, the importance of Israel and Israel advocacy for many Jewish organizations has likewise drawn the curiosity of contemporary political observers. Institutional differences pertaining to the respective governmental and interest group systems further invite comparative study, and may be suited to lead to a better appreciation of the general terms of politics in two major Western democracies.

Finally, while attempting to illuminate the larger patterns of interest group politics in Germany and the United States, this dissertation hopefully contributes to a more nuanced understanding – and demystification – of some of the most prominent yet perhaps least understood organizations in political life today.

2 Methodology and Empirical Evidence

The lacunae in research on Jewish organizations, as well as the contemporary perspective taken in this dissertation, require extensive use of primary sources. To gather firsthand information, more than 20 semi-structured interviews were conducted with leaders of the world's major Jewish organizations in Germany and the United States. Moreover, this dissertation also makes use of hitherto neglected yet highly pertinent archival sources on German and American Jewish organizations.

Accordingly, this study uses the inductive rather than the deductive method. Its argument is based on the findings of field research and does not subscribe to a single theoretical school of thought; at the theoretical level, it borrows elements from interest group theory and combines them with insights offered by the new institutionalism. The work presented here is, in this sense, more consistent with the "pragmatic" American approach to political science, as opposed to the rather deductive "Teutonic" method with its predilection for often complex and abstract theories.[1]

2.1 Interviews

The author interviews conducted with Jewish organizations in Germany and in the United States can be described as "field research", that is, as "research based on personal interaction with research subjects in their own setting".[2]

In the United States, over 20 interviews with some of the world's major Jewish organizations were conducted, including the American

---

[1] Dirk Berg-Schlosser, "Politikwissenschaft international", in: Dieter Nohlen and Rainer-Olaf Schulze (eds.), *Lexikon der Politikwissenschaft: Theorien, Methoden, Begriffe*, 2 vols. (München: Verlag C.H. Beck, 2005), vol. 2, 724, 722, respectively (quotation marks in original).

[2] Elisabeth Jean Wood, "Field Research", in: Carles Boix and Susan C. Stokes (eds.), *The Oxford Handbook of Comparative Politics* (New York: Oxford University Press, 2007), 123.

Jewish Committee, the Anti-Defamation League, the American Jewish Congress, the Conference of Presidents of Major American Jewish Organizations, the Conference on Jewish Material Claims Against Germany, the Jewish Council for Public Affairs, the Zionist Organization of America, and J Street, among others. I was also given the benefit of talking to John P. Becker of the Office of the Special Envoy for Holocaust Issues at the U.S. Department of State. Despite multiple requests, however, AIPAC was not available for interviews.[3] On the other side of the Atlantic, I had the privilege of meeting with the President of the Central Council of Jews in Germany, Charlotte Knobloch, the director of AJC Berlin, Deidre Berger, as well as with the chairman of the Union of Progressive Jews in Germany, Jan Mühlstein. Finally, numerous expert interviews with leading scholars in the field provided valuable insight both thematically and in terms of the general research design. The great majority of interviews were recorded and transcribed and are available upon request from the author.[4]

Moreover, all fieldwork meant conducting what may be termed "elite interviews",[5] that is, interviews with highly educated and highly placed respondents, who often had profound knowledge of Germany and German-Jewish affairs. Such interviews require a mainly open-ended approach because elites usually "do not like being put in the straightjacket of close-ended questions" – rather, they prefer to articulate their own views and tell their own story.[6] The present study therefore opted for

---

[3] According to AIPAC staff member Emily Ruda, the organization pursues the "strict policy" of not supporting school research of any kind. AIPAC does not publish annual reports either. Conversation (by phone) with Emily Ruda, Deputy Leadership Development Director, American Israel Public Affairs Committee, June 12, 2009.

[4] For a full list of the interviews conducted, see the annex in this dissertation.

[5] See Kenneth Goldstein, "Getting in the Door: Sampling and Completing Elite Interviews", *PS: Political Science & Politics* 35:4 (December 2002), 669-672; Jeffrey M. Berry, "Validity and Reliability Issues in Elite Interviewing", *PS: Political Science & Politics* 35:4 (December 2002), 679-682.

[6] Joel D. Aberbach and Bert A. Rockman, "Conducting and Coding Elite Interviews", *PS: Political Science & Politics* 35:4 (December 2002), 674. Malcolm Hoenlein, for instance, the executive vice chairman of the Conference of Presidents of Major American Jewish Organizations, opened the inter-

semi-structured interviews with open-ended questions, an approach that expediently combines the "journalistic" style of interviewing with elements of the "ethnographic" style. The journalistic style involves direct and very specific questions and thus gives the interviewee the impression of talking to an insider who appears to know everything already. The ethnographic style by contrast casts the interviewer as an unsuspecting outsider who appears to know very little about the topic.[7] A mix of both styles usually gives the respondents enough room to talk, while at the same time providing a topical framework for comparative questions covering the horizontal and vertical politics of the respective organization. Respondents were thus asked about the organization's founding history, membership structure, size of staff and offices, legal status, finances and budget, internal decision-making processes, coalitional behavior towards other Jewish and non-Jewish interest groups, general political orientation and specific policy positions, as well as about the organization's characteristic political approaches and strategies. In an interview with Charlotte Knobloch, pertinent primary sources such as the annual reports of the Central Council could furthermore be reviewed and their relevance discussed from a contemporary perspective.

2.2   Archival Collections

With regard to archival sources, I draw on oral history collections against which the evidence collected from the above mentioned interviews can further be tested. The first collection, entitled "Ethnic Groups and American Foreign Policy Project" was conducted by Judith Goldstein for the Columbia University Center for Oral History (COH) in the period from 1974 to 1986 and is available upon request at Columbia University. The collection is excellent and presently features 24 interviews with U.S. senators, representatives, congressional aides, as well as with other high-ranking individuals and Jewish organizational leaders.[8]

---

    view with an anecdote from a recent meeting with President Barack Obama at the White House.
[7] See Beth L. Leech, "Asking Questions: Techniques for Semistructured Interviews", *PS: Political Science & Politics* 35:4 (December 2002), 665.
[8] Most interviewees however placed restrictions on the date of publication of their memoirs. The overall number of interviews in the collection is higher, as it also comprises interviews that will be released in the near future.

The second oral history collection I make use of is the "Politics of American Jews Project" carried out by (and formerly archived at) the American Jewish Committee, now available at the Dorot Jewish Division of the New York Public Library. Recorded between 1971 and 1991, it offers a rare collection of lengthy interviews with some of America's most distinguished Jewish leaders, including Nahum Goldmann (the founder of the Claims Conference), I. L. Kenen (the founder of AIPAC), and David A. Harris (the acting executive director of the American Jewish Committee). To my knowledge, scholars have not yet systematically scrutinized any of these oral history collections – a most surprising fact given the richness and high academic standard of both projects.

In particular, the archives of the New York Public Library provided indispensable material with regard to Germany. The Dorot Jewish Division permits access to copies of the weekly newspaper *Allgemeine jüdische Wochenzeitung*, stored on microfilm from 1966 to 2001, as well as of its successor newspaper, the *Jüdische Allgemeine*, held in hard copy from 2002 up to the present. Both newspapers are edited by the Central Council of Jews in Germany and are therefore highly relevant for this dissertation. The Leo Baeck Institute New York, too, provided useful primary sources such as internal memoranda and correspondences of Jewish organizations and abundant secondary literature on German Jewish history.[9]

Moreover, the Blaustein Library of the American Jewish Committee was extremely useful thanks to the depth and diversity of its material. The Blaustein Library contains all annual reports of the Central Council of Jews in Germany (which were only published from 1960 to 1971); the entire series of the "AIPAC Papers On U.S.-Israel Relations" (also partly available at Harvard University's Widener Library); numerous annual reports of the Claims Conference; and a vast amount of secondary literature and current news coverage on virtually all major American Jewish organizations.

By considering a wide variety of sources – primary and secondary, contemporary and historical, oral histories and the written word – this dissertation hopes to present a nuanced and comprehensive perspective

---

[9] The Institute, founded in 1955, is internationally recognized as the most comprehensive archive documenting the history and culture of German-speaking Jewry.

on Jewish organizations that allows the reader to appreciate the many facets of Jewish politics in Germany and the United States.

3 Plan of the Dissertation

The fundamental objective of the dissertation is to examine the horizontal and vertical politics of the major contemporary Jewish political organizations in the United States and in Germany. Designed to fulfill this purpose, the study is divided into four parts.

The first part, which also includes the preceding two introductory chapters, delineates the intellectual terrain and proceeds with a review of the literature in chapter 4. A theoretical framework suggesting various axes for analysis, derived from the field of Jewish political studies more generally, as well as a political science approach to the study of Jewish organizations, organized around the concept of power and its horizontal and vertical applications, is subsequently developed in chapter 5.

The second part deals extensively with Jewish political organizations in the United States and unfolds in seven chapters. Chapter 1 gives an overview of the postwar trends in American Jewry and attempts to explain why Israel, and Israel advocacy in particular, has featured prominently on the agenda of many Jewish and Jewish political organizations. Chapter 2 examines more closely the society-centered model of American politics, as evidenced through the respective interest group and governmental systems, and identifies fragmentation and competition as its key characteristics. The focus of chapter 3 rests on the related political implications for Jewish organizations. Chapter 4 argues for a process-oriented typology geared specifically to the analysis of Jewish political organizations, introducing the distinction between "modern" and "new" Jewish politics as the key analytical categories. Chapter 5 is devoted to what has been termed modern Jewish politics and considers the "big three" Jewish defense organizations – the American Jewish Committee, the Anti-Defamation League, and the American Jewish Congress – as well as the major Jewish umbrellas in the United States: the Jewish Council for Public Affairs, the Conference of Presidents of Major American Jewish Organizations, and the Conference on Jewish

Material Claims Against Germany. Chapter 6 in turn provides a detailed and contrastive analysis of the two organizations typically associated with the new Jewish politics – AIPAC and J Street – and, in so doing, challenges the facile and commonplace thesis of the "Israel lobby" on various grounds. Finally, chapter 7 summarizes the empirical findings in synoptical fashion.

The third part offers a detailed empirical account of the politics of the Central Council of Jews in Germany and is organized in six chapters. Chapter 1 provides an overview of the current social structure of the German Jewish community, with a focus of attention on the major trends since 1945 and 1989 in particular. Chapter 2 examines both the institutional and non-institutional factors that account for the intertwined relationship between the Central Council and the state. Chapter 3 broadens the perspective by taking a critical look at the oft-invoked yet imperfect "special relationship" between the German state and the Jewish community. With this background established, chapter 4 deals at length with the characteristics of the political style of the Central Council. Specifically, it contains concise political portraits of the umbrella's past chairmen and presidents. Chapter 5, which includes a case study of the hitherto neglected role of the Central Council during German unification, addresses the issue of partnership and dependency from yet another angle, discussing the risk of instrumentalization and alibi politics that the umbrella is exposed to due to its close relationship with the state. Chapter 6 concludes with a summary of the main empirical findings.

The fourth part puts the previous findings back into a comparative perspective, discusses their theoretical implications, and suggests further directions for study. It also attempts to give an answer to our initial question whether the term "Jewish politics" can be a useful conceptual tool for guiding research in political and social science.

4 Review of the Literature

Depending on the respective analytical focus the scholarly literature on Jewish organizations can by and large be divided into "horizontal" and "vertical" approaches. Whereas horizontal approaches focus on the social structure of and the interaction between Jewish organizations and the Jewish communities, vertical approaches tend to be more "political" as they deal with the interaction between Jewish organizations and governmental institutions.

Despite the growing academic as well as popular interest in Jewish organizations owing to recent controversial publications such as "The Israel Lobby and U.S. Foreign Policy" by John J. Mearsheimer and Stephen M. Walt,[1] a great number of research issues still remain unaddressed or are simply taken for granted. As Michael Massing writes, "Mearsheimer and Walt provide little sense of how AIPAC and other lobbying groups work, how they seek to influence policy, and what people in government have to say about them", noting that "the lack of firsthand research" gives the book "a secondhand feel".[2]

Jerome A. Chanes provides a concise yet insightful general overview of Jewish organizations in the United States,[3] whereas Daniel J. Elazar analyzes the internal politics of the Jewish community and the various

---

[1] See John J. Mearsheimer and Stephen M. Walt, *The Israel Lobby and U.S. Foreign Policy* (New York: Farrar, Straus and Giroux, 2007).

[2] Michael Massing, "The Storm Over the Israel Lobby", *The New York Review of Books* (online), June 8, 2006. An obvious illustration of this shortcoming is the fact that Mearsheimer and Walt do not make use of the data available from IRS Form 990. If used systematically, the data from IRS Form 990 do however provide valuable insight as they help contrast and contextualize the differences in size and funds of the organizations in question.

[3] See Jerome A. Chanes, *A Primer on the American Jewish Community* (New York: AJC, 2008).

spheres of activity of Jewish organizations.[4] Mittleman, Sarna and Licht deal with the various kinds of contemporary Jewish political organizations and offer an introduction to the basic patterns of organization in the American Jewish community.[5] Other writings examine in detail the trends and developments in Jewish organizational life since 1945[6] and the rise of Jewish political action committees (PACs).[7]

On the other hand there is very scarce research available on contemporary German Jewish organizations.[8] Most notably, a monograph

[4] See Daniel J. Elazar, *Community and Polity: The Organizational Dynamics of American Jewry* (Philadelphia: The Jewish Publication Society, 1995), 277-312. Obviously, not all Jewish organizations pursue political goals. According to Elazar, there are five major spheres of activity: (1) religious-congregational; (2) educational-cultural; (3) community relations; (4) communal-welfare; and (5) Israel-overseas.

[5] See Alan Mittleman, Jonathan D. Sarna and Robert Licht (eds.), *Jewish Polity and American Civil Society. Communal Agencies and Religious Movements in the American Public Sphere* (Lanham, MD: Rowman & Littlefield Publishers, 2002), therein in particular Steven Windmueller, ""Defenders": National Jewish Community Relations Agencies", 13-66; Michael C. Kotzkin, "Local Community Relations Councils and Their National Body", 67-101; and Martin J. Raffel, "History of Israel Advocacy", 103-179.

[6] See Daniel J. Elazar, "Developments in Jewish Community Organization in the Second Postwar Generation", in: Seymour Martin Lipset (ed.), *American Pluralism and the Jewish Community* (New Brunswick, NJ: Transaction Publishers, 1990), 173-192; Jack Wertheimer, "Jewish Organizational Life in the United States Since 1945", in: AJC (ed.), *American Jewish Year Book Vol. 95* (New York: AJC, 1995), 3-98.

[7] See Lawrence Rubin, "The Emerging Jewish Public-Affairs Culture", in: Lipset (ed.) (1990), 193-202.

[8] There is, however, excellent historical scholarship on German Jewish organizations. Regarding Imperial Germany, see Barbara Suchy, "The Verein zur Abwehr des Antisemitismus (I). From Its Beginnings to the First World War", in: LBI (ed.), *LBI Year Book Vol. 28* (London: Secker & Warburg, 1983), 205-239; Marjorie Lamberti, *Jewish Activism in Imperial Germany. The Struggle for Civil Equality* (New Haven: Yale University Press, 1978); Evyatar Friesel, "The Political and Ideological Development of the Centralverein before 1914", in: LBI (ed.), *LBI Year Book Vol. 31* (London: Secker & Warburg, 1986), 121-146; Jacob Borut, "Jewish politics and generational change in Wilhemine Germany", in: Mark Roseman (ed.), *Generations in Conflict. Youth revolt and generation formation in Germany 1770-1968*

on the Central Council of Jews in Germany is still lacking, a fact mainly attributable to the paucity of relevant primary sources. Accordingly, the politics of the Central Council has only recently become the object of scholarly inquiry.[9] Comparative studies and studies undertaken from a transatlantic perspective have in particular remained a desideratum as current research on Jewish organizations has progressed in a rather disconnected fashion.[10] One salient commonality however exists: the trope of "Jewish power", as we shall see, has been a consistent feature in the literature on Jewish organizations.

4.1 Jewish Organizations in Horizontal and Vertical Perspectives

While the literature on Jewish organizations can be divided into horizontal and vertical perspectives, each perspective provides different

---

[9] (Cambridge: Cambridge University Press, 1995), 105-120; and Jehuda Reinharz, "*Deutschtum* and *Judentum* in the Ideology of the Centralverein Deutscher Staatsbürger jüdischen Glaubens 1893-1914", *Jewish Social Studies* 36:1 (January 1974), 19-39. Regarding the Weimar Republic, see Carl J. Rheins, "The Verband nationaldeutscher Juden 1921-1933", in: LBI (ed.), *LBI Year Book Vol. 25* (London: Secker & Warburg, 1980), 243-268; Barbara Suchy, "The Verein zur Abwehr des Antisemitismus (II). From the First World War to its Dissolution in 1933", in: LBI (ed.), *LBI Year Book Vol. 30* (London: Secker & Warburg, 1985), 67-103. Regarding the Third Reich, see Marjorie Lamberti, "The Jewish Defence in Germany after the National-Socialist Seizure of Power", in: LBI (ed.), *LBI Year Book Vol. 42* (London: Secker & Warburg, 1997), 135-147; Otto Dov Kulka and Esriel Hildesheimer, "The Central Organisation of German Jews in the Third Reich and its Archives (On the Completion of the Reconstruction Project)", in: LBI (ed.), *LBI Year Book Vol. 34* (London: Secker & Warburg, 1989), 187-203.

See Michael Brenner, "Von den Hintertüren der Diplomatie auf die Bühne der Öffentlichkeit: Der Wandel in der Repräsentation des Zentralrats der Juden in Deutschland", in: Fritz Backhaus, Raphael Gross and Michael Lenarz (eds.), *Ignatz Bubis. Ein jüdisches Leben in Deutschland* (Frankfurt am Main: Jüdischer Verlag im Suhrkamp Verlag, 2007), 124-133.

[10] One notable exception is Evyatar Friesel, "The Centralverein and the American Jewish Committee: A Comparative Study", in: LBI (ed.), *LBI Year Book Vol. 36* (London: Secker & Warburg, 1991), 97-125.

insights depending on its focus on the three key dimensions of political analysis: polity, policy, and politics.

4.1.1 Horizontal Perspective: the Polity

Horizontal perspectives deal with the polity in which Jewish organizations operate and focus on the internal dynamics of the Jewish community. They provide some general tools for the analysis of Jewish organizations.

Only a small number of people actually get involved in the work of Jewish organizations. In a typology by Daniel J. Elazar seven categories of participants in American Jewish life can be identified, spanning the gamut from a core of most committed individuals ("integral Jews") toward less committed individuals on the fringes ("quasi-Jews").[11] The first group, called integral Jews, regard their Jewishness as a central factor of their lives and strive to live fully according to a Jewish rhythm. They tend to express their Jewishness through intensive involvement in Jewish affairs. Approximately 5 to 10 percent of the Jewish population of the United States fall under this category. A second group – the participants – similarly take part in Jewish life on a regular, though not daily, basis. Although they do not consider their Jewishness a full-time concern, participants may seek an active role in Jewish organizations as officers, fund-raisers, or lobbyists. Approximately 10 to 12 percent of American Jews can be subsumed under this category. A third group, the affiliated Jews, includes individuals who are affiliated with a Jewish organization in some concrete way without being particularly active in it. It is estimated that this category includes between 25 to 33 percent of the American Jewish population. A fourth category consists of contributors and consumers. These are Jews who sporadically give money to support Jewish causes and periodically rely on the services of Jewish organizations. Even though they clearly identify as Jews, they are only minimally associated with the Jewish community. Estimates for this group range between 25 and 33 percent of all American Jews. Even less committed to communal affairs are members of the fifth group, the peripherals – Jews who are completely uninvolved in Jewish life and do not use, or contribute money to, Jewish organizations. It is estimated that this cate-

---

[11] See Elazar (1995), 90-100.

gory approximately includes 20 percent of the American Jewish population. A sixth category, the repudiators and converts-out, consists of Jews who actively deny and reject their Jewishness. Between 5 and 10 percent of American Jews belong to this category. Finally, there is an unknown number of what Elazar refers to as quasi-Jews, that is, individuals who cannot be clearly identified as Jewish due to intermarriage or assimilation. Between 5 to 10 percent of American Jews can be subsumed under this category.

In an attempt to classify the various types of Jewish organizations, Elazar further proposes a typology based on the functional contributions of each organization to the larger community. Again, Elazar regards the Jewish community as the environment from which Jewish organizations emerge and distinguishes four types of Jewish organizations: government-like institutions; localistic institutions and organizations; general-purpose, mass-based organizations; and special-interest institutions and organizations. Government-like institutions include comprehensive-representative organizations,[12] community services organizations,[13] and community relations organizations.[14] They "play roles and provide services on a countrywide, local, or regional basis that under other conditions would be played, provided, or controlled by governmental authorities, either predominantly or exclusively".[15] These organizations rely on professional staff and are active in fields such as social welfare and charity, education and culture, the administration of public funds, and Israel. Localistic institutions such as synagogues and *landsmanshaftn* (that is, charitable associations providing services for immigrants, today virtually inexistent) address local concerns and serve the personal needs of their members. Mass-based organizations perform multiple functions: they articulate the values, attitudes and policies of the community, offer an infrastructure for developing a communal consensus on that basis, and maintain institutionalized channels of communication between the leadership and the broad base of individuals. Mass-based organizations bridge the gap between government-like and localistic institutions because they "function as the equivalent of political parties (indeed, in

---

[12] Such as the Jewish federations.
[13] Such as the Hebrew Immigrant Aid Society (HIAS).
[14] Such as the American Jewish Committee, the Anti-Defamation League, and the American Jewish Congress.
[15] Elazar (1995), 234.

some Jewish communities in other countries they *are* political parties) to aggregate and mobilize interests in the community".[16] Akin to political parties, they provide a pool of personnel for the leadership positions within the community. Finally, special-interest organizations focus on specific issues and areas of activity. Their influence is usually fairly modest and mostly limited to the realm of local decision-making.[17]

Yet, the foremost problem with this typology is that it does not differentiate between political and apolitical organizations. As we will see in the empirical part of this dissertation, there are numerous features that set Jewish organizations apart from one another, let alone the many differences that can further be observed among the category of Jewish political organizations. Moreover, Elazar's typology does not go beyond the boundaries of the American model, for it does not discuss the possibility of centralized representative bodies that are common practice in Europe.[18] In Elazar's typology it would for instance be impossible to locate the Central Council of Jews in Germany. But even within the American context the theoretical framework suggested by Elazar is now largely "outdated", according to an assessment by the historian Jack Wertheimer, a renowned expert on American Jewish organizations.[19] It will therefore be, among other things, the task of this dissertation to elaborate an up-to-date and empirically grounded typology of Jewish political organizations in the United States.

4.1.2 Vertical Perspective: Politics and Policy

The literature on the politics of Jewish organizations essentially revolves around two policy fields: the field of foreign policy, on the one hand, and the field of German reparations and compensation policy toward the victims of Nazi persecution, on the other. In this context it is striking to observe that the bulk of the literature can in fact be localized within a

---

[16] Elazar (1995), 260 (emphasis in original).
[17] See Elazar (1995), 266-267.
[18] As is the case in Finland, France, Germany, Italy, Spain, and Sweden, among others.
[19] Conversation with Jack Wertheimer, Joseph and Martha Mendelson Professor of American Jewish History, The Jewish Theological Seminary, March 24, 2009, New York.

larger discourse on ethnic politics and, specifically, the discourse on "Jewish power".

To begin with, the academic foreign policy debate remains infused with a tendency to see Jewish organizations through the prism of ethnic lobbying. This tendency can be ascribed to an increased awareness for the concepts of transnationalism,[20] multiculturalism,[21] and ethnicity[22] since the end of the Cold War, when ethnic groups came to play an increasingly prominent role in both politics and political science.[23] As Tony Smith has argued, three major historical stages of ethnic group influence in American politics can be distinguished: first, the period from the 1910s through the 1930s, during which ethnic activism was focused on domestic affairs and was thus strongly isolationist; second, the period during the Cold War, when ethnic groups embraced a greater degree of internationalism and united behind an anti-Soviet stance; and third, the period following the Cold War, characterized by a continued but less united commitment to internationalism. Since then, increased partisan rivalries and a lack of consensus on foreign policy priorities allowed ethnic groups to play an "even more influential" role in shaping U.S. foreign policy.[24] The fact that scholars now pay more attention to ethnic groups, including Jewish organizations, reflects these changes accordingly.

The second and more prominent discourse at work is that of "Jewish power", a familiar theme linked to a vast history of anti-Semitic writings in general. "Jewish power" in fact is the title of a polemic book on

---

[20] See Gabriel Sheffer, *Diaspora Politics: At Home Abroad* (New York: Cambridge University Press, 2003); Yossi Shain, *Kinship and Diasporas in International Affairs* (Ann Arbor: University of Michigan Press, 2007).

[21] See Arthur M. Schlesinger, *The Disuniting of America*: *Reflections on a Multicultural Society* (New York: Norton, 1992).

[22] For a discussion of the concept, see Werner Sollors, *Theories of Ethnicity: A Classical Reader* (New York: New York University Press, 1996).

[23] See David C. King and Miles Pomper, "The U.S. Congress and the Contingent Influence of Diaspora Lobbies: Lessons from U.S. Policy Toward Armenia and Azerbaijan", *Journal of Armenian Studies* 8:1 (Fall-Winter 2004), 72-98.

[24] See Tony Smith, *Foreign Attachments. The Power of Ethnic Groups in the Making of American Foreign Policy* (Cambridge, MA: Harvard University Press, 2000), 47-48, 65 (quote).

American Jewish politics by the journalist J. J. Goldberg.[25] The respective discourse takes Jewish political power simply for granted, advertises it for sensationalist purposes, or is concerned with the exact measurement and normative evaluation of the latter.[26] The available literature on Jewish organizations nonetheless shares one common denominator in that it focuses nearly exclusively on the questions of "influence" and "power".[27] This is a curious fact, because interest group research clearly suggests that measuring the exact influence of any given group is an exceedingly difficult, if not impossible, task.[28]

The shared concern for power and influence notwithstanding, scholars have been far from agreeing on a common interpretation of the evidence at hand. While some authors do not make a statement on whether such influence is desirable or not, others have argued that the activism of Jewish organizations is detrimental since it allegedly impinges upon otherwise sound policies. In its most extreme form, the influence of Jewish organizations is seen as illegitimate or as altogether illegal.

The first set of authors does not pursue an own political agenda but is rather concerned with the question of "influence" from a purely scholarly perspective. The goal of such studies is to determine and to provide a more accurate measure for the "influence" wielded by Jewish organizations. David Howard Goldberg, for instance, undertakes the somewhat bizarre attempt to devise a numerical index of Jewish organizations' influence on U.S. and Canadian foreign policy.[29] While the idea of an index by itself is not objectionable, the insights it produces certainly are – and, as Goldberg candidly admits, stem from the "methodological and theoretical difficulties associated with [the] index".[30] Mitchell Bard, who

---

[25] See J. J. Goldberg, *Jewish Power: Inside the American Jewish Establishment* (Reading, MA: Addison-Wesley, 1996).

[26] See Will Maslow, "Jewish Political Power: An Assessment", *American Jewish Historical Quarterly* 66:2 (December 1976), 349-362.

[27] A critical discussion of these concepts follows in section 5.2.1 below.

[28] See Frank R. Baumgartner and Beth L. Leech, *Basic Interests: The Importance of Groups in Politics and Political Science* (Princeton: Princeton University Press, 1998), 37.

[29] See David Howard Goldberg, *Foreign Policy and Ethnic Interest Groups: American and Canadian Jews Lobby for Israel* (New York: Greenwood Press, 1990).

[30] Goldberg (1990), 12.

provides a discussion of the successes and failures of American pro-Israel groups, by contrast takes a less scholastic approach.[31] Ahrari includes in his analysis a comparative perspective and finds that Jewish organizations exercise considerably more influence than pro-Arab groups, a fact he attributes to the congruence of American and Israeli strategic interests in the Middle East.[32] A related argument is made by Lipson, who contends that lobbying is a "necessary, but not sufficient, condition of U.S. support for Israel".[33] Steven Spiegel furthermore asserts that, despite intense public activity, ethnic lobbies do not exercise a high degree of influence over U.S. Middle East policy. Because ethnic lobbies mainly work in the legislative arena, Spiegel argues, they have "only a muted and indirect influence on decisionmaking in the executive branch". Noteworthy is also Spiegel's observation that the activities of Jewish organizations are generally "less pronounced" than the contributions of individual Jews to the political process.[34] Louis Gerson reaches a similar conclusion, though for different reasons, contending that political leaders exploit ethnic groups as voting blocs to serve specific political interests.[35] Inquiring about the access points for ethnic groups in the policy process, Robert H. Trice and Paul Y. Watanabe make a distinction between Congress and the executive as spheres of influence and point to the tendency of ethnic groups to favor legislative action in their attempts to influence policy.[36] A comprehensive and methodologically sound

---

[31] See Mitchell Bard, "Ethnic Group Influence on Middle East Policy – How and When: The Cases of the Jackson-Vanik Amendment and the Sale of AWACS to Saudi Arabia", in: Mohammed E. Ahrari (ed.), *Ethnic Groups and U.S. Foreign Policy* (New York: Greenwood Press, 1987), 45-64.

[32] See Mohammed E. Ahrari, "Domestic Context of U.S. Foreign Policy Toward the Middle East", in: Ahrari (ed.) (1987), 1-22.

[33] Charles Lipson, "American Support for Israel: History, Sources, Limits", in: Gabriel Sheffer (ed.), *U.S.-Israeli Relations at the Crossroads* (London: Frank Cass, 1997), 130.

[34] Steven L. Spiegel, "Ethnic Politics and the Formulation of U.S. Policy Toward the Arab-Israeli Dispute", in: Ahrari (ed.) (1987), 23, 24, respectively.

[35] See Louis L. Gerson, "The Influence of Hyphenated Americans on U.S. Diplomacy", in: Abdul Aziz Said (ed.), *Ethnicity and U.S. Foreign Policy* (New York: Praeger Publishers, 1981), 19-31.

[36] See Robert H. Trice, "Domestic Interest Groups and a Behavioral Analysis", in: Said (ed.) (1981), 121-141; Paul Y. Watanabe, *Ethnic Groups, Congress,*

study on alleged "Jewish influence" in U.S. foreign policy was furthermore carried out by the political scientist A.F.K. Organski. According to Organski, the idea that sustained assistance to Israel is due to "pressures of U.S. Jewish votes, money, and organization [sic] is not supported by the evidence". Specifically, Organski shows that there is no meaningful causal relation between strong support for Israel in Congress and the financial and electoral support that legislators receive from American Jews. From this perspective, the influence often ascribed to lobbying groups such as AIPAC appears to be much overstated.[37]

A second set of authors by contrast deems the influence exerted by Jewish organizations excessive and claims it distorts foreign policy in ways that are incompatible with the "national interest". Authors of this category do not call into question the activities of Jewish organizations as such, which they consider to be "legitimate forms of democratic political participation".[38] Jewish organizations, they concede, act in accordance with the expectations and workings of American politics and behave no different than other lobbies. Yet, in these analyses, Jewish organizations stand accused of promoting policies in support of Israel that supposedly run counter to the national interest. Because current U.S. foreign policy toward Israel is not in America's best interest, only the political clout of what is termed the "Israel lobby" can account for this anomaly. Edward Tivnan and John Newhouse as well as John J. Mearsheimer and Stephen M. Walt make such a case.[39] This normative view of Jewish organizations in fact connects with a broader strand in the current literature on ethnic groups, which asserts that "transnational and nonnational ethnic interests have come to dominate foreign policy" in the

---

and American Foreign Policy: The Politics of the Turkish Arms Embargo (Westport, CT: Greenwood Press, 1984), xiii-xv.

[37] A.F.K. Organski, *The $36 Billion Bargain: Strategy and Politics in U.S. Assistance to Israel* (New York: Columbia University Press, 1990), 209.

[38] Mearsheimer/Walt (2007), 5.

[39] See Edward Tivnan, *The Lobby: Jewish Political Power and American Foreign Policy* (New York: Simon & Schuster, 1987); John Newhouse, "Diplomacy, Inc. The Influence of Lobbies on U.S. Foreign Policy", *Foreign Affairs* 88:3 (May/June 2009), 73-92; and John J. Mearsheimer and Stephen M. Walt, "Is It Love or The Lobby? Explaining America's Special Relationship with Israel", *Security Studies* 18:1 (January-March 2009), 58-78.

post-Cold War era.[40] While Huntington regards ethnic clout as a result of eroding American national interests, Mearsheimer and Walt turn the argument upside down: the "Israel lobby" is the cause of distorted notions that prevail with regard to the national interest and, specifically, regarding U.S. policy toward Israel. Hence, from this perspective, most Jewish and pro-Israel organizations appear in an unequivocally negative light.

A third set of authors is situated on the extreme end of the spectrum of opinion and goes so far as to assert that the influence wielded by the "Israel lobby" is illegitimate or altogether illegal. Raising the anti-Semitic specter of "dual loyalty", Grant F. Smith for example contends that AIPAC officials "conduct unauthorized diplomacy and secretly thwart debate, diplomacy, and sensible United States policies". AIPAC, portrayed as an "unregistered foreign agent" in violation of the Foreign Agents Registration Act (FARA) of 1938, is indicted for conducting "ongoing Israeli government propaganda campaigns" that allegedly "put the US Congress and the American people under the *de facto* influence of a powerful foreign interest". Smith thus claims to disclose what in his view are "AIPAC crimes up to the present day".[41] Former Congressman Paul Findley, himself the author of a similarly accusatory book,[42] praises Smith's analysis for its insight into "how AIPAC and the Israel lobby have hijacked the American political process".[43] Needless to say, these are classic conspiracy theories: the line of argument used is no different from, say, Henry Ford's infamous anti-Semitic pamphlet on "Jewish influence" in American politics.[44]

---

[40] Samuel P. Huntington, "The Erosion of American National Interests", *Foreign Affairs* 76:5 (September/October 1997), 29.

[41] Grant F. Smith, *Foreign Agents: The American Israel Public Affairs Committee From the 1963 Fulbright Hearings to the 2005 Espionage Scandal* (Washington, D.C.: Institute for Research: Middle Eastern Policy, 2007), 15 (emphasis in original), 17.

[42] See Paul Findley, *They Dare to Speak Out: People and Institutions Confront Israel's Lobby* (Chicago: Lawrence Hill, 2003).

[43] Findley quoted on blurb of Smith (2007).

[44] See Henry Ford, *The International Jew: The World's Foremost Problem*, ed. Gerald L. K. Smith (Los Angeles: Christian Nationalist Crusade, undated), especially chapters 7 ("How the Jews Use Power") and 8 ("Jewish Influence

Finally, the policy field dealing with German reparations and compensation policy – also referred to in German as *Wiedergutmachung*[45] – provides a substantial amount of historical scholarship on the role of Jewish organizations.[46] Another valuable source of information is the autobiography of Nahum Goldmann, who led the negotiations with the German government on the payment of reparations to Israel and indemnification for victims of Nazi persecution as president of the Conference on Jewish Material Claims Against Germany.[47] The Claims Conference, the foremost Jewish organization dealing with Holocaust-related issues, was established mainly at Goldmann's initiative and remains one of the world's major Jewish organizations today.[48]

Alas, in this policy field, too, the literature has produced its share of conspiracy theories. The most salient example is Norman G. Finkelstein's bizarre polemic against an alleged "Holocaust industry". His argument, however, is not simply to suggest a conspiracy by Jews against Gentiles; rather, Finkelstein accuses the Claims Conference of deliberately betraying the interests of Holocaust survivors in order to maximize its own wealth and influence. It is essentially an anti-establishment tirade in which the governing elites, the major American Jewish organizations, and the Claims Conference in particular, are accused of making common cause in the "exploitation of Jewish suffering".[49] But the book

in American Politics"). Ford, the famed carmaker, first published the book as a series of articles in *The Dearborn Independent* in the 1920s.

[45] *Wiedergutmachung* literally means "making whole again" or "making good again".

[46] See, for example, Nana Sagi, *Wiedergutmachung für Israel. Die deutschen Zahlungen und Leistungen* (Stuttgart: Seewald Verlag, 1981); Constantin Goschler, *Schuld und Schulden. Die Politik der Wiedergutmachung für NS-Verfolgte seit 1945* (Göttingen: Wallstein, 2005).

[47] See Nahum Goldmann, *The Autobiography of Nahum Goldmann. Sixty Years of Jewish Life* (New York: Holt, Rinehart and Winston, 1969), translated by Helen Sebba.

[48] See Marilyn Henry, *Confronting the Perpetrators: A History of the Claims Conference* (London: Vallentine Mitchell, 2007); Ronald W. Zweig, *German Reparations and the Jewish World: A History of the Claims Conference* (London: Frank Cass, 2001).

[49] This is the subtitle of the book by Norman G. Finkelstein, *The Holocaust Industry: Reflections on the Exploitation of Jewish Suffering* (London: Verso, 2000).

is also reminiscent of anti-Semitic slurs such as Louis-Ferdinand Céline's rambunctious *Bagatelles pour un massacre*, published in 1937: it is a work that appears to obliterate the boundaries between fact and fiction, thereby raising the question of whether it should be regarded as a non-fictional text or as a mere *exercice de style* – as the literary critic André Gide put it – in its own right.[50] Devastating criticism of Finkelstein's book and its inaccuracies is abundantly available and need not be repeated here.[51] The main point, however, is that Finkelstein links the activities of Jewish organizations to the popular theme of "Jewish power"; as we have seen earlier, the concern with power and influence remains conspicuously present in the contemporary discourse on Jewish organizations.

4.2 Summary

It is clear from our discussion of the literature that we still lack basic research about Jewish organizations since relatively little is known about the internal dynamics and specific political styles of these organizations. Comparative and decidedly transatlantic perspectives have also remained a desideratum. Studies concerned with the polity in which Jewish organizations operate provide some useful, albeit at times outdated, concepts. Analyses of the politics and policy of Jewish organizations in turn exhibit a preference for dealing with issues related to ethnic lobbying and foreign policy. The persistence of the trope of "Jewish power" is particularly striking, and has reinforced preconceived notions about the alleged political clout of Jewish organizations.

---

[50] See André Gide, "Les Juifs, Céline et Maritain", *Nouvelle Revue Française* 295 (April 1938), 630-636.

[51] See Karl Brozik, "Gegendarstellung der Jewish Claims Conference", 54-56, and Michael Brenner, "Warum man mit Finkelstein nicht diskutieren muss. Die neue Holocaust-Debatte und die deutsche Öffentlichkeit", 201-207, in: Ernst Pieper (ed.), *Gibt es wirklich eine Holocaust-Industrie? Zur Auseinandersetzung um Norman Finkelstein* (Zürich: Pendo, 2001). Also see Moshe Zuckermann, "Finkelstein und die Instrumentalisierung der Vergangenheit. Reflexionen aus israelischer Sicht", in: Rolf Surmann (ed.), *Das Finkelstein-Alibi. "Holocaust-Industrie" und Tätergesellschaft* (Köln: PapyRossa Verlag, 2001), 72-85.

This dissertation, however, takes an entirely different perspective on Jewish organizations. Unlike the bulk of previous research, it is not concerned with Jewish organizations' "influence" or "power", but rather sets out to inquire how Jewish organizations have adapted to, and operate within, the political systems of Germany and the United States. In so doing it also seeks to make a contribution to the field of Jewish political studies, a brief overview of which is provided below.

5 Theoretical Background

5.1 Jewish Political Studies and Perspectives for Analysis

Jewish political studies is a relatively recent and interdisciplinary field of inquiry and deals with all aspects of the Jewish political experience, including the activities of Jewish organizations. As a brief review of the field will show, fruitful research on Jewish politics can be structured along three major axes: functional, historical, and differential.

5.1.1 Origins of the Field

Up to date, comparatively little research has been devoted to the study of Jews and their intersection with politics. One reason is that those who have dealt with the Jewish political experience have often come from diverse academic backgrounds and are typically not trained as political scientists. But political scientists, too, have exhibited a reluctance to join the debate. As Ruth R. Wisse, a professor of Yiddish and comparative literature at Harvard University, notes: "To this day, Jews figure more prominently in the study of religion than they do in the study of government or political theory. Political science has shown little interest in a nation that doesn't fit its paradigms".[1] To address this deficiency, the newly constituted field of Jewish political studies seeks to provide a scholarly platform where Jewish studies and political science can fruitfully intersect. This does not mean that Jewish political studies is necessarily a discipline of its own; and although it is a field that may benefit from a number of interdisciplinary insights, it can (and should) first and foremost rely on the existing methods and theory of political science.

The term "Jewish political studies" was coined in the early 1970s, when Daniel J. Elazar argued the need for a field bridging the gap be-

---

[1] Ruth R. Wisse, *Jews and Power* (New York: Schocken Books, 2007), xiv.

tween Jewish studies and political science.[2] In 1974 Elazar noted that, "[d]espite many difficulties, including some psychological ones, and continued neglect, a field of Jewish political studies is emerging".[3] At the beginning of the 1990s, Jewish political studies was still regarded as "one of the most recent fields to be separately articulated within the framework of the social scientific study of the Jews".[4] While many possible subfields have been identified – ranging from Jewish political thought to Jewish public law and issues related to Israel – the boundaries of the field have remained fuzzy accordingly. For the purpose of this dissertation, it is however expedient to define "Jewish politics" – as opposed to the analytical categories of polity and policy – as the key subject matter of Jewish political studies. Let us now briefly consider how this term can be rendered operative for research.

Among the first scholars to introduce the term "Jewish politics" in the academic debate was the German-Jewish scholar Michael Wolffsohn, a professor of history at the University of the Armed Forces in Munich, who conceives of Jewish politics as the "politics that Jews actively shape or passively experience, sometimes suffer".[5] Peter Y. Medding, a political scientist at the Hebrew University of Jerusalem, offers a more elaborate definition by distinguishing between the individual and collective levels of Jewish politics. With regard to the contemporary era, Medding identifies two conceptions of Jewish politics. The first refers to "the activities of Jewish organizations in pursuit or defense of manifest

---

[2] See Daniel J. Elazar, "Jewish Political Studies", *Modern Judaism* 11:1 (February 1991), 79. Elazar however sees the origins of Jewish political studies dating back to the late 1960s – an assertion that can only be upheld if one adopts Elazar's very broad and ultimately unsatisfactory conception of the field.

[3] Daniel J. Elazar, "Jewish Political Studies as a Field of Inquiry", *Jewish Social Studies* 36:3-4 (July-October 1974), 233.

[4] Daniel J. Elazar, "Introduction – Jewish Political Studies as a Field", in: Daniel J. Elazar (ed.), *Authority, Power and Leadership in the Jewish Polity: Cases and Issues* (Lanham, MD: University Press of America, 1991), 1.

[5] Michael Wolffsohn, *Spanien, Deutschland und die "Jüdische Weltmacht". Über Moral, Realpolitik und Vergangenheitsbewältigung* (München: C. Bertelsmann Verlag, 1991), 29. Wolffsohn – perhaps deliberately – uses the controversial term "Judenpolitik" as the German translation for "Jewish politics".

Jewish concerns", a definition that will henceforth be used for the purpose of the present study. The second by contrast defines Jewish politics more broadly and "includes within its purview the activities and responses of individual Jews (not just those of organizations) in pursuit of any goals, issues and policies, not only those of intrinsically Jewish concern".[6] In this context Medding also points out that the initiative in Jewish politics does not always have to emanate from Jews themselves: "While individual Jews and Jewish organizations seek out others in their political activities, by the same token, other political actors, on their own initiative, for their own reasons, and in their own interests (...) turn politically to Jews as individuals and as a group in various ways".[7] Both Medding and Wolffsohn thus point to the risk of instrumentalization that Jewish organizations are exposed to when they get involved in the political process. Both authors also highlight the importance of institutional and historical circumstances and their impact on the terms of Jewish politics. Three different perspectives for analysis further elucidate this point.

5.1.2 Perspectives for Analysis: Functional, Historical, Differential

First, a functional view of Jewish politics deals with the style, strategy and operation of Jewish organizations, Jewish political parties, or other Jewish intermediaries. By adopting Peter Y. Medding's distinction between traditional, modern, and new Jewish politics we can further examine how the Jewish communities have adapted to the specific context of the larger polity during different periods of time.

The pattern of "traditional Jewish politics" – which never existed in the United States – spans the period from the Middle Ages to emancipation in Europe. One of its characteristics is that politics was not conducted by independent Jewish organizations but by *shtadlanim*, that is, by individuals who served as intercessors between the Jewish community and the authority.[8] Jewish politics was essentially personal politics,

---

[6] Peter Y. Medding, "Preface", in: Peter Y. Medding (ed.), *Values, Interests and Identity. Jews and Politics in a Changing World* (New York: Oxford University Press, 1995), vii.
[7] Medding (1995), vii.
[8] A *shtadlan* is a representative of the Jewish community with access to high dignitaries and legislative bodies. The name is derived from the Aramaic

and the dominant "strategy of political action relied upon personal, behind-the-scenes influence". Jews conducted politics out of a position of dependence, insecurity and weakness; devoid of rights, the Jewish political status had constantly to be renegotiated, and was fundamentally insecure and vulnerable.[9]

The subsequent pattern of "modern Jewish politics" emerged in the wake of emancipation, when Jews were granted formally equal citizenship status. This pattern is characterized by an increased activism to secure rights of Jews both abroad and at home. Still, Jewish politics of that period did not go beyond influencing public policy from the outside of the political process, that is, "without getting directly involved in the formal structure that exercised power and possessed authority".[10]

The "new Jewish politics" by contrast is an American specificity and not representative of contemporary Jewish politics as a whole. It is not an entirely novel phenomenon for it does not replace modern Jewish politics but, as Medding writes, rather "builds upon" and "enhances" it.[11] Key characteristics of this pattern are "a new spirit of activism" as well as a "greater political participation in various ways".[12] The new Jewish politics accordingly involves a more vigorous lobbying and arguably is best exemplified by organizations such as the American Israel Public Affairs Committee, which insert themselves directly and permanently in the legislative and electoral process.

Second, our understanding of Jewish politics can also benefit from the insights offered by a historical perspective. To be sure, Jewish politics does not occur in a vacuum, but is always closely linked to the

root "sh-d-l" (שדל), which in its reflexive form has the meaning "to make an effort" or "to intercede on behalf of". *Shtadlanim* had to perform the roles of intercessor, diplomat, and advocate at once, see Hanoch Avenary, "Shtadlan", in: Michael Berenbaum and Fred Skolnik (eds.), *Encyclopaedia Judaica*, 22 vols., 2nd ed. (Detroit: Macmillan Reference USA, 2007), vol. 18, 521-522.

[9] See Peter Y. Medding, "The New Jewish Politics in America", in: Robert S. Wistrich (ed.), *Terms of Survival. The Jewish World Since 1945* (London: Routledge, 1995), 86.
[10] Medding in Wistrich (ed.) (1995), 87.
[11] Medding in Wistrich (ed.) (1995), 87.
[12] Daniel J. Elazar, "The New Jewish Politics", in: Daniel J. Elazar (ed.), *The New Jewish Politics* (Lanham, MD: University Press of America, 1988), 1.

social and cultural dynamics of the surrounding polity. By drawing a comparison between the Middle Ages and the age of Absolutism and Enlightenment, David Biale has convincingly illustrated how larger institutional arrangements affect the politics of the Jewish communities.[13] The political system of the Middle Ages was characterized by a far-reaching fragmentation of power. In a system of widely dispersed sovereignty, political activity took place within the heterogeneous network of interdependent corporate structures, where hierarchies of power were continually shifting and no one actor could claim full sovereignty by its own. The Jewish community, itself an autonomous and collective actor, was part of that network. Medieval Jewish politics, then, was predicated on a contractual relationship between the *shtadlan* and the ruler; the medieval practice of shared sovereignty – with Jews having a "dependent, though not necessarily inferior, status"[14] – was in fact an integral part of the contract in *dina de-malkhuta dina*.[15]

The age of Absolutism in contrast involved a rapid expansion of the state and the concentration of all political power in the hands of the ruler and his bureaucracy. As David Biale puts it, "This new political theory thus envisioned a transfer of power from the community or corporation to the individual: the very power that had been invested in the communal structure was now to be returned to the individual Jew so he could reinvest it in the secular state".[16] Because of its potential to interfere or rival the claim upon full sovereignty of the state, Jewish political autonomy increasingly became a problem: absolutist policy did not tolerate Jews as an autonomous community or corporation, but instead sought to establish a direct relationship between the individual and the state. Similarly, the medieval doctrine of *dina de-malkhuta dina* was reinterpreted in absolutist terms and now demanded absolute loyalty to the secular state.[17] While this brief comparison shows how external – political and

[13] See David Biale, *Power and Powerlessness in Jewish History* (New York: Schocken Books, 1986).
[14] Biale (1986), 111.
[15] Literally "the law of the kingdom is law", referring to the Halakhic rule that the law of the country is binding. See Menachem Elon, "Dina de-Malkhuta Dina", in: Berenbaum/Skolnik (eds.) (2007), vol. 5, 663-669.
[16] Biale (1986), 112.
[17] The political ideology of Absolutism found support among the philosophers of the Jewish Enlightenment ("Haskalah"): the *maskilim*, who were "enthu-

ideological – changes may affect the terms of Jewish politics, it also points to the growing encroachment of the state on Jewish political activity.

Finally, we may also take a contrastive or differential perspective. This axis of analysis is concerned with the question in what respect, if any, Jewish politics is different from non-Jewish politics. As we have seen, the functional and historical approaches taken by Peter Y. Medding and David Biale militate against such a notion of differentiality. Their work suggests that Jewish politics does not follow a specifically "Jewish" pattern but, to the contrary, is shaped by (and therefore tends to reflect) the underlying social, political, or institutional constraints and opportunities of the respective political system. Ezra Mendelsohn reaches a similar conclusion when he writes that modern Jewish politics certainly "possesses its unique characteristics" while still having "much in common with the politics of other peoples".[18] Yet it would be misguided to overlook the unique structural challenge posed by the threat of anti-Semitism. As Ruth R. Wisse contends, anti-Semitism has a direct impact "[on] how Jewish politics works, and specifically the way in which [it] distort[s] and severely limit[s] Jewish options". Because it "complicates the normal expression of Jewish political interests", the ideology of anti-Semitism represents a serious impediment to the free exercise of Jewish political activity. As a result, Wisse argues that the familiar dictum of Heinrich Heine – "As the Gentiles go, so go the Jews" – is invalidated by the effect of anti-Semitism.[19] In the context of this dissertation, it is therefore instructive to note that numerous major Jewish organizations were explicitly founded not as pro-Israel lobbying groups but as "defense" organizations against anti-Semitism.[20]

---

siasts for the modern state", viewed the state as a "benevolent father", writes Biale (1986), 107.

[18] Ezra Mendelsohn, *On Modern Jewish Politics* (New York: Oxford University Press, 1993), 127.

[19] Ruth R. Wisse, "The Art of the Possible? On Modern Jewish Politics, by Ezra Mendelsohn", *Commentary*, March 1994, 56, 57.

[20] Examples include the *Centralverein deutscher Staatsbürger jüdischen Glaubens* (C.V.) as well as the *Verein zur Abwehr des Antisemitismus* ("Abwehrverein"). In the United States, the American Jewish Committee and the Anti-Defamation League were similarly established as defense organizations. The

5.2 The Politics of Jewish Organizations: a Political Science Perspective

This chapter addresses the question how a political science perspective can contribute to our understanding of Jewish organizations. As we shall see, the strength of political science lies in offering valuable insights into the nature of power relationships – in our case between Jewish organizations, the state, and society. Vertical relationships of power refer to the interaction between Jewish organizations and the state, while horizontal relationships of power are concerned with cooperation and conflict between Jewish organizations themselves. Considered against the larger background of structure and agency, both "inner-Jewish" and "outer-Jewish" factors furthermore play an important role in defining these relationships of power.

5.2.1 Politics, Power, and Political Science

It is generally understood that the term "politics" includes a fairly wide range of human activities.[21] At the most basic level politics refers to the realm of public affairs and, accordingly, political science is chiefly concerned with the analysis of private interests within the public sphere. Yet, it does not necessarily presuppose a rigid conceptual dichotomy between the public and the private, as in recent years the accurate understanding of the private as a structuring element of politics has gained particular significance; the increased awareness of cultural parameters in politics attests to this fact.[22]

The single most defining element, indeed "the essence" (V. O. Key), of politics and of political science lies in its concern with "power".[23] Max Weber defines power as "the capacity to carry through one's will in

---

French Central Council, CRIF, was founded as the *Comité Général de Défense juive*.

[21] See Rainer-Olaf Schulze, "Politik/Politikbegriffe", in: Nohlen/Schulze (eds.) (2005), vol. 2, 697-698.

[22] For a prominent and controversial example, see Samuel P. Huntington, *The Clash of Civilizations and the Remaking of World Order* (New York: Simon & Schuster, 1996).

[23] V. O. Key, *Politics, Parties & Pressure Groups* (New York: Crowell, 1964), 2.

a social relation against resistance, irrespective of the sources of that capacity".[24] Robert A. Dahl similarly emphasizes the coercive aspect of power: "A has power over B to the extent that he can get B to do something that B would not otherwise do".[25] Power, then, is the capacity of an actor – an individual, group or institution – to enforce a specific outcome of behavior of another actor by restricting that actor's freedom of action.[26]

Influence is not synonymous with power, nor does it constitute a subcategory thereof. It is not a means of coercion insofar as it does not determine specific behavioral outcomes. Its characteristic is instead the capacity to determine a set of action or choice alternatives available to an actor.[27] In other words, influence refers to an action by which A does not force B to do something A wants B to do, but merely leaves B with a restricted choice of action alternatives. Whereas the use of power enforces one single and specific behavior, the use of influence discourages a certain number of behavioral outcomes. But both concepts always presuppose an asymmetrical relation between the behavior of two actors – both are predicated on the assumption that a change in behavior of one actor will alter the behavior of the other.[28]

The foremost challenge researchers are confronted with regards not so much the operational definition of power but rather its methodological use and empirical relevance. Martha Derthick points out the pitfalls

---

[24] Quoted in R. J. Mokken and F. N. Stokman, "Power and Influence as Political Phenomena", in: Brian Barry (ed.), *Power and Political Theory: Some European Perspectives* (London: Wiley, 1976), 34.

[25] Robert A. Dahl, "The Concept of Power", *Behavioral Science* 2:3 (July 1957), 202-203.

[26] Also see Peter Bachrach and Morton S. Baratz, "Two Faces of Power", *American Political Science Review* 56:4 (December 1962), 947-952. For a formal definition of power, see William H. Riker, "Some Ambiguities in the Notion of Power", *American Political Science Review* 58:2 (June 1964), 341-349.

[27] See Mokken/Stokman (1976), 37.

[28] See Herbert A. Simon, "Notes on the Observation and Measurement of Power", in: Roderick Bell, David V. Edwards and R. Harrison Wagner (eds.), *Political Power. A Reader in Theory and Research* (New York: The Free Press, 1969), 77.

associated with linking cause and effect when applying the concept of power to the activities of an interest group:

> A fundamental difficulty is that of proving that B would not have done what A wanted him to do even in the absence of A's efforts to exert power. Although we can discover that A wanted B to take a certain action, and we can observe that A has certain resources of potential power and used the available means to bring them to bear on B, and we can observe that B took the action that A intended, we still cannot be sure that B would not have taken the action without A's efforts.[29]

In methodological terms, the attempt to prove the influence of a particular interest group by establishing a positive correlation between the perceived effect (the policy outcome) and its supposed cause (group action) is inherently flawed and involves a misleading assessment of group influence. For this reason, power analyses need to be based on a valid *negative* correlation: the existence of a causal link between action and result can only be assumed if one can prove that all other factors that possibly account for this result failed to show explanatory relevance in the first place. Because the concept of power is hardly susceptible to direct measurement,[30] it consequently has a very limited value in terms of comparability. A more objective way to appreciate the political impact of a given interest group is to look at the sources of power and the conditions and means for its exercise.[31] Indirect measurement of power then also allows us to make a more accurate statement about the potential impact of the interest group at hand.

But most importantly, power must be viewed not as a "thing" but as a relationship. For V. O. Key, power consists of "relationships of superordination and subordination, of dominance and submission, of the governors and the governed".[32] Power therefore is best understood as a relational concept: it is, writes Robert A. Dahl, "a relation among people".[33] Political science, in turn, is concerned with the study of such relation-

---

[29] Martha Derthick, *The National Guard in Politics* (Cambridge, MA: Harvard University Press, 1965), 7.
[30] See Baumgartner/Leech (1998), 37.
[31] See Simon (1969), 77.
[32] Key (1964), 2-3.
[33] Dahl (1957), 203.

ships of power. This notion of politics is also consistent with the classical approach to the field as it builds, for instance, on the approach to politics taken by Aristotle in his comparative typology of political regimes.[34] Let us now consider more in detail what kinds of relationships of power matter most for our analysis of Jewish organizations.

5.2.2 Horizontal and Vertical Relationships of Power

Power is here understood as a relational concept, with two relationships of power being of particular relevance for this dissertation: the one between Jewish organizations themselves and between Jewish organizations and other interest groups, and the one between the state and Jewish organizations.

Jewish Organizations and Society: Intergroup Coalition-Building Theories

As in other political arenas, interest group relations can be analyzed against the background of cooperation and conflict.[35] Cooperation can take the form of alliances or logrolling, which David Truman distinguishes as "[t]he two principal forms of mutual assistance" among interest groups:

> The alliance, whether formal or informal, involves the development of a common strategy among several groups in pursuit of a policy which bears some substantive relation to the interests of each. (...) Logrolling, on the other hand, involves a group's giving support to a proposal that may bear no relation or only the most tenuous relation to its own objec-

---

[34] The number of rulers defines the relationship of power with the ruled. Aristotle's typology does not imply a normative judgment about power itself, as constitutions may either be "correct" or "deviant", regardless of the formal power structure. See Fred Miller, "Aristotle's Political Theory", *Stanford Encyclopedia of Philosophy*, http://plato.stanford.edu/entries/aristotle-politics/#PolView, accessed January 22, 2010.

[35] See Robert H. Salisbury, John P. Heinz, Edward O. Laumann and Robert L. Nelson, "Who Works with Whom? Interest Group Alliances and Opposition", *American Political Science Review* 81:4 (December 1987), 1217.

tives; in return it receives similar support from the group it has assisted.[36]

Similar to an alliance, a coalition is "an ongoing mechanism for explicitly coordinating some or all of the actions" of its members.[37] Such coalitions may take different forms. So-called "disjointed coalitions" involve members with a shared goal but different overall agendas, whereas "shared core coalitions" involve groups pursuing one common agenda.[38]

Political scientists offer competing theories to explain coalition (or "alliance") formation among interest groups. Authors arguing from an institutional perspective regard the need for coalition-building as a distinct feature of majoritarian political regimes such as the United States. Due to majority rule in electoral and legislative politics, they argue, interest groups – and minority groups in particular – must form coalitions if they want to achieve their goals. Coalitions are here seen as a mere necessity given the nature of the overall institutional setting.[39] Yet this argument falls short of explaining how coalitions are actually built: it does not say anything about the factors that influence the choice of allies within such a coalition.

Another group of scholars contends that coalitions are based on the ties created by a shared minority status.[40] According to this view, similar political interests as well as ideological affinity and trust among leaders

---

[36] David Truman, *The Governmental Process. Political Interests and Public Opinion* (Westport, CT: Greenwood Press, 1981), 363.

[37] James Q. Wilson, *Political Organizations* (New York: Basic Books, 1973), 267.

[38] Jerry Gafio Watts, "Blacks and Coalition Politics: A Theoretical Reconceptualization", in: Wilbur C. Rich (ed.), *The Politics of Minority Coalitions. Race, Ethnicity, and Shared Uncertainties* (Westport, CT: Praeger, 1996), 41-43.

[39] See Truman (1981), 362; Lisa García Bedolla, *Latino Politics* (Cambridge, MA: Polity Press, 2009), 28.

[40] See Rufus Browning, Dale Marshall and David Tabb, *Protest Is Not Enough. The Struggle of Blacks and Hispanics for Equality in Urban Politics* (Berkeley: University of California Press, 1984). For further references, see Kerry L. Haynie, "Understanding the New Race Politics: Conclusions and Challenges", in: Kerry L. Haynie and Jane Junn (eds.), *New Race Politics in America. Understanding Minority and Immigrant Politics* (New York: Cambridge University Press, 2008), 170.

serve as the basis for intergroup coalitions.[41] While this argument is useful for explaining existing coalitions, it does not provide reasons for the absence of such coalitions among (and even very similar) minority groups. In fact, there is no obvious reason to assume that interethnic cooperation will just naturally occur.[42] How, then, does similarity affect the willingness to cooperate?

James Q. Wilson argues the unorthodox view that intergroup coalitions are unlikely to occur in any case – and entirely regardless of how similar organizations are.[43] Using deductive logic, Wilson proposes an autonomy-based rationale as the key paradigm for explaining intergroup coalition-building. According to Wilson, there is in fact a "normal tendency of formal organizations to resist coalition formation".[44] Given that competition is the defining feature of group relations, Wilson assumes that groups do not seek to maximize their size, wealth, or status in the first place. Rather, organizations first and foremost seek to maintain themselves. To this effect they need to develop autonomy, defined as "a distinctive area of competence, a clearly demarcated and exclusively served clientele or membership, and undisputed jurisdiction over a function, service, goal, or cause".[45] In order to distinguish themselves from others, organizations seek to occupy certain domains in which they are not exposed to competition.[46] Being highly averse to risk, organizations

---

[41] See Raphael J. Sonenshein, *Politics in Black and White. Race and Power in Los Angeles* (Princeton: Princeton University Press, 1993), 20.

[42] See James D. Fearon and David D. Laitin, "Explaining Interethnic Cooperation", *American Political Science Review* 90:4 (December 1996), 715-735.

[43] For an alternative view, see Marie Hojnacki, "Interest Groups' Decisions to Join Alliances or Work Alone", *American Journal of Political Science* 41:1 (January 1997), 61-87. Hojnacki argues that allies, context, autonomy and group character determine coalitional activity. Unlike Wilson, however, Hojnacki is unable to offer an overarching explanatory paradigm.

[44] Wilson (1973), 275.

[45] Wilson (1973), 263.

[46] The term "autonomy" refers to a claim over a given domain. It is not synonymous with the term "issue niche", for multipurpose organizations, too, can develop autonomy.

go to great lengths to avoid competitive situations which potentially threaten their survival.[47]

A high level of autonomy thus acts as a strong inhibitor of coalitions among organizations. In this case organizations have no incentive to join a coalition since this would only weaken their individual autonomy. On the other hand, organizations with low autonomy are equally reluctant to form a coalition. Low autonomy results in intense competition as each organization faces an immediate threat to its survival. Typically, the lack of autonomy prompts organizations to attack potential allies, especially important ones, rather than obvious enemies.[48]

But organizations will also resist coalitions even if these are not per se zero-sum games, that is, even if there are indeed potential rewards to be earned from the cooperative effort. Wilson's autonomy-based rationale helps better understand why the major theories about coalition-building – minimum-size theory and ideological compatibility theory – both make defective predictions as to the number of coalitions that actually form:

First, minimum-size theory suggests that coalitions depend on whether the outcome can be shared among the smallest possible number of members. The smaller the total number of members of the coalition, the higher the return an individual member will obtain in exchange for his contribution. This implies that large and powerful members will often be excluded from the winning coalition because their presence would make the coalition larger than necessary. Yet in many cases organizations do not build minimum-size coalitions: the individual contribution of each member is often hard to measure,[49] and the probability of (as well as the payoffs from) a coalition victory may be uncertain. Following Wilson's rationale, another explanation is that keeping coalitions down to minimum-size paradoxically increases the risk of losing autonomy. Ultimately all coalition members are potential rivals; thus, re-

---

[47] Political parties, however, are set up to contest elections and are therefore specifically required to compete with one another. Yet, the degree of competition is limited, for most parties try to mobilize their own supporters or appeal to swing voters rather than convert members of the rival party, writes Wilson (1973), 263.

[48] See Wilson (1973), 264-266.

[49] See Marie Hojnacki, "Organized Interests' Advocacy Behavior in Alliances", *Political Research Quarterly* 51:2 (June 1998), 437-459.

linquishing autonomy makes sense in broad coalitions only, where the potential loss of autonomy can be spread among a large number of organizations. In terms of maintaining autonomy, then, a coalition of the many is better than a coalition of the few.

Second, ideological compatibility theory starts from the basic premise that "likes attract likes".[50] Ideological compatibility is in fact one of the most frequent explanations for coalitions, in particular for those among minority groups.[51] This theory however presupposes a non-competitive environment, an assumption often at odds with political reality. Ironically, like-minded groups with shared goals and ideological beliefs may be particularly exposed to rivalry and competition. The more identical a pair of organizations, the greater is the threat to their autonomy – and the less the incentive to form a coalition.[52] Accordingly, Wilson's autonomy-based rationale suggests that coalitions are instead more likely to form among dissimilar organizations.

The main conclusion drawn from James Q. Wilson's coalition theory is that organizations have a normal tendency to avoid situations of cooperation and conflict – they do not seek coalitions and they do not wish to compete.[53] Empirical findings, too, cast doubt on the usefulness of coalitions. Baumgartner and Mahoney for instance show that coalition membership leads to lower rather than higher levels of policy success. The evidence is clear: "On average, [coalitions] are a sign of trouble brewing".[54]

Although not desirable as such, coalitions can still be a viable option under certain circumstances. Successful autonomy-driven coalitions should therefore involve a set of non-competitive and dissimilar organizations. For example, coalitions across policy domains could be an option since they would not substantially reduce autonomy. Jewish organi-

---

[50] Wilson (1973), 269 (quotation marks in original).
[51] See Sonenshein (1993); Haynie/Junn (2008).
[52] See Wilson (1973), 272.
[53] For a similar conclusion, see William P. Browne, "Organized Interests and Their Issue Niches: A Search for Pluralism in a Policy Domain", *Journal of Politics* 52:2 (May 1990), 492.
[54] Frank R. Baumgartner and Christine Mahoney, "The Determinants and Effects of Interest-Group Coalitions", paper prepared for delivery at the Annual Meeting of the American Political Science Association, Chicago, IL, September 2-5, 2004, 28.

zations, in turn, may have an incentive to seek support from non-Jewish groups as well – not simply because Jews are a minority group, but because inter-Jewish coalitions could possibly jeopardize organizational autonomy. In the same vein, ad hoc coalitions would allow for extended cooperation while at the same time maintaining a sufficient degree of autonomy.[55] Being temporary arrangements, ad hoc coalitions usually break up at some point of the legislative process.[56] Finally, cooperation based on logrolling and disjointed coalitions, organized around one specific purpose or goal, may also be a suitable way to preserve autonomy.

Jewish Organizations and the State

The institutional characteristics of the state also merit some scrutiny as they have a direct bearing on how interest groups can influence the policy process. More specifically, they shape the relationships of power between Jewish organizations and the state.

Strong States and Weak States

In analyses of the modern state, a dichotomy has sometimes been made between "strong" and "weak" states.[57] According to a definition by Kriesi et al., strong states are characterized by limited institutional accessibility, whereas weak states lack both the autonomy and the capacity to act.[58] The classification of the state as either strong or weak thus depends on the openness of access as well as on the state's capacity to

---

[55] See Wilson (1973), 277-279.
[56] See Kevin W. Hula, *Lobbying Together. Interest Group Coalitions in Legislative Politics* (Washington, D.C.: Georgetown University Press, 1999), 101, 106.
[57] See Stephen D. Krasner, *Defending the National Interest. Raw Materials Investments and U.S. Foreign Policy* (Princeton: Princeton University Press, 1978); Bertrand Badie and Pierre Birnbaum, *Sociologie de l'Etat* (Paris: Grasset, 1979); and John Zysman, *Governments, Markets, and Growth: Financial Systems and the Politics of Industrial Change* (Ithaca: Cornell University Press, 1983).
[58] See Hanspeter Kriesi, Ruud Koopmans, Jan Willem Duyvendak and Marco Giugni, *New Social Movements in Western Europe. A Comparative Analysis* (Minneapolis: University of Minnesota Press, 1995), 27.

act and implement policy. Today, the French Fifth Republic represents the paradigmatic case of a strong state, whereas the United States is widely regarded as an example of a weak state. To make general assumptions based on the rigid dichotomy between strong and weak states can however be misleading. Even in strong states an interest group may still enjoy a strong position in the policy process if it is part of a larger corporatist arrangement. On the other hand, weak states do not always confer a strong bargaining position onto interest groups, especially if the state is unable to produce or to implement the policy outcome the group desires. State strength can furthermore vary from one policy domain or one period to the other. Strong states may effectively turn out to be weak in a given policy domain, while weak states may gain strength in others.[59] A useful application of the concept therefore presupposes a disaggregated view of the state that takes into account the differences that exist between policy domains.[60]

U.S. and German Governmental Systems

The distinction between strong and weak states can be further elucidated when considered against the background of the division of governmental authority. Interest groups act very differently depending on how governmental authority is diffused in a given political system.[61] A typology proposed by Almond et al. illustrates why interest groups adapt their strategies to the overall logic of the governmental system in which they operate.

Structurally, governmental authority can be concentrated or dispersed among different branches of government in ways to create parliamentary, mixed,[62] or presidential systems. Geographically, variations in

---

[59] See Kriesi/Koopmans/Duyvendak/Giugni (1995), 27.
[60] See Michael M. Atkinson and William D. Coleman, "Strong States and Weak States: Sectoral Policy Networks in Advanced Capitalist Economies", *British Journal of Political Science* 19:1 (January 1989), 47-67.
[61] See Gabriel A. Almond, G. Bingham Powell, Russell J. Dalton and Kaare Strøm, *Comparative Politics Today: A World View* (New York: Pearson Longman, 2010), 101-102.
[62] Mixed, or "semipresidential", regimes such as France's Fifth Republic combine elements of both presidential and parliamentary regimes. See Maurice

the diffusion of authority between the central (national) government and lower levels, such as states, provinces, or municipalities, may result in confederal, federal, and unitary states, depending on the respective degree of decentralization. In the United States, the executive and legislative branches of government are elected separately and for fixed terms. In this case, no one branch of government can by ordinary means unseat the other. Yet, both are compelled to interact extensively in the legislative process and need to achieve some degree of coordination in order to make policy. The American presidential regime may thus experience periods of "divided government", and gridlock may frequently occur.[63] Owing to the structural dispersal of power between the legislature and the executive, both Congress and the presidency have "large and significant roles in policymaking".[64] Authority is furthermore distributed geographically at the central and state levels, which is why the U.S. also constitutes a federal system. The division of government authority in horizontal and vertical terms makes the United States an exemplary case of a weak state. It follows for the strategy of interest groups that, as a general rule, they will have to approach both the executive and legislative branches of government, and will possibly have to extend their advocacy efforts to the state and federal levels, too.

Parliamentary regimes like the Federal Republic of Germany are characterized by interdependent executive and legislative branches.[65] Only the legislative branch is directly elected, whereas the chief executive – the chancellor and his or her cabinet – emerges from the legislature. The executive thus rests upon the support of the legislative major-

---

Duverger (ed.), *Les régimes semi-présidentiels* (Paris: Presses Universitaires de France, 1986).

[63] The period from 1981 to 2003 was one of divided government, except of the years from 1993 to 1995. It is important to note that divided government does not necessarily entail policy stalemate, see Winand Gellner, "Effizienz und Öffentlichkeit – Entscheiden im präsidentiellen System der USA", in: Klaus Dicke (ed.), *Politisches Entscheiden* (Baden-Baden: Nomos, 2001), 79-80; David R. Mayhew, *Divided We Govern. Party Control, Lawmaking, and Investigations, 1946-2002* (New Haven: Yale University Press, 2005).

[64] Almond/Powell/Dalton/Strøm (2010), 104.

[65] See Lewis J. Edinger and Brigitte L. Nacos, *From Bonn to Berlin. German Politics in Transition* (New York: Columbia University Press, 1998), 50-54.

ity. This institutional arrangement involves an important concentration of authority at the executive level: "Since the same party (or parties) controls both branches of government, the cabinet tends to dominate policymaking, and the legislature may be less influential than under a presidential constitution".[66] Yet it would be erroneous to portray Germany as a clear-cut example of a strong state: territorial fragmentation is matched by a considerable distribution of authority on the state (*Länder*) level, where autonomous public policy may frequently apply. As a result, interest groups will mainly direct their activities toward the executive branch while at the same time coping with policy fragmentation on the state level.[67]

Pluralist and Statist Paradigms

Finally, the concept of structure and agency is key to understanding the relationship between interest groups and the state.[68] It is organized around the question of whether an interest group's agency, or rather the institutional structure of the polity, should be regarded as the determining factor of political outcomes.[69] The scholarly debate on this question essentially opposes pluralist and statist writings.[70]

---

[66] Almond/Powell/Dalton/Strøm (2010), 105.
[67] Also see Lewis J. Edinger, *West German Politics* (New York: Columbia University Press, 1986), 181-225.
[68] See Colin Hay, "Structure and Agency", in: David Marsh and Gerry Stoker (eds.), *Theory and Methods in Political Science* (Basingstoke: Macmillan, 1995), 189-206; Philip G. Cerny, *The Changing Architecture of Politics: Structure, Agency, and the Future of the State* (London: Sage Publications, 1990). By analogy, Freud's distinction between individual conscience and the *Über-Ich*, or the contrast between milieu and genetic predetermination in Naturalist literature, are further examples of how the concept of structure and agency has been applied across various disciplines.
[69] In political science, the concept of "structure" always implies a causal element and is therefore not synonymous with "context". Insight owed to a Conversation with Ira Katznelson, Ruggles Professor of Political Science and History, Department of Political Science, Columbia University, April 30, 2009, New York.
[70] See the excellent overview by Peter A. Hall, *Governing the Economy: The Politics of State Intervention in Britain and France* (New York: Oxford University Press, 1986), 13-17.

Pluralists typically regard policy as the direct product of group conflict. According to this school of thought, the behavior of the state is seen as a mere function of societal pressures. Political outcomes are ascribed to interest group influence, which is considered to be the single driving force of the overall political process. Like in a billiard ball model, the state is simply pushed around by competing interests – and therefore cannot act as a "neutral broker" among rival factions.[71] As did the school of thought following Arthur F. Bentley, the essence of politics is to be explained through the interplay between interest groups and governmental institutions. Akin to the idea of a market equilibrium model, the existing state of society was thus meant to be explained through the balance of group pressures.[72] David Truman and Mancur Olson took a similarly group-centered approach to the understanding of the governmental process.[73] But also John J. Mearsheimer and Stephen M. Walt in their much-disputed book "The Israel Lobby and U.S. Foreign Policy" present a line of argument that tends to fall under this category. While it does not deny the importance of structure during the period of the Cold War, the main thrust of the book is to attribute the outcomes of foreign policy to the pressure exerted by the "Israel lobby".

Statists, on the other hand, reject the idea of a policy process dominated by interest group influence. They base their competing vision on an image of the state as an actor with interests and policy preferences of its own. According to the central tenet of this paradigm, the state is thought to be frequently autonomous from societal pressure and to have indeed the capacity to impose its own interests and policy preferences (usually associated with some conception of the "national interest") against societal resistance.[74] As statist theory suggests, states are not only actors in the pluralist struggle of interests; they are in fact important actors that "may formulate and pursue goals that are not simply

---

[71] See Hall (1986), 17; Peter A. Hall and Rosemary C. R. Taylor, "Political Science and the Three Institutionalisms", *Political Studies* 44:5 (December 1996), 938 (quote).

[72] See Arthur F. Bentley, *The Process of Government: A Study of Social Pressures* (Chicago: University of Chicago Press, 1908).

[73] See Truman (1981); Mancur Olson, *The Logic of Collective Action: Public Goods and the Theory of Groups* (Cambridge, MA: Harvard University Press, 1965).

[74] See Hall (1986), 15.

reflective of the demands or interests of social groups, classes, or society".[75] Statists oppose a theory of pluralism that relegates the state to a minor role in the policy process and emphatically call for "bringing the state back in".[76]

For example, Stephen D. Krasner shows that key American decision makers were able to defend their conception of the "national interest" by pursuing foreign economic policy independently of domestic pressure.[77] Similarly, Eric A. Nordlinger argues that a political process governed by the principles of pluralism necessarily opens up venues for the state as an actor in its own right. The democratic state, Nordlinger writes, "is frequently autonomous in translating its own preferences into authoritative actions, and markedly autonomous in doing so even when they diverge from those held by the politically weightiest groups in civil society".[78]

5.3   Summary

Taking a political science perspective on Jewish organizations essentially means looking at the various relationships of power – vertical and horizontal – that these organizations are involved in. The institutional explanation of how power is distributed in the polity is particularly pertinent: weak states arguably provide opportunities for interest groups that strong states simply do not. This insight in fact stems from the literature associated with the "new" institutionalism,[79] a school of thought that emphasizes how states, intentionally or unintentionally, shape the mobilization and political capacities of interest groups.[80] On the other

---

[75] Peter B. Evans, Dietrich Rueschemeyer and Theda Skocpol, *Bringing the State Back In* (New York: Cambridge University Press, 1985), 9.
[76] This is the title of the book by Evans/Rueschemeyer/Skocpol (1985).
[77] See Krasner (1978).
[78] Eric A. Nordlinger, *On the Autonomy of the Democratic State* (Cambridge, MA: Harvard University Press, 1981), 203.
[79] See Ellen M. Immergut, "The Theoretical Core of the New Institutionalism", *Politics & Society* 26:1 (March 1998), 5-34; Hall/Taylor (1996), 936-957. The new institutionalism is first and foremost a rejection of behavioralism and of the group approach to politics.
[80] See Sven Steinmo, Kathleen Thelen and Frank Longstreth (eds.), *Structuring Politics. Historical Institutionalism in Comparative Analysis* (New York:

hand, the scholarly dissent between statists and pluralists raises legitimate questions about the precedence of structure over agency. Political opportunity structures theory has attempted to bridge the conceptual gap between structure and agency, though often with mixed results.[81] Its common theoretical core however rests on Giddens's contention that structures must be regarded as "dual": they are not static, but are continually reproduced by social action.[82]

This dissertation, too, is situated within the larger discourse on structure and agency in interest group politics: it borrows elements from interest group theory, and combines them with insights from the new institutionalism. Relationships of power, then, are best understood as shaped by both non-institutional and institutional factors. In other words, "inner-Jewish" and "outer-Jewish" factors alike can be expected to have a tangible impact on the politics of Jewish organizations.[83] Now that the

Cambridge University Press, 1992), 1-28; John L. Campbell and Ove K. Pedersen, *The Rise of Neoliberalism and Institutional Analysis* (Princeton: Princeton University Press, 2001), 1-17, 249-275.

[81] Political opportunity structures ("POS") theory was developed by Peter Eisinger, Sidney Tarrow and Herbert Kitschelt, among others. See David S. Meyer and Debra C. Minkoff, "Conceptualizing Political Opportunity", *Social Forces* 82:4 (June 2004), 1457-1492; Marco Giugni, "Welfare States, Political Opportunities, and the Mobilization of the Unemployed: A Cross-National Analysis", *Mobilization: An International Journal* 13:3 (September 2008), 297-310; and Hanspeter Kriesi, Ruud Koopmans, Jan Willem Duyvendak and Marco Giugni, "New social movements and political opportunities in Western Europe", *European Journal of Political Research* 22:2 (August 1992), 219-244. Political opportunity structures theory is not to be confused with the concept of "policy windows" used by scholars such as John W. Kingdon, *Agendas, Alternatives, and Public Policies* (New York: Longman, 2003).

[82] See William H. Sewell, "A Theory of Structure: Duality, Agency, and Transformation", *American Journal of Sociology* 98:1 (July 1992), 1-29; Anthony Giddens, *The Constitution of Society: Outline of the Theory of Structuration* (Berkeley: University of California Press, 1986).

[83] In adopting the analytical distinction between inner- and outer-Jewish factors, this dissertation follows Eli Bar-Chen, "Prototyp jüdischer Solidarität – Die Alliance Israélite Universelle", *Jahrbuch des Simon-Dubnow-Instituts* 1 (2002), 277-296.

theoretical background has been provided, we can turn to the empirical analysis of Jewish organizations in the United States and in Germany.

Part Two: Jewish Organizations in the United States

The second part of this dissertation deals extensively with Jewish political organizations in the United States. It offers a decidedly disaggregated view of Jewish organizations and, at the most general level, argues that the notion of an alleged "Israel lobby" as a political actor in its own right is neither intuitively plausible nor supported by the empirical evidence. To the contrary, the properties of the American political system abet significant rivalries among Jewish organizations themselves, which, as we shall see, need to carve characteristic organizational niches and distinct political styles in order to prevail in a fluid and highly competitive environment. The organizations here under review are thus illuminative of the larger pattern of society-centered politics in the United States.

This line of argument unfolds in several chapters. An introductory chapter gives an overview of the postwar trends in American Jewry and attempts to explain why Israel, and Israel advocacy in particular, has featured prominently on the agenda of many Jewish and Jewish political organizations. In the second chapter we examine more closely the society-centered model of American politics, as evidenced through the respective interest group and governmental systems, and identify fragmentation and competition as its key characteristics. A third chapter then discusses the related political implications for Jewish organizations. A fourth chapter argues for a process-oriented typology geared specifically to the analysis of Jewish political organizations, introducing the distinction between "modern" and "new" Jewish politics as the key analytical categories. Chapter 5 deals with what has been termed modern Jewish politics and analyzes the "big three" Jewish defense organizations – the American Jewish Committee, the Anti-Defamation League, and the American Jewish Congress – as well as the major Jewish umbrellas in the United States: the Jewish Council for Public Affairs, the Conference of Presidents of Major American Jewish Organizations, and the Conference on Jewish Material Claims Against Germany. The sixth chapter, in turn, provides a detailed and contrastive analysis of the two organizations typically associated with the new Jewish politics – AIPAC and J Street – and, in so doing, challenges the facile and commonplace thesis of the "Israel lobby" on various grounds. Finally, chapter 7 summarizes the key empirical findings in synoptical fashion.

1 Postwar Trends in American Jewry

Before we turn to the empirical analysis of specific Jewish organizations, some background information may first be in order. What follows is a brief discussion of the post-Second World War trends in and the contemporary structure of the American Jewish community, whereby special attention will be given to the question why Israel advocacy represents a major theme for many Jewish organizations today.

In the course of the twentieth century, American Jews not only became much more politically involved but also experienced, as Peter Y. Medding writes, a shift from powerlessness to power. "Previously, American Jews were politically weak and insignificant. (...) Today, American Jewry is widely regarded as a significant and influential political force that exercises considerable political power. (...) Once political outsiders, American Jews have become political insiders".[1] To understand this development it is necessary to examine the social history and internal dynamics of the American Jewish community. As scholars of American Jewish history have argued, two major social trends in postwar American Judaism can be identified: integrationism and survivalism.[2] The key observation is that external threats to the Jewish community vanished during integrationism, yet were quickly replaced by a series of new – now internal – challenges for Jewish survival.[3] The shift

---

[1] Medding in Wistrich (ed.) (1995), 88.
[2] See Steven M. Cohen and Leonard J. Fein, "From Integration to Survival: American Jewish Anxieties in Transition", *Annals of the American Academy of Political and Social Science* 480:1 (July 1985), 75-88; Wertheimer (1995), 4-47. A similar distinction is made by Hasia R. Diner, *The Jews of the United States, 1654 to 2000* (Berkeley: University of California Press, 2004), 259-358.
[3] This thesis is similarly spelled out by Alan M. Dershowitz, who asserts that "the long epoch of Jewish persecution is finally coming to an end and (...) a new age of internal dangers to the Jewish people is on the horizon". Alan M. Dershowitz, *The Vanishing American Jew. In Search of Jewish Identity for the Next Century* (Boston: Little, Brown and Company, 1997), 7.

49

from integrationism to survivalism also had important political implications: while political activity could express itself more freely, it also became, some authors contend, "a new form of Jewish identity".[4]

1.1 From Integrationism to Survivalism

The integrationist era spans the period from 1945 until the Six-Day War in 1967 and is characterized by the gradual disappearing of external dangers that impeded the involvement of Jews in the democratic political process. One crucial motivation for American Jews to effectively organize was the lesson of World War II with its experience of powerlessness and the failure of American Jews' lobbying efforts to save European Jews from Nazi persecution.[5] Despite intervening efforts of the American Jewish Committee, then the major Jewish organization in American politics,[6] the Roosevelt administration's response to Nazism had been disastrous: it was, as Arthur D. Morse finds, "an almost coordinated series of inactions".[7] Not only did the United States not fight the war specifically to save the Jews of Europe;[8] it also "willfully disregarded" a number of auspicious rescue opportunities.[9] The disunity of American Jewry further contributed to the inertia of the U.S. government. While the American Jewish Congress advocated a hands-on militant approach and organized a nationwide boycott of German goods, the American Jewish Committee opted for a more diplomatic approach and

---

[4] Elazar in Elazar (ed.) (1988), 1.
[5] See Elazar in Elazar (ed.) (1988), 2.
[6] See Fred A. Lazin, "Jews in American Politics: Past and Present", *Society* 43:2 (January/February 2006), 62.
[7] Arthur D. Morse, *While Six Million Died. A Chronicle of American Apathy* (Woodstock, NY: The Overlook Press, 1983), 129.
[8] See Wisse (2007), 178-180.
[9] Peter Novick, *The Holocaust in American Life* (New York: Mariner Books, 2000), 47. For a discussion of U.S. policy during the Holocaust, see David S. Wyman, *The Abandonment of the Jews: America and the Holocaust, 1941-1945* (New York: Pantheon Books, 1984); Herbert Druks, *The Failure to Rescue* (New York: R. Speller, 1977); and Saul S. Friedman, *No Haven for the Oppressed: United States Policy Toward Jewish Refugees, 1938-1945* (Detroit: Wayne State University Press, 1973).

hence refused to participate in such "noisy scenes".[10] Lacking political influence and sufficient assertiveness, Jewish organizations' response to the crisis of European Jewry remained weak and ineffectual.[11]

One of the main reasons why this was the case is the fact that, by then, anti-Semitism[12] was still very well-established in the United States. In the last decades of the nineteenth century, following the Civil War, many schools, professions, neighborhoods, hotels, resorts, and social clubs had in fact imposed quotas on Jews or excluded them altogether. In 1915, anti-Semitism infamously led to the lynching of Leo Frank, the only lynching of a Jew recorded in the history of the United States.[13] During the First World War, American Jewry had been under attack from racist groups such as the Ku Klux Klan, and in the 1920s several major universities introduced quotas to limit Jewish enrollment.[14] Anti-

---

[10] Morse (1983), 122. Morse (1983, 129) notes that "[t]he moribund immigration policy of the United States, and America's failure to reassert America's traditional defense of humanity, combined to produce total apathy".

[11] "The failure of Jewish organizations, including AJC, to move an administration that enjoyed nearly iconic status among the bulk of American Jews has cast a long and painful shadow to this day", writes David A. Harris, *American Jewish Committee at 100* (New York: AJC, 2006), 4.

[12] According to a definition by David Berger, anti-Semitism "means either of the following: (1) hostility toward Jews as a group that results from no legitimate cause or greatly exceeds any reasonable, ethical response to genuine provocation; or (2) a pejorative perception of Jewish physical or moral traits that is either utterly groundless or a result of irrational generalization and exaggeration". See David Berger, "Antisemitism: An Overview", in: David Berger (ed.), *History and Hate: The Dimensions of Anti-Semitism* (Philadelphia: The Jewish Publication Society, 1986), 3. A further distinction must be made between behavioral and attitudinal anti-Semitism, argues Jerome A. Chanes, ""America Is Different!" Myths and Realities in the Study of Antisemitism in the United States", in: Paul Berenbaum (ed.), *Not Your Father's Antisemitism: Hatred of the Jews in the Twenty-First Century* (St. Paul, MN: Paragon House, 2008), 222.

[13] See Fred Cople Jaher, "The Experience of Jews in the United States and Europe Illuminates American Exceptionalism", in: Berenbaum (ed.) (2008), 209.

[14] For example, by 1919, about 80 percent at New York's Hunter and City Colleges and roughly 40 percent of Columbia's students were Jewish. Harvard restricted Jewish enrollment by quota in 1922, on the argument that limiting

Semitism was to some degree indeed socially acceptable, and helped a known anti-Semite such as Thomas E. Watson get elected to the U.S. Senate in 1920. The rise to prominence of Father Charles Coughlin, America's foremost anti-Semitic demagogue in the 1930s, similarly illustrates this trend. Anti-Semitism reached its climax during the Second World War: surveys have shown that in 1940, 63 percent of Americans held the opinion that Jews had "objectionable qualities".[15] Needless to say, the anti-Semitism of these years severely hampered the political activities of Jewish organizations, as NYU historian Hasia R. Diner notes: "By and large, Jewish organizations shied away from airing their fears publicly, loathe to express their anger or to point out the "Jewish" angle of their political vision. Noisy demonstrations and impassioned public proclamations drawing attention to Jewish concerns did not suit their desire to be viewed as sober, respectable citizens".[16]

But also after 1945, it was the anti-Communism of the McCarthy era that "put Jews in an uncomfortable and compromised position".[17] While only few American Jews were communists, many communists were in fact Jews. The Communist Party of the United States of America (CPUSA) attracted a substantial number of Jews to its ranks. At the height of its influence and size from the mid-1930s to the early 1950s, the CPUSA enrolled roughly 50,000 Jewish members – out of a total membership of less than 100,000.[18] This, however, is not to say that a large proportion of American Jews were attracted to Communism, for the overall Jewish population in the United States constituted about 4,500,000 people during the same period.[19] The tiny percentage of the overall Jewish community that was active in the CPUSA nonetheless sufficed to raise fears and distrust among the larger population. Harvey Klehr has observed in this context that Jews have "frequently been linked" to communists in the minds of the American public, which

---

the number of Jewish students would eventually help contain anti-Semitism. See Jewish Virtual Library, "Harvard's Jewish Problem", www.jewishvirtuallibrary.org/jsource/antisemitism /harvard.html, accessed March 19, 2010.

[15] See Jaher (2008), 210.
[16] Diner (2004), 215.
[17] Diner (2004), 277.
[18] See Nathan Glazer, *The Social Basis of American Communism* (New York: Harcourt, Brace & World, 1961), 130.
[19] See Glazer (1961), 130.

viewed American communism as an essentially Jewish phenomenon.[20] The execution of Julius and Ethel Rosenberg in 1953 on charges of conspiracy to deliver atomic secrets to the Soviet Union also furthered the notion of Jews being linked to communist subversion. Indeed, the Rosenberg trials paradigmatically illustrate how American Jewry came to be associated with the "red scare" of the McCarthy era. It was not until the mid-1950s, writes the historian Jack Wertheimer, that "American Jewish groups felt sufficiently secure to espouse a strong pro-Israel position and to represent that position before government officials".[21]

By the late 1960s, the integration of American Jews into the political mainstream eventually brought about the end of integrationism. Jews now assumed prominent roles in the civil rights and anti-Vietnam War movements and later "led or were influential in most, though not all, of the political reform, feminist, consumer rights, gay rights, environmental, and other public interest groups".[22] The highly disproportional involvement of American Jews in the radical politics of the New Left is also well-documented: while Jews accounted for about one-tenth of all college students in the 1960s, they "were often half or more of the radicals on leading campuses".[23] During the subsequent era of survivalism, the internal threat of demographic decline became the major challenge for the American Jewish community. As we shall see in the next subsection, this shift had important implications for the politics of Jewish organizations.

---

[20] Harvey Klehr, *Communist Cadre. The Social Background of the American Communist Party Elite* (Stanford, CA: Hoover Institution Press, 1978), 37.
[21] Wertheimer (1995), 14.
[22] Benjamin Ginsberg, "Identity and Politics. Dilemmas of Jewish Leadership in America", in: L. Sandy Maisel and Ira N. Forman (eds.), *Jews in American Politics* (Lanham, MD: Rowman & Littlefield Publishers, 2001), 12.
[23] Stephen J. Whitfield, "Famished for Justice. The Jew as Radical", in: Maisel/Forman (eds.) (2001), 222.

1.2 A Divided Community

Today, as the historian Jonathan D. Sarna points out, "no religious group in America is more number-conscious than Jews".[24] In fact, the core Jewish population, defined as "self-identifying Jews by either religion or ethnicity who adhere to no other religion", is facing an accelerated demographic decline. According to the authoritative National Jewish Population Survey 2000-2001, the Jewish population fell in absolute numbers from 5.5 million in 1990 to 5.2 million in 2001, corresponding to a ten-year decline of about 5 percent. The American Jewish Year Book estimated the Jewish population of the U.S. at 6.4 million in 2007, or 2.2 percent of the larger population.[25] In either case Jews now constitute around 2 percent of America's total population, compared to 3.7 percent at their peak in the 1940s. This decline is indeed "historic", for it marks "the first time since colonial days that the total number of Jews in America has ever gone down".[26] Current data moreover indicate that Israel, with a Jewish population of about 5.4 million, "has overtaken the United States in hosting the largest Jewish community worldwide".[27]

Four major reasons account for the current demographic trends. First, the American Jewish community is not reproducing itself due to low fertility rates: the Jewish birthrate currently averages 1.8 children per couple, falling short of the 2.1 needed for replacement. Second, Jewish immigration to the United States is no longer sufficient to offset low fertility rates. There no longer is strong demographic support from abroad

---

[24] Jonathan D. Sarna, *American Judaism. A History* (New Haven: Yale University Press, 2004), 356.

[25] The full version of the NJPS can be downloaded at http://www.jewishfederations.org/local_includes/downloads/4606.pdf, accessed April 9, 2011. See Ira M. Sheskin and Arnold Dashefsky, "Jewish Population in the United States, 2007", in: AJC (ed.), *American Jewish Year Book Vol. 107* (New York: AJC, 2007), 134, 159-160.

[26] Sarna (2004), 357. The beginning of American Jewish history is usually dated at September 1654, when 23 Jewish refugees sailed into New Amsterdam after having been expelled from Brazil by the Portuguese. See Diner (2004), 13.

[27] Sergio DellaPergola, "World Jewish Population, 2007", in: AJC (ed.), *American Jewish Year Book Vol. 107* (New York: AJC, 2007), 551. The world Jewish population was estimated at 13.1 million at the beginning of 2007.

as in the past, especially since the influx of Jews from the Soviet Union diminished in the late 1990s. Third, the number of conversions to Judaism has fallen sharply. This development owes to the fact that Reform and Reconstructionist Judaism – both of which promote progressive forms of Jewish religious practice – have accepted the principle of patrilineal descent: in contrast to Halakhic law, they recognize children who regard themselves as Jews to be Jews even if they were born to non-Jewish mothers, thereby reducing the incentive for conversion. Finally, intermarriage has had a substantial impact on the American Jewish population totals. The main challenge associated with intermarriage is that the children of mixed couples later identify overwhelmingly with Christianity or with no religion at all; only about a quarter identify as Jews. Currently, one third of all American Jews live in mixed Jewish-Gentile households.[28] In the same vein, Rabbi Moshe Edelman of the United Synagogue of Conservative Judaism (USCJ), who officiates in weddings, estimates that about 5 percent of Orthodox Jews, over 30 percent of Conservative Jews, and 55 to 60 percent of Reform Jews do in fact intermarry.[29]

At the same time, the American Jewish community is "rapidly polarizing into two camps".[30] According to Jack Wertheimer, certain segments of the community are deepening their links with Judaism, while others are drifting away from it. "[I]n the religious sphere, a bipolar model is emerging, with a large population of Jews moving toward religious minimalism and a minority gravitating toward greater participation and deepened concern with religion".[31] Considered against the backdrop of the typology of Jewish community affiliation proposed by Daniel J. Elazar, the inner core of American Jewry – integral Jews, participants, and affiliated Jews – thus further gravitates to the center while the majority is centrifugally drawn toward the fringes. Contemporary

---

[28] See Sarna (2004), 360, 362, with further references.
[29] See Interview with Rabbi Moshe Edelman, Associate Director, United Synagogue of Conservative Judaism, June 29, 2009, New York.
[30] Jack Wertheimer, "The Truth About American Jews and Israel", *Commentary*, June 2009, 44.
[31] Jack Wertheimer, "Recent Trends in American Judaism", in: AJC (ed.), *American Jewish Year Book Vol. 89* (New York: AJC, 1989), 162.

definitions of Jewishness have accordingly become more fluid and, as Hasia Diner contends, American Jews have become "Jews by choice".[32] The trend towards individualism has made it particularly difficult to preserve Jewish unity. "If factionalism is an index of vitality", writes Ruth R. Wisse, "most American Jewish communities are thriving. (...) The American Jewish communities – for no two are alike – are ridden with factionalism and dissension on every conceivable point".[33] The divisiveness within the American Jewish community stems from a variety of causes:

For one thing, American Jews are geographically dispersed across the country, with major centers of Jewish population in California (1.19 million), Florida (655,000), New Jersey (479,000) and New England (419,000). The most densely populated state is New York with a Jewish population of 1.62 million in 2002, while New York City alone hosted a Jewish population of 972,000.[34] Second, the different religious movements in American Judaism – Orthodox, Conservative, Reform, and Reconstructionist – contribute to the fragmentation of the Jewish community. In a 2009 survey conducted by the American Jewish Committee, 9 percent of American Jews identified as Orthodox, 24 percent as Conservative, 27 percent as Reform, and 2 percent as Reconstructionist, while 36 percent said they were "just Jewish".[35] A different picture presents itself when the numbers are considered against the background of synagogue affiliation: in 2008, of those who belonged to a synagogue 21 percent affiliated with the Orthodox, 33 percent with the Conservative, 42 percent with the Reform, and 3 percent with the Reconstructionist movement.[36] Two recent trends are furthermore noteworthy. On the one hand, the Conservative movement lost market share to its main competitors, Reform and Orthodoxy, as the latter have become more open to

---

[32] Diner (2004), 358.
[33] Ruth R. Wisse, ""Peace Now" and American Jews", *Commentary*, August 1980, 21. Also see Jack Wertheimer, *A People Divided. Judaism in Contemporary America* (New York: Basic Books, 1993).
[34] See Sheskin/Dashefsky (2007), 159-160, 186.
[35] See American Jewish Committee, "2009 Annual Survey of American Jewish Opinion", http://www.ajc.org/site/apps/nlnet/content3.aspx?c=ijITI2PHKoG&b=846741&ct=7513467, accessed March 27, 2010.
[36] See Jerome A. Chanes, *A Primer on the American Jewish Community* (New York: AJC, 2008), 6.

traditional and, respectively, liberal practices. At the same time, says Rabbi Moshe Edelman, there has also been "a tremendous pushback away from the movements", prompting the creation of so-called "independent" synagogues which are not affiliated with any of the major denominations.[37]

American Jews are also divided by often sharply contrasting political views, in particular between liberal and neoconservative politics. The general liberalism of American Jews has been widely documented, and even leading Jewish neoconservatives such as the late Irving Kristol recognize that "American Jews, in their overwhelming majority, are politically rooted in a liberal tradition".[38] The liberalism of American Jews, one of the most prominent examples of "anomalous group political behaviour in American politics",[39] has intrigued psephologists and pundits alike. Despite a comparatively high socioeconomic status, American Jews have curiously remained on the Democratic side of the political spectrum by fairly solid margins.[40] As the essayist Milton Himmelfarb once put it in a much-cited aphorism, American Jews "earn like Episcopalians and vote like Puerto Ricans".[41] For example, Franklin D. Roosevelt won 82 percent of the American Jewish vote in the presidential election of 1932, 85 percent in 1936, and even 90 percent in the elections of 1940 and 1944. In 1960, John F. Kennedy obtained 82 percent of the Jewish vote, while his Democratic successor Lyndon B. Johnson went on to win another 90 percent in 1964. Bill Clinton earned 86 percent and 83 percent of the Jewish vote in 1992 and 1996, respectively, while Barack Obama earned a still impressive 78 percent of the Jewish

---

[37] Edelman (2009 Interview).
[38] Irving Kristol, "The Liberal Tradition of American Jews", in: Lipset (ed.) (1990), 109.
[39] Geoffrey Brahm Levey, "The Liberalism of American Jews – Has It Been Explained ?", *British Journal of Political Science* 26:3 (July 1996), 370.
[40] See Anna Greenberg and Kenneth D. Wald, "Still Liberal After All These Years? The Contemporary Political Behavior of American Jewry", in: Maisel/Forman (eds.) (2001), 161-194; Lana Stein, "American Jews and Their Liberal Political Behavior", in: Wilbur C. Rich (ed.), *The Politics of Minority Coalitions. Race, Ethnicity, and Shared Uncertainties* (Westport, CT: Praeger, 1996), 193-200.
[41] Quoted in Joseph Berger, "Milton Himmelfarb, Wry Essayist, 87, Dies", *The New York Times*, January 15, 2006.

vote in the presidential election of 2008.[42] Recent surveys likewise show that merely 16 percent of American Jews consider themselves Republicans, as opposed to 53 percent who identify as Democrats and 30 percent who regard themselves as independents.[43] In recent years, however, a sizable segment of the Jewish community has identified with conservative and neoconservative politics.[44] In this context some authors have suggested that the political dissensions between liberal and conservative Jews are among the main reasons that keep feeding the "culture wars" within the American Jewish community.[45]

Finally, the American Jewish community is also culturally diverse, as it has attracted immigrants from different geographic origins. It does not constitute a "diaspora" community, as some authors erroneously suggest,[46] given that large waves of Jewish immigration to the United States are essentially historical phenomena. During the first wave of immigration in the colonial period, most Jews were of Sephardic, that is, mostly Spanish or Portuguese origin, while the second wave until the end of the nineteenth century brought Jews of primarily Ashkenazic, that is, Central European origin to America. The third wave, from 1881 to 1924, was shaped by the massive influx of Jews from Russia and other parts of Eastern Europe. After 1945, Holocaust survivors flocked to the United States in large numbers, as did immigrants from the former Sovi-

---

[42] See Michael Wolffsohn, *Israel. Geschichte, Politik, Gesellschaft, Wirtschaft* (Wiesbaden: VS Verlag, 2007), 221; Marc Dollinger, *Quest for Inclusion. Jews and Liberalism in Modern America* (Princeton: Princeton University Press, 2000), 3; and Marissa Brostoff and Rebecca Spence, "Black, Jewish Vote for Obama May Signal a Renewed Tie", *Forward*, November 13, 2008.

[43] See American Jewish Committee, "2009 Annual Survey of American Jewish Opinion", http://www.ajc.org/site/apps/nlnet/content3.aspx?c=ijITI2PHKoG &b=846741&ct=7513467, accessed March 27, 2010.

[44] See Mearsheimer/Walt (2007), 126-132.

[45] See Edward Shapiro, "Right Turn? Jews and the American Conservative Movement", in: Maisel/Forman (eds.) (2001), 195-212; Murray Friedman, *The Neoconservative Revolution: Jewish Intellectuals and The Shaping of Public Policy* (New York: Cambridge University Press, 2005); and Christian Bala, *Konservatismus, Judaismus, Zionismus. "Kulturkrieg" in der US-Diaspora* (Baden-Baden: Nomos, 2006).

[46] See, for example, Sheffer (2003).

et Union after 1989.[47] America's Yiddish-speaking Jewish population further adds to the cultural diversity of the Jewish community. In light of these multiple divisions, scholars have argued the hypothesis that political activism on behalf of Israel serves as a viable means of binding the American Jewish community together, as the following section shows.

1.3 "Political Judaism" and Israel Advocacy in the United States

Various scholars have argued the hypothesis that Holocaust memory and political activism provide a common bond for uniting the heterogeneous American Jewish community. According to the historian Peter Novick, the Holocaust has become the "central symbol of Jewishness" and serves as "virtually the only common denominator" for American Jewry today. In other words, the Holocaust has achieved the status of a "consensual symbol" that provides a divided community with some sense of collective identity.[48] Harvard political scientist Stephen M. Walt takes a similar position, arguing that after 1967 American Jewish organizations have deliberately begun to highlight the Holocaust and Israel as a feature of being Jewish.[49]

Indeed, the focus on Israel is conspicuously present in the work of nearly all major Jewish organizations today. As Jack Wertheimer notes, it is "hard to think of any large national American Jewish organization that does not include Israel in its portfolio".[50] The increasingly prominent role of professional advocacy organizations such as AIPAC and the Presidents Conference likewise illustrates this trend. Set up in the 1950s for the explicit purpose of Israel advocacy, both AIPAC and the Presi-

---

[47] See Jerome A. Chanes, *A Primer on the American Jewish Community* (New York: AJC, 2008), 2-4.

[48] Novick (2000), 7. In the same vein, NYU historian Tony Judt writes that "[m]any American Jews are sadly ignorant of their religion, culture, traditional languages, or history. But they do know about Auschwitz, and that suffices". Tony Judt, "Edge People", *The New York Review of Books* (online), February 23, 2010.

[49] See Interview with Stephen M. Walt, Robert and Renée Belfer Professor of International Affairs, John F. Kennedy School of Government, Harvard University, October 6, 2008, Cambridge, MA.

[50] Jack Wertheimer, "The Truth About American Jews and Israel", *Commentary*, June 2009, 43.

dents Conference gained momentum after the Six-Day War in 1967 before rising to further prominence in the 1970s and 1980s.[51] Both are today widely regarded as key players within the "Israel lobby".[52]

The growing importance of Israel also changed the outlook of established defense organizations like the American Jewish Committee. By the end of the 1980s, AJC became explicitly Israel-bound, and now frequently used the Zionist-coined term of Jewish "peoplehood" in its publications.[53] This evolution is fairly surprising in light of the Ben Gurion-Blaustein agreement of 1950 and the critical stance AJC had taken earlier on the issue of Zionism.[54] In 1961, AJC established an office in Jerusalem and, in 1979, recommended Jewish identity programs to be conducted jointly by Israelis and American Jews. In 1982, it founded the Institute on American Jewish-Israeli Relations, an institute "dedicated entirely to strengthening ties between American Jewry and Israel".[55] Today, says AJC veteran Lawrence D. Lowenthal, Israel-related issues are the "top priority" for the American Jewish Committee and account for about 50 percent of its overall policy work.[56]

A general distinction must further be made between the terms "pro-Israelism" and "Zionism". According to a definition introduced by the sociologist Chaim I. Waxman, the former refers to American Jews who live in the United States and support Israel economically, politically or emotionally, but whose "primary source of Jewish identification is de-

[51] See Wertheimer (1995), 55.
[52] See Mearsheimer/Walt (2007), 14, 113, 116, 119, 126.
[53] See Friesel (1991), 116-117.
[54] The agreement, concluded between Jacob Blaustein, president of AJC, and then Israeli Prime Minister David Ben-Gurion affirmed the integrity of both Jewish communities and mutual non-interference. Deflecting charges of so-called dual loyalty, the agreement was specifically intended to clarify that "the Jews of the United States, as a community and as individuals, have no political attachment to Israel". American Jewish Committee, "AJC press release on the Blaustein-Ben-Gurion Agreement (Sept. 10, 1950)", http://www.ajcarchives.org/AJC_DATA/Files/508.PDF, accessed March 27, 2010.
[55] American Jewish Committee, "Continuity and Change", http://www.ajc.org/site/apps/nlnet/content3.aspx?c=ijITI2PHKoG&b=841113&ct=1052387, accessed March 27, 2010.
[56] Interview with Lawrence D. Lowenthal, National Senior Advisor, former Director of AJC Boston, American Jewish Committee, November 3, 2008, Cambridge, MA.

rived from, and oriented to, the American Jewish community". The term "Zionism" by contrast refers to individuals for whom Israel plays "a central role" in their own personal lives and in their "sense of identity and very existence".[57] Moreover, the concern for Israel intersects with the above mentioned survivalist agenda. As the Israeli scholar Eytan Gilboa has argued, the widespread pro-Israel sentiment among American Jews is also attributable to the overall perception that Israeli survival is in doubt. This in turn has favored actions and attitudes supportive of Israel at various levels.[58]

The "Israelcentric focus"[59] of many Jewish organizations has at times been a curious phenomenon, at least in the eyes of some prominent contemporary critics. Noam Chomsky for example caustically remarked that "[a] similar stance of state-worship would be difficult to find, apart from the annals of Stalinism and fascism".[60] Chomsky – one of Israel's foremost critics – however misses the point when he describes the support for the Jewish state as irrational or outlandish. For Israel advocacy indeed has a "sociological function" for the American Jewish community, as Middle East scholar Martin Kramer explains. It is not simply a form of political support extended to a foreign country, but also "very much [serves] the self-interest" of the American Jewish community.[61] In other words, Israel advocacy gives Jewish organizations a specifically Jewish purpose and is thus as political as it is relevant for communal identity. At the same time, though, the empirical evidence shows that the attachment of American Jews to Israel is less pronounced and less political than is commonly believed.

Current research indicates that the majority of American Jews not only have a superficial knowledge of Israel but also that relatively few of them have actually visited the country. Intriguingly, only 35 percent of American Jews have ever been to Israel, as opposed to two-thirds of

[57] Chaim I. Waxman, "The Centrality of Israel in American Jewish Life: A Sociological Analysis", *Judaism* 25:2 (Spring 1976), 177.
[58] See Eytan Gilboa, *American Public Opinion toward Israel and the Arab-Israeli Conflict* (Lexington, MA: Heath and Company, 1987), 264.
[59] Mearsheimer/Walt (2007), 118-119.
[60] Noam Chomsky, *Fateful Triangle. The United States, Israel, and the Palestinians* (Cambridge, MA: South End Press, 1999), 16.
[61] Interview with Martin Kramer, Senior Fellow, Weatherhead Center for International Affairs, Harvard University, November 6, 2008, Cambridge, MA.

adult Canadian Jews and nearly 75 percent of French and Australian Jews.[62] Also, very few of them make *aliyah*, that is, immigration to Israel. In 2009, a record year, only 3,800 *olim* (new immigrants) moved to Israel from the U.S. and Canada combined.[63]

As one may reasonably expect, the level of attachment to Israel varies between individuals and depends on a variety of factors. To begin with, attachment to Israel correlates strongly with religious activity. Orthodox Jews are the most attached, while Jews who do not participate in religious activities tend to have only a tenuous connection with Israel. But also the affiliation with synagogues or Jewish institutions needs to be considered: 85 percent of highly affiliated Jews maintain close ties to Israel, as compared to less than 50 percent of the unaffiliated. Moreover, intermarried Jews as well as their children are less likely to maintain a personal connection to Israel than Jews who marry Jews.[64] The younger generation of American Jews is also far less attached to – if not altogether alienated from – Israel than previous generations. At the same time, and contrary to popular belief, political views do not greatly affect the attachment to Israel. For instance, American Jews under age 35 with right-leaning political views are especially alienated from Israel, even more so than their left-leaning peers.[65] What these figures suggest is that the support for Israel must be considered within the context of the bipolar structure of the American Jewish community. According to a representative survey of the adult Jewish population in the United States in 2009, 69 percent of the respondents felt "fairly close" or "very close"

---

[62] See Jack Wertheimer, "The Truth About American Jews and Israel", *Commentary*, June 2009, 42.
[63] See Ynetnews, "2009 a record year in North American aliyah", http://www.ynetnews.com/articles/0, 7340,L-3827806,00.html, accessed March 30, 2010.
[64] See Jack Wertheimer, "The Truth About American Jews and Israel", *Commentary*, June 2009, 44.
[65] See Steven M. Cohen and Ari Y. Kelman, "Beyond Distancing: Young Adult American Jews and Their Alienation from Israel", The Jewish Identity Project of Reboot, Andrea and Charles Bronfman Philanthropies, 2007, http://www.policyarchive.org/bitstream/handle/10207/14573/Beyond%20Distancing.pdf?sequence=1, accessed March 30, 2010.

to Israel, whereas 30 percent reported they had a "fairly distant" or "very distant" relationship to the Jewish state.[66] The practice of Jewish philanthropy in the United States moreover suggests that domestic concerns clearly prevail over the support given to Israel. Citing various studies on the topic, Michael Wolffsohn points to the largely unknown fact that today merely about 30 percent of all American Jewish donations flow to Israel; in the 1960s, the same number had still averaged 60 percent.[67] What is more, the lion's share of Jewish philanthropy not only remains in the United States but is furthermore used for mainly apolitical purposes. Donations typically support cultural or educational institutions, museums, hospitals, or local community work. Only 6 percent of the financial gifts by the 123 wealthiest American Jews in 2004 were directed at Jewish institutions.[68] America's 157 Jewish federations – the local philanthropic organizations that raise and allocate funds worth $3 billion annually – spend considerably less on Israel-related issues than on domestic programs. Consider the example of Combined Jewish Philanthropies (CJP), the Jewish federation of Greater Boston. Founded in 1895 with the mission to alleviate the plight of Jewish immigrants from Eastern Europe, CJP is the oldest Jewish federation of the United States. In 2008, CJP's donor support totaled over $106 million; its total assets were $530 million.[69] About 14,000 donors of all backgrounds, primarily Jewish community members from the upper and middle classes, give to CJP, with individual donations ranging from $1 to $2 million. Donors are "very responsive to crises that affect Israel's security", says Amy Mitman, assistant vice president at CJP: during the second Lebanon war in 2006, for instance, CJP was able to raise $10 million in ten days.[70] Yet, Israel

---

[66] See American Jewish Committee, "2009 Annual Survey of American Jewish Opinion", http://www.ajc.org/site/apps/nlnet/content3.aspx?c=ijITI2PHKoG&b=846741&ct=7513467, accessed March 27, 2010.
[67] See Wolffsohn (2007), 378.
[68] See Wolffsohn (2007), 378.
[69] See Combined Jewish Philanthropies, *Jewish Boston Connected. Bringing Our Strategic Plan to Life* (Boston: CJP, 2008), 24. CJP's vast financial resources by far exceed the annual budget of major Jewish organizations such as AIPAC or the American Jewish Committee (about $50 million each).
[70] Interview with Amy Mitman, Assistant Vice President, Combined Jewish Philanthropies, November 12, 2008, Boston.

is not the main benefactor of CJP's fund-raising activities. According to its 2009 Campaign Team Book, only 23 percent of the allocated funds were earmarked for "Helping Jews in Israel and Around the World".[71] CJP also states that its "financial support of Israel is not political" and that, upon request, any gift to CJP may be directed for local use only.[72]

These findings notwithstanding, scholars have also argued that a politician's stance on Israel can often be a decisive factor in elections, because pro-Israel groups in the United States are frequently able to mount substantial pressure on candidates that are seen as unfriendly toward the Jewish state. Mearsheimer and Walt cite numerous examples of how pro-Israel groups seek to influence members of Congress and, by dint of helping candidates raise financial support, can allegedly skew the balance in tight election races.[73] In addition, pro-Israel groups purportedly have a certain weight when it comes to executive appointments which require confirmation by the U.S. Senate. A recent example is the lobbying campaign led against Charles W. Freeman Jr., a seasoned U.S. diplomat, in 2009. Freeman, who had long been critical of Israel's policies, was slated to serve as chairman of the National Intelligence Council, until critics launched a campaign to derail the appointment on grounds of Freeman's alleged anti-Israel bias. Freeman eventually withdrew from the nomination, blaming what he called "the Israel lobby" for his undoing.[74]

Yet regardless of the merits of such claims, the heightened concern with pro-Israel advocacy has arguably been a characteristic feature in American Jewish politics that, especially when considered from a transatlantic perspective, sets American Jewish organizations apart from their less politically activist counterparts in Europe.

---

[71] See Combined Jewish Philanthropies, *Jewish Boston Connected. 2009 Campaign Team Book* (Boston: CJP, 2008), 8.

[72] Combined Jewish Philanthropies, *Jewish Boston Connected. 2009 Campaign Team Book* (Boston: CJP, 2008), 12.

[73] See Mearsheimer/Walt (2007), 153-160, as well as section 6.1.2 ("AIPAC and U.S. Elections") below for further discussion.

[74] See Nathan Guttman, "Following Withdrawal From Intelligence Post, Freeman Points Finger at Israel", *Forward*, March 20, 2009; Mark Mazzetti and Helene Cooper, "Israel Stance Was Undoing of an Intelligence Nominee", *The New York Times*, March 12, 2009.

2 Society-Centered Politics in the United States: Fragmentation and Competition

Before we can turn to the empirical case study of American Jewish organizations, it is necessary to look at the institutional setting in which these organizations operate. Both the discourse on structure and agency and the literature associated with the "new" institutionalism stress the relevance of the institutional context for our understanding of interest group politics.

In this chapter we briefly examine the general institutional factors that make American interest group politics a particularly competitive arena. What follows is an analysis of the key features of the American interest group and governmental systems and their relevance for the practice of interest mediation in the United States.

2.1 Interest Group System and Current Trends

As early as in the 1830s, the shrewd observer of modern comparative politics Alexis de Tocqueville noted the proclivity of Americans for "political association".[1] Still today, the United States is commonly referred to as a "nation of organizers"[2] and as an "interest group society".[3]

The fact that interest groups play a major role in American politics may nonetheless seem surprising; after all, the American interest group system is highly fragmented and characterized by its essentially "an-

---

[1] Alexis de Tocqueville, *Democracy in America* [1835/1840], eds. Harvey C. Mansfield and Delba Winthorp (Chicago: University of Chicago Press, 2000), 180.
[2] Theda Skocpol, Marshall Ganz and Ziad Munson, "A Nation of Organizers: The Institutional Origins of Civic Voluntarism in the United States", *American Political Science Review* 94:3 (September 2000), 527-546.
[3] Jeffrey M. Berry and Clyde Wilcox, *The Interest Group Society* (New York: Pearson Longman, 2009).

archic" structure.[4] Interest groups compete not only for influence in different fields, but also with each other in the same field of policy, and rarely can a single group claim representativeness in a given sector of society. The degree of integration is also limited within each sector, as interest groups are relatively reluctant to trade their autonomy for integrated and collective organizational structures. As Graham K. Wilson points out, interest groups moreover face competition from a variety of rivals, ranging from corporations to political action committees to professional lobbying firms.[5] Structural conditions such as the ethnic segmentation of society and the rootedness of interest groups in local and federal politics further add to the fragmentation of the overall interest group system.[6]

Fragmentation can also be attributed to the dramatic increase in the number of national interest groups, which have grown almost fourfold since 1959 and are estimated at about 23,000 today. Some types of interest groups have grown at much greater rates than others: trade associations experienced a considerable loss in market share, but still remain an important part of the interest group landscape. Particularly pronounced has been the growth of groups from the nonprofit sector: health, social welfare, cultural, educational, public affairs, governmental, and religious groups together represented 59 percent of the aggregate number of groups in 1995, as opposed to only 31 percent in 1959.[7] In other words, the American interest group system experienced both a significant quantitative and qualitative increase in group activity over the past few decades.[8]

---

[4] Peter Lösche, "Verbände, Gewerkschaften und das System der Arbeitsbeziehungen", in: Peter Lösche and Hans Dietrich von Loeffelholz (eds.), *Länderbericht USA. Geschichte, Politik, Wirtschaft, Gesellschaft, Kultur* (Bonn: Bundeszentrale für politische Bildung, 2004), 353.

[5] See Graham K. Wilson, "American Interest Groups", in: Jeremy J. Richardson (ed.), *Pressure Groups* (New York: Oxford University Press, 1993), 136-140.

[6] See Lösche (2004), 353, 355.

[7] See Baumgartner/Leech (1998), 109-110.

[8] See Lösche (2004), 377; Martin Sebaldt, *Transformation der Verbändedemokratie. Die Modernisierung des Systems organisierter Interessen in den USA* (Wiesbaden: Westdeutscher Verlag, 2001).

At the same time, interest groups have become increasingly involved in electoral politics. Political action committees (PACs), designed to help candidates raise and allocate funds in election campaigns, are now a powerful political force. The number of PACs increased dramatically after the amendment of the Federal Elections Campaign Act (FECA) of 1974, from about 600 in 1974 to almost 4,500 in 2000. The rise of so-called "Jewish PACs" – those that channel campaign funds to pro-Israel candidates – has likewise been impressive. Whereas in 1980 there were almost no Jewish PACs active in American congressional elections, their number had risen to over 75 in 1986.[9] The Supreme Court decision *Buckley v. Valeo* of 1976 further stimulated the creation and activities of PACs for it specifically clarified that PACs may engage in unlimited spending on issue advocacy, that is, on advocacy that does not explicitly call for the election or defeat of a candidate. Following the landmark Supreme Court ruling in *Citizens United v. F.E.C.* in 2010, so-called "super PACs" (also referred to as independent expenditure committees) are permitted to raise unlimited funds not just from individual donors but also from corporations and unions; they can advocate for or against a candidate by name, yet may not coordinate their activities with parties or with a particular candidate's campaign. Considering that PACs are frequently organized around fairly narrow and particularistic interests, their presence adds to the overall fragmentation of the interest group landscape in the United States.[10]

Another trend that has transformed the nature of interest group politics is the shift from membership organizations to professionally managed advocacy groups and nonprofit organizations.[11] Operated by paid staffs and professionals, a growing number of interest groups do not rely on traditional mass membership. Instead, they resemble "bodyless heads", as Marshall Ganz puts it, that either represent other organi-

---

[9] See Michael J. Malbin, "Jewish PACs: A New Force in Jewish Political Action", in: Elazar (ed.) (1988), 51.

[10] See M. Margaret Conway, Joanne Connor Green and Marian Currinder, "Interest Group Money in Elections", in: Allan J. Cigler and Burdett A. Loomis (eds.), *Interest Group Politics* (Washington, D.C.: CQ Press, 2002), 120-121.

[11] See Theda Skocpol, *Diminished Democracy: From Membership to Management in American Civic Life* (Norman, OK: University of Oklahoma Press, 2003).

zations or do not have individual members at all.[12] In the same vein, conventional gatherings lose their significance as supporters are increasingly mobilized through mass mailings and the media.[13] Traditional grassroots activity has changed, too: rather than running their own local campaigns, some groups have begun to outsource this task to an "activism industry", which does the canvassing on their behalf.[14] In light of these developments, concerns over the rise of a new "pressure elite" have expectedly been voiced,[15] thereby resonating with earlier studies on elitism in American politics.[16]

In short, American interest groups operate in a fragmented and highly volatile environment. The governmental system and the practice of interest mediation further reinforce these trends as they expose interest groups to considerable competition among themselves.

2.2   Governmental System and the Practice of Interest Mediation

According to Nelson W. Polsby, some of the salient features of the contemporary American political system are:

> 1. A presidential branch increasingly separate and distinct from the executive
> 2. Competition between presidency and Congress for influence over the permanent government
> 3. A singularly important legislative branch, capable of forging alliances with interest groups

---

[12] Quoted in Skocpol (2003), 163.
[13] See Steven E. Schier, *By Invitation Only: The Rise of Exclusive Politics in the United States* (Pittsburgh: University of Pittsburgh Press, 2000).
[14] See Dana R. Fisher, "The Activism Industry", *The American Prospect* (online), September 14, 2006; Dana R. Fisher, *Activism, Inc.: How the Outsourcing of Grassroots Campaigns Is Strangling Progressive Politics in America* (Stanford: Stanford University Press, 2006).
[15] See John B. Judis, "The Pressure Elite: Inside the Narrow World of Advocacy Group Politics", *The American Prospect* (online), March 21, 1992.
[16] See C. Wright Mills, *The Power Elite* (New York: Oxford University Press, 1956); E. E. Schattschneider, *The Semisovereign People: A Realist's View of Democracy in America* (New York: Holt, Rinehart and Winston, 1960).

4. A one-hundred-party system, based in the several states, providing for some of the variation in representation that in other electoral systems is supplied by multiple national parties
5. A strong form of judicial review that underwrites frequent recourse to litigation and reliance on lawyers in ordering relations among citizens and political institutions
6. A very large population of decision makers in many policy areas and reliance on the national news media to send signals among them[17]

Political scientists typically classify the United States as a presidential regime; a system of checks and balances, it is characterized by an "antagonistic partnership" between the executive and legislative branches.[18] The legislative and executive branches of government are elected separately, and no one branch can by ordinary means unseat the other. It is a system in which neither the president rules nor one where Congress governs but one where both the president and Congress, along with the courts and independent states, share power in ways that make change difficult.[19]

The legislative initiative rests with Congress, and is driven by single representatives or senators and their staffers. In particular, congressional committees and subcommittees play a key role in the legislative process. In parliamentary regimes like Germany, by contrast, the executive and legislative branches are intertwined rather than separated: here, the executive emerges from the legislature and rests upon its majority. In Germany, therefore, the legislative initiative is clearly dominated by the executive and its bureaucracy.[20]

Interest groups adapt their lobbying strategies accordingly. Because of the separation of powers in the United States, effective access to one part of the government does not assure access to another. For the constituencies of these institutions are very different, as David Truman notes: "The representative, the senator, and the president each must give

---

[17] Nelson W. Polsby, "The Political System", in: Peter H. Schuck and James Q. Wilson (eds.), *Understanding America. The Anatomy of An Exceptional Nation* (New York: PublicAffairs, 2008), 25.
[18] Kurt L. Shell, "Das politische System", in: Lösche/Loeffelholz (eds.) (2004), 202 (quotation marks in original).
[19] See Polsby (2008), 3.
[20] See Lösche (2004), 368-369.

ear to groups that one or both of the others frequently can ignore".[21] Interest groups will thus often need to approach the presidency and the House and Senate – both of which are equal partners in the legislative process – at the same time. Lobbying Congress is particularly time-consuming: owing their election to local constituencies, members of Congress act independently as political entrepreneurs and, unlike in parliamentary regimes, are less inherently susceptible to fraction discipline. In order to be successful, interest groups have to concentrate their lobbying efforts on individual members of Congress and its committees. Their success critically depends on the ability to forge personal relationships with the legislators and staffers that are part of the "issue network" in the respective policy domain.[22]

In terms of interest mediation between state and society, the United States corresponds to the model of a pluralist interest group system.[23] First and foremost, pluralist systems are characterized by the lack of corporatist arrangements between specific groups and the government. In the U.S., the fragmented structure of the interest group system is among the main reasons that account for the lack of such (neo)-corporatist arrangements. Also, there are no business and labor peak associations in America; only 13 percent of jobholders are unionized.[24] The pluralist system of the United States does not allow interest groups to gain a corporatist edge over others – to the contrary, it exposes them to intense competition among themselves.

Moreover, the structural weakness of political parties tends to enhance the role of interest groups as the privileged link between the state and society. Over the past decades, other intermediaries such as PACs and think tanks, too, have increasingly taken on functions traditionally ascribed to political parties.[25] It is therefore not surprising that – unlike

---

[21] Truman (1981), 324.
[22] See Hugh Heclo, "Issue Networks and the Executive Establishment: Government Growth in an Age of Improvement", in: Anthony King (ed.), *The New American Political System* (Washington, D.C.: American Enterprise Institute, 1978), 87-124.
[23] See Almond/Powell/Dalton/Strøm (2010), 69.
[24] See Lösche (2004), 378.
[25] See Lösche (2004), 372; Winand Gellner, *Ideenagenturen für Politik und Öffentlichkeit: Think Tanks in den USA und in Deutschland* (Opladen: Westdeutscher Verlag, 1995).

in Weimar Germany – there has never been a Jewish political party in the United States.[26] Instead, the mediating function between the Jewish community and the state is performed by Jewish organizations and is modeled after the pattern of Jewish self-governance, as described in the chapter below.

3 Political Implications for Jewish Organizations: a Pattern of Self-Governance

The main features of the institutional environment in the United States – that is, fragmentation and competition – affect Jewish organizations in three important ways. First, they affect the ways in which Jewish communities organize political activity. Second, they help understand why organizational duplication has been a perennial issue in American Jewish politics. And third, they also explain why Jewish organizations outside of the mainstream have sometimes faced marginalization and decline.

3.1 Communal Organization

Jewish communal organization in the United States follows the pattern of voluntary participation and self-governance.[27] This means that American Jews are free to bind together as they see fit, without facing the need to create a national or local umbrella organization for external representation to the state. American pluralism, individualism, and voluntarism are the reasons why the traditional European model of a uniform, all-controlling *kehillah* – a community chartered and regulated by the secular government – could never strike root in the United States. Arthur A. Goren has shown in a study on community organization that the at-

---

[26] See Michael Brenner, "The Jüdische Volkspartei – National-Jewish Communal Politics during the Weimar Republic", in: LBI (ed.), *LBI Year Book Vol. 35* (London: Secker & Warburg, 1990), 219-243.
[27] See Hasia R. Diner, "Jewish Self-Governance, American Style", *American Jewish History* 81:3-4 (Spring/Summer 1994), 277-295.

tempts to establish a *kehillah* in New York at the beginning of the twentieth century only lasted a few years before breaking up.[28]

In addition, the constitutional separation of church and state in the United States precludes the model of the *kehillah* as an intermediary between the state and the Jewish community. Specifically, the First Amendment to the United States Constitution protects the free exercise of religion and prohibits Congress from establishing a state church; in the same vein, there is no protection for any particular religious organization.[29] It is the "aloofness of the state" – with the government placing itself above and outside matters religious – that serves as a precondition for Jewish self-governance in America.[30]

To borrow the terminology of Daniel J. Elazar, the American Jewish community is thus best understood as a prime example of a "diffused community": it is a community without government recognition or government support, an entirely voluntary community, where "an open market exists for competing Jewish organizations to emerge in every sphere and in every arena".[31] Still, while the pattern of Jewish self-governance allows for a high degree of fluidity, it is also prone to organizational duplication.

3.2 The Issue of Duplication

One of the questions that most bedevil American Jewish organizations is that of duplication. Addressing this very issue in 1951, Robert M. MacIver, a professor emeritus at Columbia University, published a report commissioned by the National Community Relations Advisory Council

---

[28] See Arthur A. Goren, *New York Jews and the Quest for Community: The Kehillah Experiment, 1908-1922* (New York: Columbia University Press, 1970), 252.

[29] See Corwin Smidt, Lyman Kellstedt, John Green and James Guth, "Religion and Politics in the United States", in: William Safran (ed.), *The Secular and the Sacred: Nation, Religion, and Politics* (London: Frank Cass, 2003), 34.

[30] Diner (1994), 287.

[31] Daniel J. Elazar, "Jewish Communal Structures Around the World", http://www.jcpa.org/dje/articles2/jewcommstruct.htm, and Daniel J. Elazar, "Representation in Five Jewish Communities: Australia, Canada, France, the Netherlands, and the USA", http://www.jcpa.org/dje/articles2/5jewcomm.htm, accessed April 19, 2010.

(NCRAC), a group that served as a forum for discussion among the American Jewish Committee, the Anti-Defamation League, the American Jewish Congress, the Jewish Labor Committee, the Jewish War Veterans, and the Union of American Hebrew Congregations. MacIver concluded that "the lack of unity, the active discord, [and] the jealous and often quarrelsome competitiveness" between these organizations made it impossible for them to develop "any clear conception of a common goal".[32] He therefore called for a "concentration of effort" and for "common planning"[33] in order to avoid "competitive waste and unprofitable duplication".[34] All fields of activity that seemed to be duplicated by two or more organizations were thus to be assigned to a single agency. Specifically, the MacIver report recommended that the separate research on anti-Semitism by the American Jewish Committee and the Anti-Defamation League be consolidated into a single fact-finding system; that AJC and ADL relinquish their veterans departments and cede that task to the Jewish War Veterans; that the Jewish Labor Committee become the only organization active in the field of labor; that the Union of American Hebrew Congregations obtain exclusive jurisdiction in the interfaith area; that only one organization shall be concerned with providing legal advice; and that AJC and ADL better coordinate their informational programs and outreach to other groups.[35]

Unsurprisingly, the organizations that stood to lose functions quickly dismissed MacIver's recommendations. In fact, both the American Jewish Committee and the Anti-Defamation League decided to secede from

---

[32] Robert MacIver, *Report on the Jewish Community Relations Agencies* (New York: National Community Relations Advisory Council, 1951), AJC Blaustein Library, 53.

[33] Robert MacIver, *Report on the Jewish Community Relations Agencies* (New York: National Community Relations Advisory Council, 1951), AJC Blaustein Library, 53.

[34] Robert MacIver, *Report on the Jewish Community Relations Agencies* (New York: National Community Relations Advisory Council, 1951), AJC Blaustein Library, 93.

[35] See Robert MacIver, *Report on the Jewish Community Relations Agencies* (New York: National Community Relations Advisory Council, 1951), AJC Blaustein Library, 131-133.

NCRAC, as they now feared a loss of autonomy.[36] In a statement of views on the report, AJC pointed out that the "preservation of organizational autonomy" was "essential" and that specific tasks could not be bundled together because each organization represented the particular convictions of a particular constituency. In the same vein, ADL charged that "the Report misses completely the part which constituency plays in the work of the ADL" and thus opposed the idea of bringing community functions under the central control of a single organization.[37] The American Jewish Congress in turn was pleased with the report and shared many of its recommendations – obviously because these involved the prospect of gaining functions at the expense of its main rivals, namely AJC and ADL. The Jewish Labor Committee, along with the Jewish War Veterans and the Union of American Hebrew Congregations, also shared the major premises of the report and welcomed its provisions for increased autonomy in their domains.[38] James Q. Wilson, in an illustration of his autonomy-based coalition theory, explains Jewish organizations' mixed reactions to the MacIver report. While the reallocation of functions would have strengthened the autonomy of some organizations, Wilson argues, it would inevitably have lessened that of others and would have reduced their appeal with current and future members.[39]

In sum, the debate on the MacIver report first and foremost shows that duplication between Jewish organizations need not be seen as a "problem" or as an organizational deficiency. Rather, it should be regarded as a direct expression of the pluralist and voluntary nature of Jewish communal organization in the United States.

---

[36] See Wertheimer (1995), 24. Both organizations however rejoined NCRAC in 1966.

[37] Quoted in Robert MacIver, *Report on the Jewish Community Relations Agencies* (New York: National Community Relations Advisory Council, 1951), AJC Blaustein Library, 173 (AJC), 225 (ADL).

[38] See Robert MacIver, *Report on the Jewish Community Relations Agencies* (New York: National Community Relations Advisory Council, 1951), AJC Blaustein Library, 179, 231, 234, 242, respectively.

[39] See Wilson (1973), 274.

3.3 Consensus and Marginalization

Because interest group politics in America takes place within a competitive market environment, Jewish organizations that position themselves at the margins of the community tend to risk further marginalization and eventual decline. Among the most well-known examples of Jewish organizations that have faced this risk are organizations such as the American Council for Judaism, Breira, New Jewish Agenda, and the Jewish Peace Lobby. Some of these organizations decided to cease their operations after only a few years of existence, while others continue to play at best a peripheral role within the Jewish community.

A curious case in American Jewish political history, the American Council for Judaism (ACJ) remains "the only American Jewish organization ever formed for the specific purpose of fighting Zionism and opposing the establishment of a Jewish state".[40] Already upon its creation by a group of Reform rabbis in Atlantic City in 1942, the American Council for Judaism differed from the rest of American Jewry in religious, social, economic, and ideological terms.[41] Consistent with its rejection of Zionism, it defined Jews not in ethnic but in purely religious terms. While the members of the ACJ saw themselves as "authentic Jews in the classical tradition of Reform Judaism", its Zionist opponents found them "unhistorical", indeed "traitorously un-Jewish".[42] The ACJ's anti-Zionist stance however backfired, and helped bring about the organization's decline, because it created a new incentive for Zionists to intensify their activities. Thus, ironically, the American Council for Judaism helped its opponents win over previously apathetic sympathizers to the Zionist cause.[43] Today, the ACJ still seeks to provide "a dis-

---

[40] Thomas A. Kolsky, *Jews Against Zionism. The American Council for Judaism, 1942-1948* (Philadelphia: Temple University Press, 1990), ix.
[41] See Samuel Halperin, "Zionist Counterpropaganda: The Case of the American Council for Judaism", *Southwestern Social Science Quarterly* 41 (March 1961), 454.
[42] Quoted in Halperin (1961), 456.
[43] See Halperin (1961), 463.

tinctive alternative vision of identity and commitment", yet continues to occupy an isolated position within the American Jewish community.[44]

In the 1970s and 1980s, two newly founded organizations – Breira and New Jewish Agenda – framed Jewish advocacy in a way that could not but challenge the communal mainstream. Associated with activists of the political left, Breira, which translates as "alternative", originated in spring 1973. It quickly stirred controversy due to its support for mutual recognition between Israelis and Palestinians after the Yom Kippur War. Fierce opposition from major Jewish organizations and in particular from the right-wing, pro-settlement group Americans for a Safe Israel (AFSI) supposedly led to its disbandment in 1978.[45] Two years later, New Jewish Agenda (NJA) followed in Breira's footsteps, adopting the mission to serve as "a Jewish voice among progressives and a progressive voice among Jews".[46] Unlike its informal predecessor, NJA was set up as a multipurpose and grassroots organization so as to enlist support from broader segments of the Jewish community. Though it was not exactly the "counter-AIPAC lobby" that Yasser Arafat once believed it to be,[47] the mainstream community perceived New Jewish Agenda to violate the prevailing consensus. As a result, New Jewish Agenda drifted ever further toward the fringes of the community and finally decided to shut down, for various reasons, in 1992.[48]

Situated on the left of the political spectrum, the dovish Jewish Peace Lobby (JPL), a small grass-roots organization established in 1989, shares some similarities with NJA. As is clear from its founding statement, JPL presents itself as an alternative lobbying organization to

---

[44] American Council for Judaism, "About Us... Learn About the American Council for Judaism", http://www.acjna.org/acjna/about.aspx, accessed April 21, 2010.

[45] See New Jewish Agenda, "NJA's early evolution & the legacy of Breira", http://www.newjewishagenda.net/breira.php, accessed April 22, 2010. NJA even asserts that Breira was "destroyed by other Jewish organizations".

[46] New Jewish Agenda, ""Agendas within Agenda": The challenge of mobilizing diverse Jewish communities", http://www.newjewishagenda.net/challenges.php, accessed April 22, 2010.

[47] See Rael Jean Isaac, "New Jewish Agenda – Outside the Consensus", *Midstream*, December 1990, 15.

[48] See New Jewish Agenda, "Why did NJA shut down?", http://www.newjewishagenda.net/whyshutdown1.php, accessed April 22, 2010.

AIPAC that seeks to enlist broad support from within and without the Jewish community. So far, it has however played a marginal role in American Jewish politics, not least because of its negative perception by some as a "Jewish lobby for the P.L.O.".[49]

---

[49] Rael Jean Isaac, "A Jewish Lobby For The P.L.O.", *Midstream*, February-March 1991, 36-37.

4 Typologies of American Jewish Organizations

In this section we undertake the attempt to categorize Jewish organizations more systematically. Following a short discussion of general typologies, we develop a process-oriented typology specifically suited for the analysis of Jewish political organizations and, correspondingly, elaborate on the basic distinction made by Peter Y. Medding between "modern" and "new" Jewish politics.

4.1 Overview and General Typologies

Nowhere else are Jewish organizations more numerous and functionally diverse than in the United States. Indeed, a 2007 survey published by the American Jewish Committee reports a total number of no less than 5,057 national Jewish organizations in seven distinct functional categories: community relations; cultural; Israel-related; overseas aid; religious, educational organizations; schools, institutions, social, mutual benefit; and social welfare. It is worthwhile to note that the total number of organizations is distributed about evenly among these functions. Considered against the backdrop of the overall spectrum of Jewish organizations, Israel-related organizations constitute only a relatively minor category. In absolute numbers, the various categories include the following types of organizations:[1]

Table 1: Overview of American Jewish Organizations, General Typology

Community Relations	605
Cultural	610
Israel-Related	618
Overseas Aid	631
Religious, Educational	633

---

[1] See American Jewish Committee, "National Jewish Organizations", in: AJC (ed.), *American Jewish Year Book Vol. 107* (New York: AJC, 2007), 605.

Schools, Institutions	645
Social, Mutual Benefit	656
Social Welfare	659
Total	5,057

The issue-related typology of Jewish organizations used in this statistic follows the approach commonly taken in the scholarly literature.² Jewish organizations are typically classified by issue involvement in one of the five major spheres of activity: religious-congregational; educational-cultural; community relations; communal-welfare; and Israel-overseas.³ This typology has the ostensible benefit of giving a handy overview of American Jewish organizational life in general as it includes the entire range of Jewish organizations. Yet, it is often difficult to identify a given organization with one single issue as many organizations are active in various domains. Consider, for example, the American Jewish Committee, which Elazar misleadingly characterizes as an "Israel-overseas" organization. While AJC in fact deals extensively with Israel and issues of international concern, it also serves as a community relations agency due to its outreach to the various Jewish and non-Jewish communities; in addition, it shares many elements of an educational, research-oriented organization.

Alternatively, one may also refer to a functional typology of Jewish organizations. According to this typology, the Jewish community represents a polity of its own, and Jewish organizations are accordingly classified based on their functional contributions to that polity. Drawing analogies to the intermediary structure of political systems in general, Elazar distinguishes four types of Jewish organizations: government-like institutions; localistic institutions and organizations; general-purpose, mass-based organizations; and special-interest institutions and organi-

---

[2] James Q. Wilson offers a different typology, using as variables the relative degree of autonomy and the relative level of resources of the organization. Wilson argues that the configuration of these variables determines the likelihood of interorganizational competition. The typology is not specifically tailored for the analysis of Jewish organizations, though. See Wilson (1973), 264-266.

[3] See Elazar (1995), 277-312.

zations.[4] Within each category, further issue-related distinctions, as noted above, can then be made.

However, even an improved issue-related typology is largely unsatisfactory since overlaps between the various functional categories may still occur. But also for other reasons, the issue-related and functional typologies proposed by Elazar are of limited value for political science analysis. This is because they do not allow for a clear distinction between the political and apolitical spheres of community activity: as a matter of fact, both typologies indifferently juxtapose political and apolitical organizations. How, then, can Jewish organizations be typologized in a way that better suits political scientists?

4.2 A Process-Oriented Typology of Jewish Political Organizations

Obviously, one preliminary step is to exclude from further analysis those organizations that do not explicitly engage in political activities. This admittedly is easier said than done. For it is perfectly reasonable to argue that prima facie non-political activities – such as Jewish philanthropy – may indeed have "political ramifications", as Stephen M. Walt contends, and may thus have at least an indirect impact on politics.[5] For the sake of clarity, however, the typology suggested in the following only includes Jewish organizations that explicitly formulate and pursue a political agenda.

Thus, organizations such as synagogues, community services organizations,[6] and the Jewish federations will be excluded from further consideration. This is to say that we need to forego the analysis of a substantial part of American Jewish organizational life; a brief remark on the outstanding role of the Jewish federations may nonetheless be in order. The federations are essentially synonymous with charities or philanthropies – their main business is local fund-raising and allocating funds for welfare services. Not least because of the work of the federations, Jewish philanthropy in America is world-renowned for its finan-

---

[4] See Elazar (1995), 234-276. Also see chapter 4.1.1 in the first part of this dissertation.
[5] Walt (2008 Interview).
[6] Here, the Hebrew Immigrant Aid Society (HIAS), founded in 1881, or the American Jewish Joint Distribution Committee (JDC), founded in 1914, are among the most well-known examples.

cial scope and dedication. Today, 157 federations and 400 independent network communities are organized within The Jewish Federations of North America (known under the name of United Jewish Communities, or UJC, until 2009), which raises and distributes more than $3 billion annually for social and welfare services.[7]

But even considering the narrow category of Jewish political organizations, a variety of distinctions can still be made. For instance, one may distinguish between stand-alone and umbrella organizations; between religious and secular political organizations; between national and local organizations; or between local political and local apolitical organizations. While these distinctions are empirically valid, they are however likely to obscure more than they reveal. Since they are not mutually exclusive, they are ill-suited to guide our research in a systematic fashion.

In order to avoid the predicament of possible overlaps, this dissertation therefore relies on a process-oriented typology of Jewish political organizations. It differentiates Jewish political organizations depending on their degree of involvement in the political process. In so doing we can fruitfully build upon Peter Y. Medding's conceptual distinction between "modern" and "new" Jewish politics, as defined below. (As we have seen earlier, the pattern of "traditional" Jewish politics, is not – and has never been – relevant in the American case.)

Modern Jewish politics describes a pattern in which Jewish organizations primarily influence the political process from the outside, that is, by appealing to the public through mass media or by staging punctual political campaigns.[8] Jewish political organizations associated with this pattern often pursue a multi-issue agenda and are not only focused on issues related to Israel; they may also pursue educational goals, for example. Only a share of their work is devoted to professional lobbying activities. The pattern of modern Jewish politics is pertinent for organizations such as the "big three" defense organizations – the American Jewish Committee, the Anti-Defamation League, and the American Jewish Congress – as well as for umbrella organizations such as the Jewish

---

[7] See The Jewish Federations of North America, "About Us", http://www.jewishfederations.org/section.aspx?id=31, accessed April 26, 2010.

[8] For a further and general discussion, see Ken Kollman, *Outside Lobbying: Public Opinion and Interest Group Strategies* (Princeton: Princeton University Press, 1998).

Council for Public Affairs, the Conference of Presidents of Major American Jewish Organizations, and the Conference on Jewish Material Claims Against Germany.

New Jewish politics by contrast refers to a pattern in which Jewish organizations are permanently involved in the political process, which they try to influence from the inside through legislative and electoral lobbying. Jewish organizations associated with this pattern are decidedly pro-active and seek to have an ex ante impact on legislation and policy decisions. Typically, their headquarters are located in Washington, D.C., rather than in New York City. The most prominent organizations pertaining to this category are the American Israel Public Affairs Committee (AIPAC) and J Street. Both were set up as single-issue organizations and are exclusively focused on pro-Israel advocacy. The pattern of new Jewish politics, it should be said, is not necessarily tied to formal organizations; it may also be characteristic of a less rigidly organized movement such as Chabad-Lubavitch, a branch of Hasidic Judaism, which has achieved remarkable results through the zealous pursuit of its goals and direct involvement in the American political process.[9]

Adopting a process-oriented typology allows for the comparison of Jewish political organizations regardless of their individual differences in terms of ideology, geography, constituency, or style. In that sense, the typology used in this dissertation is based on the notion of the Weberian ideal type: although it may not claim validity in terms of an exact representation of social reality, it still serves as a means of knowledge by highlighting the salient features of a particular case.

---

[9] See Sue Fishkoff, *The Rebbe's Army. Inside the World of Chabad-Lubavitch* (New York: Schocken, 2003), 162-200. In 2002, for example, Chabad's local *shlichim* ("emissaries") raised a budget of about $1 billion. The acronym "Chabad" stands for *hokhmah* ("wisdom"), *binah* ("comprehension"), and *da'at* ("knowledge"). Rabbi Menachem Mendel Schneerson, known as "the Rebbe", led the Lubavitch movement from 1950 to 1994.

5 Modern Jewish Politics

The analysis presented in this chapter deals with America's most prominent contemporary Jewish defense organizations – the American Jewish Committee, the Anti-Defamation League, and the American Jewish Congress – as well as with the politics of leading umbrellas such as the Jewish Council for Public Affairs, the Presidents Conference, and the Claims Conference. It shows that there are substantial differences in terms of political mission and style among these organizations. It also places these differences in the context of the respective institutional framework and specifically contends that interorganizational rivalries create substantial pressure for each of these organizations to develop a distinct character. A salient feature of modern Jewish politics, they rather try to influence the political process from the outside as opposed to being directly involved in the electoral and legislative process. At a more general level, a disaggregated view of these Jewish organizations furthermore provides a compelling argument against the widely held yet misleading notion of a solidly unified pro-Israel movement in the United States.

5.1 The "Big Three" Jewish Defense Organizations

A story told by the Jewish labor organizer Paul Jacobs[1] – retold here in a slightly abridged version by Alan M. Dershowitz – ironically alludes to the struggle of the "big three" to define their role as distinct advocacy organizations. When a Jew walks into the men's room of a New York City bar, the story goes, he notices that someone has written "Screw the Jews" on the toilet wall. He calls various Jewish organizations, which quickly jump into action, but in very different ways: "The ADL issues a press release adding this act of anti-Semitism to its list of anti-Semitic incidents and announcing that this proves that anti-Semitism is on the rise again and everyone should join the ADL. The American Jewish

---

[1] See Paul Jacobs, *Is Curly Jewish?* (New York: Atheneum, 1965), 140-141.

Congress files a lawsuit seeking to enjoin the sale of liquor to anti-Semites. The American Jewish Committee, after checking with the National Council of Churches, makes a large grant to Columbia University to study the effects of liquor on anti-Semitism and other forms of bigotry, urging everyone not to jump to any conclusions, since it is possible that an Eastern European Jew might have scrawled the graffiti".[2]

This story, however caricatural, alludes to some of the major traits of these organizations as well as anticipates an important finding of this chapter: that Jewish organizations, by virtue of operating in a competitive environment, need to craft distinct political styles and organizational identities to maintain themselves. How this plays out in detail for the American Jewish Committee, the Anti-Defamation League, and the American Jewish Congress is the subject of the following analysis.

5.1.1 The American Jewish Committee

Founding History and Internal Structure

The American Jewish Committee is the oldest Jewish defense organization in the United States.[3] It was created in 1906 in response to the Kishinev pogroms in czarist Russia and, at the outset, above all emphasized the defense of Jewish rights abroad.[4] Today, AJC describes itself more broadly as an "international think tank and advocacy organization" that attempts to promote "pluralistic and democratic societies where all minorities are protected".[5] According to its mission statement, AJC specifically "protects the rights and freedoms of Jews the world over; com-

---

[2] Dershowitz (1997), 73.

[3] For a detailed study of the Committee's early history, see Naomi W. Cohen, *Not Free to Desist. The American Jewish Committee 1906-1966* (Philadelphia: The Jewish Publication Society, 1972).

[4] Kishinev – or Chișinău, today the capital of the Republic of Moldavia – was the scene of an anti-Jewish pogrom in 1903. Israel's "national poet", the Hebrew poet Haim Nahman Bialik, deals with the Kishinev pogroms is his ode "In the City of Slaughter", see Ruth R. Wisse, *The Modern Jewish Canon. A Journey Through Language and Culture* (New York: The Free Press, 2000), 109.

[5] American Jewish Committee, "Who We Are", http://www.ajc.org/site/c.ijITI2PHKoG/b.789093/k.124/Who_We_Are.htm, accessed April 29, 2010.

bats bigotry and anti-Semitism and promotes human rights for all; works for the security of Israel and deepened understanding between Americans and Israelis; advocates public policy positions rooted in American democratic values and the perspectives of the Jewish heritage; and enhances the creative vitality of the Jewish people".[6]

Since its inception AJC has been known for its high intellectual standards as well as for its tendency towards elitism. Indeed, AJC literally started out as a "committee": founded by a small group of American Jews from the established German-Jewish community, it represented the Americanized "uptown" Jews and initially did not exceed a membership of less than one hundred (personally invited) individuals.[7] In its early days, AJC relied on the "prestige, status, and connections of its handful of members" – such as Cyrus Adler, Jacob Schiff, Oscar Straus, Louis Marshall, and Mayer Sulzberger – and had "no desire" to be a mass-based organization.[8]

Over the course of the past 100 years, though, AJC has become a much more inclusive organization. Today, it numbers 175,000 members and supporters in 33 chapters (local offices which were created after 1943) throughout the United States.[9] Its internal decision-making process follows a democratic pattern that allows for grassroots participation: local chapters, for instance, can initiate policies that are then brought to the attention of the national office. In practice, the general direction of AJC is nonetheless largely influenced by David A. Harris, the organization's executive director. After a policy decision has been made by the executive committee, one of the four major commissions (anti-Semitism, interfaith, public policy, and international) will draft a related policy statement, which is then sent to the board of governors for further consideration. The board of governors comprises about 250 members from all chapters and has the powers to overrule the decisions of both the commissions and the executive committee. In order to pass, decisions generally have to be "clear-cut". Yet while all chapters have a say in the

---

[6] David A. Harris, *American Jewish Committee at 100* (New York: AJC, 2006), inner cover page.

[7] See Interview with Eugene DuBow, former Director of AJC Berlin, American Jewish Committee, March 23, 2009, New York.

[8] Diner (2004), 195.

[9] See American Jewish Committee, *AJC by the numbers* (New York: AJC, 2007), 7.

decision-making process, they also have to abide by the national policy once a final decision is made. Chapters may not opt out of national policies, as the example of same-sex marriage shows. After a local vote of 19 to 6 in favor of same-sex marriage, AJC's Boston chapter recently decided to draft a statement for national consideration. Following a controversial debate and vote at the national level, the initiative prepared by AJC Boston however failed to pass. As a result, advocacy on behalf of same-sex marriage is now no longer possible in any of the AJC chapters, including Boston.[10]

Upper-level membership in AJC tends to be costly as financial contributions generally increase the likelihood of getting appointed to one of the key decision-making bodies. A donation of at least $50,000 is expected from members of the executive committee; at least $10,000 is expected from members of the board of governors; at the chapter level, members of the board of directors donate at least $1,500. But money alone, says Lawrence D. Lowenthal, ultimately does not suffice to get appointed, since AJC is "a very intellectual organization" and thus is "very demanding". In this sense, AJC can still be considered an elitist organization, or as AJC memoirist Gary Rubin explains: "[Y]es, absolutely, we are and should be an elite organization. (...) The word elite means the best (...) in this very competitive atmosphere for membership (...) that attracts the best, that attracts the allegiance of the leading American Jews, who are many now".[11] It accordingly has a distinguished membership: "There are many Jewish members of the top law firms, of the top business corporations. There are many Jews who have easy access to the political arena, who speak to their congresspeople every day (...)".[12] As the only American Jewish political organization with a permanent representation in Germany, AJC furthermore maintains excellent relations with the country's political elites. For example,

---

[10] See Lowenthal (2008 Interview).
[11] Interview with Gary Rubin, November 12, 1990, The New York Public Library-American Jewish Committee Oral History Collection, Dorot Jewish Division, The New York Public Library, Astor, Lenox and Tilden Foundations, 135-136.
[12] Interview with Gary Rubin, November 12, 1990, Dorot Jewish Division, NYPL, 134. For a list of some of AJC's most prominent supporters, see American Jewish Committee, *AJC 2008 Annual Report* (New York: AJC, 2009), 14-15, 17-19.

on the occasion of the tenth anniversary of the opening of its Berlin office, AJC received personal greetings from many of Germany's top political leaders.[13]

To finance its activities the American Jewish Committee relies mostly on contributions and membership dues. AJC reported an annual budget of about $55 million (up from $29 million in 2004 and $31 million in 2003) and total assets worth over $138 million in 2008.[14] It ranked fourth by expenses and third by assets in a nationwide survey of civil rights, social action and advocacy organizations published by the Urban Institute in 2007.[15] As a nonprofit organization under the regulations of section 501(c)(3) of the Internal Revenue Code, AJC benefits from tax exemption.[16]

---

[13] Among the congratulators were Frank-Walter Steinmeier (minister for foreign affairs), Klaus Kinkel (former minister for foreign affairs), Norbert Lammert (president of the German Bundestag), Rita Süssmuth (former president of the German Bundestag), Wolfgang Schäuble (minister of the interior), Otto Schily (former minister of the interior), Franz Josef Jung (minister of defense), Brigitte Zypries (minister of justice), and Klaus Wowereit (governing mayor of Berlin). On the occasion of its centennial anniversary, AJC received greetings from Chancellor Angela Merkel, former Federal President Richard von Weizsäcker, and former Foreign Minister Joschka Fischer, among others. See American Jewish Committee, *A tribute to the AJC in Germany on the occasion of the American Jewish Committee's centennial anniversary* (Berlin: AJC, 2006), 1, 10.

[14] Contributions account for 86 percent of the overall budget. See American Jewish Committee, *AJC 2008 Annual Report* (New York: AJC, 2009), 20-21. For the 2003 and 2004 numbers, see The Foundation for Public Affairs (ed.), *Public Interest Group Profiles 2004-2005* (Washington, D.C.: CQ Press, 2004), 51.

[15] See The Urban Institute, National Center for Charitable Statistics, "NCCS – Display Largest Public Charities", http://nccsdataweb.urban.org/PubApps/showTopOrgs.php?cat=R&amt=exps, and http://nccsdataweb.urban.org/PubApps/showTopOrgs.php?cat=R&amt=ass_eoy, accessed April 30, 2010.

[16] The Internal Revenue Code is part of the United States Code which contains the general and permanent laws of the United States. For detailed information on the 501(c)(3) status, see United States Code Annotated, *Title 26. Internal Revenue Code §§ 501 to 640* (St. Paul, MN: West Group, 2002), 12-146, especially 13 and 71-72. The related government agency is the Internal Revenue Service (IRS) of the U.S. Department of the Treasury.

AJC positions itself as a multi-issue organization engaging in advocacy on a diverse spectrum of issues, including human rights, interfaith dialogue, Jewish life, anti-Semitism, Israel, Iran, world affairs (with special attention paid to the United Nations, Europe, Latin America, and Africa), and even environmental issues. AJC remains solidly committed to a broad agenda although the focus on Jewish as well as general political and civic issues inevitably entails increased competition from single-issue "boutique organizations".[17] Gary Rubin explains AJC's rationale:

> [T]he question, in terms of competitive marketing, is what is your niche, and I do believe that there is a niche in the American Jewish community for a broad-based organization, and that's who we are. And I think that if we try to abandon our niche and identify ourselves, say, only with anti-Semitism or only with Israel, there are other organizations that have already filled those niches and we will essentially be pale imitators of the ADL or of AIPAC. (...) [W]e won't be very good institutionally if what we do is compete institutionally with them in their niches. We have to promote ours, and ours is the agency that (...) is willing to fight for a broad rather than narrow view of what the Jewish agenda should be. I believe that there are significant numbers of American Jews who want to be associated with an agency like that, and so especially in a competitive marketing situation, one has to go to one's strength and I believe that the broad agenda is specifically our strength.[18]

Despite being a multi-issue organization, AJC is primarily concerned with international affairs and with issues relating to its mission of "Glo-

---

[17] Interview with Gary Rubin, November 12, 1990, Dorot Jewish Division, NYPL, 128. "Boutique organizations" are organizations geared to one single issue, such as Israel or anti-Semitism, and which raise funds from members who are strictly concerned about that one issue. It should also be noted that there is no single or obvious definition of what "Jewish" concerns are: involvement in interfaith dialogue or in environmental advocacy, for example, can also be inferred from the Jewish religious tradition, in particular from the precepts of *zedakah* ("righteousness") and *tikkun olam* ("repairing the world").

[18] Interview with Gary Rubin, November 12, 1990, Dorot Jewish Division, NYPL, 132-133.

bal Jewish Advocacy".[19] The founding director of AJC's Berlin office, Eugene DuBow, points to the fact that AJC "was filling a niche" when it developed a decidedly international outlook after David A. Harris had assumed office as executive director in 1990.[20] An AJC community organizer of more than four decades, DuBow cautions that a yet broader selection of issues would possibly put the organization at risk: given that Jewish organizations operate in a competitive environment, they are particularly dependent on individual contributions to fund their activities; contributors however are often focused on specific issues and thus "reluctant to give" to broad-based organizations.[21] Moreover, AJC's internationalist outlook was already somewhat visible upon its creation in 1906, when it reacted to pogroms against Jews in Russia. Initially founded as a non-Zionist organization, AJC has evolved over the years into "a profoundly pro-Israel organization".[22] It shed its former reluctance to espouse the idea of Jewish peoplehood and now is openly committed to the religious, secular, and ethnic definitions of American Jewish identity.[23]

Political Style: Horizontal and Vertical Politics

The internal characteristics of the American Jewish Committee affect its political style in two important ways. First, by pursuing a relatively broad agenda, AJC is able to work in coalitions with various other interest groups. Second, due to its strong international presence and global advocacy work, it has fostered its image as the "embassy of American

---

[19] This slogan is stated repeatedly on AJC's website, see for example American Jewish Committee, "About Us", http://www.ajc.org/site/c.ijITI2PHKoG/b.789089/k.D39C/About_Us.htm, accessed May 1, 2010.

[20] When he began his career at AJC in 1966, says DuBow (2009 Interview), 75 percent of AJC's work was focused on civil rights issues – it was "domestic work".

[21] DuBow (2009 Interview).

[22] Marianne R. Sanua, *Let Us Prove Strong. The American Jewish Committee, 1945-2006* (Waltham, MA: Brandeis University Press, 2007), xiii.

[23] That is, "Judaism", "Israelism", and "tribalism", see the Interview with David A. Harris, October 7, 1991, The New York Public Library-American Jewish Committee Oral History Collection, Dorot Jewish Division, The New York Public Library, Astor, Lenox and Tilden Foundations, 26-27.

Jews" abroad. Accordingly, AJC is known for its quiet and diplomatic approach to politics – with some exceptions, as a brief case study will show.

Horizontal Politics

In terms of intergroup politics, the American Jewish Committee typically engages in what has been termed "disjointed coalitions", that is, in coalitions with groups that share common goals but have a different overall agenda. It works with Jewish as well as non-Jewish groups alike. Indeed, as David A. Harris avers, AJC is "friendly with non-Jewish organizations" and seeks to build broad coalitions against the background of shared interests. "Rather than looking inward, we reach out", Harris says. The policy of intergroup dialogue and public outreach has not failed to elicit criticism from some Jews in the Hasidic community, however, who regard the outspoken "coalitioning" promoted by AJC as "the beginning of the end for Judaism".[24]

The American Jewish Committee is especially known for its coalitional work in the field of interreligious and interethnic dialogue. AJC maintains ongoing relationships with 21 denominations in the United States,[25] including programs to promote Christian-Jewish, Muslim-Jewish, and Hindu-Jewish relations as well as outreach initiatives to the Latino community.[26] AJC had also been a strong supporter of African Americans during the civil rights movement: in 1954, the U.S. Supreme Court quoted social science research commissioned by AJC in its landmark decision in *Brown v. Board of Education*, which declared racial segregation in public schools to be in violation of the Fourteenth Amendment of the U.S. Constitution.[27]

---

[24] Interview with David A. Harris, October 7, 1991, Dorot Jewish Division, NYPL, 47, 46.

[25] See American Jewish Committee, *AJC by the numbers* (New York: AJC, 2007), 11.

[26] See American Jewish Committee, "Interfaith", http://www.ajc.org/site/c.ijIT I2PHKoG/b.823789/k.7F9/Interfaith.htm, accessed May 4, 2010.

[27] See Sanua (2007), x. Amendment XIV was ratified in 1868 as one of the Reconstruction Amendments (that is, Amendments XIII-XV) following the Civil War.

But AJC's broad-based agenda is only a necessary, though not sufficient, condition for successful coalition-building. Even more important is the fact that AJC views itself as an "international think tank" and as a "research institute".[28] By developing policy positions on a wide range of issues it creates the preconditions for subsequent intergroup outreach and coalitional work. According to Gary Rubin, there is no other Jewish organization "that invests as many resources as [AJC does] on American policy development and in participation in policy debates".[29] To serve these ends, AJC employs 24 "staff experts" in a total of 13 policy fields.[30] In addition to publishing activities in these policy fields, the American Jewish Committee is noted for its regular surveys of American Jewish opinion and, in particular, for publishing the American Jewish Year Book, the foremost reference source about the Jewish communities and Jewish life in the U.S. and worldwide.[31] The influential monthly *Commentary* magazine, today a leading voice of neoconservatism, was founded by AJC in 1945 and published under its auspices until 2006.[32] All these intellectual contributions have further enhanced AJC's ability to have its views considered on various policy issues.

Given its coalitional approach to politics, it is maybe not surprising that, in terms of political orientation, the American Jewish Committee defines itself as a "centrist organization".[33] This is to say that AJC stands neither clearly on the conservative nor the liberal side of the political spectrum as there is "a genuine constituency for both groups"

---

[28] Lowenthal (2008 Interview).
[29] Interview with Gary Rubin, November 12, 1990, Dorot Jewish Division, NYPL, 121.
[30] See American Jewish Committee, "AJC Experts", http://www.ajc.org/site/ c.ijITI2PHKoG/b.789101/k. 2E0C/AJC_Experts.htm, accessed May 5, 2010. The related policy fields are: anti-Semitism, energy independence, international affairs, intergroup relations, interreligious affairs, Israel, Jewish life, Latin American and Latino affairs, legal affairs and domestic policy, Russian Jewish community, terrorism, United Nations, and young leadership.
[31] See American Jewish Committee, "American Jewish Year Book", http:// www.ajcarchives.org/main.php?GroupingId=40, accessed May 5, 2010.
[32] See Gabrielle Birkner, "Commentary, American Jewish Committee Separate", *The New York Sun*, December 21, 2006.
[33] Interview with David A. Harris, October 7, 1991, Dorot Jewish Division, NYPL, 51.

and "genuine respect for differences of perspective". But it is fair to say that, at least as far as domestic matters are concerned, AJC has often taken policy positions that are usually identified with liberal politics. While it "does reach out to both sides", Gary Rubin says, "the predominant direction of our agenda is liberal. It's true on poverty, it's true on immigration. (...) I think that basically (...) our immigration policy (...) is in keeping with political liberalism. And that's also true about church-state policy, [and] of our civil-rights policy".[34] The liberal bent regarding domestic issues notwithstanding, it would however be erroneous to label AJC an overall "liberal" organization. Its overall agenda, including foreign affairs and Israel, especially when compared to other Jewish organizations, is more consistent with centrist politics.[35]

What distinguishes AJC from its peers is not only its strong international focus but, most importantly, its niche position as the "embassy of American Jews".[36] Ever since the appointment of David A. Harris as executive director in 1990, AJC has expanded significantly into the realm of international relations. Today, it maintains affiliations with Jewish organizations in 23 countries and operates offices and bureaus in eight cities – Berlin, Brussels, Geneva, Jerusalem, Mumbai, Paris, Rome, and Warsaw. In Brussels, AJC hosts its Transatlantic Institute, while Geneva is home to UN Watch, monitoring United Nations actions regarding Israel.[37] Since the opening of its Berlin office in 1998, AJC has been the only American Jewish political organization with a permanent representation in Germany.[38] In line with its decision to make international affairs a more prominent feature on its agenda, the Committee furthermore joined the Conference of Presidents of Major American Jewish Organizations in 1991, a Jewish umbrella organization that deals

---

[34] Interview with Gary Rubin, November 12, 1990, Dorot Jewish Division, NYPL, 118.
[35] As confirmed independently in the interviews with Lowenthal (2008 Interview) and with Deidre Berger, Director of AJC Berlin, American Jewish Committee, May 19, 2009, Berlin.
[36] DuBow (2009 Interview).
[37] See American Jewish Committee, *AJC by the numbers* (New York: AJC, 2007), 13.
[38] With the arguable exception of the Claims Conference, an umbrella organization based in New York City, which also has a permanent office in Germany.

predominantly with Israel and international issues. For many years, in fact, AJC had refrained from joining the Presidents Conference out of its non-Zionist tradition and predominant focus on American domestic concerns.[39]

In an effort to cultivate "long-term diplomatic relationships", AJC staff and lay leaders visit about 60 countries per year and meet with heads of state, foreign ministers, and other government officials. In the same vein, AJC embarks on a "diplomatic marathon" during the yearly sessions of the United Nations General Assembly, where it "meets privately with the presidents, prime ministers, and foreign ministers of at least 70 UN member states".[40] Honing its image as a quasi-diplomatic institution, AJC even subsumes its domestic coalitional politics under the larger heading of diplomacy, stating that "350 AJC members and professional staff" effectively act as "domestic diplomats, engaging leaders of other ethnic groups and faiths in discussions that move beyond polite dialogue to frank exchanges and, when possible, to alliances that help achieve shared political and public policy objectives".[41] AJC's strong focus on diplomacy is also evident in the programming of its annual meetings, which have featured a number of international government representatives and ministers of foreign affairs.[42]

The American Jewish Committee has thus gained a reputation for being the key Jewish organization providing diplomatic as well as trans-

[39] See Jerome Chanes, "Conference of Presidents of Major American Jewish Organizations", in: Berenbaum/Skolnik (eds.) (2007), vol. 5, 143. The adhesion to the Conference however was more of a symbolic step: AJC had already enjoyed an "observer" status with the Presidents Conference since 1967 and had therefore "participated in all activities of the Conference (...) during this period", says the related communiqué issued by AJC, March 15, 1991, AJC Blaustein Library.

[40] American Jewish Committee, *AJC by the numbers* (New York: AJC, 2007), 8.

[41] American Jewish Committee, *AJC by the numbers* (New York: AJC, 2007), 14.

[42] In 2010, U.S. Secretary of State Hillary Clinton, Minister of Foreign Affairs of the Netherlands Maxime Verhagen, Israel's Defense Minister Ehud Barak, and Israel's Ambassador to the U.S. Michael Oren addressed the meeting. See American Jewish Committee, "Annual Meeting Highlights", http://www.ajc.org/site/c.ijITI2PHKoG/b.5353475/k.8D7D/Meeting_Home.htm, accessed May 6, 2010.

atlantic links between foreign leaders and American Jews. Eugene DuBow, the founding director of AJC's Berlin office from 1998 to 2000, recalls how he was – in his view mistakenly – believed to be "the ambassador of American Jews" in Germany.[43] But "[p]erception in some cases develops into reality", notes DuBow, who quickly found himself "rubbing shoulders with the diplomats and government leaders".[44] In recognition of AJC's role as the first Jewish organization to promote dialogue with Germany after 1945, and not least because of its commitment to support German unification as the first Jewish organization outside Germany, Federal President Horst Köhler bestowed praise on AJC for its having been part of the "avant-garde" in the field of German-Jewish relations for over 50 years.[45] In the same vein, Eugene DuBow concludes that the American Jewish Committee "remains the most important player on the American Jewish-German diplomatic scene" today.[46]

Vertical Politics

The Committee is therefore known for its diplomatic approach to politics – it preferably relies on the method of working "behind the scenes"

---

[43] DuBow (2009 Interview).

[44] Eugene DuBow, "American Jewish Diplomacy & Germany", http://www.dubowdigest.typepad.com/, accessed March 29, 2009. For example, DuBow was invited to a small dinner given by Chancellor Kohl and Federal President Herzog for U.S. President Clinton and also attended a six-person lunch with former Israeli Prime Minister Shimon Peres.

[45] Horst Köhler, "Rede anlässlich der Jahresversammlung des American Jewish Committee", http://www.bundespraesident.de/dokumente/-,2.11969/Rede/dokument.htm, accessed May 6, 2010. In recognition of its role in facilitating transatlantic lines of communication, it was the American Jewish Committee Horst Köhler chose to address when he gave his first speech as federal president in the United States. On the relationship between AJC and Germany, also see Beate Neuss, "Not Frozen in the Past. The American Jewish Committee's Policy towards Germany", *Frankfurter Allgemeine Zeitung*, February 14, 1998, AJC Blaustein Library (reprinted in English); Jeffrey M. Peck, *A Continuous Tradition of Dialogue and Tolerance: AJC in Germany* (Berlin: AJC, 2006).

[46] Eugene DuBow, "American Jewish Diplomacy & Germany", http://www.dubowdigest.typepad.com/, accessed March 29, 2009.

as opposed to engaging in public confrontation.⁴⁷ The strategy of discreet pressure and quiet diplomacy has characterized AJC through much of its history. Examples include AJC's backstairs diplomacy in support for German Jewry during the 1930s, its background role leading up to the Luxembourg Agreements in 1952, as well as its efforts to negotiate a cancellation of the joint Bitburg visit by U.S. President Ronald Reagan and Chancellor Helmut Kohl in 1985.⁴⁸

This being said, we shall now turn to a case study of AJC's politics toward the German government on the issue of Holocaust compensation that illustrates ex contrario the limits of behind-the-scenes advocacy. A short yet highly publicized episode with considerable political impact, it serves as an instructive example of the traditional strategy followed by the American Jewish Committee – that is, to combine "moral suasion and sophisticated diplomacy leveraged by public opinion".⁴⁹

In May 1997, the American Jewish Committee featured a large advertisement in the *New York Times*: "Guess Which One Receives a War Victims Pension from the German Government", the ad reads, featuring two photographs below the headline, one of a survivor of a Nazi ghetto in Eastern Europe, the other of a veteran of the Latvian Legionnaires and the Waffen-SS. "If you guessed the survivor, you're wrong, sad to say", the ad, quoted here in full, continues:

> While Holocaust survivors in other parts of the world are eligible to receive German pensions, Holocaust survivors in Eastern Europe and the former Soviet Union have never received a pension of any kind from Bonn. Inexplicably, the German government has simply drawn the line at providing such direct assistance to this group of survivors. Not so, however, for many of the survivors' former tormentors. Believe it or not, the German government provides generous monthly pensions to Nazi war veterans, whose injuries or even mild, chronic ailments qualify them for "war victims pensions." In the U.S. alone, there are 3,377 pensions sent each month to veterans of the armies of the Third Reich or their dependents! After the fall of communism, many Waffen-SS veterans in the

---

⁴⁷ Lowenthal (2008 Interview).
⁴⁸ See Sanua (2007), 7, 9, 12, 14, 16, 68, 89, 306.
⁴⁹ American Jewish Committee, *AJC by the numbers* (New York: AJC, 2007), 5.

Baltic states and elsewhere in Eastern Europe discovered they, too, were eligible and are now receiving such pensions from Germany, while their victims are not. Today, an estimated 15,000-20,000 Jewish survivors of ghettos and concentration camps live in Eastern Europe and the former Soviet Union. They are old, many are in poor health and financially destitute. Surely, they deserve some help and comfort in the last years of their lives. Join our call to the German government to correct this grievous wrong. Bring justice to the real victims of the Holocaust. Contact us to see how you can help.[50]

On the same day the ad appeared, AJC organized a press conference on Capitol Hill to point to the inequity of the situation and shortly thereafter met with top White House officials, who promised that President Clinton would raise the matter directly with Chancellor Kohl. Then in August 1997, AJC initiated a campaign in the U.S. Senate to draft an open letter of bipartisan appeal to Chancellor Kohl urging pensions for the survivors. Sponsored by Senators Christopher Dodd (D-CT) and Kay Bailey Hutchinson (R-TX), the letter was signed by 82 senators and featured in a full-page AJC ad in the *New York Times* and the *International Herald Tribune*.[51] Only three days later, and after years of resistance, Germany agreed to resume negotiations with the Claims Conference. In January 1998, the German government eventually announced it would allocate DM 200 million to a new program – later known as the Central and Eastern European Fund – to provide pension payments for needy victims of Nazi persecution in the East. As Marilyn Henry notes, the ad campaign launched by AJC had "created a political and public relations nightmare that the German government could not ignore".[52] This finding

---

[50] American Jewish Committee, "Guess Which One Receives a War Victims Pension from the German Government", newspaper advertisement reprinted from the *New York Times*, May 7, 1997, AJC Blaustein Library.

[51] The senators expressed their "deep concern about the continued refusal of the German government to pay pensions" to Eastern European Holocaust survivors even as it paid "generous "war victims pensions" (...) to veterans of the Waffen-SS" and urged Chancellor Kohl "to address this matter with the utmost speed". American Jewish Committee, United States Senate Letter, August 1, 1997, AJC Blaustein Library.

[52] Henry (2007), 97. Henry (2007, 98) further notes that the German government's initial reaction to the ad campaign was "indignation at being pres-

is also confirmed by John P. Becker, a senior diplomat at the Office of the Special Envoy for Holocaust Issues at the U.S. Department of State, who recalls how "the German government was thoroughly panicked" and how the incident "caused them enormous amounts of embarrassment", eventually prompting Germany to negotiate a settlement "so this horrible embarrassment come to an end".[53]

The strategy of going public was not initially pursued by AJC. Rather, it was a strategy of last resort after all other diplomatic means of communication had been exhausted. AJC had in fact held multiple meetings on the topic with German officials since 1995, involving "virtually the entire spectrum of German political leadership", including the federal president, chancellor, foreign minister and various Bundestag members, in the hopes of reversing Germany's recalcitrant stand on the issue. With the passage of time, AJC however became "increasingly frustrated by the lack of progress" despite its "non-confrontational approach" and "unprecedented access based on four decades of work in Germany". Following an unsuccessful meeting with Chancellor Kohl's chief of staff in February 1997, AJC advised the German government that it would go public with its campaign in two months time if no progress were forthcoming. It also spelled out the steps it planned to take, including the ad campaign. At first it seemed as if a breakthrough was possible, which led AJC to postpone the ad by two weeks; but after mediation efforts had failed, AJC resumed its plans.[54] Realizing that "quiet diplomacy was not working", it eventually launched its successful newspaper campaign in May 1997.[55]

Why did AJC succeed with its campaign? The organization's top leaders, Robert S. Rifkind and David A. Harris, regard elements of AJC's diplomatic and coalitional approach to politics as having been decisive. In their view, the key reasons for success are to be found in the

sured for additional compensation". Only after public pressure had mounted were negotiations resumed.

[53] Interview with John P. Becker, Property Restitution Advisor, Office of the Special Envoy for Holocaust Issues, U.S. Department of State, July 9, 2009, Washington, D.C.

[54] See Robert S. Rifkind and David A. Harris, Letter to Members, January 28, 1998, AJC Blaustein Library. All previous quotations cited from ibid., 2.

[55] American Jewish Committee, "Germany to Compensate Double Victims", *AJC Journal*, April 1998, AJC Blaustein Library, front page.

links that its international programming forged with the Jewish communities in Eastern Europe; the many years of AJC dialogue with top German officials and the credibility it helped establish; the "willingness to give quiet diplomacy every opportunity to succeed" before going public; its strong presence in Washington, which allowed for effective cooperation with the administration and the U.S. Congress; and its chapter network across the country, which helped raise the issue on a national level. In addition to AJC's own efforts, the pressure exercised by the Department of State as well as the Senate resolution endorsed by 82 senators also supported its cause.[56] The strategy of engaging public opinion and spurring media coverage thus effectively yielded the intended results; two years later, AJC adopted a similar strategy when it raised public pressure on German companies that had used forced and slave labor during the Nazi era, but had failed to provide compensation.[57]

As this brief – and admittedly unrepresentative – case study suggests, the political style of the American Jewish Committee may occasionally involve more than its characteristic behind-the-scenes diplomacy. At the same time, the Committee still relies extensively on a coalitional and, by virtue of its own research activities, on an educational approach to politics: it is as much a Jewish defense agency as it is an internationally oriented think tank and lobbying organization.

5.1.2 The Anti-Defamation League

Founding History and Internal Structure

While the American Jewish Committee was established in reaction to anti-Jewish pogroms abroad, the Anti-Defamation League came into being in reaction to an incident of domestic anti-Semitism, known as the Leo Frank case, in 1913. That same year, the young Jewish businessman Frank was sentenced to death for allegedly raping and murdering a girl

---

[56] See Robert S. Rifkind and David A. Harris, Letter to Members, January 28, 1998, AJC Blaustein Library, 1, 3 (quote).

[57] At a press conference in Berlin and New York, AJC released a list of over 250 German companies, see American Jewish Committee, "AJC Turns Up the Heat on German Industry", *AJC Journal*, February 2000, AJC Blaustein Library, front page.

who worked in his factory in Atlanta. Considering the flimsiness of the evidence and other procedural problems of the trial, the governor of Georgia commuted the sentence to life in prison in 1915. This decision in turn drew the ire of a (white Christian Georgian) mob, which bluntly abducted Leo Frank from jail and hanged him.[58] Against the background of this incident, indeed an American analogy to the Dreyfus affair in France, the "Anti-Defamation League of B'nai B'rith" was eventually established as a Jewish defense organization.[59]

Since its inception the immediate object of the League has been to "stop, by appeals to reason and conscience and, if necessary, by appeals to law, the defamation of the Jewish people. Its ultimate purpose is to secure justice and fair treatment to all citizens alike and to put an end forever to unjust and unfair discrimination against and ridicule of any sect or body of citizens".[60] ADL insofar pursues a dual mission: in addition to fighting anti-Semitism and promoting Jewish security, its activities extend beyond the Jewish community through its defense of civil rights more generally. As an example one may cite ADL's concern with McCarthyism in the 1950s, which it saw "as a threat to the security of all Americans and not as a Jewish problem per se". Benjamin R. Epstein, former national director, thus characterized ADL as "both a defense of Jewish rights organization as well as a broad general human-rights in-

---

[58] The Leo Frank case also decisively contributed to the revival of the Ku Klux Klan, see Diner (2004), 171; Leonard Dinnerstein, *The Leo Frank Case* (New York: Columbia University Press, 1968).

[59] Although ADL still maintains a legal connection with B'nai B'rith, today both are fully autonomous from each other. B'nai B'rith – literally "sons of the convenant" – was founded as a social, fraternal organization in 1843; it is America's oldest Jewish organization. See Jerome Chanes, "Anti-Defamation League (ADL)", in: Berenbaum/Skolnik (eds.) (2007), vol. 2, 195.

[60] Anti-Defamation League, "About the Anti-Defamation League", http://www.adl.org/about.asp?s=top menu, accessed May 13, 2010.

stitution".[61] Tellingly, ADL today employs many non-Jewish staff, even though it remains "first and foremost a Jewish organization".[62]

Based in New York City only a short walk from the United Nations headquarters, ADL works out of 28 regional offices that serve as multipliers for its advocacy work throughout the United States. Unlike AJC with its strong focus on transatlantic relations, ADL does not maintain offices in Europe, but has representations in Ontario, Moscow, and Jerusalem. The League also maintains continuous contact with Congress and the administration through a permanent office in Washington, D.C., staffed with three representatives. ADL is above all a grassroots organization: it predominantly operates on the local level, not least to ensure its effectiveness in monitoring and reporting anti-Semitic incidents in rural areas.[63]

In contrast to the American Jewish Committee or the American Jewish Congress, ADL is not a membership organization. It is staffed by career professionals and governed by a large National Commission, which currently comprises 703 commissioners.[64] Given its lack of individual members ADL is informally known for its "pyramidical" decision-making structure and for being "a one-man organization";[65] most decisions are said to be made by its national director, Abraham H. Foxman, who has led ADL since 1987.

Instead of membership dues ADL therefore relies on one-time (as well as monthly) gifts from individual supporters, typically ranging from $25 to $1,000, as well as on charitable gifts in the form of planned giv-

---

[61] Interview with Benjamin R. Epstein, July 5, 1973, The New York Public Library-American Jewish Committee Oral History Collection, Dorot Jewish Division, The New York Public Library, Astor, Lenox and Tilden Foundations, 4, 1, respectively.
[62] Interview with Kenneth Jacobson, Deputy National Director, Anti-Defamation League, June 17, 2009, New York.
[63] See Kramer (2008 Interview).
[64] See Anti-Defamation League, *Leading The Fight. Anti-Defamation League Annual Report 2008* (New York: ADL, 2009), 38-41.
[65] As stated independently by leaders of two Jewish organizations interviewed for this dissertation who, for reasons of confidentiality, shall not be identified here.

ing through legacy and endowments.[66] Another important source of income are corporate donations and transfers from the ADL Foundation, which give the League sufficient financial firepower to support its activities.[67] In a recent survey by the Urban Institute on civil rights, social action and advocacy organizations, ADL ranks first nationwide in terms of overall expenses. Endowed with more than $180 million, the ADL Foundation furthermore ranks second nationwide, only eclipsed by the funds of the American Civil Liberties Union Foundation.[68] In 2007, the League reported an annual budget in excess of $68 million,[69] the largest budget among the "big three" Jewish defense organizations.

Consistent with the idea of pursuing a dual – both Jewish and general – mission, ADL combats anti-Semitism and bigotry from many different perspectives and engages in advocacy on a variety of issues. Its major policy fields include anti-Semitism and civil rights; extremism and hate-motivated crimes; education and religious freedom; Hispanic and interfaith affairs; Israel and the Holocaust; and terrorism and international affairs. Akin to the American Jewish Committee, the Anti-Defamation League can therefore be characterized as a multi-issue organization.

Contrary to assertions made in the scholarly literature, Israel and U.S. foreign policy are neither "front and center" on ADL's website[70] nor on its overall policy agenda. Considering that Israel advocacy does not con-

---

[66] See Anti-Defamation League, "Fighting Anti-Semitism, Bigotry and Extremism", http://www.adl.org/donations.asp?s=topmenu, accessed May 12, 2010.

[67] Given its dual mission, ADL is able to raise money from companies that value its general agenda, such as its work on workplace diversity. See Jacobson (2009 Interview).

[68] See The Urban Institute, National Center for Charitable Statistics, "NCCS – Display Largest Public Charities", http://nccsdataweb.urban.org/PubApps/shoowTopOrgs.php?cat=R&amt=exps, and http://nccsdataweb.urban.org/PubApps/showTopOrgs.php?cat=R&amt=ass_eoy, accessed May 12, 2010.

[69] Contributions accounted for about 71 percent of total revenue in 2007, while transfers from the ADL Foundation accounted for about 26 percent; the remainder was referred to as "other income". Calculations based on Anti-Defamation League, *Leading The Fight. Anti-Defamation League Annual Report 2008* (New York: ADL, 2009), 33.

[70] Mearsheimer/Walt (2007), 145.

stitute the sole – and in fact not even the foremost[71]– field of activity for ADL, it is hard to see why Mearsheimer and Walt regard the Anti-Defamation League as a "part of the core" of the "Israel lobby".[72] It is instructive to note in this context that ADL, highlighting its role as a grassroots organization, currently spends 49 percent of its total program services on regional operations. ADL's local offices typically deal with incidents of anti-Semitism, racism and other forms of hate crimes, the separation of church and state in public schools, or the promotion of diversity and respect in local communities. An additional 15 percent of its program services are destined to support civil rights advocacy, while another combined 20 percent are spent on education, international affairs, and interfaith programs. There is no explicit reference to Israel in ADL's budget plan.[73]

Regarding its issue priorities the Anti-Defamation League has carved a distinct niche as the leading Jewish organization in the field of First Amendment advocacy. ADL strongly supports church-state separation, as it "believes that a high wall of separation is essential to the continued flourishing of religious practice in America, and to the protection of minority religions and their adherents".[74] In the same vein, it is committed to upholding the freedom of speech and of the press. This has proven to be a particularly challenging task, not least because ADL itself has repeatedly stood accused of trying to "stifle legitimate criticism".[75]

---

[71] Even regarding Israel advocacy, ADL does not necessarily engage in direct lobbying itself. For example, ADL supports Israel through publications that provide activists with background information and talking points, see Anti-Defamation League, *Israel: A Guide for Activists* (New York: ADL, 2008).

[72] Mearsheimer/Walt (2007), 113.

[73] See Anti-Defamation League, *Leading The Fight. Anti-Defamation League Annual Report 2008* (New York: ADL, 2009), 33, 26-31; Anti-Defamation League, *Anti-Defamation League Annual Report 2007* (New York: ADL, 2008), 27-38.

[74] Anti-Defamation League, "ADL's Agenda For The New Administration", *ADL on the Frontline*, Fall 2008-Winter 2009 (New York: ADL, 2008), 5.

[75] According to deputy national director Kenneth Jacobson, precisely this charge is brought against ADL's advocacy work on a regular basis, especially when the United Nations General Assembly gathers in New York for a new round of meetings. Similar charges have also been raised by Mearsheimer/Walt (2007), 168, 185-187, and Chomsky (1999), 14.

Clarifying ADL's approach on the issue, deputy national director Kenneth Jacobson explains the three kinds of criticism distinguished by ADL: first, legitimate criticism of Israel; second, illegitimate criticism of Israel that equals anti-Semitism; and third, distorted criticism of Israel that, although not by itself anti-Semitic, creates an environment for anti-Semitism. ADL combats both of the latter two categories. For example, it regards publications such as "The Israel Lobby and U.S. Foreign Policy" as pertaining to the second category, that is, as "classic anti-Semitism".[76] Part of the reason is that ADL strives to "keep hate on the extremes" and to prevent it from entering the mainstream.[77] At the same time, Jacobson also avers that "legitimate criticism" of Israel is "of course possible", and that "a lot of criticism" actually is "legitimate".[78]

Political Style: Horizontal and Vertical Politics

The political style of the Anti-Defamation League exhibits two major characteristics. As a multi-issue organization, ADL on the one hand builds support through intergroup coalitions and through cooperation with government agencies. On the other hand, it also cultivates an image as a decidedly "tough" organization and thus differentiates itself clearly from the more diplomatic approach to politics of the competing American Jewish Committee.

Horizontal Politics

Since it pursues a dual mission as a Jewish and general civil rights organization the Anti-Defamation League is able to engage in disjointed coalitions with other interest groups. An important focus of its work is

---

[76] Jacobson (2009 Interview). Jacobson cites the charge "It is easier to criticize Israel in Israel than in the U.S." as an example of the third category, that is, as illegitimate criticism of Israel that creates an environment for anti-Semitism.
[77] "We really get nervous when hate enters the mainstream", Jacobson says, adding that ADL regards publications from "extremist[s]" like Noam Chomsky as being "less dangerous" than the more widely read Mearsheimer and Walt or Jimmy Carter, *Palestine: Peace Not Apartheid* (New York: Simon & Schuster, 2006).
[78] Jacobson (2009 Interview).

for example the strengthening of ties with the Hispanic community. Like previous generations of Jews, Hispanic Americans, too, have faced verbal and physical attacks motivated by anti-immigrant bias; at the same time, anti-Semitic beliefs are still widespread among Hispanics. To tackle these issues, ADL cooperates closely with the National Council of La Raza (NCLR), the largest national Hispanic civil rights and advocacy organization in the United States. In the same vein, the League has also voiced its strong opposition to the recent signing into law of Arizona Senate Bill 1070, which it considers to establish harsh rules on immigration enforcement.[79] Given its concern with civil rights issues ADL has another potential ally and competitor: the American Civil Liberties Union (ACLU). Sustained by over 500,000 supporters and members and with staffed offices in all 50 states, the ACLU has played an important role in civil rights advocacy in America.[80] But as the ACLU tends to focus more narrowly on First Amendment rights as opposed to ADL's multi-issue agenda, there is no significant rivalry between both organizations;[81] they attract supporters from fairly different constituencies and neither ally nor compete with each other.

In terms of political orientation, the Anti-Defamation League thinks of itself as a "non-partisan" organization, one that does not fully align itself with either the Republican or the Democratic platforms: "We are the kind of institution that believes that we work with whatever political

---

[79] S.B. 1070 is based on racial profiling, as it requires law enforcement officials who have "reasonable suspicion" about someone's immigrant status to check for relevant documentation. Critics see the bill to be in violation of the Fourth Amendment, which protects against "unreasonable searches and seizures". ADL urged the governor of Arizona, Janice Kay Brewer (R), to veto the bill, which was however signed into law on April 23, 2010. See Anti-Defamation League, "ADL Laments Arizona Governor Brewer's Decision to Sign SB 1070 Into Law", http://www.adl.org/PresRele/CvlRt_32/5743_32.htm, accessed May 13, 2010.

[80] See American Civil Liberties Union, "About the ACLU", http://www.aclu.org/about-aclu-0, accessed May 13, 2010. Another important civil rights organization is the National Urban League (NUL), which specifically advocates for the rights of African Americans, see National Urban League, "Mission and History", http://www.nul.org/who-we-are/mission-and-history, accessed May 13, 2010.

[81] See Jacobson (2009 Interview).

group is in authority", Epstein says, underscoring ADL's pragmatism in the pursuit of its political goals.[82] Critics such as John J. Mearsheimer and Stephen M. Walt however discern a more explicit ideological orientation, arguing that the League, just like the Zionist Organization of America (ZOA), is biased to espouse "right-of-center views".[83] Curiously enough, the very opposite charge has frequently been raised by a number of well-identified right-wing groups themselves, including the ZOA, all of which accuse ADL of being "left-wing".[84] To make sense of this apparent contradiction, it is necessary to draw a distinction between domestic and international issues. While ADL generally maintains "much easier relations" with Democratic administrations owing to shared positions on domestic issues such as the separation of church and state, it still evinces more commonalities with the Republican Party as far as domestic security is concerned.[85] On matters related to Israel, ADL seeks to build support based on a nonpartisan consensus and, historically, has been able to maintain good relations with either administration.

What is more, ADL has been misleadingly associated with right-leaning politics due to its outspoken and forceful political style, which sets it apart from more restrained organizations such as the American Jewish Committee. "We're tough Jews", Kenneth Jacobson says, adding that "there's a little bit of a bias [with ADL] to speak out forcefully".[86] Tellingly, some of ADL's major publications are entitled *ADL on the Frontline* or *Leading the Fight*, thereby affirming and advertising its image as a "tough" organization.[87] In this sense, the style of the Anti-Defamation League reflects in some way the idea of the *Muskeljude* (literally "muscle Jew") put forward by the *fin de siècle* Zionist and Ger-

[82] Interview with Benjamin R. Epstein, July 5, 1973, Dorot Jewish Division, NYPL, 5.
[83] Mearsheimer/Walt (2007), 128.
[84] Jacobson (2009 Interview).
[85] This, however, did not hinder ADL to take a clear stand against the Bush administration's detention policy on Guantánamo Bay, for example.
[86] Jacobson (2009 Interview).
[87] See, for example, Anti-Defamation League, "ADL's Agenda For The New Administration", *ADL on the Frontline*, Fall 2008-Winter 2009 (New York: ADL, 2008); Anti-Defamation League, *Leading The Fight. Anti-Defamation League Annual Report 2008* (New York: ADL, 2009).

man-Jewish cultural critic Max Nordau who, not least with a view to realizing the goal of a national state in Palestine, envisioned a bold and new "genus" of Jews.[88]

At the same time, ADL also maintains a "softer side" through its outreach and educational programs, which provide some sort of counterweight to the organization's "tough" stance on other issues. According to Kenneth Jacobson, it is indeed the combination of both approaches that makes "the real strength of ADL" since it creates a "unique" organizational identity and a competitive edge with regard to other Jewish organizations.[89]

Vertical Politics

This, however, does not imply that the Anti-Defamation League will necessarily adopt a confrontative style to advance its political agenda. As one may reasonably expect, ADL's preparedness to speak out in strong terms indeed "depends on the issue. Many things we do quietly. [But if] there's no other way to get the message across, sometimes we need to take out ads to get the attention of the government and of the people we want to reach", Jacobson says. ADL for instance featured a series of advertisements in major American and European newspapers to criticize the Swiss government for contracting to buy $28 billion in natural gas from Iran, arguing that such an investment subsidized Iran's drive to develop nuclear weapons. "Guess who is the world's newest financier of terrorism?", the headline asks, before revealing the answer in bold letters: "Switzerland". The strategy of leveraging public opinion – just like the American Jewish Committee had done in its successful newspaper campaign – yielded the desired effect for ADL: "We knew our Swiss ads were effective when a European diplomat told us, 'I don't want to wake up one morning and find my country in one of these ads in *The New York Times*,'" an ADL official is quoted as saying in the

---

[88] Max Nordau first called for a "muscular Judaism" at the Second Zionist Congress in 1898. A few years later, Nordau fully articulated the concept in two articles published in *Die Jüdische Turnzeitung*, see Todd Samuel Presner, *Muscular Judaism: the Jewish body and the politics of regeneration* (New York: Routledge, 2007), 58.

[89] Jacobson (2009 Interview).

organization's 2009 annual report.[90] Even though the Swiss government, which distanced itself from the ad, did not rescind the deal, it still suffered a serious blow to its public image abroad.[91]

In addition to building coalitions with like-minded interest groups, the Anti-Defamation League forges close links with law enforcement and government agencies. The League for example cooperates with the 56 members of the Organization for Security and Co-operation in Europe (OSCE), where it is one of two U.S. representatives to a drafting committee on hate crime legislation. It also recently presented a set of recommendations to the OSCE's Office for Democratic Institutions and Human Rights (ODIHR) on how to more effectively address Internet inspired hate crimes.[92] In the United States, ADL first drafted model hate crime legislation in 1981; 45 states have since enacted laws based on or similar to the model.[93]

---

[90] Anti-Defamation League, *Leading The Fight. Anti-Defamation League Annual Report 2008* (New York: ADL, 2009), 22.

[91] The Swiss foreign ministry, the *Eidgenössisches Departement für auswärtige Angelegenheiten* (EDA), declared in this context that the energy deal with Iran was not in violation of any United Nations sanctions against Iran. See Neue Zürcher Zeitung, "Der Gasliefervertrag wirft weitere Wellen", April 8, 2008. Critics might argue that ADL's ad itself raises legitimate questions about the admissibility of such a campaign in the court of public opinion as states, too, may enjoy the right to reputation. For an intriguing general discussion of this idea, see Elad Peled, "Should States Have a Legal Right to Reputation? Applying the Rationales of Defamation Law to the International Arena", *Brooklyn International Journal of Law* 35:1 (2010), 107-153.

[92] See Anti-Defamation League, *Leading The Fight. Anti-Defamation League Annual Report 2008* (New York: ADL, 2009), 23; Anti-Defamation League, "ADL Offers Recommendations to OSCE for Combating Internet Inspired Hate Crimes", http://www.adl.org/PresRele/HatCr_51/5723_51.htm, accessed May 17, 2010. The OSCE, a regional organization under Chapter VIII of the Charter of the United Nations, promotes human rights, minority rights, tolerance and non-discrimination, among other things, in Europe. The ODIHR offices are based in Warsaw.

[93] See Anti-Defamation League, "About the Anti-Defamation League", unpublished pamphlet (New York: ADL, 2006). In its decision in *Wisconsin v. Mitchell*, 508 U.S. 476 (1993), the U.S. Supreme Court upheld a Wisconsin crime statute based on ADL model legislation. See Anti-Defamation League,

ADL also supplies law enforcement personnel with comprehensive and updated information on hate groups and extremists. To this effect, ADL has set up a Law Enforcement Resource Network and provided training on hate crimes for a large number of law enforcement officers on the federal, state, and local levels. ADL is a valuable source of information for government agencies because it continuously tracks extremism of all types: its Investigative Researchers track right-wing, left-wing, and Islamic extremists on the ground, while its Research Analysts, including Arabic speakers, track them over the Internet. In October 2008, the U.S. Justice Department's Bureau of Alcohol, Tobacco, Firearms and Explosives (ATF) turned to ADL with a request for information about suspects involved in an alleged plot to kill more than 100 African Americans, including then-presidential candidate Barack Obama.[94] The League, which had been tracking the suspects, responded quickly with a dossier of information, winning accolades for its cooperative effort. "ADL's information on extremists is a treasure trove for us", an official at the ATF said, underscoring that it would take his agency "weeks and months" to gather the same information.[95]

In this context it is worthwhile to note that the American Jewish Committee – as AJC's program specialist on anti-Semitism and extremism, Kenneth Stern, remarks – "for many years, had an operation equal to, if not better than, the ADL in terms of data collection".[96] Today, the former overlaps are hardly perceptible: the American Jewish Committee has since the 1990s sharpened its profile as an internationally oriented organization with a strong focus on Jewish diplomacy,[97] while

---

"Hate Crimes Laws / I. Introduction", http://www.adl.org/99hatecrime/intro.asp, accessed May 17, 2010.

[94] See Anti-Defamation League, *ADL In Action. White Supremacists and President-Elect Obama: Two Reports* (New York: ADL, 2008).

[95] Anti-Defamation League, *Leading The Fight. Anti-Defamation League Annual Report 2008* (New York: ADL, 2009), 21.

[96] Interview with Kenneth S. Stern, December 6, 1990, The New York Public Library-American Jewish Committee Oral History Collection, Dorot Jewish Division, The New York Public Library, Astor, Lenox and Tilden Foundations, 28.

[97] See Interview with Kenneth S. Stern, December 6, 1990, Dorot Jewish Division, NYPL, 56. In the same vein, Stern tellingly states his intention to get

the Anti-Defamation League has further honed its reputation as an uncompromising leader in the combat against anti-Semitism and bigotry. Again, organizational niches were elaborated and henceforth occupied; the institutional logic of the American polity required both organizations to develop distinct styles and identities to maintain their appeal in the increasingly competitive marketplace of Jewish politics.

5.1.3 The American Jewish Congress

Founding History and Internal Structure

Founded in 1918, the American Jewish Congress is the only one of the "big three" Jewish defense organizations that has been strongly supportive of Zionism since its early beginnings and throughout its history.[98] Following the Balfour Declaration of 1917, in which the British government vaguely stated to "view with favour the establishment in Palestine of a national home for the Jewish people", the Congress was established with the purpose to push for a Jewish state at the Paris Peace Conference, leading up to the Treaty of Versailles.[99] Formally dissolved after the peace talks, and then reorganized under the leadership of Reform Rabbi Stephen S. Wise, the American Jewish Congress attracted to its ranks Zionist luminaries such as Golda Meir, who later served as Israel's foreign and prime minister, as well as the Supreme Court justices Felix Frankfurter and Louis Brandeis, the first Jew ever to be appointed to that

---

"a little more involved in international issues" and to look at anti-Semitism and bigotry from a more international perspective.

[98] "I have been an American all my life, but I've been a Jew for 4,000 years", the organization's early leader, Stephen S. Wise, is quoted as saying in Cohen (1972), 220.

[99] The "shadow of Lemberg" – referring to the anti-Jewish pogrom of 1918 in what by then was the Polish city of Lwów, and now is the Ukrainian city of Lviv – acted as a further impetus for the American Jewish Congress to mobilize in support of the Jews of Europe at the Paris Peace Conference, writes Carole Fink, *Defending the Rights of Others: The Great Powers, the Jews, and International Minority Protection, 1878-1938* (New York: Cambridge University Press, 2004), 126.

position.[100] Dissatisfied with the American Jewish Committee, which it regarded as a self-appointed group of a handful of German-Jewish elites, the Congress was explicitly set up as a broad-based organization, articulating the interests of the Eastern European and Polish Jewish masses in a democratically elected and representative body. Accordingly, more than 350,000 Jews from throughout the United States cast their ballots to elect the delegates of the first American Jewish "Congress", a forerunner of the then institutionalized organization. In addition to class differences, the participation of women in the politics of the Congress also set it apart from the older and more established defense organizations.[101]

Clarifying its mission today, the American Jewish Congress describes itself as "an association of Jewish Americans organized to defend Jewish interests at home and abroad through public policy advocacy – using diplomacy, legislation, and the courts".[102] It currently maintains seven offices in the United States as well as one office in Jerusalem. Though, with a membership of about 25,000 in 2009 – down from about 50,000 a few years ago[103] – the Congress hardly resembles the Jewish mass-based organization of its early days. As a result the Congress has also become "less fully-democratic than it was before",[104] assistant executive director Marc D. Stern admits, citing the now relatively small number of offices and the physical distances between them as the main reason for less frequent national meetings and, hence, for increased autonomy on the regional level.

What is more, the structure of its internal decision-making system – the National Leadership Council (NLC) – contains elements of elitism that are hardly compatible with the original image of the Congress as an all-inclusive egalitarian organization. Indeed, membership in the NLC is

---

[100] Alan M. Dershowitz, a staunch supporter of Israel and the Felix Frankfurter Professor of Law at Harvard Law School, currently serves as honorary chair on the Legal Action Task Force of the American Jewish Congress, see American Jewish Congress, *American Jewish Congress National Leadership Council. A Prospectus for Leadership* (New York: AJCongress, undated), 8.

[101] See Diner (2004), 197-199.

[102] American Jewish Congress, "About Us", http://ajc.convio.net/site/PageServer?pagename=about, accessed May 19, 2010.

[103] See Foundation for Public Affairs (ed.) (2004), 54.

[104] Interview with Marc D. Stern, General Counsel and Assistant Executive Director, American Jewish Congress, June 10, 2009, New York.

"by invitation only, and is open only to those who otherwise meet the eligibility criteria": for members to serve on one of the key governing bodies, a given annual contribution is required, ranging from at least $1,000 to be part of the Regional Leadership Roundtable to at least $5,000 for members of the National Board of Advisors; at the top levels, a minimum of $10,000 is required for the National Board of Overseers, while members of the National Board of Trustees are expected to contribute at least $25,000.[105] In this respect, ironically, the American Jewish Congress has wound up embracing the very elitism in opposition to which it was originally founded.

It is yet another irony of history that the American Jewish Congress, once the voice of the Jewish masses, now faces an existential threat to its continuity not so much because of its shrinking membership base, but because of its disastrous decision to entrust a substantial part of its assets to the man now infamous for running the largest Ponzi scheme ever encountered: Bernard L. Madoff. In 2003, struggling to sustain its funding, the Congress sold its Manhattan headquarters and invested part of the proceeds with Madoff, and in 2004 transferred another large sum to Madoff's investment firm. As a result of the fraud, which was uncovered in 2008, the Congress lost a staggering $21 million of the $24 million (or roughly 90 percent) in endowments that supported its operations.[106] According to the *Forward*, the endowments funded about one-fourth of the organization's annual budget, which plunged dramatically from $6.2 million in 2006 to $2.5 million in 2009.[107] Amid the tough financial situation, the Congress also reduced its staff to 15 employees, down from 40 employees in 2004.[108]

In addition to the Madoff scandal, the Congress's budget woes are further exacerbated by its own fund-raising strategy – that is, to rely on a

---

[105] See American Jewish Congress, *American Jewish Congress National Leadership Council. A Prospectus for Leadership* (New York: AJCongress, undated), 2 (quote), 4-5.

[106] See Anthony Weiss, "AJCongress Crippled by Madoff Scandal", *Forward*, January 16, 2009.

[107] See Stern (2009 Interview). The 2009 annual budget is quoted from Stern (2009 Interview). For the 2006 numbers, see Weiss (2009), footnote above.

[108] See Interview (follow-up) with Marc D. Stern, General Counsel and Assistant Executive Director, June 12, 2009, New York. For the 2004 numbers, see Foundation for Public Affairs (ed.) (2004), 54.

large number of small gifts rather than on select donations from "big donors" – a strategy that has proven to be ineffective, Stern says. Also, the decision to generate revenue through its in-house travel department, which organizes tours to Israel and to other destinations, rather than by developing a solid fund-raising base of individual members appears to have been "a big mistake".[109] As of 2006, the Congress received 40 percent of its funding from individuals, 20 percent from membership dues; 25 percent from special events and projects; and 15 percent from other sources.[110]

While it tends to be more narrowly focused in its advocacy work than AJC or ADL, the American Jewish Congress nonetheless comes close to the type of a multi-issue organization, splitting its budget more or less evenly between domestic and international issues.[111] Major fields of activity include advocacy for the safety and security of Israel; Israel and NATO; energy independence; advocacy for religious freedom in the U.S. and the separation of church and state; free speech; and women's rights.[112] Along with its attachment to the Zionist idea, the Congress has been strongly committed to the advocacy for women's rights, an issue that has played an important role ever since the organization was founded.

Indeed, when elections were held during the first American Jewish Congress in 1917, women enjoyed both the right to active and passive suffrage – that is, three years before women obtained the unrestricted right to vote with the ratification of the Nineteenth Amendment to the U.S. Constitution.[113] Upon the initiative of Louise Waterman Wise, the

---

[109] According to the judgment of an officer of a Jewish organization interviewed for this dissertation who, for reasons of confidentiality, shall not be identified here.

[110] See The Foundation for Public Affairs (ed.), *Public Interest Group Profiles 2006-2007* (Washington, D.C.: CQ Press, 2006), 49.

[111] See Stern (2009 Interview).

[112] See American Jewish Congress, "About Us", http://www.ajcongress.org/site/PageServer?pagename=about, accessed May 20, 2010.

[113] Amendment XIX, which stipulates that "[t]he right of citizens of the United States to vote shall not be denied or abridged by the United States or by any State on account of sex", was ratified on August 18, 1920. See U.S Government Printing Office, "Amendments to the Constitution of the United States

American Jewish Congress established a Women's Division in 1933, thereby underlining its dedication to the issue of women's rights. Moreover, the Congress became the first Jewish organization to call for the elimination of all restrictive abortion laws in 1964, well before the landmark decision of the U.S. Supreme Court in *Roe v. Wade* in 1973. Women also took on substantial leadership roles within the organization: Naomi B. Levine was named executive director in 1972, the first woman to lead a national Jewish organization in the United States. The Congress further established a Commission for Women's Equality, chaired by a number of noted Jewish feminists in politics and government (such as Bella Abzug and Elizabeth Holtzman), media and the arts (Letty Pogrebin, Francine Klagsbrun, and Cynthia Ozick), and religious life (such as the Orthodox feminist Blu Greenberg). On the international level, it joined forces with Israel's "Women of the Wall" in an effort to improve the rights for women to hold prayer services at the Western Wall in Jerusalem. Advocacy for women's rights thus remains a signature issue on the contemporary agenda of the American Jewish Congress.[114]

But along with the general trend in interest group politics toward ever more specialized organizations, the American Jewish Congress, too, had to narrow down both its focus and the scope of its activities. Most Jewish organizations have become more particularistic in their outlook since virtually every conceivable issue is also covered by non-Jewish lobbying groups. "Today", Marc D. Stern says, "Jews would rather join a specialized non-Jewish organization than a Jewish organization that happens to have the issue in its larger portfolio".[115]

---

of America", http://www.gpoaccess.gov/constitution/pdf2002/007.pdf, accessed May 20, 2010.

[114] See American Jewish Congress, *The AJCongress Women's Division: A History* (New York: AJCongress, undated); Stuart Svonkin, "American Jewish Congress", *Jewish Women: A Comprehensive Historical Encyclopedia*, http://jwa.org/encyclopedia/article/american-jewish-congress, accessed May 20, 2009.

[115] Stern (2009 Interview). In the 1950s, says Stern, Jewish organizations were the only groups to deal with issues such as abortion and women's equality, whereas today this obviously is no longer the case.

Political Style: Horizontal and Vertical Politics

In addition to its financial difficulties, the American Jewish Congress has been struggling to develop a distinct niche of activity so as to differentiate itself from ADL and AJC. By borrowing elements of the political style and policy agenda of its main competitors, the American Jewish Congress has maneuvered itself into a situation of intense rivalry with both Jewish defense organizations, not least because it has adopted policy positions similar to those of its rivals.

Horizontal Politics

Quite similar to the Committee or the League, part of the political style of the American Jewish Congress is to build coalitions with like-minded interest groups. The Congress, too, engages in disjointed coalitions, often working with religious and ethnic groups that have little knowledge of Israel or relationship with Jews. Citing the Jewish tradition of social justice as well as the minority position of Jews in the United States as the key impetus for its coalitional work,[116] the organization reaches out to a variety of ethnic communities. Likewise, it has played a central role in the civil rights movement and has a history of promoting Black-Jewish relations.[117] Yet with the breakdown of the formerly broad coalition between Jews and African Americans – an alliance that had already been under strain since the late 1960s –, and following the Andrew Young affair of 1979, the Congress lost a traditional field of activity as well as a number of potential allies.[118]

---

[116] See American Jewish Congress, *What We Stand For...Who We Are* (New York: AJCongress, undated, probably 2008), 12; American Jewish Congress, *Rights & Justice: The Separation of Church and State* (New York: AJCongress, undated), 3.

[117] See Stern (2009 Interview); American Jewish Congress, *American Jewish Congress National Leadership Council. A Prospectus for Leadership* (New York: AJCongress, undated), 9.

[118] In 1979, sources revealed that Andrew Young, the first African American to serve as U.S. ambassador to the United Nations, had met in secret with PLO officials. Jewish organizations criticized Young publicly, but did not call for his resignation. President Carter reacted by removing Young from his post.

As a general rule, coalition-building between the American Jewish Congress and non-Jewish organizations is based on personal relations rather than on abstract strategic rationales. This is to say that coalitions first and foremost are not restricted to a particular type of organization or ideology: "The most important question", explains Stern, "is not whom you join with but rather with whom you don't join with (...), with whom you can't deal".[119] For example, one of the groups that the Congress explicitly denies any form of cooperation is the militant Jewish Defense League (JDL), a group that claims to be "the most controversial, yet the most effective of all Jewish organizations".[120] The Congress has also refrained from engaging in coalitions with the Council on American-Islamic Relations (CAIR), an organization which has been accused of providing a platform for anti-Israel and anti-Semitic voices.[121] In the 1980s, the American Jewish Congress openly boycotted Louis Farrakhan and his anti-Semitic Nation of Islam, although it generally reaches out to the Muslim community: one of its current initiatives for instance involves the close cooperation with the International Quranic Center, an organization that promotes a vision of a moderate Islam and interreligious dialogue.

Since the American Jewish Congress has been active in domains commonly associated with the American Jewish Committee, such as international affairs and Jewish diplomacy, it has come under increased pressure to maintain its organizational distinctiveness. By engaging issues such as energy independence or Israel's relationship with NATO –

This decision in turn led to angry reactions in the African American press, which blamed the Jews for Young's dismissal. See Diner (2004), 339.

[119] Stern (2009 Interview).

[120] Jewish Defense League, "About JDL", http://www.jdl.org/index.php/about-jdl/, accessed May 22, 2010. Founded in Brooklyn by the Orthodox Rabbi Meir Kahane amid heightened Black-Jewish tensions in 1968, the Jewish Defense League relies on a "raw show of force – including the use of arms", if necessary, to protect Jews and Jewish interests. JDL was unequivocally rejected by the leadership of the mainstream Jewish organizations, who sought to "distance themselves as much as possible from the extremist organization", notes Diner (2004), 341.

[121] See Anti-Defamation League, "Council on American-Islamic Relations", http://www.adl.org/Israel/cair/default.asp, accessed May 22, 2010.

both of which figure prominently on the Congress's agenda[122] – it faces direct competition from the highly professionalized AJC, which has a clear comparative advantage both in terms of resources and experience in advocating for these issues.

One the other hand, the American Jewish Congress has also engaged in First Amendment advocacy,[123] a traditional stronghold of the Anti-Defamation League. In its Coalition to Defend Free Speech, for example, the Congress seeks to bring together a broad spectrum of groups to counter attacks against the freedom of expression and, in particular, against the criminalization of speech deemed to be defamatory of religion. It essentially advocates the same policy as ADL, for it opposes the prosecution of hate speech through legal action, adding that it regards the German practice of penalizing Holocaust denial under Section 130 of the German Criminal Code (StGB) as "a mistake".[124] Again, the Congress is exposed to competition with an organization that has a clear comparative advantage in its field of activity – not to mention the additional rivalry presented by leading civil rights organizations such as the ACLU.

But even regarding the issue of women's empowerment – one of the Congress's key issues not covered by AJC or ADL – Hadassah, the Women's Zionist Organization of America, represents a dauntingly powerful competitor. With more than 300,000 members, Hadassah is in fact the largest Zionist, women's, and general Jewish organization in the United States.[125] It is thus doubtful that the issue of women's rights will be sufficient to help the Congress develop a genuine niche that sets it apart from competing Jewish organizations.

---

[122] See American Jewish Congress, *Redefining Israel's Relationship with NATO* (New York: AJCongress, undated); American Jewish Congress, *Protecting Our Future: Energy Independence for the 21st Century* (New York: AJCongress, undated).

[123] See, for example, American Jewish Congress, *Rights & Justice: The Separation of Church and State* (New York: AJCongress, undated); American Jewish Congress, *Public Schools & Religious Communities. A First Amendment Guide* (New York: AJCongress, undated).

[124] Stern (2009 Interview).

[125] Hadassah was founded in 1912 by the American Zionist organizer Henrietta Szold. See Erica Simmons, "Hadassah, The Women's Zionist Organization of America", in: Berenbaum/Skolnik (eds.) (2007), vol. 8, 185-188.

Finally, this predicament is further exacerbated by the fact that the American Jewish Congress does not differ substantially from ADL and AJC in terms of political orientation. "The differences are now smaller than before", says Marc D. Stern, indicating that the organization, while historically rather oriented toward left-of-center politics, has now increasingly embraced a more centrist stance.[126]

Vertical Politics

The American Jewish Congress, intent on fostering a distinct organizational identity, has long defined its political style most clearly in opposition to the diplomatic approach of the American Jewish Committee. In a thinly veiled reference to AJC, the Congress explicitly points out that "quiet diplomacy and a "keep still" attitude are no way to win", declaring that it is "the courage to take a stand where others are less bold (...) that makes the American Jewish Congress unique".[127] Further highlighting its contrast with AJC, the Congress even describes itself as a "rambunctious"[128] organization that – "unlike others" – is "not satisfied with mere words" but "demand[s] results".[129]

This basic difference between both organizations had already been obvious during the 1930s, when the American Jewish Congress openly supported a boycott of German goods, while AJC cautioned against such a measure. Moreover, in its self-ascribed role as "The Attorney General for the Jewish People",[130] the Congress pioneered the use of law and public policy advocacy as a means of protecting Jewish religious freedom, a strategy that was opposed by many Jewish organizations, including AJC and ADL.[131] But that niche, too, has vanished: "While, at the time, nearly everyone criticized our aggressive stand", the Congress

---

[126] Stern (2009 Interview).
[127] American Jewish Congress, *American Jewish Congress National Leadership Council. A Prospectus for Leadership* (New York: AJCongress, undated), 6.
[128] Stern (2009 Interview).
[129] American Jewish Congress, *What We Stand For...Who We Are* (New York: AJCongress, undated, probably 2008), 9.
[130] American Jewish Congress, *What We Stand For...Who We Are* (New York: AJCongress, 2005), 2.
[131] See Jerome Chanes, "American Jewish Congress (AJCongress)", in: Berenbaum/Skolnik (eds.) (2007), vol. 2, 57.

writes retrospectively, "today, nearly every other Jewish organization has mimicked our approach".[132] In particular, the assertive political style of the American Jewish Congress bears obvious similarities with the "tough" approach to politics taken by the Anti-Defamation League: hence, though this approach helps the Congress better distinguish itself from AJC, it adds to the rivalry with ADL at the same time.

Since it is "committed to influencing government", as Marc D. Stern points out, the American Jewish Congress essentially relies on personal contacts with legislators, litigation, and media campaigns to advocate its policy agenda. Given its reputation as an expert in legal matters, the Congress is also approached by individual legislators, who may turn to the organization for advice on the constitutionality of a given initiative. For the purpose of dealing with legal matters the Congress has established a Legal Action Task Force, which is staffed by distinguished legal scholars: for example, Alan M. Dershowitz, a vocal supporter of Israel and the Felix Frankfurter Professor of Law at Harvard Law School, currently serves as honorary chair of the task force.[133] There is, however, no single or preferred strategy pursued by the Congress: as is often the case with multi-issue organizations, it rather adapts its approaches to the nature of the respective issue.[134]

This being said, and in light of the multiple difficulties the American Jewish Congress is facing, it is not entirely certain that the organization will be able to sustain itself and continue as one of the "big three" Jewish defense organizations in the future. Crippled by the Madoff swindle and struggling to find a distinct niche of activity somewhere between its powerful rivals, the American Jewish Congress has purportedly entered into merger talks with the American Jewish Committee in April 2010 as a way out of the crisis.[135] Indeed, addressing the question of general developments in the Jewish organizational world, Marc D. Stern had opined earlier in 2009 that "contractions and mergers" could be ex-

---

[132] American Jewish Congress, *American Jewish Congress National Leadership Council. A Prospectus for Leadership* (New York: AJCongress, undated), 6.
[133] See American Jewish Congress, *American Jewish Congress National Leadership Council. A Prospectus for Leadership* (New York: AJCongress, undated), 8.
[134] See Stern (2009 Interview).
[135] See Haviv Rettig Gur, "After Madoff, AJCongress looks for merger", *The Jerusalem Post*, April 26, 2010.

pected to occur in the future.[136] Whether or not the alleged talks with the American Jewish Committee will yield any results remains to be seen; it should however be reminded that a similar effort to initiate a merger of sorts between both organizations had failed in the 1990s – also at a time when many observers airily predicted the demise of the Congress.[137] Meanwhile, the American Jewish Congress has suspended its operations as of July 2010.[138]

Table 2: Comparison of "Big Three" Jewish Defense Organizations, Main Features

	AJC	ADL	AJCongress
Type	Membership organization	No individual members	Membership organization
Founding impetus	Kishinev pogroms	Leo Frank case	Paris Peace Conference
Founding year	1906	1913	1918
Legal status	501(c)(3)	501(c)(3)	501(c)(3)
Membership	175,000	n/a	25,000
Offices	33	28	2
Headquarters	New York	New York	New York
Budget	$55 million	$68 million	$2.5 million

Note: AJC budget in 2008, ADL budget in 2007, AJCongress budget in 2009. Membership figures as of 2009.

5.2 Umbrellas

The following chapter analyzes the politics of the most important Jewish political umbrellas in the United States: the Jewish Council for Public Affairs (JCPA), the Conference of Presidents of Major American Jewish Organizations (Presidents Conference), and the Conference on Jewish

---

[136] Stern (2009 Interview).
[137] See Jerome Chanes, "American Jewish Congress (AJCongress)", in: Berenbaum/Skolnik (eds.) (2007), vol. 2, 58.
[138] See Forward, "AJCongress Suspends Activities", July 18, 2010.

Material Claims Against Germany (Claims Conference). As we shall see, these umbrellas have similarly developed specific organizational niches and distinct political styles to differentiate themselves from each other. Discernible differences exist between the JCPA and the Presidents Conference, both of which serve as the key coordinating bodies for Jewish organizations at the national level. The Claims Conference, however, constitutes a special case: although formally organized as an umbrella of international organizations and concerned exclusively with Holocaust issues, it can be qualified, for several reasons, as an essentially American organization and will therefore also be discussed in this chapter. Despite a general reluctance to transfer part of their organizational domains and autonomy to a larger coordinating body, as the MacIver report of 1951 has shown, a large number of Jewish organizations, including the "big three" Jewish defense organizations, have participated in and shaped the politics of these umbrellas.

5.2.1 The Jewish Council for Public Affairs

Founding History and Internal Structure

When the JCPA was founded under the name of the National Community Relations Advisory Council (NCRAC) in 1944, it was not quite manifest that this was a Jewish organization. For, tellingly, its founders had carefully left out the word "Jewish", most likely in an attempt to keep a low profile in a society still characterized by a considerable degree of anti-Jewish bias. By 1971, the organization eventually felt comfortable enough to change its name to the National Jewish Community Relations Advisory Council (NJCRAC), now emphasizing its role as a Jewish organization. In 1997, the name was once again changed to the Jewish Council for Public Affairs, which stated the organization's purpose more accurately.[139]

---

[139] See Wertheimer (1995), 13; Diner (2004), 324; Jewish Council for Public Affairs, "About the JCPA", http://www.jewishpublicaffairs.org/organization s713f.html?action=printContentItem&orgid=54&typeID=1366&itemID=21 761m, accessed May 25, 2010. Michael Berenbaum, "Jewish Council on [sic] Public Affairs", in: Berenbaum/Skolnik (eds.) (2007), vol. 11, 288, however writes that NCRAC was renamed NJCRAC in 1968.

According to Article II of its 2008 by-laws, the mission of the Jewish Council for Public Affairs is "to serve as the representative voice of the organized American Jewish community". In so doing, the JCPA pursues a dual mission, combining both Jewish and general advocacy, as it is expressed in three interrelated goals: first, to safeguard the rights of Jews in the United States and around the world; second, to dedicate itself to the safety and security of the state of Israel; and third, to protect, preserve and promote a democratic and pluralistic society that furthers harmonious interreligious, interethnic, interracial, and other intergroup relations. The JCPA further points out that these goals are "informed by Jewish values" and reflect "the profound Jewish commitment to tikkun olam, the repair of the world" as well as "the conviction of the organized Jewish community that it must be active in the effort to build a just society".[140]

The Jewish Council for Public Affairs is headquartered in New York, with a staff of 17 employees, and maintains a second office in Washington, D.C., staffed with five employees.[141] Given its role as a coordinating body the JCPA obviously is not a membership organization; it is an organization of organizations that provides a mechanism to identify issues, formulate policies, and develop joint initiatives between 14 national and 125 local independent partner agencies.[142]

First, the JCPA's national member agencies include leading Jewish political organizations such as the American Jewish Committee, the American Jewish Congress, or the Anti-Defamation League. The Jewish Labor Committee – once considered part of the "big four" together with AJC, ADL, and the Congress – is a founding member of the JCPA and its predecessor organizations. Moreover, religious organizations such as the Orthodox Union, the United Synagogue of Conservative Judaism,

---

[140] Jewish Council for Public Affairs, *By Laws* (New York: JCPA, 2008), 2-3 ("tikkun olam" underlined in original); Jewish Council for Public Affairs, "About the JCPA", http://www.jewishpublicaffairs.org/organizations713f.html?action=printContentItem&orgid=54&typeID=1366&itemID=21761m, accessed May 25, 2010.

[141] See Interview with Ethan Felson, Vice President, Jewish Council for Public Affairs, May 8, 2009, New York.

[142] See Jewish Council for Public Affairs, "About the JCPA", http://www.jewishpublicaffairs.org/organizations713f.html?action=printContentItem&orgid=54&typeID=1366&itemID=21761, accessed May 31, 2010.

the Union for Reform Judaism, and the Jewish Reconstructionist Federation as well as women's organizations such as Hadassah, the National Council of Jewish Women, and the Women's League for Conservative Judaism are also among JCPA's national member agencies. Other members include ORT America, one of the world's largest non-governmental educational organizations; B'nai B'rith International, a Jewish humanitarian organization; and the Jewish War Veterans of the USA, founded in 1896. The Jewish Federations of North America, the umbrella of the local Jewish philanthropic organizations (the "federations"), and Hillel: The Foundation for Jewish Campus Life, the world's largest Jewish campus organization, are among the various additional, affiliated member agencies.

Second, the JCPA's 125 local independent members comprise two kinds of organizations: they refer to both the apolitical local Jewish organizations, that is, the above mentioned federations, and to the explicitly political local Jewish organizations – the Community Relations Councils ("CRCs") or, as they are sometimes also called, the Jewish Community Relations Councils ("JCRCs"). By virtue of its broad-based structure, the JCPA thus is in a position to reach a considerable part of the American Jewish community.

However, not all member organizations are granted the same political weight in the JCPA's Plenary Session, the highest governing body of the Council. The plenum, which meets at least annually, elects the officers and directors of the JCPA and adopts policies, formulates programs and develops an annual agenda for the field.[143] Similar to the representational pattern of the U.S. Congress, each of the 14 national organizations receives a fixed number of 23 votes in the plenary session, regardless of membership or size, whereas each community relations council receives votes in accordance with the Jewish population of its respective community.[144] Depending on the local community population, the votes allotted to the CRCs are divided into 19 brackets and range between a minimum of two votes for community populations of fewer than 5,000 up to 38 votes for populations of more than 1 million. For

---

[143] See Jewish Council for Public Affairs, *By Laws* (New York: JCPA, 2008), 5.
[144] The votes of the federation system are exercised en bloc by The Jewish Federations of North America (formerly known under the name of United Jewish Communities), which receives 23 votes, like the other 14 national member agencies.

instance, CRCs with a Jewish community population of over 100,000 are allotted 14 votes, while CRCs receive 20 votes for communities larger than 200,000. Community relations councils representing a community population of more than 500,000 are entitled to at least 28 votes. Given the geographic distribution of the Jewish population in the United States, the CRCs of California, Florida, Illinois, and the Northeast region including Washington, D.C. together hold the largest number of votes and hence wield the most influence in the JCPA's plenary session.[145]

With an annual budget of about $3 million in 2009, the Jewish Council for Public Affairs is admittedly less well-endowed than its member agencies. Yet it would be erroneous to assume that political effectiveness can only result from financial strength. As in the case of the Presidents Conference, which will be discussed at a later point, the significance of the JCPA stems not from abundant organizational funds but from its ability to coordinate policy and political action between its members. This perhaps explains why 50 percent of the annual expenses of the JCPA were spent on staff salaries in 2007, while an additional 12 percent was directed at administration and travel costs. Thus, inter-organizational networking and coordinating efforts are by far more important than the JCPA's own programs, at least in financial terms – only 7 percent of the budget was dedicated to programs in 2007.[146] As a rule of thumb, the JCPA receives roughly one-third of its funding from allocations made by the federations, and another third from membership dues paid by the national agencies and CRCs as well as from private philanthropy; yet another third of its budget is financed through grants from foundations such as George Soros's Open Society Institute, the Nathan Cummings Foundation, and the Jacob and Hilda Blaustein Foundation.[147]

While the political agenda of the Jewish Council for Public Affairs spans a wide variety of issues, there has been a noticeable trend over the

---

[145] See Jewish Council for Public Affairs, *By Laws* (New York: JCPA, 2008), 6. For an overview of the Jewish population of the United States by individual states, see Sarna (2004), 358-359, and Sheskin/Dashefsky (2007), 159-160, 186.

[146] See Jewish Council for Public Affairs, *2007 Annual Report* (New York: JCPA, 2008), 12-13.

[147] See Felson (2009 Interview).

past two decades towards placing more emphasis on domestic concerns. This development, which has helped the Council sharpen its profile and distinguish itself more clearly from the competing Presidents Conference, becomes evident upon a brief comparison of the organization's program plans and the priorities accorded to the respective policy positions. For instance, in 1990-1991, the JCPA – by then under the name of NJCRAC – still devoted 27 pages to domestic issues and 30 pages to Israel and international issues, whereas in 2009 it reserved no less than 42 pages for domestic issues, but only 18 pages for Israel and international issues.[148] Despite the shift towards domestic concerns the JCPA is nonetheless committed to covering the entire spectrum of the contemporary policy debate,[149] thereby reflecting its stated mission to be the representative voice of the organized American Jewish community.

Political Style: Horizontal and Vertical Politics

As for horizontal interaction, it is instructive to examine the coalitional politics of the JCPA with outside groups and, in particular, the internal politics among JCPA's member organizations. Even though the Council has fundamentally reformed its practice of policy coordination, it is still limited in its ability to act as a powerful player in the political process. As for vertical interaction, the CRCs, which are represented in the JCPA, do however play an important role due to their involvement in local Jewish politics.

Horizontal Politics

Since it deals disproportionally with domestic issues, the Jewish Council for Public Affairs, consistent with the mainstream political orientation of American Jewry more generally, has long been associated with left-wing politics. The tendency toward embracing liberal positions stems from the political background of the organization's leadership as well as from the composition of its member organizations.

---

[148] See National Jewish Community Relations Advisory Council, *Joint Program Plan 1990-91* (New York: NJCRAC, 1991); Jewish Council for Public Affairs, *Policy Compendium* (New York: JCPA, 2009).

[149] See Felson (2009 Interview).

To begin with, it is worthwhile to note that the Council's acting executive director, Steve Gutow, previously served as head of the National Jewish Democratic Council (NJDC) before joining the JCPA.[150] The NJDC is an important liaison between American Jews and the Democratic Party and regards itself as the "national voice of Jewish Democrats", though it works alongside the party, not within it.[151] Further indicative of a certain liberal bent is the fact that Gutow, listed by the *Forward* as one of the most influential American Jews in 2007, is an ordained Reconstructionist rabbi.[152] Reconstructionist Judaism in fact is one of the most progressive religious movements in the United States and has therefore been characterized as being "decidedly liberal" in nature.[153]

The political outlook of its member organizations further adds to the overall liberal cast of the Jewish Council for Public Affairs. This is true for the American Jewish Committee, the Anti-Defamation League, and the American Jewish Congress, all of which pursue liberal agendas as far as domestic issues are concerned; and it is particularly true for the Jewish Labor Committee (JLC), which represents the interests of the Jewish community to the labor movement and the interests of labor within the Jewish community. As one of NCRAC's founding members, the JLC has a long history of involvement in the politics of the umbrella

---

[150] See Ellen G. Witman, "National Jewish Democratic Council", *The Philadelphia Jewish Voice*, May 28, 2010. NJDC was founded in 1990. It is the counterpart of the Republican Jewish Coalition (RJC), which was established in 1985. Both organizations are based in Washington, D.C.

[151] National Jewish Democratic Council, "Mission", http://www.njdc.org/site/page/mission, accessed May 28, 2010.

[152] See Forward, "Forward 50, 2007", http://www.forward.com/forward-50-2007/#religion, accessed May 28, 2010.

[153] Jerome A. Chanes, *A Primer on the American Jewish Community* (New York: AJC, 2008), 9. Owing its inspiration to Mordecai Menahem Kaplan, Reconstructionist Judaism rejects a God-centered theology and instead conceives of Judaism in universal cultural terms. It redefines Judaism not as a religion based on the traditional authority of *halakhah* (Jewish law) but as a constantly evolving civilization where no one belief or dogma is necessarily permanent. See Mordecai M. Kaplan, *Judaism as a Civilization: Toward a Reconstruction of American-Jewish Life* (New York: Macmillan, 1934). Today, approximately 2 to 3 percent of American Jews identify as Reconstructionist.

organization and is well-known for its left-wing political orientation rooted in the ideology of Bundism.[154] "The JCPA is the most important umbrella for us", says Arieh Lebovitz, communications director of the Jewish Labor Committee, citing the JCPA's "record of supporting unions and labor issues" as the main reasons for JLC's support.[155] Commenting on the overall composition of the JCPA, Lebovitz further notes that the organization "by its nature (...) attracts people who have a liberal social agenda".[156] Finally, some of the larger Jewish federations such as the Jewish Federation of Greater Los Angeles have similarly been referred to as "left-wing" organizations. No wonder, then, that a genuinely conservative Jewish organization like the Orthodox Union – largely outnumbered by its liberal counterparts – describes itself as "probably the most right-wing by far on the JCPA".[157]

[154] Bundism is a secular, Yiddish-based, cultural-political worldview that originated in the late nineteenth century in Eastern Europe. The *Algemeyner Yidisher Arbeter Bund in Lite, Poyln un Rusland*, or simply the Bund, was founded as a Jewish socialist party in Russia in 1897. Bundists subscribed to the idea of Jewish life as lived out in Eastern Europe and thus sharply opposed "Zionism and other conceptions of a world-embracing Jewish national identity", writes Moshe Mishkinsky, "Bund", in: Berenbaum/Skolnik (eds.) (2007), vol. 4, 278.

[155] Interview with Arieh Lebovitz, Communications Director, Jewish Labor Committee, June 26, 2009, New York. The Jewish Labor Committee was founded in New York in 1934. Considered one of the "big four" Jewish defense organizations until the 1950s, the JLC has had to deal with a steep decline in membership and overall significance over the past decades. Today, says Lebovitz, it has a full-time national staff of seven employees, four of whom work in New York, and unofficially counts between 2,300 and 2,400 members.

[156] It may thus not be a mere coincidence that Lebovitz formerly held a position with Americans for Progressive Israel (API), a left-wing Zionist organization that later became an affiliate of the JLC. However, the Jewish Labor Committee has historically been a Bundist, not a Zionist, organization wedded to a social-democratic, not a socialist, political agenda. Although the JLC, through affiliates like API, "always had a left Zionist labor component to it", Lebovitz (2009 Interview) says, it "was generally non-Zionist to anti-Zionist".

[157] Interview with Howard Beigelman, Deputy Director of Public Policy, Orthodox Union, June 22, 2009, New York.

As a result of the bias toward left-wing politics the Jewish Council for Public Affairs has experienced considerable internal conflicts in the past, which eventually led to a general overhaul of the decision-making process along with the rebranding of the organization in 1997. Under the old system, the national staff of NCRAC would annually draft a joint program plan in December, which was then submitted to the plenum ten months later. One of the flaws with this practice was that the final draft, which typically reflected the left-wing positions of NCRAC's national leadership, was often met with criticism at the more moderate grassroots level. Working from a top-down approach, NCRAC "rather tried to forge than find a consensus", Ethan Felson says, adding that "the issues that were shaped weren't organic", and thus increasingly came to be challenged by some of its member organizations. Under the "new, but imperfect" system of resolutions, says Felson, the JCPA has replaced the joint program plans by a permanent policy compendium, the "authoritative record of the current positions of the JCPA".[158] Resolutions are instruments through which the JCPA makes changes in its policy compendium on matters that it has identified as key priorities for which there is inadequate existing policy.[159] Unlike the joint program plans, the policy compendium is not negotiated anew at the annual meeting, but is merely updated when new resolutions have been adopted.[160] With this reformed system, the JCPA intends to "provide a common table, through an open, representative, inclusive and consensus-driven process around which the agencies meet to identify issues, articulate positions, develop strategies, programs and approaches designed to advance the public affairs goals and objectives of the organized Jewish community".[161]

In practice, however, the internal conflicts appear to have prevailed: in 2000, the *Forward* still found the Council an organization where "Jewish factions come together not to find common ground but to impose their own views", seeking "victory, not consensus".[162] In the same vein, UJA-Federation of New York, the largest Jewish federation in

[158] Jewish Council for Public Affairs, *Policy Compendium* (New York: JCPA, 2008), 1.
[159] See Jewish Council for Public Affairs, "Process for Adoption of Policy" (unpublished paper, 2009) 1.
[160] See Felson (2009 Interview).
[161] Jewish Council for Public Affairs, *By Laws* (New York: JCPA, 2008), 3.
[162] Forward, "Assault on Jewish Democracy", September 22, 2000.

North America and a member of the JCPA, chided the organization in an open letter for being "out of touch" with the Jewish community and further expressed its concern that the "JCPA's domestic legislative agenda ignores views held by many in our community about important issues".[163] The second largest federation, the Jewish Federation of Metropolitan Chicago, also said it was "very unhappy" with the JCPA's performance, referring specifically to issues such as school vouchers and government subsidies, which had originally touched off the controversy. Because of the unusual public exposure of the disagreements, some commentators regard this episode as heralding the end of the "liberal orthodoxy" that had obtained in the community for decades.[164]

One of the possible reasons that explain this rift is to be found in the abolition of the general veto, which had been common practice under NCRAC. Since every national member organization was formerly entitled to a veto, it could effectively stall deliberations and block decisions, which "happened quite a bit", Felson recalls. Under the new system, this is no longer the case: "Council determinations, decisions and public statements are not binding on individual member agencies, and, correlatively, no member agency can block a public action or statement by the Council". While decisions cannot be blocked by ordinary members, they can however be watered down by religious organizations, as these retain the right to exercise a religious veto: "on a matter that any denominational body chooses to define as an issue of religious conviction", stipulates Article IX Section 7 of the JCPA's by-laws, "that body can require that the proposed statement or action not be taken in the name of the Council". The abandoning of the general veto in favor of a religious veto

---

[163] James S. Tisch and Stephen D. Solender, "The Public Policy Shift", *Forward*, October 29, 1999.

[164] Ira Stoll, "End of Liberal Consensus Is Bruited by UJA-Federation", *Forward*, October 29, 1999. Marshall Breger, who formerly served as President Reagan's Jewish liaison, was quoted as saying in this context: "When I was in the White House, at times I thought that saving the whales and aid to children without parents were the major Jewish community concerns. There's no doubt that there is a change in the community. The liberal shibboleths are no longer accepted in an unexamined manner".

is thus intended to strengthen both public affairs effectiveness and community cohesion.[165]

But, crucially, while the exercise (and mere threat) of the religious veto has helped foster moderation and compromise among its member organizations, it has also prevented the JCPA from adopting straightforward and unequivocal positions on some of the most salient contemporary issues. For example, as a result of the religious veto exercised by the Orthodox Union, the JCPA has no coherent policy on settlement activity in Israel, the two-state solution and the status of Jerusalem, or the issue of same-sex marriage in the United States. As for settlements, the JCPA's resolution merely goes beyond recognizing "that within our own community there are divergent views about current and future policies of the Israeli government".[166] Regarding the two-state solution and Jerusalem, it also falls short of formulating a compelling standpoint as the Orthodox Union "disagrees with and dissents from" various statements of the JCPA's resolution.[167] "Yerushalayim must not be divided", says Howard Beigelman,[168] deputy director of public policy at the Orthodox Union, in reiteration of the organization's stated policy that Jerusalem remain the "eternal and indivisible capital of Israel".[169] Owing to the opposition of the OU – which in general "actively lobb[ies] against gay rights legislation" [170] – the Council also has no policy on same-sex mar-

---

[165] See Jewish Council for Public Affairs, *By Laws* (New York: JCPA, 2008), 14.

[166] Jewish Council for Public Affairs, *Policy Compendium* (New York: JCPA, 2008), 4.

[167] Jewish Council for Public Affairs, *Policy Compendium* (New York: JCPA, 2008), 5.

[168] Beigelman (2009 Interview).

[169] The Orthodox Union, "Sign the Petition to President Obama in Support of Jerusalem", http://www.ou.org/public_affairs/jerusalem_petition, accessed May 30, 2010.

[170] Beigelman (2009 Interview). For example, the OU lobbied against same-sex marriage in California, where it supported "Proposition 8" (see footnote below). Also, the OU "does not approve gay rights legislation in New England", says Beigelman.

riage; the respective resolution merely states that "the agency has taken no position on questions pertaining to homosexual life-styles".[171]

In addition to the restraints imposed by the religious veto, the JCPA's political effectiveness at the national level is further limited by a variety of other factors. First of all, the Council is unable to enforce policies in its member organizations: although the member agencies "come together in the spirit of cooperation and voluntarism", they are still "autonomous" and "determine and implement their own agencies' positions, policies, and programs".[172] Accordingly, as noted earlier, resolutions adopted in the plenum of the Council are not binding on its individual member agencies.

Second, the JCPA lacks the presence of a powerful Jewish organization such as AIPAC, a lobby that would add substantial political clout to the Council. AIPAC, by contrast, is a member of the Presidents Conference – an umbrella organization capable of acting much more forcefully than the JCPA.[173]

Third, the Jewish Council for Public Affairs has increasingly come to be perceived as a rival organization by some of its most important members. It is worthwhile to recall that, as early as in the 1950s, both the American Jewish Committee and the Anti-Defamation League had in fact seceded from NCRAC in protest against what they saw as a loss of autonomy following the proposals for organizational restructuring made in the MacIver report. The "big three" – which also compete among themselves – have since kept a wary eye on the politics of the organization. This is particularly true for the period after 1997, when the JCPA, as the heir to NJCRAC, expanded its role and tried to position itself as a national player in its own right. Yet precisely because of that, the Council ended up weaker than before as the national member agen-

---

[171] Jewish Council for Public Affairs, *Policy Compendium* (New York: JCPA, 2008), 34. As of May 2011, same-sex marriage is granted in five American states (in chronological order of approval: Massachusetts, Connecticut, Iowa, Vermont, and New Hampshire) and, since March 2010, in Washington, D.C. Following Massachusetts, same-sex marriage was granted in California in June 2008. In an amendment to the state constitution ("Proposition 8"), Californian voters however reversed the policy in November 2008.

[172] Jewish Council for Public Affairs, *By Laws* (New York: JCPA, 2008), 3.

[173] See chapters 5.2.2 and 6.1 below.

cies "began losing interest".[174] Indeed, when the national agencies sensed "a competitor", writes the *Forward*, they "reduced their cooperation".[175] Today, the American Jewish Congress, not least because of its own precarious situation, represents one of the most outspoken critics of the JCPA, which it considers a key rival. "It's a useless organization", says Marc D. Stern of the American Jewish Congress, airing his views on how the JCPA has "changed from a coordinating body to an agency like us".[176] The tension between both organizations is all the more acute since the American Jewish Congress, in contrast to its competitors AJC and ADL, is still struggling to find a distinct niche of activity.

In light of these various shortcomings the Jewish Council for Public Affairs has not been spared its share of criticism in the Jewish press either. The journalist Jeffrey Goldberg, for example, bluntly characterized the Council as being "irrelevant" and, even more scathingly, as "a Model U.N. for grownups".[177] In reality, however, this sort of polemic is not supported by the evidence, as a brief analysis of the JCPA's vertical politics will show.

Vertical Politics

A first indication of the political relevance of the Jewish Council for Public Affairs is its contact with lawmakers and staffers in Washington, D.C., who, says Howard Beigelman of the Orthodox Union, turn to the Council "to feel the consensus of the Jewish community on certain issues".[178] For this purpose, the JCPA specifically maintains a permanent liaison office in the capital, staffed with five employees. Further illustrative of the links between government officials and the JCPA leadership is the example of the former director of the JCPA Washington office, Reva Price, who left her position in 2006 to join the staff of Representative Nancy Pelosi (D-CA), then House Minority Leader.[179] The ensuing director of the JCPA office in Washington, Hadar Susskind, was

---

[174] Forward, "Assault on Jewish Democracy", September 22, 2000.
[175] Forward, "Wanted: Referee", July 20, 2001.
[176] Stern (2009 Interview).
[177] Jeffrey Goldberg, "The Relevancy Standard", *Forward*, March 13, 1998.
[178] Beigelman (2009 Interview).
[179] See Matthew E. Berger, "Pelosi's Price is Right for Jewish Community", *Forward*, November 24, 2006.

named one of the 50 most influential American Jews in 2008, along with prominent figures such as the national director of ADL, Abraham Foxman, or the executive director of AIPAC, Howard Kohr. According to the *Forward*, Susskind is reputed to be known by "almost everyone who's anyone on Capitol Hill".[180]

It must also be taken into account that a good deal of the criticism leveled against the JCPA refers to the period of the Bush administration, which, as Ethan Felson says, "often was not in line with the JCPA on domestic issues". As noted before, the JCPA devotes a large and growing share of its work to domestic concerns and moreover has a clear bent for liberal politics; it is therefore not at all surprising that the effectiveness of the Council to influence public policy remained limited in the face of the various disagreements with the conservative Republican agenda. Tellingly, the Bush administration was especially reluctant to provide speakers for any of the JCPA's conferences, says Felson. Democratic administrations, by contrast, provide more common ground in terms of policy and thus politically "benefit the JCPA".[181]

Second, the Jewish Council for Public Affairs can partly compensate for the structural limitations on its effectiveness because it relies extensively on coalitional arrangements with other interest groups.[182] "Cooperation with non-Jewish organizations is very important", says Felson, pointing out that in fact "every issue is done with coalitions".[183] A statement adopted by the 2009 JCPA plenum similarly spells out that the goals of the JCPA "are often advanced through coalition work with a broad range of constituencies including issue-based organizations, religious and ethnic groups. Often, we are aligned with groups on some issues and find ourselves in opposition on others", the statement continues, indicating that intergroup cooperation in many cases takes place

---

[180] Forward, "Forward 50, 2008", http://www.forward.com/forward-50-2008/, accessed May 31, 2010. Susskind now serves as vice president of policy and strategy at the lobbying organization J Street.

[181] Felson (2009 Interview).

[182] See, for example, Jewish Council for Public Affairs, *Building One Nation. Race, Ethnicity & Public Policy* (New York: JCPA, undated), as well as the article by its former chairman Leonard A. Cole, "The Politics of Coalition-Building", *Forward*, July 27, 2001.

[183] Felson (2009 Interview).

within disjointed coalitions.[184] Such coalitions have previously involved joint efforts with mainline Protestants as well as with the Muslim community;[185] the JCPA also supports initiatives to build pro-Israel coalitions on American campuses as part of a larger network of national Jewish organizations, including the Zionist Organization of America, the Presidents Conference, and AIPAC.[186] Coalitions with the African American community, though less based on a shared identity or a similar socioeconomic status, are equally valuable as they "open up possibilities for logrolling in the future".[187]

Finally, and most importantly, the JCPA can leverage the weight of its 125 independent local member agencies – that is, the federations and the CRCs – to increase its political standing at the national level. Although the federations and the community relations councils are fully autonomous in their decisions and policy, they nonetheless maintain close working relationships with the Council. In return, the JCPA provides the federations and CRCs with policy memoranda and talking points on topics of immediate concern for the larger Jewish community;[188] rather than imposing its own views, it "serves" the local member agencies by providing them with assistance on a wide range of issues.[189] Reaching into the local communities is the particular strength of the JCPA and one of the key features that sets it apart from other umbrellas such as the Conference of Presidents.

---

[184] Jewish Council for Public Affairs, "Task Force Concern on Challenges in Coalition Building" (unpublished paper, 2009), 1.

[185] See Jewish Council for Public Affairs, *Israel Advocacy with Mainline Protestant Influentials* (New York: JCPA, 2008); Jewish Council for Public Affairs, "Task Force Concern on Muslim Jewish Relations" (unpublished paper, 2009).

[186] See Jewish Council for Public Affairs, *A Guide to Coalition-Building on American Campuses* (New York: JCPA, undated).

[187] Felson (2009 Interview).

[188] See, for example, the internal (unpublished) policy memorandum "Community Relations Implications of the Visit to Israel by Pope Benedict XVI", May 6, 2009, sent to all federations, CRCs, and other member agencies. The memorandum contains a draft of a written statement regarding the papal trip as well as background information on the itinerary. It also suggests numerous talking points on the trip and on related topics.

[189] Felson (2009 Interview).

Of course, the Jewish federations operate as charities and not as public affairs groups; only the CRCs are political organizations. However, many CRCs are in fact supported, and in some cases even completely directed, by their local federation, says Amy Mitman of CJP Boston, the oldest Jewish federation in the United States and a member of the JCPA.[190] While the federations do not get directly involved in politics, they however play an important role in funding part of the operations of the local community relations councils. Consider, for example, the UJA-Federation of New York, the country's largest local philanthropy, which currently supports the local Jewish community relations council with an annual grant of $1.3 million.[191] A glance at IRS Form 990,[192] indicating assets of more than $1 billion and over 600 employees in 2008-2009, quite accurately reveals the status of the New York federation as the "400-pound gorilla" that it surely is.[193]

The community relations councils, on the other hand, are highly effective in terms of grassroots advocacy and are crucial allies for the JCPA on the local level. Alan S. Ronkin, deputy director of the JCRC of Greater Boston, the largest community relations council in terms of staff and projects in the United States, refers to the JCPA as "essentially our professional organization" that "provides assistance [and] leadership for us". The JCRC Boston, too, is a body of constituent organizations and unites 42 member agencies under its tent. It is therefore in a comfortable position to build grassroots support and form coalitions with other local interest groups. In smaller cities, says Ronkin, the JCRCs in fact "work closely with AIPAC" and thereby enhance their political clout.[194] In

---

[190] See Mitman (2008 Interview). The JCRC Boston operates independently, but receives part of its funding from CJP. In other cities – for example in Cincinnati, Ohio – the JCRC is entirely part of the local Jewish federation, says Mitman.

[191] See UJA-Federation of New York, "Grants", http://www.ujafedny.org/grants/, accessed June 1, 2010.

[192] See UJA-Federation of New York, "2009 Federal Tax Return Form 990", http://www.ujafedny.org/get/10026, accessed June 1, 2010.

[193] Interview with Stephen Steiner, Director of Public Relations, Orthodox Union, June 22, 2009, New York.

[194] Interview with Alan S. Ronkin, Deputy Director, Jewish Community Relations Council of Greater Boston, December 8, 2008, Boston. In large cities, however, the work of the JCRCs and AIPAC is separate. The JCRC Boston

Boston, the JCRC operates with an annual budget of $3 million and employs a staff of 26 professionals; like the JCPA, it is a multi-issue organization.[195]

It is thus fair to say that the Jewish Council for Public Affairs, while it remains comparatively weak in terms of national politics, does not fall short of its original purpose: that is, being a coordinating body rather than a player in its own right. Ultimately, the strength of the JCPA is not so much inherent in the organization itself, but depends largely on the willingness of its members to take the lead and translate policy into action. Forging consensus among a large number of national and local organizations is without doubt a challenging task; yet despite its shortcomings, the JCPA still acts as an important seismograph recording the by and large representative positions of the organized Jewish community.

5.2.2 The Conference of Presidents of Major American Jewish Organizations

Founding History and Internal Structure

A curious exception to the classic organizational pattern in American Jewish politics, the Conference of Presidents of Major American Jewish Organizations, though intended to serve as an umbrella organization, was not created at the initiative of the American Jewish community but owes its existence to the impetus of the U.S. Department of State and to the Zionist leader Nahum Goldmann. Frustrated with the multiplicity of Jewish organizations petitioning their offices, Secretary of State John Foster Dulles and Assistant Secretary Henry A. Byroade, under the presidency of Dwight D. Eisenhower, urged the creation of a single body that would represent the American Jewish community to the administration. Abba Solomon Eban, the ambassador of Israel to the United States, similarly endorsed such a step. In 1954, the cosmopolitan Jewish states-

---

was founded in 1944 in reaction to local incidents of anti-Semitism; the Holocaust was not the primary motive for its creation, says Ronkin.

[195] See Interview with Ari Alexenberg, Director, Israel Action Center, Jewish Community Relations Council of Greater Boston, December 16, 2008, Boston.

man Nahum Goldmann[196] convened what came to be known as the Presidents Club, thereby laying the foundation for the Conference of Presidents of Major American Jewish Organizations, formally established in 1959.[197] Another major transformation occurred in 1966, when the Conference became a body of constituent organizations, as opposed to merely one of presidents.

But it was not only for the influence of Abba Eban and Nahum Goldmann that the Presidents Conference started out as a strongly Zionist organization. In fact, upon its creation, eight of the 15 founding organizations of the Conference were affiliated with the Zionist movement.[198] The historical context also played a role: after the establishment of the state of Israel in 1948, the American Zionist organizations were facing the threat of redundancy since their political activities were now taken over by Israeli officials.[199] The Presidents Conference, in turn,

---

[196] Nahum Goldmann (1895-1982) was born in Visznevo, a *shtetl* in Lithuania, and grew up in Germany. Goldmann, who during his lifetime held seven different citizenships, served as the first chairman of the Presidents Conference, as chairman of the Jewish Agency for Israel, and as president of the World Zionist Organization, the World Zionist Congress, and the Conference on Jewish Material Claims Against Germany. See Goldmann (1969).

[197] See Interview with Malcolm Hoenlein, Executive Vice Chairman, Conference of Presidents of Major American Jewish Organizations, October 29, 2009, New York; Jerome Chanes, "Conference of Presidents of Major American Jewish Organizations", in: Berenbaum/Skolnik (eds.) (2007), vol. 5, 141. This is to say that the nature of the organization was ultimately modeled after the designs of John F. Dulles and Nahum Goldmann rather than those of Abba Eban and Philip Klutznick, the president of B'nai B'rith, who also played a key role in the creation of the Conference. The latter both envisaged an informal club rather than a centralized, binding organization. See Conference of Presidents of Major American Jewish Organizations, *Conference of Presidents of Major American Jewish Organizations. Celebrating 40 Years of Making American Jewish History* (New York: Conference of Presidents, 1996), 33.

[198] See Conference of Presidents of Major American Jewish Organizations, *Conference of Presidents of Major American Jewish Organizations. Celebrating 40 Years of Making American Jewish History* (New York: Conference of Presidents, 1996), 34.

[199] See Conference of Presidents of Major American Jewish Organizations, *Conference of Presidents of Major American Jewish Organizations. Cele-*

provided a consummate opportunity for them to reactivate their mission and redefine their purpose – small wonder that it was warmly embraced by organizations such as the American Zionist Committee for Public Affairs (the precursor to AIPAC), the American Zionist Council, and the Zionist Organization of America, among others.[200]

The mandate of the Presidents Conference today is to act as "the voice of organized American Jewry, speaking and acting on the basis of consensus on issues of vital international and national concern". In so doing, the Conference intends to be "the central forum for key American, Israeli and other world leaders to address critical issues of concern to the American Jewish community", such as U.S.-Israel relations, the United Nations, terrorism and arms proliferation, and global anti-Semitism. The Conference of Presidents has broadened its issue focus since Malcolm Hoenlein took office as executive vice chairman, the organization's key leadership position, in 1986; it does not deal with local issues, though.[201]

Located in Midtown Manhattan without representations or affiliates elsewhere in the United States or abroad and a small staff of 12 employees in 2009, the Conference of Presidents has remarkably few resources of its own.[202] But with a comprehensive membership of currently 52 national member agencies, up from just over 30 in 1986, the Conference virtually spans the gamut of American Jewish organizational life: among its most prominent members are Jewish defense organizations such as AJC, ADL, the American Jewish Congress and the

---

brating 40 Years of Making American Jewish History (New York: Conference of Presidents, 1996), 33.

[200] See the untitled memorandum of the 20 Jewish organizations gathered for a Conference of Jewish Organizations, held at the Shoreham Hotel, Washington, D.C., on March 5-6, 1955, AJC Blaustein Library. Other explicitly Zionist organizations present at the Conference include the Labor Zionist Organization of America, the Progressive Zionist League – Hashomer Hatzair, the Zionists – Revisionists of America, the United Zionist Labor Party, and Hadassah, the Women's Zionist Organization of America.

[201] See Conference of Presidents of Major American Jewish Organizations, "About the Conference", http://conferenceofpresidents.org/content.asp?id=52, accessed June 9, 2010.

[202] See Foundation Center, "990 Finder", http://dynamodata.fdncenter.org/990s/990search/esearch.php, accessed June 8, 2010. The same is true for the Conference's budget, see below.

Jewish Labor Committee; the pro-Israel lobbying organization AIPAC; Hadassah, the Women's Zionist Organization of America, and WIZO, the Women's International Zionist Organization, as well as four other independent women's organizations; the umbrella organization JCPA; religious organizations such as the (Orthodox) Rabbinical Council of America, the Orthodox Union, the United Synagogue of Conservative Judaism, the Union for Reform Judaism, and the Jewish Reconstructionist Federation; left-wing groups such as Americans for Peace Now and right-wing groups such as the Zionist Organization of America; and finally, other heavyweight organizations like ORT America, B'nai B'rith International, and Hillel: The Foundation for Jewish Campus Life.[203]

Still, the question whether the Conference of Presidents indeed constitutes an umbrella of *major* Jewish organizations is a subject worthy of debate and has been disputed by some of its constituent members. Commenting on the composition of the Presidents Conference, and especially on the trend toward integrating an increasing number of relatively small organizations, the national director of the Anti-Defamation League, Abraham Foxman, was quoted as saying that the name "really [is] a misnomer" and that the organization should be more accurately referred to as "the Conference of Minor Jewish Organizations".[204] While this is arguably true for a segment of the Conference's constituent members, the large majority of organizations can nonetheless be considered to have the necessary size and standing so as to be legitimately included in the Presidents Conference, especially since all candidates for membership must undergo an application procedure based on a set of objective criteria. First, as a preliminary condition, the candidate organization is required to operate at least two national offices, and must also have an own constituency not duplicated by any other organization. Second, once the membership committee of the Conference has voted on the application, it makes a recommendation to the full body, where another vote is held. Votes in the full body to be successful require approval by

---

[203] See Conference of Presidents of Major American Jewish Organizations, "Member Organizations", http://conferenceofpresidents.org/content.asp?id=55, accessed June 8, 2010. In contrast to the JCPA, however, the Presidents Conference does not have any local Jewish member organizations.

[204] Lawrence Cohler-Esses, "Dissension In The Ranks", *The Jewish Week*, August 8, 1997.

two-thirds majority. In accordance with this procedure, Hillel, the world's largest Jewish campus organization, was the most recent organization to be admitted to the Presidents Conference.[205] Judging from the procedural rules established by the Conference, the acceptance of genuinely minor organizations therefore seems unlikely to occur – and even less so on a regular basis.

What distinguishes the Conference of Presidents most clearly from the JCPA is its decision-making structure characterized by a lack of regular votes. Unlike the JCPA, which relies on an institutionalized voting process including the possibility to block decisions by the exercise of a religious veto, the Conference of Presidents as a general rule does not proceed to vote on its policy positions. Even though it has procedures to do so if necessary, the Conference's leadership is supported by what might be termed the intuitive consent of its members: "Decisions are made by consensus, which doesn't mean unanimity. (...) It's actually something you can't quantify, but you know it when you have it", executive vice chairman Hoenlein explains in almost Potter-Stewartian language.[206] "It doesn't usually come to a vote. When it comes to a vote, you already have a problem", Hoenlein further argues, "because consensus is something that should be obvious". Unsurprisingly, votes at the Conference thus rarely occur and, according to Hoenlein, are held only "once in five years".[207] In this regard, the Conference of Presidents still operates much in the way it did during its early days, that is, as "essentially a chairman and an executive director. (...) Most of the statements are just made by the chairman and myself", says Hoenlein. The Conference nonetheless maintains an ongoing dialogue with its member organizations through various weekly events and briefings, but not nec-

---

[205] See Hoenlein (2009 Interview).

[206] Referring to U.S. Supreme Court Associate Justice Potter Stewart, who, in his concurring opinion on the difficulties of defining obscenity in the decision in *Jacobellis v. Ohio*, 378 U.S. 184, of 1964 famously wrote that "I know it when I see it".

[207] This is why Michael Massing's line of argument that, since all member organizations have a single vote regardless of size, the "smaller conservative groups (...) decisively outnumber the larger liberal ones and so can neutralize their influence" is not convincing. The chairman of the Conference is elected by the whole body, though. See Michael Massing, "Deal Breakers", *The American Prospect*, March 11, 2002.

essarily in the form of business meetings. This is why, at least in theory, the Conference comes together "all the time"; in practice, however, its member organizations do not regularly attend these weekly gatherings.[208]

Since it is run informally as a coordinating body and furthermore renounces complex decision-making procedures, the Conference of Presidents, unlike most of its member agencies, is not in need of a strong budget to maintain its political significance. In 2008, the Conference reported a modest total revenue of about $667,000, total expenses of $426,000, and total assets of $828,000. Salaries, other compensation, and employee benefits amounted to roughly $287,000, making up 67 percent of the organization's total expenses, while the remainder was consumed by administrative costs. The stated revenue was generated almost entirely from membership dues.[209] A related organization, the tax-exempt Conference of Presidents Fund, was established in 1982 as an additional fund-raising tool to help offset some of the costs of the Presidents Conference. In 2008, the net assets of the Fund approximated $3.1 million, with revenues of roughly $1.9 million and expenses of about $1.8 million.[210] Transactions from the Fund to the Conference involved over $972,000 in 2008.[211] Yet, as in the case of the JCPA, the relevance and impact of the Presidents Conference stems less from its limited financial resources than from its access to the corridors of power and its ability to act as the political voice of the organized Jewish community.

---

[208] Hoenlein (2009 Interview). This leadership style has been repeatedly called into question by some of the Conference's member organizations and has led to considerable tension among them. See section 5.2.2 ("Horizontal Politics") below.

[209] According to Form 990, see The Urban Institute, NCCS, "Conference of Presidents of Major American Jewish Organizations", http://nccsdataweb.urban.org/PubApps/showVals.php?ft=bmf&ein=132500881, accessed June 9, 2010. These figures also remained under $1 million each for the years 2005 through 2008.

[210] See Charity Navigator, "Conference of Presidents of Major American Jewish Organizations Fund", http://www.charitynavigator.org/index.cfm?bay=search.summary&orgid=9365, accessed June 9, 2010.

[211] See The Urban Institute, NCCS, "Conference of Presidents of Major American Jewish Organizations", http://nccsdataweb.urban.org/PubApps/showVals.php?ft=bmf&ein=132500881, accessed June 9, 2010.

Political Style: Horizontal and Vertical Politics

The key implication of the above described informal leadership style is that the Conference of Presidents continually risks alienating the very organizations it crucially depends on for its own success. This is why its member organizations have been especially wary of seeing the umbrella develop into an unchecked player in its own right that competes with, rather than represents, its constituent organizations. At the same time, the lack of rigid structures is among the key reasons that account for the political clout of the Presidents Conference.

Horizontal Politics

"The Presidents Conference's real problem", writes Rabbi Eric Yoffie, a prominent Jewish leader and president of the Union for Reform Judaism,[212] "is that the organization is unrepresentative and structurally flawed; that no established procedures exist for decision making, setting priorities or arriving at consensus positions; that virtually all power resides in the hands of the chairman and executive vice-chairman, and that the normal procedural safeguards, transparency and internal debate that characterize virtually all major Jewish organizations are absent in the conference".[213] While Yoffie's comments added fuel to the abiding debate among his and other member organizations on the validity of the governance procedures at the Presidents Conference,[214] Theodore Mann, a former chairman of the Conference, took the criticism yet one step further by boldly calling into question – and indeed denying – the overall legitimacy of the organization he once headed. Curiously enough, in a strongly worded opinion piece published in the *Forward*, Mann called

---

[212] See Forward, "Forward 50, 2009", http://www.forward.com/forward-50-200 9/, accessed June 16, 2010.

[213] Eric Yoffie, "Reform the Presidents Conference", *Forward*, August 2, 2002. Founded in 1873 by Rabbi Isaac Mayer Wise as the Union of American Hebrew Congregations, the Union for Reform Judaism – as it was renamed in 2003 – represents an estimated 1.5 million Jews. Reform Judaism represents the largest religious stream within American Judaism in terms of members and synagogues.

[214] See Lawrence Cohler-Esses, "Dissension In The Ranks", *The Jewish Week*, August 8, 1997.

the Presidents Conference "an undemocratic institution" that, in his view, "is not worthy of our great Jewish community". Already the circumstances of its founding, Mann insinuates, deprive the umbrella of a fair right to exist: "The whole notion of a Jewish organization created at the request of the government of a nation in which Jews live – reeking as it does of Old World patterns – is highly offensive". Recent attempts at reforming the Conference, writes Mann, are therefore "mistaken. The Presidents Conference does not need to be reformed; it needs to be abolished".[215]

While the Conference of Presidents has weathered such attacks, the "numerous attempts" (Hoenlein) to reform the umbrella have meanwhile failed to gain traction. Plans to create an executive committee[216] with rotating seats and permanent seats for the largest member organizations did not win sufficient support.[217] Moreover, the former chairmen of the Presidents Conference, some of whom remain as informal counsel, are also presumed to act as "a protective layer" impeding reform.[218] One possible reason is that the creation of an executive committee could alienate a large number of member organizations due to the permanent imbalances associated with such a body. Unlike the JCPA, which con-

---

[215] Theodore Mann, "Do American Jews Need a Conference of Presidents?", *Forward*, August 23, 2002.

[216] See Eric Yoffie, "Reform the Presidents Conference", *Forward*, August 2, 2002; Nacha Cattan, "Rabbi's Call For Change Spurs Fight At Top Body", *Forward*, August 12, 2002.

[217] In fact, as Hoenlein (2009 Interview) points out, only those organizations would agree to the proposed changes that also expected to sit on the yet to be created committee. Hoenlein also made it clear that he had supported the idea of creating an executive committee.

[218] According to ADL's Abraham Foxman, quoted in Matthew E. Berger, "Presidential Moves", *The Jerusalem Report*, July 9, 2007. Former chairmen of the Presidents Conference, who served non-recurring terms of one or two years, have included, beginning with Nahum Goldmann: Philip Klutznick, Joachim Prinz, Israel Miller, Alexander M. Schindler, Theodore Mann, Julius Berman, Kenneth J. Bialkin, Morris B. Abram, Seymour D. Reich, Shoshana S. Cardin, and Leon Levy, among others. See Conference of Presidents of Major American Jewish Organizations, "The Conference of Presidents of Major Jewish [sic] Organizations: 40 Years of Making American Jewish History" (New York: undated leaflet [classified on October 14, 1996]), AJC Blaustein Library, 2.

sists of local and national organizations different in size and numbers, the Conference of Presidents is composed exclusively of major American Jewish organizations. Weighted voting rights would in all likelihood be hardly agreeable to organizations that consider themselves to be on an equal footing with each other.[219]

But the recent proposals for reforming the Presidents Conference must also be seen as motivated by turf concerns and as a means for the largest agencies to rein in the leadership of the Presidents Conference. As the Conference, akin to the JCPA, gradually evolved from an ad-hoc coordinating body into a functional agency of its own, the fear of being relegated to secondary roles has become topical for some of its member organizations. "If the Presidents Conference appears strong", says Kenneth J. Bialkin, a past chairman of the Conference, its constituent organizations react by viewing it "as a competitor".[220] Concerns about autonomy were in fact among the main reasons why the American Jewish Committee held aloof from membership in the Presidents Conference until 1991. When reconsidering its position in the late 1970s, AJC still noted the "expansion of (...) activities" of the Presidents Conference.[221] In a memorandum weighing the potential benefits of membership, AJC concluded that it would be institutionally "weakened" as a member of the Conference for it would lose its "visibility as an agency" as well as the "support among some influential segments of the Jewish community who look to AJC as an independent voice".[222]

---

[219] This perhaps explains why the former chairmen of the Presidents Conference "insisted that each group in the conference should have equal weight in the voting process", quoted from Lawrence Cohler-Esses, "Dissension In The Ranks", *The Jewish Week*, August 8, 1997. The principle of intuitive consent, as opposed to a regular voting procedure, also seems to have gained wide acceptance. Instead of losing members due to its discretionary leadership style, the Conference of Presidents, to the contrary, has attracted to its ranks a large number of Jewish organizations over the past decades.

[220] Quoted in Lawrence Cohler-Esses, "Dissension In The Ranks", *The Jewish Week*, August 8, 1997.

[221] American Jewish Committee, *AJC's Relations With The Conference of Presidents of Major American Jewish Organizations* (New York: AJC, 1978), AJC Blaustein Library, 11.

[222] American Jewish Committee, *AJC's Relations With The Conference of Presidents of Major American Jewish Organizations* (New York: AJC, 1978), 2.

Similarly, when the Presidents Conference adopted new confidentiality regulations in 1999, a heated debate ensued. Under the new regulations, member organizations "have imposed limitations on their dissent from Conference policy positions in order to maintain the effectiveness of the Conference"; no member organization may therefore, "expressly or by nuance, demean or denigrate consensus statements of the Conference".[223] But also the disclosure of the hitherto apparently unknown Conference of Presidents Fund in 1997,[224] which supports some of the umbrella's activities, "raised questions for some members about whether the conference may be beholden to a separate, previously unacknowledged constituency of wealthy donors".[225] Among the contributors to the fund were high-profile individuals like Mortimer B. Zuckerman and Ronald S. Lauder. Concerns over the potential outside influence of big donors quickly mounted, not least because Zuckerman and Lauder both served at the helm of two member organizations of the Presidents Conference at the time the fund became publicly known.[226] Although it is unlikely that these contributions had a lasting, if any, impact on poli-

---

As reasons supporting membership in the Presidents Conference, AJC (ibid., 1-2) noted for example that it was already a member of other Jewish umbrellas; that the threat to the security and well-being of Israel was after all a unifying issue; and that, over the years, the distinctions between Zionists and non-Zionists had virtually disappeared. It also believed, presumably in allusion to its own non-Zionist origins, that full membership in the Conference might dissipate "some of the vestiges of the old prejudices against AJC that still exist".

[223] Quoted in Rebecca Spence, "Lauder, Conference Bigs Erupt in Public Feuding Over Leaks and Dissent", *Forward*, September 17, 1999.

[224] While Hoenlein asserted that all member organizations knew about the fund, a former chairman of the Conference, who was in fact listed as one of the fund's directors, said he knew nothing about it. See Lawrence Cohler-Esses, "Dissension In The Ranks", *The Jewish Week*, August 8, 1997. Robert Rifkind, president of the American Jewish Committee, said he, too, had not had "any idea who was supporting the Presidents Conference other than its members up to this time". Quoted in Seth Gitell, "Conference Disclosing Details of Its Finances", *Forward*, July 25, 1997.

[225] Lawrence Cohler-Esses, "Dissension In The Ranks", *The Jewish Week*, August 8, 1997.

[226] Zuckerman served as honorary president of the America-Israel Friendship League and Lauder as the chairman of the Jewish National Fund.

cy,[227] this brief episode may well have impaired the mutual trust between the leadership and some of the member agencies of the Presidents Conference.[228]

A related issue that the Conference of Presidents has been confronted with is the dispute about whether it primarily represents the interests of its constituent agencies, on the one hand, or those of the state of Israel, on the other. Consider the example of the American Jewish Committee, an organization that observed the Conference's earlier policy toward Israel with a decidedly critical eye. In an internal communication regarding the Israeli incursion into Jordan in November 1966, AJC distanced itself in plain terms from the Presidents Conference, scolding the umbrella for taking "a pro-Israel stand that is more royalist than the king".[229] AJC consequently refused to subscribe to a related statement issued by the Presidents Conference, on the argument that the "choice of the wording gave it the tone of a whitewash and endorsement of the Israeli action. To refer to Israel's military counterattack as "an expedition" seems to us less than candid", AJC noted in its "strictly confidential" memorandum.[230] Likewise, in a review of arguments against membership in the Conference, AJC noted somewhat ambivalently in 1978 that "influential segments of opinion (...) correctly or incorrectly see the Presidents Conference as essentially an instrument of Israel and not an independent American Jewish voice".[231] Addressing the question

---

[227] First, Zuckerman and Lauder merely contributed $25,000 each; second, the Conference of Presidents Fund only covered part of the Conference's overall expenses; and third, the budget of the Conference did not even exceed $1 million at the time the fund became publicly known. The use of outside funds is moreover widely practiced among Jewish organizations: the JCPA, for example, receives one-third of its funding from foundations.

[228] Figures taken from Cohler-Esses (1997) and Gitell (1997), see footnotes above.

[229] American Jewish Committee, Foreign Affairs Department, "Memorandum", December 1, 1966, AJC Blaustein Library, 2.

[230] American Jewish Committee, Foreign Affairs Department, "Memorandum", December 1, 1966, AJC Blaustein Library, 1. The one-page statement of the Conference of Presidents, released on November 22, 1966, is available at the AJC Blaustein Library.

[231] American Jewish Committee, *AJC's Relations With The Conference of Presidents of Major American Jewish Organizations* (New York: AJC, 1978), 2.

of Israel advocacy today, Malcolm Hoenlein however avers that the Conference unequivocally "represent[s] the American Jewish constituency" and "take[s] positions based upon the assessment of what the positions are of the American Jewish community".[232] True, the Presidents Conference had shown a strong interest in Israel-related affairs already upon its creation; but it is fair to say that this did not contradict the organization's internal consensus, reflective as it was of the positions of the then dominant Zionist member agencies.

In terms of political orientation, the claim has sometimes been made that the Conference of Presidents comes close to the epitome of a right-wing organization. Scholars such as John J. Mearsheimer and Stephen M. Walt contend that the umbrella has "become increasingly conservative over time" and is "now led by hard-liners who support the positions of their hawkish counterparts in Israel".[233] In the same vein, journalist Matthew Berger writes that previous chairmen of the Presidents Conference – such as the cosmetics heir Ronald Lauder, the publisher Mortimer Zuckerman, or the CEO of Loews Corporation, James Tisch – all had "a few things in common: large bank accounts, household-name status within the Jewish community and beyond and hawkish views on Israel".[234] In 2002, the rejection of two left-wing groups, Meretz USA and the Reconstructionist Rabbinical Association, by the membership committee of the Presidents Conference was seen as a further indication of bias against prospective members from the political left.[235] Dissatisfaction with the organization's leadership had also surfaced back in 1996, when several liberal groups issued blunt calls for an ouster of Malcolm Hoenlein, the long-time executive vice chairman and key leader of the Presidents Conference.[236]

A few critical remarks are nonetheless in order. First, it can be reasonably argued that the "traditional and committed support for the

---

[232] Hoenlein (2009 Interview).
[233] Mearsheimer/Walt (2007), 126.
[234] Matthew E. Berger, "Presidential Moves", *The Jerusalem Report*, July 9, 2007.
[235] See Rachel Pomerance, "Presidents Conference rejects two left-wing groups; some claim bias", *JTA Daily News Bulletin*, December 20, 2002.
[236] See Forward, "Hoenlein Ouster Emerges as Aim of Dovish Camp", March 22, 1996.

elected government of Israel",[237] indeed a central tenet of Conference policy, rather reflects the political shifts in Israeli politics than the inherent ideological positions of the member organizations themselves.[238] For instance, Rabbi Alexander Schindler, a former chairman of the Conference associated with political liberalism, still supported the government of Menachem Begin and worked to secure wider acceptance for it within the Jewish community.[239] Second, the political affiliations of the past chairmen of the Conference contradict the claim of a consistent right-wing bias of the Conference. Although former chairman Ronald Lauder is a member of the Republican Party, the acting chairman of the Conference, Chicago attorney and community leader Alan Solow, is in fact, as *Haaretz* reports, "a key supporter and confidante of Barack Obama".[240] If such a bias existed, it would be difficult to explain how Solow was able to gather the majority of votes needed for his election. It is also worthwhile to recall that the more conservative chairmen such as Zuckerman or Tisch all served during the Bush administration;[241] Solow's appointment in turn appears to underline the pragmatic consideration of the Presidents Conference to also maintain privileged ties with the Obama administration.

Third, if the Conference of Presidents were unflinchingly biased toward right-wing politics, it would be hard to conceive how an ostensibly

---

[237] As pointed out in a joint letter by chairman Leon Levy and 11 past chairmen of the Presidents Conference, published in the *Forward*, "Why Israel's Interference Would Be Unwise", March 29, 1996.

[238] It was not until 1977, following the election victory of Menachem Begin, that Israel was for the first time governed by the right-wing Likud, after nearly three decades of continued rule by the left-wing parties Mapai and Alignment (the latter being a merger of Mapai and Ahdut ha-Avodah). Since 1977, Israel has been led by either Likud or Kadima prime ministers, with the exceptions of Shimon Peres (1984-1986, Alignment, and 1995-1996, Labor), Yitzhak Rabin (1992-1995, Labor), and Ehud Barak (1999-2001, One Israel/Labor).

[239] See Jerome Chanes, "Conference of Presidents of Major American Jewish Organizations", in: Berenbaum/Skolnik (eds.) (2007), vol. 5, 141.

[240] Bradley Burston, "Key Obama backer, confidante Alan Solow tipped to head U.S. Jewry's top body", *Haaretz*, December 21, 2008.

[241] Ronald S. Lauder, already chairman during Bill Clinton's second term, served as Conference chairman during the Bush administration until May 2001, when he was succeeded by Mortimer Zuckerman.

left-wing organization such as Americans for Peace Now (APN) was ever accepted as a member. The politically and religiously variegated composition of the Conference, formed over more than five decades, by contrast suggests that candidates have been admitted or rejected according to the set of objective criteria described above.[242] This is why the left-wing pro-Israel lobbying group J Street, for purely formal reasons, would currently not be eligible for membership in the first place.[243]

At the same time, certain reservations toward J Street's progressive agenda are clearly noticeable in the ranks of the Conference. "It's very questionable if they are in fact pro-Israel and what they are", says Malcolm Hoenlein, arguing his belief that, while "[a]nybody can purport to be pro-Israel", J Street had "not evidenced it yet".[244] Although the Conference of Presidents is decidedly less liberal in outlook than the JCPA, it cannot be labeled per se as a right-wing or hawkish organization; the vertical politics of the Presidents Conference, subject to further inquiry in the next subsection, illustrates the point.

Vertical Politics

Allegations that the Conference of Presidents is predisposed to espouse views of the political right are rejected in resolute terms by Malcolm Hoenlein himself, the organization's key leader who has represented the position of the Conference to all U.S. administrations from George H. W. Bush to Barack Obama. "[W]e work with whatever administration it is", says Hoenlein, "we're not Republicans or Democrats, liberal or conservative. We are representing the American Jewish community and, with that, we work with everybody". To honor the commitment to bipartisan appeal, the Presidents Conference maintains "very close and regular discussions" with, and has been well received by, officials from both

---

[242] Meretz USA and the Reconstructionist Rabbinical Association were in fact not turned down on political grounds, but because their budget and membership were deemed too small for a member of the Conference of Presidents of *Major* American Jewish Organizations. See Pomerance (2002), footnote above.

[243] Only organizations that have been in business for at least five years are eligible for membership, says Hoenlein (2009 Interview). J Street was founded in April 2008.

[244] Hoenlein (2009 Interview).

Democratic and Republican administrations.[245] Being a 501(c)(4) organization, it would not be able to engage in partisan advocacy in either case without losing its tax-exempt status – a rather unattractive option, given the already limited budget of the Presidents Conference. And although it could legally devote a substantive amount of its activities to lobbying, it is "not a lobby per se", says Hoenlein, even as the organization "obviously advocate[s] and tr[ies] to educate on issues of concern". Instead, the Presidents Conference likes to see itself more as an educational organization: in its political style, suggests the executive vice chairman, the umbrella therefore relies less on the exercise of pressure but rather gains respect through its credibility and "by people learning that you tell the truth".[246]

A different reading of the political style of the Presidents Conference is offered by Stephen M. Walt of Harvard's Kennedy School, who points to the coalitional relationship between AIPAC and the Presidents Conference. According to Stephen Walt, both organizations are effectively "linked" and "mutually reinforce their bargaining positions due to the logic of the American political system. The more power AIPAC has over Congress", Walt contends, "the more power the Presidents Conference has over the executive branch".[247] This statement obviously implies the existence of tangible organizational and strategic links between the two organizations – a claim that is clearly supported by the evidence. In fact, AIPAC is a member organization of the Presidents Conference and already its functional predecessor, the American Zionist Committee for Public Affairs, was among the founding members of the Conference in 1959. At the same time, all presidents of the Conference's member organizations are represented on the board of AIPAC, thereby further enhancing the ties between both organizations.

In their advocacy work, however, AIPAC and the Presidents Conference focus on distinct branches of government. While AIPAC deals nearly exclusively with Congress, the Presidents Conference is "much more charged with the administration" and, not least due to limited personnel resources, does "not spend a bulk of (...) time meeting with

---

[245] Hoenlein (2009 Interview).
[246] Hoenlein (2009 Interview).
[247] Walt (2008 Interview).

Congressmen".[248] This does not exclude that the Conference also gets involved in legislative advocacy, as memoirist and former chairman Israel Miller explains in an interview for Columbia University's Ethnic Groups and American Foreign Policy Project: "I deal as the chairman primarily with the executive rather than with the legislative, but there is of course a spillover. (...) In the main we deal with the President, the Secretary of State, Assistant Secretaries, (...) [but] sometimes the lines of demarcation are rather fuzzy and blurred, and we are dealing with issues that go across those lines, and therefore there are occasions when I would deal with the legislative".[249] According to Malcolm Hoenlein, AIPAC and the Conference of Presidents "do work closely together", even though the Conference often has "a broader agenda" and generally addresses a wider range of issues than AIPAC. "But the truth is that it works very well between us", says Hoenlein.[250]

The close cooperation with AIPAC is not the only reason why the Conference of Presidents is recognized as a highly effective and politically significant organization. As a result of its informal decision-making structure that forgoes regular votes, the Conference of Presidents tends to be perceived by the administration as a united political force. It is able to avoid public exposure of internal policy differences, and thereby appears less divided. As we have seen, the Presidents Conference nonetheless has been challenged by some of its member organizations over its political orientation and leadership style. But since internal dissent is not institutionalized by policy statements based on formal voting procedures, the leadership of the Conference – in contrast to the JCPA – enjoys great latitude in how to represent its views to government officials. The flexibility to do so may occasionally threaten the cohesion among its members, which jealously seek to guard their individual autonomy; yet ultimately, the effectiveness of the Conference depends on taking that risk.

---

[248] Hoenlein (2009 Interview).
[249] Reminiscences of Rabbi Israel Miller (August 11, 1975), Ethnic Groups and American Foreign Policy Project, page 2 in the Columbia University Center for Oral History Collection. Underlining the importance of contacts with the executive, Miller (ibid., 9) however also says that "ten minutes alone with the Secretary of State [Henry Kissinger]" are "more important to [him] than five conferences".
[250] Hoenlein (2009 Interview).

Moreover, the Conference of Presidents has been led by highly placed and influential individuals, a fact that has helped the organization gain access to the corridors of power in politics and beyond. Malcolm Hoenlein, ranked by the *Forward* as one of America's foremost Jewish leaders,[251] maintains excellent working relationships with key policy makers, having served more than 24 years as the head of the umbrella organization.[252] As noted above, its acting chairman is Alan Solow, a graduate of Harvard Law School and a close friend of Barack Obama's. The past chairmen of the Presidents Conference – beginning with the exceptional leader Nahum Goldmann, who advanced the Zionist cause through his deftness in European diplomacy – also boasted distinguished backgrounds and can be considered extraordinarily well-connected individuals. Mortimer B. Zuckerman, for example, is the owner of both *U.S World & News Report* and the New York *Daily News*, while Ronald S. Lauder, a former U.S. ambassador to Austria, is known as a major philanthropist in the U.S. and abroad. Both Zuckerman and Lauder are listed by *Forbes* magazine as being among the wealthiest individuals in the world.[253]

Finally, as the representative voice of organized American Jewry, the Conference of Presidents can draw on the support of a total of 52 major national Jewish organizations, which adds substantially to its clout. By way of comparison, the second most important national Jewish umbrella, the JCPA, only musters a membership of 14 national member agencies. Yet, local Jewish organizations such as federations or CRCs – an important power base for the Jewish Council for Public Affairs – are not represented in the Presidents Conference. This prima facie disadvantage is however compensated for indirectly since the JCPA itself is a member of the Presidents Conference. The very fact that the JCPA is a member

---

[251] See Forward, "Forward 50", http://www.forward.com/forward-50-2006/, accessed June 19, 2010.

[252] In contrast to the Conference's chairman, Hoenlein serves an unlimited term but can be unseated by the members of the Conference at any time, according to Hoenlein (2009 Interview).

[253] In 2010, Lauder and Zuckerman owned $2.6 billion and $1.6 billion, respectively, see Forbes, "#367 Ronald Lauder", http://www.forbes.com/lists/2010/10/billionaires-2010_Ronald-Lauder_R9VK.html, and Forbes, "#616 Mortimer Zuckerman", http://www.forbes.com/lists/2010/10/billionaires-2010_Mortimer-Zuckerman_W07H.html, accessed June 14, 2010.

of the Presidents Conference – and not the other way around – further illustrates the differences in power and prestige between both umbrella organizations.

Among the most significant political achievements of the Conference of Presidents was its "instrumental role"[254] in rescinding the infamous United Nations Resolution 3379, which equated Zionism with racism. In a critical show of contempt for Israel's founding ideology, the U.N. General Assembly had in fact determined in 1975 by a vote of 72 to 35 with 32 abstentions that "Zionism is a form of racism and racial discrimination".[255] It was not until over 16 years later, after the end of the Cold War, that the defamatory statement was finally revoked with the adoption of U.N. General Assembly Resolution 46/86 in 1991. The revocation marked an important step toward mending, at least to some degree, the difficult and at times antagonistic relationship between Israel and the United Nations.[256]

Another well-known advocacy initiative of the Presidents Conference was its assistance in helping secure $10 billion in U.S. loan guarantees for Israel at the beginning of the 1990s. Israeli Prime Minister Yitzhak Shamir had requested the commercial loan guarantees over a five-year period in order to finance the resettlement of immigrants ar-

---

[254] Conference of Presidents of Major American Jewish Organizations, "The Conference of Presidents of Major Jewish [sic] Organizations: 40 Years of Making American Jewish History" (New York: undated leaflet [classified on October 14, 1996]), AJC Blaustein Library, 1. The American Jewish Committee also deserves credit for leading the effort, especially in 1990 and after.

[255] For an overview of the voting patterns, see Edmund Jan Osmańczyk, *The Encyclopedia of the United Nations and International Relations* (London: Taylor & Francis, 1990), 1077. Romania, the Republic of South Africa, and Spain did not participate in the voting. Brazil, China, Portugal, the German Democratic Republic, and the USSR (and its satellites, by virtue of the Brezhnev doctrine), along with a large number of Muslim and Arab states, were among those that voted in favor of the Resolution. The voting patterns by and large reflected the political block alignment of the East-West conflict.

[256] Resolution 3379 was adopted at the plenary meeting of the U.N. General Assembly on November 10, 1975. It was revoked on December 16, 1991. For the text of both resolutions, see United Nations, "GA Resolutions", http://www.un.org/documents/resga.htm, accessed June 20, 2010. U.N. General Assembly Resolutions are not legally binding, but only recommendatory in nature.

riving from the collapsing Soviet Union, a request that President George H. W. Bush made conditional on Israel's willingness to stop building settlements in the occupied territories. As a means of putting pressure on the Bush administration, the Conference of Presidents mounted a large campaign in support of the guarantees, organizing a national advocacy day in Washington, D.C. for September 12, 1991, where over 1,000 Jewish leaders representing various local and national agencies joined in a call to protest Bush's policy. That same day, Bush held a special press conference on the Middle East in which he said he was "up against some powerful political forces" bent on thwarting the deal.[257] While the efforts led by the Presidents Conference were ultimately not sufficient to overcome Bush's resistance, the episode illustrates well the difficulties of challenging a president, even through the exercise of public pressure, on foreign policy issues.[258]

The political effectiveness of the Conference finally explains why it has won broad acceptance within the organized Jewish community despite the downside of being a highly discretionary organization. By the same token, it is precisely the lack of rigid structures that makes the Conference of Presidents – much more than the JCPA – an influential political force and key umbrella for the American Jewish community.

5.2.3 The Conference on Jewish Material Claims Against Germany

Founding History and Internal Structure

In pursuit of its mission to act as "the lobby of the persecuted",[259] the Conference on Jewish Material Claims Against Germany has strived to obtain "a small measure of justice"[260] for Jewish victims of Nazism ever

---

[257] See John T. Woolley and Gerhard Peters, The American Presidency Project, "The President's News Conference, September 12, 1991", http://www.presidency.ucsb.edu/ws/index.php?pid=19969, accessed June 20, 2010.

[258] See Raffel (2002), 135-136; Mearsheimer/Walt (2007), 39. The loan guarantees were eventually approved once Yitzhak Rabin replaced Shamir as prime minister in 1992.

[259] Conference on Jewish Material Claims Against Germany, *Claims Conference Informationen* (Frankfurt am Main: Claims Conference, 2007), 11.

[260] Conference on Jewish Material Claims Against Germany, *2007 Annual Report with 2008 Highlights* (New York: Claims Conference, 2008), 5.

since it was established in late October 1951. Under the deft leadership of its president Nahum Goldmann,[261] the Claims Conference gained historic significance as early as in 1952, when it became the first non-governmental organization to sign a formal agreement on reparations[262] with a sovereign state as part of the so-called Luxembourg Agreements.[263] A novelty in both international politics and public international law, the Luxembourg Agreements represented a caesura with the hitherto accepted practice according to which reparations were paid only between states, but not between states and individuals. Moreover, all three entities involved in the agreements – West Germany, Israel, and the Claims Conference – had not existed at the time of World War II, yet all concluded an agreement for compensation for crimes perpetrated during that time. Since the Claims Conference could not sign a treaty with a foreign state due to its status as a non-governmental organization, the agreements with West Germany were called "protocols";[264] covering in-

---

[261] Goldmann initiated the Conference shortly after Konrad Adenauer had given a landmark address on the issue before a special session of the Bundestag. Goldmann served as the president of the Claims Conference until his death in 1982.

[262] The London Debt Agreement of 1953 determined that reparations resulting from World War II were deferred until the conclusion of a final peace treaty with Germany (which was never formally concluded, as the Two-Plus-Four Treaty of 1990 only served as the equivalent of a peace treaty). However, the Luxembourg Agreements established de facto reparations to Israel and to the Claims Conference.

[263] The Luxembourg Agreements were signed on September 10, 1952, and comprise two separate accords. First, the indemnification agreement between West Germany and Israel, signed by Konrad Adenauer and Israel's first foreign minister, Moshe Sharett, under which Germany agreed to pay DM 3 billion in annual instalments to Israel in the form of goods and services, over the course of 12 years. Second, the two protocols concluded between West Germany and the Claims Conference, signed by Konrad Adenauer and Nahum Goldmann. The negotiations preceding the Luxembourg Agreements were held in Wassenaar, near Den Haag, in the Netherlands. See Henry (2007), 11-13.

[264] See Henry (2007), 25.

dividual and collective claims, they provided a legal framework for the future work of the Claims Conference.[265]

A specialized agency for Holocaust issues, the Claims Conference is "unique in its mission", says Saul Kagan, who has worked in key leadership positions at the JCC for over 50 years.[266] Indeed, there is no other Jewish organization that is exclusively devoted to advocacy on behalf of Holocaust survivors, one that negotiates internationally on individual compensation claims, that allocates funds to individuals and organizations, and that presses the recovery of looted Jewish property. Over its history, the Claims Conference has negotiated for compensation for injuries inflicted upon individual Jewish victims of Nazi persecution, as well as for the return of and restitution for Jewish-owned properties and assets confiscated and destroyed by the Nazis; obtained funds for the relief, rehabilitation and resettlement of Jewish victims of Nazi persecution, and supported the rebuilding of Jewish communities and institutions devastated by the Nazis; administered individual compensation programs for Holocaust survivors; recovered and sold unclaimed East German Jewish property and disbursed the proceeds to institutions that provide social services to elderly, needy Nazi victims and that engage in Holocaust research, education, and documentation.[267] Today, the question of addressing the needs of the aging population of Jewish survivors

---

[265] Under Protocol I, West Germany agreed to enact federal legislation to provide compensation and restitution to individual victims of Nazi persecution. Under Protocol II, which addresses the Conference's collective claims, West Germany was obliged to provide the Claims Conference with DM 450 million over a 12-year period for the relief, rehabilitation and resettlement of Jewish victims of National Socialist persecution, according to the urgency of need as determined by the Claims Conference, see Henry (2007), 11.

[266] Interview with Saul Kagan, Secretary, Conference on Jewish Material Claims Against Germany, June 5, 2009, New York. Born in interwar Poland, Kagan emigrated to the United States in 1940. A naturalized American citizen, Kagan, who speaks fluent German, later worked for the U.S. military government in Berlin. He became the first executive director of the Claims Conference in 1951, with Nahum Goldmann as president.

[267] See Conference on Jewish Material Claims Against Germany, *2007 Annual Report with 2008 Highlights* (New York: Claims Conference, 2008), 2.

in Israel and Eastern Europe remains the "top issue" for the Claims Conference, says Kagan.[268]

Given its nature as an international umbrella of highly diverse Jewish organizations, it may at first seem mistaken to regard the Conference on Jewish Material Claims Against Germany as an American Jewish organization. After all, it comprises a variegated membership of 25 independent Jewish organizations, including Argentinean, Australian, British, Canadian, French, German, Israeli, and South African Jewish organizations. Among its most prominent members are, for instance, the American Jewish Committee, the American Jewish Congress, and the Jewish Labor Committee; the Central Council of Jews in Germany, as well as its French counterpart, CRIF;[269] and organizations that themselves are umbrellas, such as the European Jewish Congress and the World Union for Progressive Judaism.[270] Two survivor organizations – the American Gathering of Jewish Holocaust Survivors and the Centre of Organizations of Holocaust Survivors in Israel – were admitted in 1989, thereby changing the umbrella's postwar membership structure: in fact, when the Claims Conference was founded, Holocaust survivors had no organization of their own and were not represented in the Conference.[271] In 2008, the World Federation of Jewish Child Survivors of the Holocaust became a member organization. Still deficient, however, is

---

[268] Kagan (2009 Interview). See also Conference on Jewish Material Claims Against Germany, *2007 Annual Report with 2008 Highlights* (New York: Claims Conference, 2008), 86. Demographic studies show there will be a significant number of elderly Nazi victims in poor conditions needing ongoing services such as homecare. Still in 2022, the JCC projects the number of survivors eligible for supplemental homecare at 11,100. As the income of the JCC from current restitution sources keeps declining, negotiations on the issue are thus likely to continue.

[269] For an analysis of the political role played by the *Conseil Représentatif des Institutions juives de France* (CRIF), see Sebastian Hoepfner, *Die Stellung der jüdischen Organisationen im politischen System Frankreichs*, Dipl. thesis, University of Passau, 2006.

[270] For an overview of member organizations, see Conference on Jewish Material Claims Against Germany, *Claims Conference Informationen* (Frankfurt am Main: Claims Conference, 2007), 1.

[271] See Henry (2007), 222.

the representation from Central and Eastern Europe, even as the region has increasingly been the focus for the work of the JCC since the 1990s.

Notwithstanding its international membership, the Claims Conference locates itself within the larger spectrum of American interest groups. "It's an American organization", avers Saul Kagan, pointing to the fact that the JCC, a 501(c)(4) organization, is not only incorporated in the state of New York and headquartered in New York City, but also employs senior staff that "happens to be American".[272] Kagan's argument is indeed consistent with the concepts commonly used in public international law to determine the nationality of juridical persons: under the terms of either the "incorporation", the "real seat", and the "control" theories, the Claims Conference clearly is to be considered an American organization.[273]

At the same time, all member organizations have a participatory role in both the appointment of the leadership positions and in the permanent work of the Conference. Each organization designates two representatives to the board of directors, which gathers once a year and appoints the organization's leadership positions such as the chairman and the executive vice president. The executive vice president appoints his staff as well as the respective committees, which develop policies for specialized fields.[274] Out of the 27 different committees, the executive committee, which meets at least twice a year, the allocations committee, and the negotiating committee for Germany are of particular importance. Through participation in the various committees, representatives of the member organizations are routinely involved in the work of the Claims Conference.[275] With three additional offices in Frankfurt am Main,

---

[272] With the exceptions of Gideon Taylor, the organization's executive vice president, who is Irish; the chairman of the executive committee, Reuven Merhav, and the first vice president, Zeev Bielski, who are Israeli; and two of the ten vice presidents, Ben Helfgott, who is British, and Ady Steg, who is French, as Kagan (2009 Interview) explains.

[273] See Rudolf Dolzer, "Wirtschaft und Kultur im Völkerrecht", in: Wolfgang Graf Vitzthum (ed.), *Völkerrecht* (Berlin: de Gruyter, 2007), 491-576, here 524-525.

[274] See Kagan (2009 Interview).

[275] See Conference on Jewish Material Claims Against Germany, *2007 Annual Report with 2008 Highlights* (New York: Claims Conference, 2008), 94-95.

Vienna and Tel Aviv, some of the Conference's work is furthermore conducted outside of the United States.

The Claims Conference is endowed with significant financial resources to fund its activities. As of December 2007, it reported funds totaling $841 million, as expenses amounted to $657 million; total liabilities and net assets were $1.18 billion.[276] In addition to payments from the German government benefiting individual survivors in accordance with various compensation programs, the major source of income is generated by the Claims Conference itself, namely by the Successor Organization of the Claims Conference.[277] The Successor Organization recovers and sells or receives compensation for unclaimed Jewish property in the former East Germany, for which the JCC is the legal successor.[278] About 80 percent of the proceeds, says Kagan, are used to fund organizations and institutions that assist needy Jewish survivors, while the remainder is spent on cultural programs such as Shoah research, documentation, or education. The Conference is free to decide on the allocation of institutional grants whereas, regarding payments to individual survivors, it administers the funds according to the criteria set by

---

Not all member organizations participate in the work of the committees, though.

[276] See Conference on Jewish Material Claims Against Germany, *2007 Annual Report with 2008 Highlights* (New York: Claims Conference, 2008), 89-91.

[277] German government funding, primarily for the Hardship Fund (created in 1980), the Article 2 Fund (1992), and the Central and Eastern European Fund (1998), amounted to $308 million. The Successor Organization generated another $309 million. To date, the Successor Organization has been responsible for approximately $960 million in grants, primarily to social welfare agencies, worldwide.

[278] A prominent case of property restitution involves the legal tussle between the Claims Conference, the German government, and the German retail chain Karstadt over the Wertheim property in Berlin. Seized and "aryanized" by the Nazis, the property was acquired by Karstadt in 1933. After German reunification, the JCC filed claims for the property, which, by then, the German government had given to Karstadt. In 2007 a settlement was reached, primarily regarding the Lenné Triangle at Potsdamer Platz, which Karstadt had sold to the Beisheim Group. Under the settlement, Karstadt paid the JCC $88 million. See Conference on Jewish Material Claims Against Germany, "The Wertheim Property", http://www.claimscon.org/?url=successor_org/wertheim, accessed August 16, 2010.

the German government and is thus bound to transfer the funds directly to eligible survivors.

Some misguided critics have marveled rather maliciously why the Claims Conference, after almost 60 years of negotiations with the German government, is still in "business". What else, if not reckless greed and moral bankruptcy, could have kept the organization in existence for such a long time?[279] These allegations, however, are baseless if not outright defamatory; as a matter of fact, the continued mission of the Claims Conference has been motivated not by avarice, but by the necessity to deal with the numerous shortcomings in German compensation policy.

From its inception, the policies regarding *Wiedergutmachung* have been characterized by substantial and often appalling imperfections. The initial Federal Indemnification Law (BEG), enacted in 1953, was widely viewed as inadequate in the amount of compensation offered and the categories of beneficiaries it covered;[280] and the revised BEG of 1956 did not apply to all victims as it only provided compensation for German citizens and for individuals who could prove, via language examinations, that they belonged to the German linguistic and cultural circle.[281] In 1965, despite the existing shortcomings, the German government quite bluntly stated its intention to draw a line under the past with the enactment of the Final Federal Indemnification Law (*BEG-Schlussgesetz*). Eastern European survivors did not receive compensation until 1998, when the Central and Eastern European Fund (CEEF) was established. Moreover, the issue of providing compensation for former slave and forced laborers was not settled until 2000, when the Foundation "Remembrance, Responsibility, and the Future" (*Stiftung "Erinnerung, Verantwortung und Zukunft"*, or EVZ) was created. Because the Holocaust was seen as an essentially European phenomenon, survivors of labor camps in North Africa had been overlooked until well into this

---

[279] See the bizarre polemic by Finkelstein (2000) as well as Christoph Schult and Andreas Wassermann, "Heiliges Geld", *Der Spiegel*, 23/2008, 54-56, who refer to the JCC as "a business enterprise sitting on assets worth hundreds of millions of dollars".

[280] See Conference on Jewish Material Claims Against Germany, *History of the Claims Conference: A Chronology* (New York: Claims Conference, 2001), 13.

[281] See Henry (2007), 37.

decade.[282] So-called "ghetto pensions" – German social security pensions for survivors who were employed for some form of wages during their internment in Nazi ghettos annexed to the Third Reich – have been available since 1997, yet 61,000 applicants out of 70,000 have been rejected.[283] The Article 2 Fund of 1992, a major compensation program currently in operation, still bars some Holocaust survivors from obtaining payments due to its strict eligibility criteria.[284]

To address these deficiencies, the Claims Conference has maintained annual negotiations with the German government. Negotiations are also necessary because the JCC administers and disburses monthly pensions, the terms of which are at times adjusted;[285] in addition, Eastern Euro-

---

[282] See Henry (2007), 227.

[283] See Conference on Jewish Material Claims Against Germany, *2007 Annual Report with 2008 Highlights* (New York: Claims Conference, 2008), 12.

[284] See Conference on Jewish Material Claims Against Germany, *2007 Annual Report with 2008 Highlights* (New York: Claims Conference, 2008), 18-19. The Article 2 Fund – based on the Implementation Agreement to the German Unification Treaty of October 3, 1990 – provides monthly pensions of currently 291 euros. In 2007, over 75,000 survivors had received payments from the Fund, bringing the total amount so far disbursed to approximately $2.3 billion.

[285] As of December 2006, Germany had paid a total of over 64 billion euros in indemnification for Nazi persecution; pensions paid under the BEG accounted for about 45 billion. According to the federal ministry of finance, there were over 59,000 current pensions being paid to survivors under the BEG, at the total annual cost of over 32 million euros, as of December 2006. About 15 percent of pensions remain within Germany, 85 percent are transferred abroad. In 1972, the peak year, more than 277,000 pensions were paid. The pensions, or *Renten*, are paid for three categories of damages: damages to life (*A-Renten*), damages to health (*B-Renten*) and damages to profession or vocation (*C-Renten*). Over 53,000 pensions are currently paid as *B-Renten*. Between 1953 and 1987, over 4,384,000 claims for compensation under BEG were filed, of which about 2 million were approved. The number of claimants is not identical with the total number of claims, but lower, as claimants usually filed more than one claim. From 1988 onward, the (small) number of new claims has not been recorded statistically. The ministry of finance "guardedly estimates" the cost of future payments at a "double-digit number in the range of billions of euros". See the internal memorandum and correspondence between Georg Heuberger, head of the JCC Frankfurt office,

pean survivors, says Kagan, have received less under the CEEF than Western survivors received under the BEG, thus prompting the need to renegotiate the agreement.[286] Finally, the ongoing needs of elderly survivors will make adjustments to existing programs inevitable for the time to come.

Political Style: Horizontal and Vertical Politics

Subject to the political dynamics in Germany, Israel, and the United States, the Claims Conference faces a variety of political challenges from without, rather than from within the organization itself. While the United States has traditionally supported the work of the JCC, the Israeli government in turn has been far less accommodating. The German government on the other hand has been a reliable, though at times uneasy, partner for the Claims Conference, as the following analysis shows.

Horizontal Politics

The Conference started out as an improvised collective of otherwise unrelated, even antagonistic, Jewish organizations that had put aside their intense political, ideological and religious differences to coalesce around one shared goal: aid to victims of Nazi persecution.[287] A single-issue organization, the JCC has nearly exclusive responsibility for the issue of Holocaust compensation and restitution; merely the presence of survivor organizations accounts for some duplication. This explains why, throughout its history, the Claims Conference has been the subject of criticism from outsiders, particularly from survivors in Israel, rather than being challenged from within by its constituent member organizations.

In Jewish public life, the question of whether or not to negotiate with Germany only a few years after the Holocaust was "a very bitter and a very controversial issue", as memoirist Saul Kagan recalls the early days of the Conference.[288] Many survivors vehemently rejected compensation

and Saul Kagan, December 3, 2007, citing data from the federal ministry of finance.

[286] See Kagan (2009 Interview).
[287] See Henry (2007), 4, 224.
[288] Interview with Saul Kagan, December 10, 1977, The New York Public Library-American Jewish Committee Oral History Collection, Dorot Jewish

payments, spurned as "blood money" (Kagan), from the German government.[289] Meetings of the Claims Conference, Kagan recounts, caused "turmoil and riots and demonstrations and everything else",[290] including "some very unpleasant episodes with representatives of groups of survivors. (...) [W]e had sit-in strikes by amputee victims of Nazi persecution, one of whom one day unscrewed part of his wooden leg and was about ready to crack my head open".[291] Similarly, Nahum Goldmann, who led the negotiations, was reviled by a large part of Jewish public opinion both in Israel and abroad as a "betrayer of Jewish honor" and had to travel accompanied by a bodyguard.[292]

Tensions with survivors are still perceptible today, resulting not least from a JCC agreement with West Germany in 1980 on the creation of the Hardship Fund, which "changed the fundamental nature" of the organization.[293] This is because the JCC has ever since been responsible for administering the Fund, along with the compensation programs for lifetime pensions, according to the criteria set by the German government.[294] The Conference thus became an operating agency responsible for processing and approving – or denying – applications for compensation claims; it is bound to administer the funds under the very guidelines it may at the same time seek to renegotiate. Transformed into an administrative partner of the German government, the Claims Conference has been in charge of a highly unpopular task – that of rejecting ineligible

---

Division, The New York Public Library, Astor, Lenox and Tilden Foundations, 10.

[289] Struggling with the legacy of the 1948 war and the challenge to absorb new waves of immigrants, Israel faced serious economic problems and thus had few choices but to negotiate with Germany for compensation under the Luxembourg Agreements, according to Jewish history scholar Derek Penslar, Zionism and the State of Israel, class taught at Columbia University, Spring 2009.

[290] Interview with Saul Kagan, December 10, 1977, Dorot Jewish Division, NYPL, 11.

[291] Interview with Saul Kagan, December 10, 1977, Dorot Jewish Division, NYPL, 35-36.

[292] Goldmann (1969), 250.

[293] Marilyn Henry, "Fifty Years of Holocaust Compensation", in: AJC (ed.), *American Jewish Year Book Vol. 102* (New York: AJC, 2002), 22.

[294] See Kagan (2009 Interview).

claims. While working to benefit victims of Nazi persecution, it often must do so "at the expense of its relationship with those victims".[295]

There are furthermore no restrictions imposed by the German government on how the proceeds from the sales of unclaimed Jewish property in the former East Germany can be used.[296] Under its current policy the JCC disburses 80 percent thereof to organizations around the world that provide essential social services for needy survivors. To receive an allocation, these organizations must however apply with the Conference, which, owing to an overall limited budget, may be forced to turn down certain requests.[297] Also, the current practice of allocating up to 20 percent of the proceeds of unclaimed Jewish property to Shoah research, education, and documentation rather than paying out the money to Holocaust survivors has not gone unchallenged.[298] Due to the very discretion it maintains over the use of these funds the Claims Conference has been subject to special scrutiny from survivors, especially in light of the large sums of money involved. Since 1980, for instance, the JCC has distributed a total of roughly $5.3 billion to Jewish victims of Nazi persecution worldwide, while in 2008 alone it disbursed more than $372 million.[299]

---

[295] Henry (2007), 228.

[296] The German government imposed a deadline for original Jewish owners and heirs to file claims for property restitution. Upon pressure by the JCC, the deadline was extended until 1992. In 1994, the JCC became the legal successor to all unclaimed Jewish property in the former East Germany. Had it not taken this step, unclaimed Jewish property would have remained with the owners at the time or reverted to the German government. Former owners who had failed to meet the German deadline of 1992 could however still receive a payment from the Claims Conference Goodwill Fund, which had a final filing deadline of 2004. As of December 2007, the JCC has paid approximately $520 million out of the Goodwill Fund, see Conference on Jewish Material Claims Against Germany, *2007 Annual Report with 2008 Highlights* (New York: Claims Conference, 2008), 42-45.

[297] See Kagan (2009 Interview).

[298] There arguably is a strong moral argument for remembering those who did not survive the Holocaust and had no share in receiving compensation. For a selection of letters debating the topic, see Conference on Jewish Material Claims Against Germany, "Allocations History and Reports", http://www.claimscon.org/?url=letters_board, accessed August 17, 2010.

[299] In 2008, the largest part – $278 million – was paid under the Article 2 Fund. See Conference on Jewish Material Claims Against Germany, *Claims Con-*

Relations with Israel, too, have at times been difficult. While in no other state Nazi victims have received more compensation than in Israel, criticism of the Claims Conference has been particularly acrimonious in that country. The Jewish state is by far the largest beneficiary of Claims Conference funds: as of December 2007, payments for more than 219,000 Nazi victims living in Israel had been approved under the Article 2 Fund and the Hardship Fund combined, out of a total of about 392,000 such approvals worldwide.[300] Yet, the Claims Conference has stood accused of withholding funds from needy Israeli survivors, a charge raised by two Israeli journalists – Guy Meroz and Orli Vilnai-Federbush – in their recent documentary "Musar Hashilumim", or "The Morality of Payments". The Conference has meanwhile responded with a defamation lawsuit against the filmmakers.[301] But the attacks continued at the political level when, after a hearing of both journalists, "[m]ost of the Knesset members (...) spoke out against the conference".[302] A rift between the Israeli government and the Claims Conference further opened up in 2007, when the Israeli minister of pensioners' affairs, Rafi Eitan, accused the JCC of neglecting the needs of Holocaust survivors.[303] Earlier, Eitan had pushed aggressively for the right to appoint half the members of the executive of the Conference, calling into question the representativeness of the umbrella organization.[304]

The harshness of Israeli criticism can be ascribed to a variety of reasons. For one thing, it is important to recall that the Conference essentially operates as an American organization – a fact that has appar-

---

ference 2008 Annual Report with 2009 Highlights (New York: Claims Conference, 2009), 28.

[300] Calculations based on Conference on Jewish Material Claims Against Germany, *2007 Annual Report with 2008 Highlights* (New York: Claims Conference, 2008), 22. By way of comparison, in the United States about 117,000 survivors had been approved for payments over the same period.

[301] See Haviv Rettig, "Claims Conference sues over Israeli documentary that "made us look like a mafia"", *The Jerusalem Post*, September 5, 2008.

[302] Dan Izenberg, "Knesset calls for state comptroller to investigate Claims Conference", *The Jerusalem Post*, June 17, 2008.

[303] See Spiegel Online, "Germany Refuses to Negotiate with Israel over New Claims", December 17, 2007.

[304] See Amiram Barkat, "Israel, local survivors seek control of Holocaust Claims Conference", *Haaretz*, November 29, 2006.

ently stirred opposition in Israel, where survivors resent their limited representation.[305] Second, the high level of poverty among Israel's Holocaust survivors may account for the charges leveled both against the Israeli government and the Claims Conference. As of 2008, the number of Holocaust survivors in Israel was estimated at approximately 233,000, or 32 percent of the age group over 65.[306] About one-third of Israeli Holocaust survivors, NGOs say, live below the poverty line.[307] This in turn raises substantial pressure on the Israeli government and the JCC to alleviate their plight. Because Israel is a functioning democracy, its leaders cannot simply turn a deaf ear to the concerns of the electorate;[308] as a result, official Israeli policy towards the Claims Conference has sometimes been less accommodating than one might expect.

Indeed, notes Stuart E. Eizenstat, a former U.S. ambassador and head of the U.S. delegations at the Washington and Prague Conferences On Holocaust Era Assets,[309] Israel has no particular incentive to obtain compensation for survivors living outside its borders. Recounting experiences from his government service, Eizenstat recalls "the lack of engagement of the state of Israel (...). They were engaged only at a secondary level, if at all, in the major negotiations I conducted", Eizenstat says. "Plain and simple, the Israeli state since its founding has been based upon the powerful Zionist idea that the real home for the world's Jews is Israel (...). Israeli governments have always sought as many im-

---

[305] To address Israeli needs, the Claims Conference however maintains a specialized committee, namely the Israeli Advisory Committee on Social Welfare Allocations, staffed with 16 officers, including key leaders of the Conference. See Conference on Jewish Material Claims Against Germany, *2007 Annual Report with 2008 Highlights* (New York: Claims Conference, 2008), 94.

[306] See JDC-ESHEL, "Israel's Elderly. Facts and Figures 2009", http://brookda le.jdc.org.il/_Uploads/dbsAttachedFiles/Aging-facts-figures09-ENG.pdf, accessed April 9, 2011. About 708,000, or 10 percent of the general population, are aged 65 or over.

[307] See Haaretz Service, "NGOs: One out of every three Holocaust survivors lives in poverty", *Haaretz*, September 11, 2009.

[308] See, for example, Matthew Gutman, "Jerusalem Offers Aid After Holocaust Survivors March On Israel's Streets", *Forward*, August 22, 2007.

[309] The Washington and Prague Conferences were held in 1998 and 2009, respectively.

migrants as possible (...). The Israeli government is not eager for these [Eastern European] communities to dig deep roots in their countries; they want them in Israel instead".[310]

What seems counterintuitive at first is a political reality for the Claims Conference: rather than from the Israeli government, the JCC has to seek support from Germany and, in particular, from the United States. Curiously enough, Holocaust reparations are "not an explicit aspect of Israeli foreign affairs"[311] – very much in contrast to the U.S., which has been strongly supportive of the work of the Claims Conference.

Vertical Politics

As a result of negotiations with the Claims Conference, the German government has paid over 66 billion euros, in nominal value and as of December 2008, in indemnification for suffering and losses resulting from Nazi persecution.[312] The political background of the negotiations is complex, but a few points deserve to be pointed out in detail.

Negotiations with the German Government

First, it is important to note that both the Claims Conference and the German government have held fundamentally different conceptions of how to deal with the question of *Wiedergutmachung*. The Jewish side flatly rejected the German term as inadequate: Israel has instead used the word *shilumim*, an Old Testament expression with the literal meaning of "payments" or "retribution", one that does not imply the notion of guilt

---

[310] Stuart E. Eizenstat, *Imperfect Justice. Looted Assets, Slave Labor, and the Unfinished Business of World War II* (New York: PublicAffairs, 2003), foreword by Elie Wiesel, 342-343.

[311] Henry (2007), 220.

[312] See Auswärtiges Amt, "Entschädigung für in der Zeit des Nationalsozialismus begangenes Unrecht", http://www.auswaertiges-amt.de/diplo/de/Aussenpolitik/InternatRecht/Entschaedigung.html, accessed August 13, 2010. Sometimes the argument is made that Germany has provided exemplary compensation programs compared to other states that did little or nothing to compensate Holocaust survivors. Given that Nazi Germany was responsible for perpetrating the crimes, this obviously is a bogus argument.

and eventual forgiveness.[313] Similarly, "the point of departure for the Claims Conference is that there is no adequate compensation", says Saul Kagan, arguing that there can only be "a degree of compensation", but no "making whole" for the losses suffered by Jews in the Shoah. While the German government has repeatedly called for a "Schlussstrich", that is, for drawing the line under the chapter of Holocaust-related claims, the Jewish side has conceived of the issue "mostly as an open, essentially interminable process".[314] And whereas the German government continues to emphasize the voluntary nature of its compensation programs, the Claims Conference insists that its demands are "not *Wohlfahrt* [social welfare], but legal claims".[315]

Second, the issue of *Wiedergutmachung* has played a distinctive role in German foreign policy but has also been subject to the latter's very limitations.[316] For instance, the larger political context of the Cold War made it impossible for the JCC to successfully negotiate compensation payments for survivors living behind the Iron Curtain. As a result of the Hallstein doctrine,[317] according to which West Germany would not maintain diplomatic relations with states that recognized the GDR, survivors living in Eastern Europe were effectively barred from receiving West German compensation. Specifically, the "sacrosanct territoriality principle"[318] made it exceedingly difficult, if not impossible, for Eastern European survivors – the so-called "double victims" of National Social-

---

[313] See Goschler (2005), 11-12. Israeli Foreign Minister Moshe Sharett coined the use of the term *shilumim* in the early 1950s. Compensation to individuals is called *pitzuim*, or "severance pays", see Conference on Jewish Material Claims Against Germany, *History of the Claims Conference: A Chronology* (New York: Claims Conference, 2001), 2.

[314] Goschler (2005), 12.

[315] Kagan (2009 Interview).

[316] It is worthwhile to recall that Adenauer also served as Germany's first foreign minister until 1955.

[317] The Hallstein doctrine was developed by Walter Hallstein, state secretary in the federal foreign office, and his collaborator Wilhelm Grewe shortly after the visit of Konrad Adenauer to Moscow in 1955. The doctrine was first applied to Yugoslavia, with which West Germany broke off diplomatic relations in 1957. The West German *Ostpolitik* since 1969 effectively ended the practice of the doctrine.

[318] Goschler (2005), 324.

ism and Communism – to receive payments. Nahum Goldmann apparently recognized this reality in 1958, when he wrote that the efforts of the Conference were "tempered by the knowledge that limitations beyond our control have sprung up at many times".[319] The powerful structural constraints of the Cold War thus had a direct bearing on the work of the Claims Conference, in particular since West Germany itself was at the time still a semi-sovereign state. This explains why many crucial issues remained unsettled until after German unification, when Holocaust-era claims became an early test of character for the Berlin Republic.[320]

Third, the impact of moral considerations on Germany's decision to provide compensation for Holocaust survivors should not be overestimated.[321] True, Adenauer on the one hand held the conviction that indemnification was a moral duty, indeed a "debt of honor"[322] for the German people, a tenet similarly espoused by his successor Ludwig Erhard.[323] But on the other hand, Adenauer also understood the significance of *Wiedergutmachung* for anchoring the Federal Republic in the Western alliance. This is why, according to Harvard professor Karl Kaiser, compensation for Nazi victims constituted a "plus factor" in terms of German-American relations. At the same time, it complemented Adenauer's larger goal of seeking reconciliation with three parti-

---

[319] Conference on Jewish Material Claims Against Germany, *Five Years Later. Activities of the Conference on Jewish Material Claims Against Germany* (New York: Claims Conference, 1958), 12.

[320] A responsibility it has however assumed in the tradition of the Bonn Republic – as opposed to the former GDR, which, in assertion of its anti-fascist founding ideology, refused to make amends for the Nazi past, see Goschler (2005), 10, 485, 413-477. For a general assessment of the Berlin Republic, see Winand Gellner and John D. Robertson (eds.), *The Berlin Republic: German Unification and A Decade of Changes* (London: Frank Cass, 2003).

[321] The question of morality in the process of *Wiedergutmachung* has been a popular theme in research, see, for example, Yeshayahu A. Jelinek (ed.), *Zwischen Moral und Realpolitik. Deutsch-israelische Beziehungen 1945-1965* (Gerlingen: Bleicher Verlag, 1997).

[322] Adenauer quoted in Goldmann (1969), 260.

[323] Erhard quoted in Conference on Jewish Material Claims Against Germany, *Conference on Jewish Material Claims Against Germany Annual Report 1965* (New York: Claims Conference, 1966), 11.

cular countries: Israel, France, and Poland.[324] In his political calculus Adenauer also overestimated the alleged "power of Jewry", especially that of Jews in the United States, even though Jewish organizations by then only had a "marginal" impact on the U.S. administration.[325] Political rather than moral considerations also played a conspicuous role in the Global Agreements, concluded bilaterally from 1959 to 1964, under which West Germany provided Western European governments with funds to compensate Holocaust survivors in their countries.[326] Striking examples of realpolitik, the amounts of payments made under the Global Agreements were essentially geared to the political importance of the respective countries.[327] Furthermore, the current eligibility criteria for the Article 2 Fund bar survivors who exceed certain income limits from

---

[324] Conversations with Karl Kaiser, Director, Program on Transatlantic Relations, Weatherhead Center for International Affairs, Adjunct Professor of Public Policy, John F. Kennedy School of Government, Harvard University, October 2008, Cambridge, MA.

[325] Niels Hansen, "Moral als Staatsräson – Zur Bewertung der Rolle Konrad Adenauers heute", in: Karl Brozik and Konrad Matschke (eds.), *Claims Conference. Luxemburger Abkommen – 50 Jahre Entschädigung für NS-Unrecht* (Frankfurt am Main: Societäts-Verlag, 2004), 86. "*Erstens aus einem Gefühl der Gerechtigkeit. Wir hatten den Juden (...) soviel (...) Unrecht angetan, wir hatten solche Verbrechen an ihnen begangen, daß sie irgendwie gesühnt werden mußten oder wiedergutgemacht werden mußten, wenn wir wieder Ansehen unter den Völkern der Erde gewinnen wollten. Und weiter: Die Macht der Juden, auch heute noch, insbesondere in Amerika soll man nicht unterschätzen. Und daher habe ich sehr überlegt und sehr bewußt, und das war von jeher meine Meinung, meine ganze Kraft d[a]rangesetzt, so gut es ging, eine Versöhnung herbeizuführen zwischen dem jüdischen Volk und dem deutschen Volk*". Adenauer quoted in Julius H. Schoeps, "Juden", in: Werner Weidenfeld and Karl-Rudolf Korte (eds.), *Handbuch zur deutschen Einheit 1949 – 1989 – 1999* (Bonn: Bundeszentrale für politische Bildung, 1999), 470.

[326] The recipient states distributed the money according to different national criteria. In France, for instance, indemnification had no specifically Jewish dimension. Jewish survivors were not treated as a separate group, as most payments were in fact doled out to former fighters of the Résistance, writes Hans Günter Hockerts, "Gewisse Stille", *Frankfurter Allgemeine Zeitung*, August 29, 2006.

[327] See Goschler (2005), 290.

receiving payments, a fact that also raises doubts about the alleged moral aspect of the compensation programs.[328]

Fourth, it must be recalled that a negative attitude toward Holocaust reparations had prevailed not only in Israel, but also in postwar Germany itself. The very idea that things had to be "made good again" lacked broad-based public support, as various surveys reveal. According to a poll conducted by the Allensbach Institute for Public Opinion Research in August 1949, only 54 percent of the respondents said that Germany had a "duty of *Wiedergutmachung*", while 31 percent responded in the negative and 15 percent were undecided. Jewish victims of Nazi persecution also ranged comparatively low on the overall hierarchy of victims in West German society. A survey carried out by the U.S. High Commission in October 1951 showed that while 68 percent of those polled approved of assistance services for Jews, an imposing 96 percent of the interviewees were in favor of aid for war widows and orphans, 93 percent for victims of aerial warfare, and 90 percent for displaced persons from the East. The approval rate for aid to the family of the failed Hitler assassins of 1944 was 73 percent, still higher than the approval rate for aid to Jews.[329] These attitudes further correspond with the finding that civic engagement on behalf of compensation for Nazi victims likewise remained on a rather low level.[330] Perhaps unsurprisingly, then, only 11 percent declared themselves "unreservedly favorable" to the Luxembourg Agreements, according to an Allensbach survey of August 1952.[331]

The German political parties, too, were deeply divided over the issue. The only fraction in the German Bundestag that unanimously voted in favor of the ratification of the Luxembourg Agreements on March 18, 1953, was the SPD – with a total of 125 favorable votes. By contrast, only 84 members of Adenauer's own fraction, the CDU/CSU, cast a "yes" vote, while 39 members abstained, and another four CDU/CSU members voted "no". The FDP, a partner in Adenauer's governing coalition, did not support the agreements: five FDP members voted against,

---

[328] See Conference on Jewish Material Claims Against Germany, *2007 Annual Report with 2008 Highlights* (New York: Claims Conference, 2008), 19.
[329] Both surveys cited in Goschler (2005), 133-134.
[330] See Goschler (2005), 136.
[331] See Goschler (2005), 134, citing data from the Allensbach Yearbook of Public Opinion.

and 19 members abstained from voting. The communist KPD unanimously opposed the agreements.[332]

Indeed, the politics of *Wiedergutmachung* – referring to official German policy regarding Holocaust-era claims – has never been associated with a single political party or governing coalition. As Constantin Goschler writes, the CDU did not regard the question of *Wiedergutmachung* as a particular priority on its overall policy agenda. The same was true for the CSU, where prominent individuals like Fritz Schäffer and Franz Josef Strauß feared for the integrity of German-Arab relations. With the notable exception of Federal President Theodor Heuss, the FDP was altogether ambivalent, and tepid at best, in its response to Holocaust reparations.[333] Only the opposition SPD,[334] which upon the request of the American Jewish Committee had already advocated the inclusion of a clause about *Wiedergutmachung* in the German Basic Law in 1948, stood out due to its unequivocal backing of the Luxembourg Agreements.[335] Still, despite SPD-led governing coalitions since 1969, the Claims Conference long remained unable to achieve any major policy victories: no major progress was made between 1965 (when the BEG was amended) and 1980 (when the Hardship Fund was eventually created). In 2000, however, Chancellor Gerhard Schröder (SPD) together with his coalition partner Alliance 90/The Greens actively led the effort in establishing the foundation "Remembrance, Responsibility, and the Future", endowed with funds of DM 10 billion, to compensate form-

---

[332] See Wolffsohn (2007), 230.
[333] A 1949 Bundestag election poster of the FDP not only called for "drawing the line" ("*Schlußstrich drunter!*") under "denazification[,] disenfranchisement [and] incapacitation", but also brazenly grouped together the three terms. On display at Stiftung Haus der Geschichte der Bundesrepublik Deutschland, EB-Nr. 1987/3/105, Bonn.
[334] In the same vein, the first German chancellor to make an official visit to Israel was Willy Brandt, not Adenauer, in 1973. It was also Brandt who spontaneously fell to his knees before a memorial to the victims of the Warsaw ghetto in Poland in 1970. Diplomatic relations with Israel were established in 1965, during the government of Ludwig Erhard, with Gerhard Schröder (CDU) as foreign minister.
[335] See Goschler (2005), 137 (CDU), 140, 171 (CSU), 141 (FDP), 142 (SPD). Within the CDU, however, individuals like Franz Böhm or Eugen Gerstenmaier were committed supporters of *Wiedergutmachung*.

er slave and forced laborers; the previous government of Helmut Kohl had by and large regarded the question of Holocaust-era claims as a "closed chapter".[336]

The first implication of the above analysis is that the Claims Conference cannot rely on a single partner in its advocacy efforts. Instead, it must build broad bipartisan support and forge coalitions across the entire political spectrum. Accordingly, it explicitly describes itself as a "non-political and non-partisan body".[337] Relations with the German bureaucracy are furthermore essential: in particular, the Conference is in permanent dialogue with the federal ministry of finance (BMF) through its German office in Frankfurt am Main. The BMF represents the "primary contact" for the Claims Conference in the German government, although the umbrella also meets with representatives of the ministry of labor and social affairs, the ministry of health, and the federal chancellery.[338] No less important is the contact with the parliamentary groups in the German Bundestag, which are typically consulted following the meetings at the ministerial level, says Kagan. Since compensation payments are funded by the German government, the Claims Conference requires the support of the Bundestag. The latter has the power of the purse and must approve the payments in its annual budgetary plans. The advocacy work of the Claims Conference thus takes place both at the executive and legislative levels: in an effort to secure favorable policy outcomes, the JCC must seek out "close cooperation" with the executive and foster "good understanding" with the legislative branch.[339]

The second implication is that the Claims Conference has to be willing to compromise and to engage in constructive dialogue rather than in confrontative political standoffs. In fact, the JCC has no intention to raise public pressure on the German government – by dint of high-profile newspaper campaigns, for instance – to press its agenda. "The

---

[336] Goschler (2005), 452. The reluctance of the Kohl government had prompted the American Jewish Committee to publish a full-page ad in the *New York Times* in 1997 to press for compensation for Eastern European Holocaust survivors, see section 5.1.1 ("Vertical Politics") above.

[337] Conference on Jewish Material Claims Against Germany, *2007 Annual Report with 2008 Highlights* (New York: Claims Conference, 2008), 7.

[338] Kagan (2009 Interview).

[339] Conference on Jewish Material Claims Against Germany, *Claims Conference Informationen* (Frankfurt am Main: Claims Conference, 2007), 9.

Claims Conference doesn't negotiate through newspapers", says Kagan, adding that such a strategy would contradict the long-standing working relationship between the German government and the Conference. "You don't put an ad in a newspaper when you have worked with a government for 57 years", Kagan avers.[340] At the same time, its member organizations have been far more assertive in their political style. Marilyn Henry phrases it well, writing the Claims Conference may be an apolitical umbrella, but some of its members may nonetheless be "highly politicized".[341]

Negotiations with the German government are routinely held once or twice per year.[342] According to the German diplomat Onno Hückmann, the former head of the legal division on war-related claims in the federal foreign office, the Claims Conference clearly dominates the agenda-setting process. On average, says Hückmann, who participated in the negotiations on behalf of the foreign ministry, the Conference presents a "catalogue of demands" consisting of about ten to 12 requests. Typically, these requests are organized around one specific issue and one-third thereof is usually accepted by the BMF. Hückmann also points to the fact that *Wiedergutmachung* still is a foreign policy issue: the initial responsibility for indemnification policy was vested in the foreign ministry, but was later transferred to the BMF.[343] Today, the BMF maintains an entire department dedicated to Holocaust-era claims, whereas the foreign office relies on a far smaller unit. The shift from foreign policy to fiscal policy has also had a profound impact on the practice of *Wiedergutmachung* itself. Whereas the federal foreign office has traditionally been favorable to *Wiedergutmachung*, the BMF has often acted as a "footdragger", says Hückmann. This has at times led to tensions between both ministries.[344]

---

[340] Kagan (2009 Interview). Obviously, though, the campaigns of its member organizations, such as the ad sponsored by AJC in the *New York Times* in 1997 clearly backed up the JCC's negotiating position.

[341] Henry (2007), 225.

[342] See Kagan (2009 Interview).

[343] The shift probably occurred in the mid-1950s when Adenauer gave up his position as foreign minister.

[344] Conversation with Onno Hückmann, Fellow (Federal Foreign Office), Weatherhead Center for International Affairs, Harvard University, November 19, 2008, Cambridge, MA.

Moreover, following the Adenauer era, German indemnification policy was driven by pressure from the Claims Conference – important questions, Hückmann says, were only resolved when the JCC exerted pressure on the German government. According to Hückmann, the Claims Conference is in fact able to build up substantial political pressure in the United States when Jewish organizations and supporters get mobilized on its behalf. This however does not mean that the Claims Conference is able to dictate indemnification policy, Hückmann adds, explaining that the ministry of finance "has the last word. (...) The budget is a fixed parameter".[345] Due to the dominant role of the BMF and the Bundestag, the Claims Conference indeed appears more like a petitioner than a principal – it can merely negotiate for the best possible results within the legal and financial framework set by the German government.

Role of the U.S. Government in Claims Conference Negotiations

The traditional bilateralism characteristic of the relationship between the German government and the Claims Conference has gradually given way to a multilateral constellation of political actors since the 1980s, along with the larger trends towards pluralization and transformation of the public sphere in German society.[346] The U.S. government has emerged as a powerful player and has played an increasingly important and often decisive role in Claims Conference negotiations with Germany. Echoing both the Wilsonian and Rooseveltian thrusts in American foreign policy,[347] the United States was motivated by moral considerations and the imperatives of its national interest: U.S. policy reflected the idea of reeducation as well as the necessity to deal with domestic pressure from Holocaust survivors.

Beginning with U.S. Military Law 59, which was enacted in the American zone as the first property restitution law in occupied Germany on November 10, 1947, the United States has been a steadfast supporter

---

[345] Conversation with Onno Hückmann, Fellow (Federal Foreign Office), Weatherhead Center for International Affairs, Harvard University, October 28, 2008, Cambridge, MA.
[346] See Goschler (2005), 21.
[347] See Henry Kissinger, *Diplomacy* (New York: Simon & Schuster, 1994), 29-55.

of compensation and restitution programs.[348] Its commitment to indemnification was also visible in the Luxembourg Agreements. High Commissioner John J. McCloy, who had "great sympathy" for the mission of the Claims Conference,[349] insisted that West Germany make amends, reminding Adenauer that reconciliation with the Jewish people was "so significant" for the international standing of the Federal Republic.[350] After the end of the Cold War, the United States still was the "most powerful and steadfast proponent of property restitution in Central and Eastern Europe".[351] Moreover, Article 2 of the Implementation Agreement to the German Unification Treaty of October 3, 1990, obligated the unified Germany to compensate Holocaust survivors who had previously received little or no compensation – an agreement that the JCC was able to reach "[w]ith the active support of the U.S. government".[352]

Domestic pressure from Holocaust survivors in the United States moreover led to the establishment within the U.S. Department of State of the Office of the Special Envoy for Holocaust Issues in 1998. "That's the root of our interest, from a political point of view. But we aren't just politically oriented, we Americans have a humanitarian side as well. So doing the right thing is something rather typical of the United States, and that's what the Department has been trying to do for this decade a little bit", John P. Becker says.[353] The Office of the Special Envoy arguably is the most obvious illustration of the U.S. commitment to supporting Hol-

---

[348] See Conference on Jewish Material Claims Against Germany, *History of the Claims Conference: A Chronology* (New York: Claims Conference, 2001), 6. By August 1947, four German states in the American zone of occupation had promulgated laws to provide financial indemnification to victims of Nazi persecution.

[349] Goldmann (1969), 265.

[350] McCloy quoted in Henry (2002), 18.

[351] Henry (2002), 53.

[352] Conference on Jewish Material Claims Against Germany, *2006 Annual Report with 2007 Highlights* (New York: Claims Conference, 2007), 23. Article 2 reads: "The Federal Government is prepared, in continuation of the policy of the German Federal Republic, to enter into agreements with the Claims Conference for additional Fund arrangements in order to provide hardship payments to persecutees who thus far received no or only minimal compensation according to the legislative provisions of the German Federal Republic", see ibid., 23-24.

[353] Becker (2009 Interview).

ocaust survivors, and its political weight clearly enhances the negotiating position of the Claims Conference.[354]

A frequent misrepresentation is to portray the Claims Conference as the driving force behind an alleged "Holocaust industry" in the United States. But as the empirical evidence shows, the Conference has not been shy about resisting domestic pressure from Holocaust survivors, taking sides with the German government instead. The Holocaust Assurance Accountability Act of 2008, or H.R. 1746, is a case in point. Sponsored by Representative Ileana Ros-Lethinen (R-FL), H.R. 1746 aims at making obligatory the disclosure of Holocaust-era policies by insurers and at establishing a federal cause of action for claims arising out of a covered policy. Although discussed in the House at the committee level, the bill never became law, not least because the Claims Conference, along with some of its member organizations and in a joint effort with the German government, actively lobbied against it.[355] The JCC did so because H.R. 1746 stands in sharp contradiction with the Berlin Accords of July 2000 – the U.S.-German Executive Agreement between President Clinton and Chancellor Schröder, under which the United States offered Germany "legal peace" regarding any possible lawsuits brought against German companies in the U.S. The United States committed to file a "Statement of Interest" recommending the dismissal of related lawsuits in American courts, complete with an affidavit by the U.S. secretary of state, and citing the overriding foreign policy considerations that led the U.S. government to conclude that the German foundation *"Erinnerung, Verantwortung und Zukunft"* was the exclusive remedy for such claims.[356] The Claims Conference, fearing for future cutbacks on payments from Germany, thus "defended the German position", Hückmann recalls.[357]

---

[354] The Office, says Becker (2009 Interview), works "fairly closely" with the Claims Conference.

[355] See Holocaust Survivors' Foundation – USA, "Vast sums devoted to defeat H.R. 1746. Several Jewish organizations, German Embassy join efforts", http://hsf-usa.org/HR1746.htm, accessed September 18, 2010.

[356] See J. D. Bindenagel, "Justice, Apology, Reconciliation, and the German Foundation: "Remembrance, Responsibility, and the Future"", in: Elazar Barkan and Alexander Karn (eds.), *Taking Wrongs Seriously. Apologies and Reconciliation* (Stanford: Stanford University Press, 2006), 300-302.

[357] Hückmann (2008 Interview, November).

Given the nature of the American political system, the Berlin Accords are of limited reliability, though. Members of Congress are not bound by the executive agreement and, being answerable to their electoral districts only, may support policies that challenge the very notion of "legal peace" between Germany and the United States. Consequently, the question of *Wiedergutmachung* is "not a closed chapter".[358] In fact, H.R. 1746 has meanwhile been reintroduced as H.R. 4596, which declares that, under certain conditions, "no executive agreement between the United States and any foreign country shall invalidate or preempt any state law creating a cause of action against an insurer or related company".[359] At the same time, neither of both House resolutions have ever represented the "concrete danger" that the German government believed them to be.[360] For sessions of Congress are limited to two years time, and all proposed bills are cleared from the books once a new session begins. As research has furthermore shown, 80 percent of all bills introduced in the House and 75 percent of those introduced in the Senate die already at the committee level. In addition, 50 percent of the bills that have either passed the House or the Senate still fail to become law. Of all legislative initiatives introduced in the U.S. Congress from 1947 to 2000, only 4.3 percent (or about 18,000 out of 419,000) have on average become law, and most of them in abridged form.[361] It is thus hardly surprising that neither the House nor the Senate ever came to vote on H.R. 1746.

As the above example suggests, the political clout of the Claims Conference must not be overestimated. In the United States, at least, Holocaust-era issues have long taken on a peculiar dynamics of their

---

[358] Hückmann (2008 Interview, November).
[359] See Govtrack, "H.R. 4596: Holocaust Insurance Accountability Act of 2010", http://www.govtrack.us/congress/bill.xpd?bill=h111-4596&tab=summary, accessed September 19, 2010.
[360] See Deutscher Bundestag, "Elfter Bericht der Bundesregierung über den Stand der Rechtssicherheit für deutsche Unternehmen im Zusammenhang mit der Stiftung "Erinnerung, Verantwortung und Zukunft"", Drucksache 17/1398 (Berlin: Deutscher Bundestag, 2010), 3.
[361] See Winand Gellner and Martin Kleiber, *Das Regierungssystem der USA. Eine Einführung* (Baden-Baden: Nomos, 2007), 33.

own.[362] Groups of Holocaust survivors and elected officials may at times pursue actions that are indifferent or even contrary to the interests of the Claims Conference. Similarly, as noted before, the structural constraints of the Cold War limited the JCC's political impact. East Germany, for instance, refused to pay compensation altogether. Only when the decline of the GDR came to a head did Erich Honecker reach out to the JCC with an offer for compensation – an entirely cynical and opportunistic move, as Saul Kagan recalls the 1987 Berlin meeting.[363] Finally, it is worthwhile recalling that the political significance of the Claims Conference extends far beyond matters of monetary compensation. Among the most important achievements of the Claims Conference are the "barriers of conscience" it has helped erect and which act as a deterrent to prevent similar injustices in the future.[364] This political and moral legacy will undoubtedly remain intact well after the end of the next decade, when negotiations with the German government will in all likelihood have come to an end.

---

[362] See Gabriel Schoenfeld, "Holocaust Reparations – A Growing Scandal", *Commentary*, September 2000, 25-34, who writes that politicians' "tears for the six million are exquisitely synchronized with their need for campaign contributions and applauding headlines", 34.

[363] See Kagan (2009 Interview). The JCC meeting nearly coincided with Honecker's long-anticipated first official visit to West Germany, made in September 1987.

[364] Bindenagel (2006), 309.

Table 3: Comparison of Largest American Jewish Umbrellas, Main Features

	JCPA	Presidents Conference	Claims Conference
Founding year	1944	1959	1951
Legal status	501(c)(3)	501(c)(4)	501(c)(4)
Member organizations	139	52	25
Offices	2	1	4
Budget	$3 million	$667,000	Varies ($372 million in 2008)
Headquarters	New York	New York	New York
Staff	22	12	35 (senior staff)

Note: JCPA budget in 2009, Presidents Conference budget in 2008.

5.3 Summary

As we have seen, American Jewish organizations operate in an essentially pluralistic and highly competitive environment. As a result of intense peer competition, they need to craft distinct identities and characteristic political styles to differentiate themselves from their rivals. Our analysis of the "big three" Jewish defense organizations confirms this point. Whereas the American Jewish Committee is known for its quiet and diplomatic approach to politics, the Anti-Defamation League has carved out a reputation for practicing a bolder and more outspoken approach. The American Jewish Congress in turn is still struggling to find a viable niche of activity between its two powerful rivals, a dilemma that continues to pose an existential threat for the organization.

For umbrellas like the JCPA and the Conference of Presidents, the main challenge has been to skillfully walk the line between representing their constituent organizations, on the one hand, and assuming independent powers of their own, on the other. Fearing for new competitors, the constituent organizations have been especially wary of seeing the coordinating bodies become players in their own right. Depending on the internal structure of the respective umbrellas, this fear has been more or less pronounced. While the JCPA's complex decision-making system strengthens its internal cohesion, it also imposes serious limits on its political effectiveness. And while the Conference of Presidents has relied on a fairly discretionary yet politically effective leadership style, it has also done so at the constant risk of alienating the very organizations it depends upon for its own success.

Another important finding is that umbrella organizations can further enhance their political relevance by fostering a decidedly bipartisan outlook. Due to its clearly liberal bent, the JCPA is therefore to be considered a comparatively weak organization. By contrast, the bipartisanship of the Presidents Conference has made the umbrella less vulnerable to changes in Congress and the administration, thereby adding to its political clout.

At the theoretical level, the discussion in this chapter leads to the conclusion that coalition theories can neither be clearly confirmed nor rejected. In fact, it appears that most coalition theories, often based on abstract premises that hardly match real-world conditions, are ill-suited to explain the coalitional behavior among the Jewish organizations in question. As the example of the Claims Conference suggests, viable and lasting coalitions among interest groups can be formed even in spite of pronounced antagonisms between the individual coalition partners. An overwhelming common purpose may in effect take precedence over tensions that would otherwise hamper interorganizational cooperation. Moreover, the examples of the JCPA and the Presidents Conference show that interest groups may still coalesce within coordinating bodies even though those very bodies may either have limited effectiveness (as in the case of the JCPA) or may be difficult to keep in check (as in the case of the Presidents Conference).

Wilson's autonomy-based coalition theory however offers a plausible explanation for the behavior among the "big three" Jewish defense organizations. Rivalry for distinct organizational niches has made the organizations especially reluctant to grant the JCPA the status of a player in its own right. Operating in a competitive setting has had yet another effect: intent on guarding their autonomy, the "big three" also engage in disjointed coalitions with non-Jewish organizations, particularly with those that share similar goals. Wilson's autonomy-based rationale is superior to the explanation offered by ideological compatibility theory since Jewish organizations arguably are more similar to each other than to their non-Jewish counterparts. The "big three" defense organizations are therefore often referred to as "community relations" organizations – an apposite description, considering that the willingness to reach out beyond the Jewish community has been a characteristic feature of organizations like AJC, ADL, and the American Jewish Congress.

6 New Jewish Politics

Jewish organizations associated with the pattern termed "new" Jewish politics differ from their more traditional counterparts in that they make full use of the democratic opportunities afforded by the American political system. Pro-Israel organizations such as AIPAC and J Street have come to embody precisely this kind of Jewish politics, as they insert themselves directly and permanently in the legislative and electoral process. While AIPAC has skillfully pioneered both congressional and grassroots lobbying, J Street has been a forerunner especially in online advocacy. Perusing a distinction made by Martin Kramer,[1] the following analysis shows that both organizations represent two starkly different models of pro-Israel lobbying. AIPAC, on the one hand, engages in what is henceforth referred to as "Israel advocacy": it advocates for the policies of the elected government of the state of Israel, irrespective of the latter's political agenda. J Street by contrast is committed to what shall be termed "policy advocacy": it pursues an own partisan agenda that may at times be at odds with the policy preferences of the Israeli government. In so doing the analysis presented in this chapter yet again dispels the notion of Jewish organizations forming an alleged "Israel lobby" as a single and coherent political actor. In fact, AIPAC and J Street have been political rivals on Capitol Hill, operating in similar, but still clearly distinctive ways.

6.1 American Israel Public Affairs Committee

6.1.1 Founding History and Internal Structure

When the *New Yorker*'s Jeffrey Goldberg asked former AIPAC official Steven Rosen to comment on AIPAC's influence in Washington, Rosen is said to simply have pushed a napkin across the table. "You see this

---

[1] See Kramer (2008 Interview).

napkin?" Rosen asked. "In twenty-four hours, we could have the signatures of seventy senators on this napkin".[2]

Arguably the most striking illustration of a new kind of Jewish advocacy that emerged in post-Second World War America, the American Israel Public Affairs Committee has come to be viewed – and both praised and scorned – as the epitome of the "Israel lobby" in the United States. Its political clout in American politics is hardly doubted by anyone: political scientists like John J. Mearsheimer and Stephen M. Walt refer to AIPAC as "the most influential pro-Israel lobbying organization",[3] while the *New York Times* describes AIPAC as "the most important organization affecting America's relationship with Israel". AIPAC itself, too, proudly advertises its prominent role as "America's leading pro-Israel lobby".[4] In fact, as early as in 1975, the organization had been identified as the "spearhead" of the increasingly influential "Israel lobby" inside the Washington Beltway.[5] That it has indeed the standing to be taken seriously by U.S. politicians suggests a 2006 survey, where AIPAC was ranked the fourth most influential interest group in the United States, only eclipsed by the National Federation of Independent Business, the American Association of Retired Persons (AARP), and the National Rifle Association (NRA), which was ranked first.[6] According to an informal and tentative ranking by the historian Jack Wertheimer, AIPAC can be considered the "most important" American Jewish organization today, still ahead of the Presidents Conference, itself an influential umbrella of various Jewish organizations.[7]

A single-issue agency solely focused on the purpose of pro-Israel advocacy, AIPAC is an organization with "explicitly Zionist roots".[8] Its founder, Isaiah ("Si") L. Kenen, initiated the American Zionist Council

---

[2] Quoted in Jeffrey Goldberg, "Real Insiders", *The New Yorker*, July 4, 2005.
[3] Mearsheimer/Walt (2007), 49.
[4] AIPAC, "About AIPAC", http://.aipac.org/about_AIPAC/default.asp, accessed October 1, 2010. *New York Times* quoted on AIPAC's website.
[5] David Binder, "The Israel Lobby in Washington Is Small and Effective", *The New York Times*, August 8, 1975.
[6] See George C. Edwards III, Martin P. Wattenberg and Robert L. Lineberry, *Government in America. People, Politics, and Policy* (New York: Longman, 2006), 329.
[7] Wertheimer (2009 Conversation).
[8] Mearsheimer/Walt (2007), 118.

(AZC) in 1951, a registered foreign lobbying group, to press Congress for aid to Israel. Since it could not engage in substantial lobbying due to its nonprofit status, Kenen reorganized the AZC in 1954, and created the American Zionist Committee for Public Affairs – the precursor to AIPAC – as a separate and henceforth domestic lobbying organization.[9] In 1959, the new organization eventually changed its name to AIPAC to better reflect the reality that many non-Zionists also supported its cause.[10]

From its early days as a "small pro-Israel public affairs boutique in the 1950s",[11] AIPAC has evolved over the decades into one of the largest and mass-based Jewish organizations in the United States.[12] A major organizational transformation occurred when Kenen retired in 1974: under the leadership of Morris Amitay, who replaced Kenen as AIPAC's executive director, and under Amitay's successor Tom Dine, the organization considerably expanded both in terms of budget and staff size. According to IRS Form 990, AIPAC employs a total number of 382 employees, as of 2009. Likewise, its budget soared from about $300,000 in 1973 to about $50 million today, with total assets worth $93 million and total liabilities amounting to $43 million.[13] Not least in light of its comparatively large staff and financial resources, AIPAC has earned a reputation for being one of the most professional and most effective American lobbying groups today.

The structure of AIPAC's decision-making system, while formally inclusive, is fairly elitist in the way decisions are actually made. On the one hand, its executive committee consists of several hundred members,

---

[9] AIPAC's founding thus predates the Suez War of 1956. Forced into retreat by the United States and the USSR, Israel returned the Sinai, which it had captured during the war, to Egypt in 1957.

[10] See Lawrence Rubin, "American Israel Public Affairs Committee (AIPAC)", in: Berenbaum/Skolnik (eds.) (2007), vol. 2, 50.

[11] AIPAC, "About AIPAC", http://www.aipac.org/about_AIPAC/default.asp, accessed October 1, 2010.

[12] See Daniel J. Elazar, "Developments in Jewish Community Organization in the Second Postwar Generation", in: Lipset (ed.) (1990), 185.

[13] See AIPAC IRS Form 990, http://dynamodata.fdncenter.org/990_pdf_archive/530/530217164/530217164_200909_990O.pdf, accessed October 1, 2010. Mearsheimer/Walt (2007, 119) use obsolete data here, modestly estimating the staff size at "more than 150" employees.

reflecting the wide array of left-wing to right-wing American Jewish organizations, and includes all presidents of the Presidents Conference's member organizations. It gathers four times a year to decide on AIPAC policy. Yet, as Michael Massing reports, the executive committee only "has little real power". Instead, the power is vested within the board of directors, a group of about 50 members that are appointed "not according to how well they represent AIPAC's members but according to how much money they give and raise".[14] Within the board, power is further concentrated in six subgroups, in particular within the so-called Minyan Club, which requires a minimum annual contribution of $100,000. The Minyan Club is "AIPAC's most exclusive club – an elite circle of several hundred of AIPAC's most dedicated members", the organization's website reads.[15] Membership in AIPAC's other political clubs also requires a substantial financial commitment. To sit on the Chairman's Council, an annual contribution of at least $36,000 is required, while members of the President's Cabinet are expected to contribute at least $25,000 annually; membership in the Senate Club still requires a minimum donation of $10,000. Finally, members in the Capitol Club and the Washington Club are expected to contribute at least $3,600 and $1,500 per year, respectively, thereby allowing the organization to form subgroups of committed supporters at the broader local level.[16] In order to become more closely involved in AIPAC's decision-making process, members can thus simply leverage their willingness to pay: "All you have to do is send money", says Stephen M. Walt, pointing to AIPAC's nature as a large grassroots organization.[17]

Despite the presumed reference in its name, AIPAC is not a political action committee (PAC). Rather, and according to its own characterization, AIPAC operates as a "national grassroots movement". Its foremost goal is to create a network of "citizen advocates" with a view to providing support for its mission on a local level. "The core of AIPAC's mission is building a base of citizen advocates who team with our expert

---

[14] Michael Massing, "The Storm over the Israel Lobby", *The New York Review of Books* (online), June 8, 2006.
[15] AIPAC, "Learn About AIPAC", http://www.aipac.org/about_AIPAC/29_319.asp, accessed October 4, 2010.
[16] See AIPAC, "Learn About AIPAC", http://www.aipac.org/about_AIPAC/29_319.asp, accessed October 4, 2010.
[17] Walt (2008 Interview).

staff to educate America's elected officials, policy makers and opinion leaders",[18] AIPAC states on its website, the only current source of primary information about the lobby.[19] To build political pressure at the grassroots level, AIPAC can rely on its membership of currently 100,000 local activists, up from 65,000 members in 2005,[20] as well as on a network of 19 regional and satellite offices across the country. Indicative of its direct involvement in the political process – a distinct feature associated with the "new" Jewish politics –, the organization is furthermore headquartered in Washington, D.C. It is registered as a domestic lobby and supported financially by private donations; it receives no funding from Israel, from any national organization or any foreign group. Due to its legal status of a 501(c)(4) organization, contributions to AIPAC are not tax deductible.[21]

Though AIPAC embodies an entirely new and unparalleled conception of Jewish politics, it did not start out very differently from other hitherto existing Jewish organizations. During its early history, AIPAC simply did what by and large all Jewish organizations had done so far: it kept a low profile and relied on personal contacts with key legislators rather than on public campaigns or instruments of mass mobilization.[22] The October War of 1973 and the retirement of AIPAC's founder I. L. Kenen in 1974 however marked the beginning of a profound transformation in the politics of the lobby, as the archival record shows. In his "confidential proposal to AIPAC", Kenen's successor Morris Amitay spelled out the necessity to reconceptualize the political style of the organization. Inferring from the current political situation in Israel and the U.S., Amitay forthrightly concludes that "new approaches must be taken to meet these threats".[23] The following section discusses in detail what these new approaches are and how their application has helped

---

[18] AIPAC, "Learn About AIPAC", http://www.aipac.org/about_AIPAC/Learn_About_AIPAC/26.asp, accessed October 1, 2010.
[19] See Ruda (2009 Conversation).
[20] See Rubin (2007), 51.
[21] See AIPAC IRS Form 990, http://nccsdataweb.urban.org/orgs/profile/530217164?popup=1, accessed October 1, 2010.
[22] See Mearsheimer/Walt (2007), 118.
[23] Morris J. Amitay, Memorandum to I. L. Kenen, September 12, 1974, CJH Archives P-680, #3-32, 4. Curiously, Amitay addresses his memorandum to the "American-Israeli Public Affairs Committee".

AIPAC become one of the most powerful and effective foreign policy interest groups in the United States.

6.1.2 Political Style: Horizontal and Vertical Politics

Both a characteristic of its political style and the recipe for its success, AIPAC inserts itself directly and permanently in the legislative process. While it has also lobbied the executive branch, its clout is most visible in lobbying the U.S. Congress. It is however less the electoral and financial support from American Jews than the predisposed sympathy for Israel that explains why a considerable number of members of Congress have voted in favor of pro-Israel positions. AIPAC thus relies far more frequently on persuasion than on threat to make its case. Numerous interviews from the New York Public Library and Columbia University oral history collections are adduced to support these points.

Horizontal Politics

Pro-Israel Groups and Think Tanks

More than any other group AIPAC has been portrayed as a key organization within the "Israel lobby", that is, "the loose coalition of individuals and organizations that actively work to shape U.S. foreign policy in a pro-Israel direction".[24] Mearsheimer and Walt contend that, while the lobby is "not a single, unified movement with a central leadership" and hence not some sort of cabal or conspiracy, it still is a powerful group with unrivaled effectiveness in influencing U.S. foreign policy. One major reason for this success, says Stephen M. Walt, is the broad-based support that AIPAC and other organizations can count on when it comes to advocating for Israel. "It's very much a networked community. (...) There is a fair bit of evidence of how interconnected different people are", Walt says. "When something happens that affects the Jewish community, lots of people get mobilized, like when my book came out", Walt says, adding that the Israel lobby had "understood the power and importance of organizations".[25] Due to its prominent role in pro-Israel

---

[24] Mearsheimer/Walt (2007), 112. Also see Elazar in Elazar (ed.) (1988), 1-12.
[25] Walt (2008 Interview).

advocacy, the American Israel Public Affairs Committee is often viewed as one of the key players within this very network; AIPAC's links to think tanks and Christian Zionists, Mearsheimer and Walt argue, can be cited to back up this claim.

Think tanks in the United States have increasingly assumed functions formerly ascribed to political parties and play an important role in shaping public discourse as well as policy alternatives regarding key issues.[26] Therefore, shared goals or personal ties with think tanks such as the Washington Institute for Near East Policy (WINEP) and the Brookings Institution can be regarded as potential assets for advancing AIPAC's political agenda. A telling example is WINEP, a think tank founded in 1985 by former AIPAC president Larry Weinberg and his wife Barbi, together with AIPAC's vice president and the AIPAC deputy director for research, Martin Indyk. The close links between WINEP and the pro-Israel community have been documented since the 1990s, albeit WINEP has sought to downplay its links to AIPAC.[27] Moreover, the institute shares obvious similarities with AIPAC's core mission since it is "funded and run by individuals who are deeply committed to advancing Israel's agenda".[28] The evolution of the Brookings Institution furthermore suggests that AIPAC can advance its cause through the support from this influential Washington think tank. In 2002, Brookings established the Saban Center for Middle East Policy, endowed with a $13 million grant and primarily financed by the American-Israeli billionaire and "ardent Zionist" Haim Saban.[29] Saban has been a staunch supporter of the Jewish state, once describing himself as "a one-issue guy, and my issue is Israel".[30] Martin Indyk, the above mentioned former Clinton administration official with ties to AIPAC and WINEP, was in fact chosen to run the Saban Center. Hence, as Mearsheimer and Walt conclude, "[i]t is hard to imagine that a research institute funded by Saban and directed by Indyk is going to be anything but pro-Israel".[31]

In addition to sympathetic think tanks such as WINEP and the Saban Center, AIPAC benefits from the backing of the religious right. Chris-

[26] See Gellner (1995).
[27] See Gellner (1995), 154-155.
[28] Mearsheimer/Walt (2007), 175-176.
[29] Mearsheimer/Walt (2007), 176.
[30] Quoted in Mearsheimer/Walt (2007), 176.
[31] Mearsheimer/Walt (2007), 177.

tian Zionists count among Israel's most vocal supporters in the United States and thus represent an important "junior partner" for AIPAC and various other pro-Israel groups.[32] A prominent example for a Christian Zionist organization is Christians United for Israel (CUFI), characterized by its founder, the San Antonio-based television evangelist John Hagee, as "a Christian version of the American Israel Public Affairs Committee".[33] Hagee, who is the CEO of Global Evangelism Television, initiated CUFI in 2006 to provide a nationwide platform for evangelical activists. Its sole purpose is to defend and support the state of Israel.[34] An illustration of CUFI's growing ties with AIPAC, Hagee was for instance invited to speak at the 2007 AIPAC Policy Conference, where he received an enthusiastic reception from those in attendance. Hagee's appearance was anything but a matter of course, given the various offensive remarks he had previously made with regard to Jews and anti-Semitism. Notwithstanding the lingering concerns that Christian Zionists seek to advance a Christian agenda in the United States and to convert Jews to Christianity, some Jewish organizations – including AIPAC – have eventually "welcomed this alliance".[35] In fact, as Mearsheimer and Walt point out, AIPAC has established its own liaison office to allow for closer cooperation with the evangelical movement.[36]

Another Christian Zionist group that adds to the political activities of CUFI is the Christians' Israel Public Action Campaign (CIPAC). CIPAC is a policy advocacy organization that categorically rejects the two-state solution, a reason why it would be a potentially difficult partner for a more politically flexible organization like AIPAC. Because it is far

---

[32] Mearsheimer/Walt (2007), 132 (quotation marks in original).
[33] Hagee quoted in Mearsheimer/Walt (2007), 134. Christian Zionists form a subgroup within the broader politically oriented Christian Right. Christian Zionism traces its origins to the theology of dispensationalism, a biblical school of thought that emerged in nineteenth-century England. A central tenet of dispensationalism is that Christ's return is foretold in the Bible and that the return of the Jews to Palestine will eventually lead to the Second Coming, see Mearsheimer/Walt (2007), 132-133.
[34] See John Hagee, *In Defense of Israel* (Lake Mary, FL: FrontLine, 2007), viii.
[35] Mearsheimer/Walt (2007), 136.
[36] See Mearsheimer/Walt (2007), 136.

more hawkish than most American pro-Israel organizations, CIPAC claims to be "The Completely Pro-Israel Lobby".[37]

To be sure, the actual political influence of AIPAC's Christian Zionist allies such as CUFI must not be overstated. For one thing, as Mearsheimer and Walt caution, Christian Zionists fall short of the organizational capacity to offer in-depth analysis on national security topics, nor can they offer specific legislative guidance on foreign policy issues. Moreover, albeit CUFI is a single-issue organization, the broader evangelical movement regards Israel as only one of many items on a larger list of concerns. Christian Zionists also lack the financial power of leading pro-Israel groups such as AIPAC and do not have the same media presence as far as Middle East issues are concerned.[38]

AIPAC's Political Orientation

As an Israel advocacy organization, AIPAC does not promote a specific set of invariably upheld policies, but advocates for the positions of the elected Israeli – indeed, any Israeli – government. Not least in light of its links to the Christian Right, AIPAC has however been portrayed as an "increasingly conservative" and allegedly "hawkish" Jewish organization.[39] This point is made by Mearsheimer and Walt, who argue that "AIPAC and other hard-line groups have occasionally backed more extreme positions than those favored by the Israeli government".[40] Various examples are cited by the authors to support this claim.

A first illustration is AIPAC's ambivalent role in the failed Oslo peace process of the 1990s. Although AIPAC formally endorsed the 1993 Oslo Accords, it still "did little to make [them] work", the authors argue. AIPAC moreover helped sponsor the Jerusalem Embassy Act of 1995, which requires the United States to move its embassy from Tel Aviv to Jerusalem – a stance that has been viewed in the literature as "a transparent attempt to disrupt the peace process".[41] As one may expect, AIPAC's embrace of a right-wing response to Oslo eventually led to a

---

[37] Christians' Israel Public Action Campaign, "About CIPAC", http://cipaconli ne.org/about/745-2/, accessed December 12, 2010.
[38] See Mearsheimer/Walt (2007), 138-139.
[39] Mearsheimer/Walt (2007), 126.
[40] Mearsheimer/Walt (2007), 127.
[41] Mearsheimer/Walt (2007), 127.

critical fallout with the Labor government of Yitzhak Rabin: irritated with AIPAC's alleged "pro-Likud bias", Rabin responded by excluding the organization from key decisions.[42] Citing yet another example for the organization's tilt toward the political right, Mearsheimer and Walt point out that AIPAC's top leadership is "considerably more hawkish on Middle East issues" than the mainstream of the American Jewish community. Specifically, conservative voices are represented on AIPAC's board of directors as well as within the organization's various financially selective clubs.[43] But also AIPAC's own events have sometimes been associated with partisan – and indeed conservative – politics. George W. Bush, for instance, was greeted with chants of "four more years, four more years" at the 2004 AIPAC Policy Conference. As Lawrence Rubin writes in the *Encyclopaedia Judaica*, the obvious display of sympathies for the Republican president effectively gave the event "the semblance of a partisan atmosphere".[44] It is likewise instructive to note that AIPAC expects the 112th U.S. Congress – following midterm elections in November 2010 in which Republicans won additional seats in the Senate and a landslide victory in the House of Representatives, giving the GOP its biggest House majority since the 1940s – to be "the most pro-Israel Congress ever".[45]

While these findings apparently seem to confirm that AIPAC comes close to the model of a right-wing policy advocacy organization, a few critical points are nonetheless in order. As we have seen in the case of the Presidents Conference, the umbrella's political agenda is not merely reflective of the views of its members, but rather is influenced by the current positions of the Israeli government. Since 1977, Israeli governments have been predominantly conservative – a circumstance that can be reasonably assumed to also have influenced AIPAC's own political outlook. As in the case of the Presidents Conference, this political outlook is furthermore subject to the changing dynamics of American politics, the political framework within which these organizations operate. Against the backdrop of the second term of the George W. Bush administration, Mearsheimer and Walt are quick to characterize AIPAC as

---

[42] Wertheimer (1995), 57.
[43] Mearsheimer/Walt (2007), 127.
[44] Rubin (2007), 52.
[45] AIPAC, "Near East Report, November 19, 2010", http://www.aipac.org/NearEastReport/pdf/NER-20101119.pdf, accessed April 9, 2011.

a politically conservative, even hawkish organization. Yet it should be recalled that AIPAC, akin to the Presidents Conference, needs to be on sympathetic terms with the U.S. president in office and his administration in order to gain meaningful access to policy-making. Lobbying organizations will therefore attempt to reciprocate, at least to some degree, the political orientation of those currently in power. Typically this is best achieved through personal contacts at the staff level, and seems to explain why AIPAC decided to recruit professionals who had previously worked for the Republican administration when the Republican Party controlled the executive branch in the 1980s.[46] Thus it is fair to assume that the political outlook of both the Israeli government and the American administration have a tangible impact on how AIPAC frames Middle East policy. It is also reasonable to argue that, rather than pushing conservative politics itself, AIPAC is partly reflective of the positions that have shaped the government agendas in those countries.[47]

The argument that AIPAC reflexively espouses views of the political right is least convincing when one draws a direct comparison with a right-wing policy advocacy organization such as the Zionist Organization of America. The second largest American Jewish lobbying organization after AIPAC, the ZOA leaves no doubt about its one-sided political orientation. Unlike AIPAC, which is open to advocate for the positions of any Israeli government, the ZOA follows a narrowly defined agenda and routinely lobbies for hawkish positions; it can be arguably characterized as the most hawkish of all major American Jewish organizations. In contrast to AIPAC, the ZOA does not take into account – and sometimes openly opposes – the current position of the Israeli government. "Part of our problem, to be honest with you, is the Israeli government", says Gary Ratner, ZOA's national executive director, at the organization's New York headquarters. As Ratner points out, the ZOA does not necessarily endorse the policies of the Israeli government. Rather, it advocates only for its "own positions", supporting only "what we believe is the historic truth".[48] Accordingly the ZOA views

---

[46] See Peter Y. Medding, *The Transformation of American Jewish Politics* (New York: AJC, 1989), 12, 19.

[47] For a similar take, see Matthew E. Berger, "AIPAC's agenda changes with Israeli, U.S. governments", *JTA Daily News Bulletin*, March 16, 2001.

[48] Interview with Gary Ratner, National Executive Director, Zionist Organization of America, June 26, 2009, New York. The ZOA was founded in 1897

key organizations such as AIPAC with a decidedly critical eye. While conceding that AIPAC can still be regarded as being "pro-Israel", the organization is nonetheless "wrong on the issues", Ratner avers. This stance has at times complicated the ZOA's lobbying efforts in Washington and, in particular, has hampered collaborative efforts with AIPAC. In several instances, the ZOA has clashed with AIPAC on Capitol Hill, where it had to explain to a bevy of puzzled Congressmen who had just been briefed by AIPAC why precisely "AIPAC happens to be wrong" on that given issue.[49] Because it is a right-wing policy advocacy organization, the ZOA – unlike AIPAC – is quite obviously limited in its political flexibility: "It's a problem that we face, it's one of the difficulties being the kind of organization that we are, who is just trying to get the truth out there, irrespective of what the Israeli government thinks, irrespective of what the majority of the Jewish community thinks, irrespective of what AIPAC thinks or what anybody else thinks", Ratner says. "We've got our views, that we think are based on facts and history, and if you understand that, then these are the positions that you have to hold".[50]

Another question that has been raised in this context is whether or not AIPAC can in fact be properly considered a "Jewish organization". For one thing, it does not even make such a reference in its name, "American Israel Public Affairs Committee". But also in its daily advocacy work, AIPAC has maintained its profile as a single-issue and independent organization since it does not co-sponsor events with other Jewish groups.[51] AIPAC's reluctance to enter into close cooperation with other major Jewish organizations has not gone unchallenged, though. In 1989, AJC, ADL, and the American Jewish Congress sent a letter to AIPAC's president, complaining the organization was not consulting widely enough with others in the Jewish community, and stating they might form their own joint committee in counterpoint to AIPAC.[52]

---

for the express purpose of lobbying and advocating for a Jewish state in Palestine. A 501(c)(3) organization, it has a membership of 30,000 individual members nationally. Its president is Morton A. Klein.

[49] Ratner (2009 Interview).
[50] Ratner (2009 Interview).
[51] See Ronkin (2008 Interview).
[52] See Chuck Alston, "AIPAC Working to Shore Up Its Clout With Congress", *CQ Congressional Quarterly*, February 18, 1989.

Yet, given its role as a major reference point for political activism within the American Jewish community, it still seems fair to categorize AIPAC as a Jewish organization.

What sets AIPAC apart from other American interest groups is its extraordinary effectiveness. Built on its aptitude to fully and permanently insert itself in the political process, AIPAC has come to set a new standard in foreign policy lobbying, even to the point of being emulated by its peers. Already in the late 1970s, AIPAC had earned a reputation strong enough to prompt related foreign policy interest groups such as the American Hellenic Institute Public Affairs Committee (AHEPA) to "use AIPAC as a model of organization", as AHEPA official Eugene Rossides confirms.[53] It is to AIPAC's political style and operations that we now turn in detail in the next section.

Vertical Politics

In this section we discuss how AIPAC has interacted with the legislative and executive branches of government, whereby special attention will be given to the organization's role in congressional lobbying and in U.S. elections.

AIPAC and the Legislative Branch

Overview

While AIPAC has sought to influence both the legislative and executive branches of government, its successes have been largely confined to congressional politics. Legislative activity in the U.S. Congress has long been at the center of attention of pro-Israel groups in the United States: this holds true at least since the time the Jackson-Vanik Amendment to the Trade Act of 1974 was passed.[54] Officially known as the Mills-Vanik Bill in the House of Representatives and the Jackson Amendment

---

[53] Reminiscences of Eugene Rossides (May 10, 1977), Ethnic Groups and American Foreign Policy Project, page 39 in the Columbia University COH Collection.

[54] See Yaakov Ro'i, "Jackson-Vanik Amendment", *The YIVO Encyclopedia of Jews in Eastern Europe*, http://www.yivoencyclopedia.org/article.aspx/Jackson-Vanik_Amendment, accessed April 8, 2011.

in the Senate, the amendment linked most-favored nation trading status for the Soviet Union to Moscow's willingness to allow for greater Jewish emigration.[55]

More importantly, the U.S. Congress has been the focal point for budget negotiations on foreign assistance, a routine in which AIPAC has proved itself a reliable advocate for Israel's needs. According to figures quoted by Mearsheimer and Walt, Israel currently receives on average about $3 billion in direct foreign assistance each year, a sum that roughly equals one-sixth of the overall U.S. foreign assistance budget and amounts to about 2 percent of Israel's GDP. In per capita terms, this level of direct foreign aid equals a direct subsidy of more than $500 per year for each Israeli citizen – an amount that is especially striking given that Israel is a modern industrial power with a per capita income that the International Monetary Fund ranked twenty-ninth in the world in 2006. Israel's per capita GDP is nearly double that of Hungary and the Czech Republic, substantially higher than Portugal's, South Korea's and Taiwan's, and far exceeds every country in Latin America and Africa. It also ranks twenty-third in the United Nations' 2006 Human Development Report and was placed thirty-eighth in the Economist Intelligence Unit's 2005 "quality of life" ranking. By way of comparison, the number two recipient of U.S. foreign aid, Egypt, receives only $20 per person, and developing countries such as Pakistan and Haiti receive roughly $5 and $27 per person, respectively.[56]

This level of generosity is of relatively recent date. Israel did not receive U.S. military assistance until 1963, when John F. Kennedy authorized the first major sale of U.S. weaponry to Israel. Following the Six-Day War in June 1967, another sea change occurred: after averaging $63 million annually from 1949 to 1965, average aid to Israel increased to $102 million per year from 1966 to 1970. Assistance then soared to more than $634 million in 1971, and more than quintupled after the Yom Kippur War of 1973. By 1973, Israel had become the largest annu-

---

[55] Seen with a critical eye by Richard Nixon and Henry Kissinger, who feared for a potential damage to the American policy of détente, the amendment was eventually signed into law by President Gerald Ford in 1975. Its passing is significant because it made "Soviet emigration practices a subject of not just public diplomacy but of legislative action", writes Kissinger (1994), 754.

[56] See Mearsheimer/Walt (2007), 26, 30, with further references.

al recipient of U.S. foreign aid, a position it has retained ever since.[57] The current level of aid to Israel, albeit requiring annual approval by the legislature and the President, is not entirely a product of unforeseeable deliberation in Congress; it is geared to a long-term agreement, a memorandum of understanding (MOU), reached between the United States and Israel in 2007. The MOU contains provisions under which Israel is slated to receive $30 billion over the next ten years in U.S. security assistance.[58]

Not least against the background of the steadfast and generous U.S. foreign aid to Israel, Mearsheimer and Walt argue that AIPAC effectively has an "almost unchallenged hold on Congress".[59] An early proponent of this theory was Senator J. William Fulbright (D-AR), who during the Yom Kippur War declared on CBS' *Face the Nation* that "Israelis control the policy in the Congress. (...) On every test, on everything the Israelis are interested in, in the Senate the Israelis have 75 to 80 votes". Noteworthy is also the claim made by former AIPAC official Steven Rosen, who vaunted that, in 24 hours, AIPAC could gather the support of "70 senators" on any given issue involving Israel.[60]

One of the main reasons for AIPAC's clout lies in its ability to garner bipartisan support from members of Congress. Unlike most other lobbies, AIPAC does not make political endorsements and, accordingly, does not take a partisan stance during election campaigns. "AIPAC never endorses candidates; we never make contributions to candidates; we don't tell people to contribute to campaigns", AIPAC founder Isaiah L. Kenen says. "We insist that we must be non-partisan, rallying both candidates, both parties, to the platform proposals that we project. (...) [W]e

---

[57] See Mearsheimer/Walt (2007), 25-26.
[58] See AIPAC, "Key Provisions of U.S. Security Assistance to Israel", http://www.aipac.org/Publications/AIPACAnalysesMemos/Key_Provisions_of_Aid.pdf, accessed November 28, 2010.
[59] Mearsheimer/Walt (2007), 162.
[60] Fulbright quoted in Rubin (2007), 51. That the same question – whether or not "the so-called Jewish lobby" could get 70-odd votes on any issue of importance to it – was among the key questions asked by Columbia researcher Judith Goldberg in the oral history series "Ethnic Groups and American Foreign Policy Project" is quite revealing of AIPAC's apparent notoriety as one of the most powerful pressure groups in Washington, D.C. already by the late 1970s.

are interested in all the candidates, we want all the candidates to be our friend".[61] This view is also shared by Kenen's successor Morris Amitay, who, in a confidential strategy paper, objects to the idea of a partisan role for AIPAC. As Amitay writes, the organization "must be apolitical in its approaches, and seek staff people and committee members of diverse political backgrounds".[62] The commitment to bipartisanship can also be interpreted as the appropriate organizational response to the breakdown of the liberal consensus within the American Jewish community and the emergence of neoconservative intellectuals and activists – hence AIPAC's reluctance to take sides with either liberal or conservative positions.[63] Isaiah L. Kenen recounts his organization being bipartisan as well, going "through open doors in many offices in Washington, conservative as well as liberal".[64] Similar to the Presidents Conference, Kenen highlights the organization's rather educational outlook, stating that he "always felt that our office was more of an information center".[65] As opposed to partisan advocacy, Kenen analyzes AIPAC's clout more as the corollary of a fairly modest effort: "to bring the facts to both political parties".[66]

According to Stephen M. Walt, however, AIPAC's political effectiveness hinges just as much on various other factors. To begin with, Walt points to the fact that AIPAC is a very professionally managed organization, and therefore able to react quickly to current events. In contrast to its pro-Arab and pro-Palestinian competitors, it also has at its disposal sufficiently large resources to finance its operations. But even more importantly, AIPAC can build enough leverage to tilt the cost-benefit calculation of every congressional candidate who is running for

[61] Interview with I. L. Kenen, July 11, 1973, The New York Public Library-American Jewish Committee Oral History Collection, Dorot Jewish Division, The New York Public Library, Astor, Lenox and Tilden Foundations, 32, 39.
[62] Morris J. Amitay, Memorandum to I. L. Kenen, September 12, 1974, CJH Archives P-680, #3-32, 4.
[63] See Elazar (1990), 185.
[64] Interview with I. L. Kenen, July 11, 1973, Dorot Jewish Division, NYPL, 30.
[65] Reminiscences of Isaiah L. Kenen (June 2, 1975), Ethnic Groups and American Foreign Policy Project, page 60 in the Columbia University COH Collection.
[66] I. L. Kenen, ""Secrets" of Israel lobby's success in United States", *Jewish Chronicle*, September 26, 1975, AJC Blaustein Library.

office or up for re-election. If somebody turns out to be "very bad news", Walt says, AIPAC will go to considerable lengths to "drive [that person] out of office". Since a Congressman's decision to confront AIPAC comes with a political price tag – in the form of letters and phone calls from prominent members of one's electoral district –, there is little incentive to confront the lobby, particularly as the decision to go along with AIPAC will not stir effective opposition among voters. "So the question is, what do I gain by quarrelling with them?", Walt summarizes the political calculation that in his view accounts for the high degree of congressional support for AIPAC.[67] Rather than challenging AIPAC on a given issue, members of Congress will seek to accommodate the lobby, because they can be confident that their constituents – who often are largely indifferent to the Middle East conflict – will not penalize them for doing so. AIPAC thus benefits from organizational advantages that stem from its being a relatively small, but highly professional and dedicated single-issue organization.[68] Political science research has shown that yielding to the demands of a small but powerful group can be a cost-effective way for politicians to win crucial votes and future allies, whereas seeking confrontation with such a group will often result in disproportionate political costs.[69] Specifically, Walt argues that AIPAC relies on the strategies of "persuasion" and "threat" in order to enlist support from legislators and congressional candidates.[70]

"Persuasion" and "Threat"

Persuasion is a strategy designed to convey a positive image of Israel to members of Congress. Its main effort is directed at giving Israel "a good brand name" by advertising the country as a fellow democracy and as a state that shares America's fundamental values.[71] In practice, this is achieved in part through the *Near East Report* (NER), AIPAC's bi-weekly newsletter, which is distributed to all members of Congress, providing them with concise background information on issues related to Israel. In many congressional offices, therefore, the NER has become

---

[67] Walt (2008 Interview).
[68] See Mearsheimer/Walt (2007), 140.
[69] See, for example, Olson (1965).
[70] Walt (2008 Interview).
[71] Walt (2008 Interview).

"required reading".⁷² Its most obvious merit lies in framing the legislative debate – or as Isaiah L. Kenen puts it, it "has an impact each week because it seeks to interpret the issues".⁷³ In addition to the NER, AIPAC has published an extensive monograph series – entitled the *AIPAC Papers On U.S.-Israel Relations* – to promote a strong relationship between both countries. The *AIPAC Papers*, which have appeared from 1982 to 2000 in the form of short booklets, focus in large part on Israel's strategic importance and the benefits of U.S.-Israeli military cooperation.⁷⁴ Another claim frequently made by AIPAC is that America's interests and Israel's interests are essentially one and the same. "Helping Israel helps America and it is AIPAC which makes sure that this message is heard", former AIPAC president Mayer Mitchell and executive director Thomas A. Dine put it pithily in an advertising letter to prospective members and donors.⁷⁵

There is a genuine necessity to constantly portray Israel in a positive light, Mearsheimer and Walt contend, because neither strategic nor moral rationales can justify the current level of American backing it receives. It is also impossible for two countries to always have identical interests, the authors argue, since this is "just not the way international politics works". They point to the instances in the past where U.S. and Israeli interests have clearly diverged, such as Israel's aspiration to acquire nuclear weapons in the 1960s or Israel's decision to invade Lebanon in

---

⁷² Rubin (2007), 50.
⁷³ Interview with I. L. Kenen, July 11, 1973, Dorot Jewish Division, NYPL, 30. At the time the interview was conducted, the NER, then "in its sixteenth year", was still a weekly publication.
⁷⁴ See AIPAC, *AIPAC Papers On U.S.-Israel Relations* (Washington, D.C.: AIPAC, 1982-2000), AJC Blaustein Library and Widener Library, especially No.1 *The Strategic Value of Israel*, No. 2 *Israel and the U.S. Air Force*, No. 4 *Israel and the U.S. Navy*, No. 5 *Israeli Medical Support for the U.S. Armed Forces*, No. 8 *U.S. Procurement of Israeli Defense Goods and Services*, No. 9 *A U.S.-Israel Free Trade Area: How Both Sides Gain*, No. 10 *How Americans Feel About Israel*, No. 13 *The Reagan Administration and Israel: Key Statements*, No. 14 *Israel's Agricultural Achievements: Their Significance for Americans*, and No. 17 *U.S.-Israel Relations: Looking To The Year 2000*.
⁷⁵ Mayer Mitchell and Thomas A. Dine, Untitled Letter, November 1991, AJC Blaustein Library, 1 (quote underlined in original).

1982.[76] Hence the efforts made by organizations like AIPAC to preserve positive attitudes toward Israel in the media:

> Channeling public discourse in a pro-Israel direction is critically important, because an open and candid discussion of Israeli policy in the Occupied Territories, Israeli history, and the lobby's role in shaping America's Middle East policy might easily lead more Americans to question existing policy toward Israel and to call for a relationship with Israel that more effectively serves the U.S. national interest.[77]

Even AIPAC itself leaves no doubt about the importance of steering public opinion in a pro-Israel direction. "A strong U.S.-Israel relationship is no accident and must not be taken for granted. Rather, it is the result of years of hard work and effective education by the pro-Israel community in general, and very specifically by AIPAC, the pro-Israel lobby", AIPAC leaders Mitchell and Dine candidly admit.[78] This is a curious statement indeed, for AIPAC commonly argues that strong U.S.-Israeli ties are not so much the product of lobbying efforts but rather the result of strategic imperatives[79] and Americans' general sympathy for Israel.

Surveys do however show that Americans clearly have favorable perceptions of Israel. For example, a Gallup poll conducted in 2007 identified Israel as the only country a majority of Americans both viewed "favorable" and perceived as "important". Furthermore, from 1996 through 2007, about 60 to 70 percent of those polled had an overall opinion of Israel that was "mostly favorable" or "very favorable".[80] But

---

[76] Mearsheimer/Walt (2007), 148. Israel, along with India and Pakistan, is not a signatory of the Non-Proliferation Treaty (NPT), which was signed in 1968 and entered into effect in 1970. As a matter of policy, Israel has never officially acknowledged or denied to possess nuclear weapons, although internationally it is widely regarded as a nuclear state.

[77] Mearsheimer/Walt (2007), 168.

[78] Mayer Mitchell and Thomas A. Dine, Untitled Letter, November 1991, AJC Blaustein Library, 1 (last four words underlined in original).

[79] See Mearsheimer/Walt (2007), 49-77.

[80] See Eytan Gilboa, "The public dimension of US-Israel relations: a comparative analysis", in: Eytan Gilboa and Efraim Inbar (eds.), *US-Israeli Relations*

the level of public support for Israel should not be overstated: one reason, Mearsheimer and Walt caution, is that the American people are "considerably more critical of some Israeli actions than U.S. politicians are", a claim that is supported by various surveys. In a *Time/CNN* poll taken in 2002, only 35 percent thought the Israeli Prime Minister Sharon was trustworthy, while 35 percent saw him as a warmonger, 20 percent considered him a terrorist, and 25 percent viewed him as an enemy of the United States. In 2003, another survey revealed that 60 percent of Americans said aid to Israel should be cut off if it resisted U.S. pressure to settle its conflict with the Palestinians, and 73 percent said the United States should not take sides in the conflict. Two years later, a survey conducted by ADL similarly found that 78 percent of Americans think their government should favor neither Israel nor the Palestinians.[81]

As to whether strategic reasons, the power of an alleged Israel lobby, or shared democratic values account for the strong U.S.-Israel relationship, the Israeli and American publics hold by and large similar opinions. Marked differences can however be observed between the general, elite, and Jewish opinion within the U.S., as Table 4 shows. What is striking is that only 9 percent of American Jews believe that their alleged "power" is the main reason for the close U.S.-Israeli relations, whereas 18 percent of the American elites and 24 percent of the general American public do. By contrast, 61 percent of American Jews consider strategic reasons as being decisive for the U.S.-Israel relationship, as opposed to only 42 percent of the general American public. At the same time, only 20 percent of the larger American public consider the similar democratic tradition of both countries to be the main reason for strong ties with Israel:

---

in a New Era: Issues and Challenges After 9/11 (London: Routledge, 2009), 56-58.

[81] See Mearsheimer/Walt (2007), 226-227, 109 (quote), 110, with further references.

Table 4: Reasons for Close U.S.-Israeli Relations, Survey of Public Opinion

Main reason	Israelis (%)	Americans (%)		
		Public	Elites	Jews
Strategic interests	48	42	52	61
Political Power of American Jews	30	24	18	9
Similar democratic tradition	17	20	23	32

Source: Gilboa (2009), 61, based on various other surveys.

In order to win sympathy for Israel in the U.S. Congress, AIPAC routinely invites politicians on "study missions" to Israel. AIPAC sponsors free congressional trips to Israel, funded through its sister organization, the American Israel Education Foundation (AIEF). Such visits usually have predictable benefits for both sides. On the one hand, they are an apt means for politicians to demonstrate to AIPAC their interest in Israel; on the other, they tend to positively affect politicians' perceptions of the Jewish state. According to Mitchell Bard, a former editor of AIPAC's *Near East Report*, "Once officials have direct exposure to the country, its leaders, geography, and security dilemmas, they typically return more sympathetic to Israel".[82] In 2005, over 100 members of Congress visited Israel, some of them multiple times.[83] About 10 percent of all congressional trips overseas are to Israel; from January 2000 to mid-2005, AIPAC's AIEF spent nearly $1 million on such visits.[84]

This, however, does not imply that favorable attitudes toward Israel in Congress are necessarily generated by AIPAC. Rather, as is evident from Columbia University's oral history collections, there has been a reliable degree of sympathy in congressional opinion predating AIPAC's lobbying efforts. It is this kind of predisposed sentiment for the Jewish state which helps explain why a large number of roughly 70 senators

---

[82] Mitchell Bard, "AIPAC and US Middle East policy", in: Gilboa/Inbar (eds.) (2009), 79.
[83] See Bard (2009), 79. It should be noted that AIPAC is the most active, but not the only, Jewish organization that sponsors such trips.
[84] See Mearsheimer/Walt (2007), 161.

have often voted along AIPAC's party line. Representative Benjamin S. Rosenthal (D-NY) for example notes the "sympathy with the American people" as well as "a warm feeling towards Israel by many members of the Congress".[85] Likewise, Senator Jacob K. Javits (R-NY) says there is "an affirmative feeling" in Congress toward pro-Israel groups, whose concerns would thus "fall upon sympathetic ears".[86] This assessment is shared by the diplomat Sol M. Linowitz, who holds the view that pro-Israel groups "could not have been effective if [they] went counter to what these people [members of Congress] themselves believed".[87] In the same vein, Senator Clifford P. Case (R-NJ) says he has "been of the same view in regard to Israel for longer than [he] can remember" and, in general, "found [his] own thinking entirely compatible with the aspirations of the socalled [sic] American Jewish lobby".[88] AJC's Hyman H. Bookbinder also ascribes the fact that "[r]oughly two thirds of the Senate has in the last few years been basically sympathetic to what might be called pro-Israel moves" to the "overwhelming American sympathy for Israel".[89] Finally, AIPAC founder I. L. Kenen explains that pro-Israel advocacy in Congress falls on fertile ground because "[t]here has always been strong support in Congress for the creation and survival of a Jewish state. (...) We had more than 70 senators way back in the '40s", Kenen

---

[85] Reminiscences of Benjamin S. Rosenthal (October 7, 1975), Ethnic Groups and American Foreign Policy Project, page 9 in the Columbia University COH Collection. Rosenthal (ibid., 10) nonetheless warns that "if the Arabs use the oil money that they have available in unlimited quantities to propagandize the American people, some of that could be eroded".

[86] Reminiscences of Jacob Javits (November 12, 1975), Ethnic Groups and American Foreign Policy Project, page 1 in the Columbia University COH Collection.

[87] Reminiscences of Sol N. Linowitz (May 28, 1976), Ethnic Groups and American Foreign Policy Project, page 22 in the Columbia University COH Collection.

[88] Reminiscences of Clifford P. Case (June 12, 1979), Ethnic Groups and American Foreign Policy Project, pages 8, 2 in the Columbia University COH Collection.

[89] Reminiscences of Hyman H. Bookbinder (October 6, 1975), Ethnic Groups and American Foreign Policy Project, pages 2, 3 in the Columbia University COH Collection.

says.[90] The assertion that congressional support for Israel predates the creation of AIPAC and of Israel itself cannot be easily dismissed, considering that the U.S. Congress had for instance endorsed the Balfour Declaration in September 1922, at a time when anti-Semitism was still socially acceptable and widespread in daily American life.[91] In addition, sympathy for Israel to some extent is rooted in the American cultural memory, and can therefore be easily mobilized for political ends.[92] The evidence presented here thus appears to indicate that AIPAC's efforts have been met with congressional sympathy in the first place, as opposed to generating it.

If sympathy and persuasion do not work, AIPAC is said to rely on "threat" as the second strategy to get reluctant Congressmen to follow its lead.[93] Nonetheless, it would be more than surprising if that were the case: AIPAC's commitment to nonpartisanship in Congress and its pledge not to endorse candidates militates strongly against the notion of exerting hard-nosed pressure. And it is precisely because of the insist-

---

[90] Reminiscences of Isaiah L. Kenen (June 2, 1975), Ethnic Groups and American Foreign Policy Project, page 2 in the Columbia University COH Collection.

[91] See Jewish Virtual Library, "U.S. Congress Endorses the Balfour Declaration", http://www.jewishvirtuallibrary.org/jsource/History/Congress_Endorses_the_Balfour_Declaration.html, accessed December 2, 2010. Also see section 1.1 above, with further references on anti-Semitism in America.

[92] George Washington, for example, has tellingly been portrayed as the "American Moses" (as arguably did Emanuel Leutze in his famous 1851 painting *Washington Crossing the Delaware*), see Karsten Fitz, *The American Revolution Remembered, 1830s to 1850s. Competing Images and Conflicting Narratives* (Heidelberg: Universitätsverlag Winter, 2010), 265-296. With Arthur M. Schlesinger, one may further draw a parallel between the ideological foundations of the United States and Israel, and hence between the idea of America as an "experiment" and as a "destiny". Zionist ideology resonates with the American historical experience because Zionism is both a revolutionary ideology (and thus an experiment) as well as a restorative utopian design (and thus preordained by destiny). See Arthur M. Schlesinger, "America: Experiment or Destiny?", *American Historical Review* 82:3 (June 1977), 505-522.

[93] See Walt (2008 Interview), Mearsheimer/Walt (2007), 159, and Findley (2003).

ence on nonpartisanship that AIPAC is, at least in I. L. Kenen's view, "one of the mildest lobbies".[94]

But AIPAC meticulously monitors the legislative activity of members of Congress and makes these records available to its members, who can then make an informed decision on which candidate to support. As Richard N. Perle, a leading figure of neoconservatism today and then a legislative assistant to Senator Henry Jackson (D-WA, the sponsor of the Jackson-Vanik amendment) discloses, "the American Israel Public Affairs Committee keeps very detailed records. I've seen the record that they keep on Jackson -- it goes back to the 1940s".[95] AIPAC also published elaborate profiles of American organizations and individuals in the third volume of the *AIPAC Papers On U.S.-Israel Relations*, where several U.S. diplomats and politicians, such as Senator James Abourezk (D-SD) and former U.S. Ambassador to the U.N. and Under Secretary of State George Ball, are accused of harboring an anti-Israel bias.[96]

What is more, AIPAC has taken sides politically in a few instances, thereby violating its stated principle of remaining outside the partisan fray. In the late 1970s, AIPAC took an "[u]nusually tough" stance on Senator Charles Percy (R-IL), as memoirist I. L. Kenen concedes.[97] Percy, to whom Mearsheimer and Walt refer as "the most renowned example of the costs that can befall a politician who crosses AIPAC", suffered a narrow defeat in 1984, not least because his opponents had received large sums from pro-Israel PACs. A generally pro-Israel voting

---

[94] Reminiscences of Isaiah L. Kenen (June 2, 1975), Ethnic Groups and American Foreign Policy Project, page 93 in the Columbia University COH Collection.

[95] Reminiscences of Richard N. Perle (February 7, 1975), Ethnic Groups and American Foreign Policy Project, page 5 in the Columbia University COH Collection.

[96] See AIPAC, *AIPAC Papers On U.S.-Israel Relations*, No. 3 *The Campaign to Discredit Israel* (Washington, D.C.: AIPAC, 1983), eds. Amy Kaufman Goot and Steven Rosen, 93-137. Even Israeli citizenship does not exempt individuals from scrutiny by AIPAC. "Israel Shahak is an outspoken critic of Israel", one profile says about a professor of chemistry at the Hebrew University, who is also a Holocaust survivor.

[97] Reminiscences of Isaiah L. Kenen (June 2, 1975), Ethnic Groups and American Foreign Policy Project, page 92 in the Columbia University COH Collection.

record notwithstanding, Percy had allegedly fallen out of favor with AIPAC by declining to sign an AIPAC-sponsored letter protesting President Gerald Ford's threatened reassessment of U.S. Middle East policy in 1975.[98] Another well-known example of partisan involvement is AIPAC's bid to recruit the Illinois attorney Richard Durbin to run against incumbent Representative Paul Findley (R-IL) in 1982. Former AIPAC president Robert Asher helped solicit funds on behalf of Durbin, who received about $104,000 from 31 different pro-Israel PACs, whereas in the same election other Illinois candidates received an average of about $3,700 from the same groups. Durbin had never held elected office, yet went on to narrowly beat Findley despite the latter's experience of having served 11 previous terms.[99] AIPAC is likewise credited with leading the effort to oust Representative Earl Hilliard (D-AL) in 2002: Hilliard's campaign, too, suffered a critical blow when his opponent got financial help from AIPAC supporters. AIPAC also "played an important role" in defeating various other politicians it found disagreeable, from Representative Pete McCloskey (R-CA) to Senators J. William Fulbright (D-AR) and Roger Jepson (R-IA).[100] "The basic message is clear: any senator or representative who crosses AIPAC is playing with fire", Mearsheimer and Walt conclude.[101]

Hyperbolic as it is, this statement is also misguided, because it portrays AIPAC as an almost all-powerful and politically aggressive organization. But neither is the case. First, AIPAC's efforts are never the only reason a candidate faces electoral challenge or suffers defeat – a fact that Mearsheimer and Walt do acknowledge, yet one that invalidates much of their argument – and there are indeed several instances in which congressional candidates have succeeded while distancing themselves from AIPAC.[102] Second, instead of relying on the use of threat, AIPAC has been far more restrained in its political style than Mearsheimer and Walt

---

[98] See Mearsheimer/Walt (2007), 158.
[99] See Mearsheimer/Walt (2007), 157.
[100] Mearsheimer/Walt (2007), 157. Mearsheimer and Walt (2007, 158) also discuss the case of Senator Adlai Stevenson (D-IL) but do not specify what kind of role, if any, AIPAC played in his race for governor, and subsequent defeat, in 1982.
[101] Mearsheimer/Walt (2007), 160.
[102] This holds true for some candidates backed by J Street, see section 6.2.2 ("Vertical Politics") below.

suggest. According to Stephen J. Solarz (D-NY), a leading voice in the House on foreign affairs, AIPAC does not push hard on every issue of concern. Rather, "as any sophisticated lobbying organization it presses more vigorously on some matters than on others, making very careful calibrations depending on the significance of the issue, the prospects for success, the attitude of the people involved". [103] As discussed above, the generally positive attitude towards Israel in Congress and in American public opinion suggests that AIPAC needs to employ persuasion, let alone threat, less frequently than its detractors commonly assume.

In this context, an interesting hypothesis further argues that the lack of accountability in U.S. foreign policy makes it easy for members of Congress to take whatever partisan positions they see fit. Because the United States is so extraordinarily secure, and because most Americans are insulated from the direct effects of foreign policy blunders, misguided policies tend to have little or no personal consequences for those who approved them, Stephen M. Walt writes on his *Foreign Policy* blog.[104] By analogy, one may infer that AIPAC's advocacy efforts are similarly facilitated, as members of Congress do not face direct political reprisals for potential failures in U.S. Middle East policy and can thus go along with AIPAC more easily than they would otherwise be able to do. In fact, given the way the American political system works, the blame for foreign policy failures is usually meted out to the U.S. president, who has the ultimate decision-making power and is chiefly responsible for the implementation of foreign policy matters.

AIPAC and U.S. Elections

Another key element in AIPAC's success is its capacity to influence campaign contributions. This is all the more important since money is critical to U.S. elections, which have become increasingly expensive to run. AIPAC inserts itself in the electoral process in essentially two ways. On the one hand, the individuals who bankroll AIPAC, and especially

---

[103] Reminiscences of Stephen J. Solarz (May 9, 1977), Ethnic Groups and American Foreign Policy Project, page 3 in the Columbia University COH Collection.

[104] See Stephen M. Walt, "More reasons for U.S. foreign policy foolishness", November 24, 2010, http://walt.foreignpolicy.com/posts/2010/11/24/more_reasons_for_us_foreign_policy_foolishness, accessed December 6, 2010.

the members of its board of directors, are also important donors to pro-Israel PACs and candidates.[105] On the other, AIPAC acts as an intermediary connecting candidates to potential donors and funds from pro-Israel PACs. As mentioned before, AIPAC itself is not a political action committee and does not endorse candidates or contribute financially to their campaigns. Instead, it arranges meetings with candidates and donors and fund-raisers – provided the candidate expresses strong sympathies with Israel.[106] AIPAC not only meets with every candidate running for Congress and provides them with in-depth briefings on Israel and the Middle East, but also asks these candidates to author a position paper in order to clarify what their views are on the U.S.-Israel relationship.[107] As George W. Ball, under secretary of state in the Kennedy and Johnson administrations, recounts in his memoirs, the stance on Israel is indeed critical for a candidate to attract campaign contributions:

> I have been through several political campaigns myself (...) and I know the technique, which was for a spokesman for significant financial interests amongst the pro-Israeli community to appear at some point in the middle of the campaign and curry the candidate on just what his views were, indicating that there was a very substantial amount of financial support that was awaiting him if his views would only be put forward in a fairly specific fashion.[108]

It is however important to note that AIPAC does not exercise control over the various pro-Israel PACs that contribute to candidates in congressional elections. In 1991, the Federal Election Commission (F.E.C.), after investigations following the complaints of AIPAC critics such as former Representative Paul Findley (R-IL), exonerated AIPAC of the charge of directly forwarding campaign contributions to pro-Israel PACs. In a unanimous decision, the F.E.C. found that there was "insufficient evidence" to believe the PACs were affiliated with AIPAC. The F.E.C.

---

[105] See Mearsheimer/Walt (2007), 154, with further references.
[106] See Michael Massing, "The Storm over the Israel Lobby", *The New York Review of Books* (online), June 8, 2006.
[107] See Mearsheimer/Walt (2007), 154.
[108] Reminiscences of George W. Ball (May 21, 1976), Ethnic Groups and American Foreign Policy Project, pages 2-3 in the Columbia University COH Collection.

also found that simultaneous membership in a PAC and on an AIPAC policy-making body – as evidenced between AIPAC and 24 different PACs – did not by itself prove an affiliation relationship between the two entities. Federal elections rules prohibit PACs from coordinating their contributions, and do not allow 501(c)(4) organizations such as AIPAC to establish, finance, control, or maintain more than one PAC.[109]

A distinction must further be made between candidates running for office in districts with high Jewish populations and those in districts with low Jewish populations. As one may expect, in districts where Jews represent a high percentage of the overall population, the Jewish vote is an important one and candidates typically try to court their Jewish electorate by espousing pro-Israel positions. Consider the example of former Congressman Stephen J. Solarz (D-NY), who represented the largest Jewish district in the U.S.[110] and, early in his career, quickly grasped the importance of supporting Israel in Congress. When he was elected to the House in 1974, the *New York Times* reports, Solarz "finagled a seat on the Foreign Affairs Committee with the idea that he could appeal to his largely Jewish district by attending to the needs of Israel".[111] In districts with low Jewish populations, the evidence is less straightforward. Stephen M. Walt and Michael Massing for example contend that politicians from such districts are just as vulnerable to the pressures of the lobby. In states where the electorate is not particularly involved in Middle East issues, candidates have no incentive to confront AIPAC as they would pay a political price for doing so; at the same time, they can reap political benefits by aligning with AIPAC to mobilize financial support for their electoral campaigns. Hence, no matter whether a district has a large or

---

[109] See Larry Cohler, "FEC clears AIPAC on charges that it directs pro-Israel PACs", *Washington Jewish Week*, December 27, 1990; Howard Rosenberg, "AIPAC cleared by FEC of charges it directs campaign contributions", *Jewish Telegraphic Agency*, December 25, 1990.

[110] See Reminiscences of Stephen J. Solarz (May 9, 1977), Ethnic Groups and American Foreign Policy Project, page 8 in the Columbia University COH Collection.

[111] Douglas Martin, "Stephen J. Solarz, Former N.Y. Congressman, Dies at 70", *The New York Times*, November 30, 2010.

small Jewish constituency, candidates will always seek to go along with AIPAC.[112]

However, the opposite scenario is no less plausible, and is indeed backed by empirical evidence. Illustrative is the example of Senator Daniel Inouye (D-HI), who has at times strayed from the largely pro-Israel majority in the Senate, bluntly saying "I don't consider myself one of the seventy". Very specifically, Inouye points out that his "Jewish constituency is almost nil, and from a very practical standpoint, it wouldn't make any difference if they all voted against me. I got in by eighty-three per cent last year (...) -- so far, the professionals would say I have a safe seat". What is more, and contrary to widespread charges, Inouye's testimony strongly suggests that pro-Israel lobbying groups such as AIPAC are unable to silence obstinate critics in Congress. "As a friend, I believe I can be critical with them", Inouye says. "And I don't just criticize privately. I do it publicly and openly".[113]

The relation between the size of Jewish constituencies and senatorial support for Israel, as well as the relation between senatorial support for pro-Israel measures and the financial contributions from Jewish sources, was examined in a detailed empirical study by the political scientist A.F.K. Organski. For the period from 1969 to 1982, Organski compared the voting record of senators from states with relatively large Jewish populations (where Jews represented at least 2 percent in the state's population) with the voting record of senators who have few Jewish constituents. The aim was then to determine whether the differences in voting behavior between the two sets of senators suggested that Jewish voters are a key factor in determining senatorial support for Israel. Organski found a clearly positive correlation between support for Israel and the size of the constituencies: in a sample of 170 senators in the time period analyzed, senators with Jewish constituencies between 2 and 3 percent supported pro-Israel positions 79 percent of the time, whereas those with Jewish constituencies larger than 3 percent supported pro-Israel positions as frequently as 90 percent of the time and higher. This is not exactly surprising; but Organski also found that senators with Jewish

---

[112] See Walt (2008 Interview), as discussed in section 6.1.2 ("Overview"), and Massing (2006), footnote above.

[113] Reminiscences of Daniel K. Inouye (October 22, 1975), Ethnic Groups and American Foreign Policy Project, pages 8, 10, 11 in the Columbia University COH Collection.

populations between 1 and 2 percent supported pro-Israel positions 66 percent of the time, while senators with 1 percent or less Jews in their constituency still favored pro-Israel positions 63 percent of the time. In other words, the fear of Jewish retribution at the polls is not the reason that leads senators with tiny Jewish constituencies to give their legislative support to Israel.[114] How, then, can we explain the high level of senatorial support for Israel even in small Jewish constituencies?

Before we can answer this question, we need to turn to an analysis of pro-Israel money and its effect on senatorial support for Israel. The understanding of this relation is crucial, since one may argue that the power of the pro-Israel lobby is not rooted in its numerical weight but in money. Financial contributions from Jewish sources, and not the senatorial concern for Jewish votes in their districts, would then explain why senators take pro-Israel positions. In his analysis Organski therefore looked at individual and PAC contributions matched against senators' voting records on measures of importance to Israel. As the total amount of financial contributions from Jewish sources will vary with the size of the Jewish population in the district – in large Jewish constituencies it can be expected to be higher than in small Jewish constituencies – Organski did not compare absolute numbers, but examined the proportion of contributions from Jewish sources to total contributions a senator received. Organski found a very strong association between levels of funding from Jewish sources and levels of senatorial support for Israel: the senators who received a very substantial fraction (5 percent and above) of their total receipts from Jewish sources favored Israel between 83 and 93 percent of the time, while the senators who received between 2 and 5 percent of their receipts from Jewish sources supported pro-Israel positions nearly 76 percent of the time. But also the senators who received 2 percent or less of their total receipts from Jewish sources still voted in favor of pro-Israel positions 51.5 percent of the time.[115] We are thus left wondering why those senators who receive but a small fraction of their total receipts from Jewish sources also take positions favoring Israel a majority of the time.

This leads us directly to the logical fallacy inherent in many arguments about the power of AIPAC and the pro-Israel lobby. It is predi-

---

[114] See Organski (1990), 65-68 (numbers rounded).
[115] See Organski (1990), 70-72.

cated on the idea that pro-Israel money buys candidates into supporting pro-Israel positions. And indeed, as we have seen, a high level of funding from Jewish sources corresponds to a high level of support for Israel. Yet it is false to claim a unidirectional causal nexus between both variables, for the opposite may equally be the case. This is precisely what Organski infers from his analysis – that money does not necessarily explain why senators support Israel, but that it may just as well be the senators' favorable predisposition toward Israel that helps them attract money from pro-Israel sources:

> [M]oney goes to those who have in the past already taken and defended positions that future contributors approve of. The money senators receive does not, then, account for their *voting* behavior. Money is not being used here to *change* a senator's mind; it reflects the fact that a senator's mind has already been favorably *made up*. Financial support is *the result*, not the cause, of what senators do.[116]

Another serious flaw in analyses which attempt to establish a correlation between the size of the Jewish constituencies, Jewish financial support, and pro-Israel voting behavior in Congress is that such a correlation can be explained in more than one ways. Support for Israel in Congress is derived not simply from the fear of Jewish constituents or the dependence on money from Jewish sources. We know this because the legislators who received minimal or no electoral or financial support from the Jewish community still supported Israel in a substantial way. Organski thus concludes that attempts to relate the strong senatorial support for Israel to the financial and electoral support they receive from American Jews constitute "a classic case of a spurious correlation. The two variables are related only through a third factor that causes both".[117] The "third factor" Organski refers to is essentially to be found in the overwhelming sympathy that American public opinion and members of Congress have professed for the Jewish state. The favorable predisposition toward Israel must accordingly be regarded as the main reason for the

---

[116] Organski (1990), 73 (emphasis in original). Instead, Organski (1990, 73-74) argues, financial contributions to pro-Israel senators serve the purpose of helping them keep their position.
[117] Organski (1990), 210.

high level of support for Israel among members of Congress.[118] Consequently, it is only fair to assume that AIPAC's actual leverage over Congress is much less pronounced than critics commonly assert.

AIPAC and the Executive Branch

In addition to lobbying Congress, AIPAC has also sought to influence the executive branch. An obvious illustration of these efforts is AIPAC's Annual Policy Conference, a gathering that draws over 6,000 participants and is regularly attended by high-ranking leaders from both branches of government.[119] Though today it is considered "a command performance for prominent politicians",[120] the conference had a difficult start and "did not always run smoothly. In the 1960s very few students came, and of those who did many were hostile and, on occasion, disruptive", I. L. Kenen recounts in his autobiography.[121] Meanwhile, however, both acting and aspiring U.S. presidents have made their appearance at the conference. In June 2008, for example, all three presidential nominees – Barack Obama, Hillary Rodham Clinton, and John McCain – attended AIPAC's annual meeting in order to showcase their pro-Israel credentials. Because of its high political profile, and because of the nominees' intense and sometimes fanciful display of affection for Israel, it was not long before the event made its way into American popular culture: it was featured at length in Comedy Central's *The Daily*

---

[118] Organski (1990, 75-78) offers a different, though less convincing, explanation when he identifies the "degree of internationalism" among senators as the third factor that resolves the puzzle. Organski (1990, 210) argues that senators "have supported Israel as they have supported helping all countries they perceived as beleaguered and in need of military or economic assistance". Israel however has received U.S. foreign aid to a much larger extent than any other comparable country, see section 6.1.2 ("Overview") above.

[119] See Neil A. Lewis, "At Annual Meeting, Pro-Israel Group Reasserts Clout", *The New York Times*, May 5, 2009.

[120] Mearsheimer/Walt (2007), 160.

[121] I. L. Kenen, *All My Causes* (Washington, D.C.: Near East Research, 1985), 81.

Show with Jon Stewart, a widely viewed satirical American late-night program.[122]

Although American presidents are less exposed to pressure than members of Congress are, and therefore have more leeway to take critical positions toward Israel, they cannot easily ignore the impact of Jewish voters in presidential elections. Mearsheimer and Walt contend that pro-Israel groups like AIPAC can "exert significant leverage over the executive branch", partly due to the importance of money and votes from the Jewish community.[123] American Jews represent less than 3 percent of the overall population yet make disproportionately large campaign donations to candidates from both parties. It is estimated that American Jews supply between 20 and 50 percent of the contributions made to the Democratic Party and its candidates. In addition, Jewish voters have high turnout rates and are concentrated in key states such as California, Florida, Illinois, New Jersey, New York, and Pennsylvania.[124] This is why, Mearsheimer and Walt purport, the so-called Jewish vote in these states can tip the balance in tight election races:

> Because Jewish voters matter in close elections, presidential candidates go to considerable lengths to cultivate their support. (...) Candidates are especially eager to appeal to AIPAC and other organizations in the lobby – and not just to Jewish voters as a bloc – because they know that the seal of approval from these prominent organizations will facilitate fund-raising and encourage higher turnout on their behalf.[125]

---

[122] At AIPAC's 2008 Policy Conference, John McCain in his speech referred to his recent "trip to Jerusalem with Senator Lieberman", while Hillary Rodham Clinton was reminded "of a passage in Isaiah". Barack Obama, who scored lowest on Stewart's "kosh-o-meter", attempted to woo the audience by revealing that he had, in fact, "had a camp counselor who was an American Jew but had lived in Israel for a time". Quoted from Comedy Central, *The Daily Show with Jon Stewart*, "Indecision 5768", http://www.thedailyshow.com/watch/thu-june-5-2008/indecision-5768, accessed November 29, 2010.
[123] Mearsheimer/Walt (2007), 163.
[124] See Mearsheimer/Walt (2007), 163.
[125] Mearsheimer/Walt (2007), 163-164.

Once in office, U.S. presidents allegedly still pander to the pro-Israel lobbying groups they partly relied upon to win the elections. Mearsheimer and Walt point to the fact that officials with close ties to leading pro-Israel organizations "heavily shaped" Middle East policy during the Clinton administration.[126] A prominent example is Martin Indyk, the former deputy director of research at AIPAC, who served on Clinton's National Security Council, as ambassador to Israel, and as assistant secretary of state. By the same token, individuals who are seen as critical of Israel are reportedly barred from being appointed to important foreign policy jobs. The authors cite the example of George Ball, whom Jimmy Carter wanted to make his first secretary of state until he realized that Ball was perceived as critical of Israel and that pro-Israel groups opposed the appointment.[127]

On close inspection, however, the claims made by Mearsheimer and Walt are hardly convincing. As we have seen in the analysis presented by Organski, the financial and electoral weight attributed to the American Jewish community is often overrated and is not necessarily indicative of the presumed power of AIPAC or other pro-Israel lobbies. First, the claim that Jewish voters can effectively decide an election is misguided and does not stand up to close scrutiny. It is a logical fallacy, for every vote has the same political weight, and precisely every voter – and, hence, no single voter or group of voters – can tip the electoral balance. This claim would only have significance if Jews were overwhelmingly and disproportionately swing voters in these key states – which they are clearly not. American Jews have remained firmly anchored in the Democratic camp for decades, with President Obama receiving 78 percent of the Jewish vote in the presidential election of 2008.[128]

Second, it would be erroneous to assume that Israel represents the key issue for the American Jewish community in presidential elections. Although campaign donations from Jewish sources are significant, there is no evidence to support the claim that these donations are first and foremost made to secure pro-Israel positions. Israel, in fact, ranks fairly low on the list of issue priorities: in 2007, the Annual Survey of American Jewish Opinion conducted by the American Jewish Committee

---

[126] Mearsheimer/Walt (2007), 165.
[127] See Mearsheimer/Walt (2007), 167.
[128] See section 1.2 above.

found that only 6 percent of those polled said support for Israel was the "most important" issue in deciding who to elect president next year, whereas 23 percent identified the economy and jobs, health care (19 percent), the war in Iraq (16 percent), and terrorism and national security (14 percent) as the most important issue. Support for Israel was tied with immigration and the energy crisis (both 6 percent).[129] Similarly, AJC's 2008 Annual Survey of American Jewish Opinion found that 3 percent of the respondents said Israel was the one issue they would most like the candidates for president discuss during the 2008 presidential campaign; at the same time, 54 percent said the economy was the top issue, followed by health care (11 percent), the war in Iraq (6 percent), energy, and terrorism (both 5 percent).[130]

Third, the memoirs of George Ball clearly show that it was not his criticism of Israel, but rather his exuberant personality, which precluded his presumptive appointment to be secretary of state. Ball is quoted as saying, "I don't think I would have been Secretary of State anyway, because I don't think, for many reasons, that Mr. Carter would have wanted me. Partly because I'm a man of fairly strong views, and I don't think he wanted anyone quite that emphatic around him. And he didn't want dissent".[131] Moreover, Ball was considered for the appointment though he had brusquely declined an invitation from "three people in New York, (...) all Jewish lawyers", to visit Israel before the elections since, as they hinted, "this could have a very important influence on any role you might play in the future Carter administration". Ball turned down the invitation, replying "it is not my habit to try to placate a foreign govern-

---

[129] See American Jewish Committee, "2007 Annual Survey of American Jewish Opinion", http://www.ajc.org/site/c.ijITI2PHKoG/b.3642951/k.9F5F/National_Affairs__2007_Annual_Survey_of_Jewish_Opinion.htm, accessed December 10, 2010.

[130] See American Jewish Committee, "2008 Annual Survey of American Jewish Opinion", http://www.ajc.org/site/apps/nlnet/content3.aspx?c=ijITI2PHKoG&b=846741&ct=5989933, accessed December 10, 2010.

[131] Reminiscences of George Ball (June 14, 1978), Ethnic Groups and American Foreign Policy Project, page 39 in the Columbia University COH Collection.

ment in order to get a job in my own".[132] If pro-Israel groups had as much leverage over the executive branch as its critics purport, it is hard to imagine how Ball was considered for the position as secretary of state in the first place.

It is also worthwhile to note that, today, AIPAC devotes a smaller share of its activities to executive lobbying than before. Until the 1980s, AIPAC's executive branch lobbying was by and large successful – with the exception of its defeat over the AWACS sale to Saudi Arabia in 1981, for example – because President Reagan regarded Israel as a strategic asset in the East-West conflict. The end of the Cold War, and the end of Reagan's term, however marked a sea change. Following the collapse of the Soviet Union, the strategic value of the U.S.-Israel relationship became subject to reassessment; at the same time, the first Bush administration took a bolder approach towards Israel, as exemplified by the presidential initiative in 1991 to pressure the government of Yitzhak Shamir to stop settlement construction and to attend a peace conference by withholding $10 billion in loan guarantees. As the *Washington Jewish Week* remarked in an editorial in 1990, AIPAC was "caught flat-footed and taken by surprise" by the policy change under George H. W. Bush, and unable to organize effective opposition to it. Being a large national grassroots organization, AIPAC has traditionally lobbied Congress instead of the executive branch, and rather than shaping U.S. Middle East policy at its source – in the White House or the U.S. Department of State – AIPAC has always built its success on its ability to organize coalitions in Congress. AIPAC has no viable means to ex ante thwart White House initiatives because of the institutional primacy of the president in foreign policy matters. In light of the sobering outlook after 1989, AIPAC thus refocused its activities on Congress, realizing that coalition-building on Capitol Hill – and the power to block or amend legislation – remains the most effective way to exert limited influence over the executive branch.[133] A sustained engagement in executive lobbying would also have exposed AIPAC to rivalry from the Conference of Presidents of Major American Jewish Organizations, the

---

[132] Reminiscences of George Ball (June 14, 1978), Ethnic Groups and American Foreign Policy Project, pages 39, 40 in the Columbia University COH Collection; last quote quotation marks in original.

[133] See Washington Jewish Week, "Executive lobbying?", March 22, 1990.

Jewish umbrella organization that has traditionally focused on the executive branch.[134]

6.1.3 Summary

Not only because of its commitment to bipartisanship has AIPAC shied away from engaging in coalitions with other pro-Israel groups. For AIPAC also is what has here been termed an "Israel advocacy" organization, and therefore by and large supports the policies of the current Israeli government – irrespective of the latter's political outlook. Engaging in this type of pro-Israel advocacy may at first glance seem like an unnecessary relinquishing of organizational autonomy, since it entails the adoption of policy positions that lie without the organization's domain of control. From a theoretical standpoint, one may thus assume that AIPAC-style Israel advocacy would be a fairly unattractive option for any lobbying group. Yet, as evidenced by AIPAC's formidable strength, Israel advocacy can also be the source of a competitive edge in lobbying Congress. As a nonpartisan organization that supports whatever Israeli government is in office, AIPAC is more politically flexible than its policy advocacy counterparts (such as the ZOA), which facilitates its efforts to build coalitions with members of Congress. By dealing with Israel advocacy as a decidedly nonpartisan issue, AIPAC is in a convenient position to enlist support from both political parties.

Particularly striking is AIPAC's clout in the U.S. Congress, a fact that is not only acknowledged by its critics but also by the organization itself. Though this dissertation does not aim at assessing the "power" or "influence" of Jewish organizations, the analysis presented here nonetheless shows that AIPAC is often misleadingly credited as the single most decisive factor in congressional support for Israel. As A.F.K. Organski has convincingly argued, Jewish votes as well as financial support from Jewish sources are the result, not the cause, of senatorial support for Israel. While AIPAC actively lobbies for its goals, it also benefits considerably from the predisposed sympathy for Israel in Congress. All this is to say that we must be careful not to overrate AIPAC's actual political impact: that it is far from holding a position of unrivaled

---

[134] See section 5.2.2 above. Given that AIPAC is a member of the Presidents Conference, there also is little need for duplication.

authority over congressional policy toward Israel is furthermore evidenced by the growing popularity of J Street – a newly founded Jewish organization that has cast itself as an alternative to AIPAC.

6.2 J Street

6.2.1 Founding History and Internal Structure

What is perhaps most striking about the creation of J Street, a self-described "pro-Israel, pro-peace" lobby launched in April 2008, is the very argument on which it was founded. Its main purpose is to fill a void in the political map of Washington, D.C. by promoting "a new direction for American policy in the Middle East and a broad public and policy debate about the U.S. role in the region".[135] Given the diversity of American Jewish organizations, this claim requires further explanation: as noted before, there are more than 600 Israel-related organizations in the U.S., which often differ considerably in terms of mission, operations, and, where applicable, political orientation. Yet according to J Street founder and executive director Jeremy Ben-Ami, there still is a need for a liberal organization like J Street. Because it acts as a counterweight to what it perceives as the excessive influence of the political right on U.S. policy toward Israel, J Street seeks to provide a new and alternative platform within the Jewish community: "For too long, the loudest voices dominating American political debate on Israel and the Middle East have come from the far right. (...) We knew that those voices – whether neoconservatives, Christian Zionists or right-wing American Jews – did not speak for us", Ben-Ami writes in the preface of J Street's first annual report.[136]

But also the group's name is a multiple play on words that underscores its ambition "to complement the work of existing organizations

---

[135] J Street, *J Street Media Kit 2-2010* (Washington, D.C.: J Street, 2010), http://www.jstreet.org/files/J%20Street%20Media%20Kit%202-2010.pdf, accessed December 28, 2010.

[136] J Street, *J Street 2008 Blazing A New Path* (Washington, D.C.: J Street, 2008), 1.

and individuals that share [its] agenda".[137] Although the streets of Washington are named for letters in the alphabet, there is no J Street to be found between I and K. The name furthermore projects a public affairs image due to its symbolic proximity to K Street, a shorthand term for the Washington lobbying industry and the area where many lobbyists' offices are located. The letter "J", in turn, suggests a specifically Jewish cause.[138]

A single-issue organization dedicated to pro-Israel advocacy, J Street is more accurately described as a family of organizations comprising three separate and legally independent entities. Its main organization, J Street, is a 501(c)(4) lobbying organization, whose advocacy efforts are directed at both the U.S. Congress and the executive branch. The second entity, JStreetPAC, is a legally independent political action committee which endorses and raises funds for candidates who support J Street's policy positions. Finally, the J Street Education Fund, Inc. is a 501(c)(3) charitable organization which aims to educate targeted audiences about Israel and the Israeli-Palestinian conflict. J Street Local, J Street's national field program and J Street U, J Street's on campus movement, are programs run by the J Street Education Fund.[139] The J Street family of organizations currently employs 41 staff members, while J Street had a core staff of 16 in 2009, including a legislative team consisting of six lobbyists who work on Capitol Hill on a daily basis.[140] The organization

---

[137] J Street, *J Street Media Kit 2-2010* (Washington, D.C.: J Street, 2010), http://www.jstreet.org/files/J%20Street%20Media%20Kit%202-2010.pdf, accessed December 28, 2010.

[138] See Neil A. Lewis, "U.S. Jews Create New Lobby to Temper Israel Policy", *The New York Times*, April 25, 2008.

[139] See J Street, *J Street Media Kit 2-2010* (Washington, D.C.: J Street, 2010), http://www.jstreet.org/files/J%20Street%20Media%20Kit%202-2010.pdf, accessed December 28, 2010.

[140] See J Street, *J Street Media Kit 2-2010* (Washington, D.C.: J Street, 2010), http://www.jstreet.org/files/J%20Street%20Media%20Kit%202-2010.pdf, accessed December 28, 2010.

reports a third-year budget of over $4 million,[141] up from $3 million in 2009, which was the double of its initial budget of 2008.[142]

Akin to AIPAC, J Street is based in Washington, D.C. and operates as a large national grassroots movement, reporting a membership of nearly 140,000 online supporters in 2010.[143] According to Amy Spitalnick, J Street's press secretary, the Internet indeed serves as the main instrument for recruiting J Street supporters, who can join the organization free of charge.[144] J Street thus "is still as much an Internet presence, launching volleys of e-mail messages from the netroots, as it is a shoe-leather operation", the *New York Times* writes.[145] In addition, the strategic acquisition of the left-wing group Brit Tzedek V'Shalom in 2009 has helped J Street expand its reach beyond a mere network of online supporters. The merger with Brit Tzedek, a large and like-minded grassroots organization, allows J Street to tap into an active network of 48,000 volunteers in local chapters across the United States. It was preceded by J Street's 2008 takeover of the Union of Progressive Zionists, a small left-leaning campus organization, undertaken in a bid to bolster its outreach to young American Jews.[146] In so doing, J Street has brought about a certain consolidation of the hitherto largely fragmented Jewish political left. Groups like the moderately dovish Israel Policy Forum however rejected a merger on grounds that "the way J Street was positioning itself and the people that were associated with it, starting with Jeremy [Ben-Ami] himself, were too far to the left for most of us in the

---

[141] See J Street, *J Street Media Kit 2-2010* (Washington, D.C.: J Street, 2010), http://www.jstreet.org/files/J%20Street%20Media%20Kit%202-2010.pdf, accessed December 28, 2010.

[142] See J Street, *J Street 2009 Driving Change, Securing Peace* (Washington, D.C.: J Street, 2009), 1.

[143] See J Street, *J Street Media Kit 2-2010* (Washington, D.C.: J Street, 2010), http://www.jstreet.org/files/J%20Street%20Media%20Kit%202-2010.pdf, accessed December 28, 2010.

[144] See Interview with Amy Spitalnick, Press Secretary, J Street, June 9, 2009, Washington, D.C.

[145] James Traub, "The New Israel Lobby", *The New York Times*, September 9, 2009.

[146] See Nathan Guttman, "J Street Makes a Strategic Acquisition as Other Groups on the Left Struggle", *Forward*, September 18, 2009.

Israel Policy Forum".[147] As of December 2010, J Street operated a network of 37 local field programs in a total of 23 states, which serves as the basis for its grassroots activity.[148]

Though inclusive in the way it builds its membership base both online and locally, a substantial financial commitment is nonetheless required of those who seek further involvement in the organization. For instance, J Street's Political Action Network (J-NET) is "made up of donors and activists who are interested in taking a leadership role in J Street's lobbying and advocacy work" and who serve as liaisons to members of Congress and national officials. J-NET members are expected to contribute at least $1,800 annually, while J-NET trailblazers, the next higher category of membership, contribute between $5,000 and $9,999 per year. J Street's Director's Circle is a similar subgroup within the organization, with required donations ranging from $10,000 ("Groundbreakers") to $100,000 ("Architects"). Members of the Director's Circle receive invitations to private receptions with elected officials and key policy makers at the organization's annual national conference. They are also invited to participate in briefings and strategy calls with J Street's National Advisory Council,[149] a body consisting of "[h]undreds of prominent former public officials, policy experts, community and academic leaders".[150] Another way of getting involved in J Street's politics is through membership in the JStreetPAC Finance Committee, where a contribution of $10,000 or more over a two-year cycle to the PAC itself or through the PAC to its endorsed candidates is required. Members of the finance committee "are deeply engaged in the PAC's endorsement process, participating in candidate interviews and providing input on endorsement decisions and strategy". They furthermore receive briefings from elected officials and policy makers and attend J Street Advisory

---

[147] Quoted in Mandy Katz, "The Man on J Street: The Story of Jeremy Ben-Ami", *Moment Magazine* (online), March/April 2010.

[148] See J Street Local, "Find J Street in your community", http://local.jstreet.org/#, accessed December 28, 2010.

[149] See J Street, *J Street 2008 Blazing A New Path* (Washington, D.C.: J Street, 2008), 14.

[150] J Street, *J Street 2009 Driving Change, Securing Peace* (Washington, D.C.: J Street, 2009), 9.

Council meetings. In 2009, there were over 60 individuals serving on the finance committee.[151]

But also the funding of J Street's operations is concentrated in the hands of a few individuals. As a 501(c)(4) organization J Street has the benefit of generally not having to disclose its donors;[152] yet it was shaken by unfettered public criticism when its ties to George Soros were revealed in 2010. Soros, a Holocaust survivor and billionaire known for his philanthropic work and support for progressive causes, had given J Street $750,000 since 2008 even though J Street's website had misleadingly stated that Soros was not a donor.[153] The disclosure of Soros's funding of J Street had an immediate negative impact on the group's credibility on Capitol Hill.[154] Moreover, nearly half of J Street's budget from mid-2008 to mid-2009 – a total of almost $812,000 – came from a single Hong Kong-based donor, a businesswoman named Consolacion Esdicul. It is Esdicul's enigmatic background that, as the conservative *Weekly Standard* writes, has bestowed on J Street the aura of a "mysterious organization".[155] In its political operations, however, J Street has followed in many respects the well-known modus operandi of its competitor AIPAC. It is to the political style of J Street and its similarities and differences with AIPAC that we now turn.

---

[151] See J Street, *J Street 2009 Driving Change, Securing Peace* (Washington, D.C.: J Street, 2009), 17.

[152] Unlike so-called 527 political organizations, 501(c)(4) organizations have the advantage of not having to disclose their donors' identity, unless the contributor gives money for a specific political advertisement. 527 organizations have increasingly been supplanted by 501(c)(4) organizations, see Michael Luo and Stephanie Strom, "Donor Names Remain Secret As Rules Shift", *The New York Times*, September 21, 2010.

[153] See Eli Lake, "Soros revealed as funder of liberal American-Jewish lobby", *The Washington Times*, September 24, 2010; Gil Shefler, "Soros a secret J Street donor since '08", *The Jerusalem Post*, September 25, 2010; and Nathan Guttman, "J Street Flap Shines Spotlight On George Soros And His Money", *Forward*, October 8, 2010.

[154] See James D. Besser, "J Street Reeling After Soros Money Revelation", *The Jewish Week*, September 29, 2010.

[155] Daniel Halper, "TWS Contest: Who is Consolacion Esdicul?", *The Weekly Standard* (online), September 28, 2010.

6.2.2 Political Style: Horizontal and Vertical Politics

J Street has cast itself not only as an alternative to established Jewish organizations, but also as a liberal start-up targeting American Jews of the post-Holocaust generation. Though it shares many similarities with its competitor AIPAC, J Street has been limited in its ability to build broad-based political support. Its decidedly partisan outlook – the characteristic of policy advocacy – accounts for the persistence of this challenge.

Horizontal Politics

One of the most salient features that distinguish J Street from its traditional Jewish counterparts is its extraordinary appeal with young American Jews. Most conspicuously, J Street itself is a very young organization: as the average age of its staff members is about 30, it speaks for, and to, the post-Holocaust generation.[156] As press secretary Amy Spitalnick, herself a recent graduate of Tufts University, points out, J Street has a particular interest in attracting to its ranks the younger generation of American Jews: "J Street is giving a voice especially to those younger American Jews who feel disenchanted and who feel they didn't have a voice in the previous pro-Israel organizations", Spitalnick says. "We provide a voice especially for people who are in this younger generation".[157] To engage this group of potential supporters, J Street makes extensive use of the Internet and of social media like Facebook and Twitter. Social media have become increasingly popular in recent years, particularly among younger people, and played an important role in Barack Obama's victory in the presidential race of 2008.[158] As of December 2010, J Street counted nearly 11,000 fans on its Facebook site and more than 3,500 followers on Twitter.[159]

---

[156] See James Traub, "The New Israel Lobby", *The New York Times*, September 9, 2009.

[157] Spitalnick (2009 Interview).

[158] See Claire Cain Miller, "How Obama's Internet Campaign Changed Politics", *The New York Times* (online), November 7, 2008.

[159] In 2010, Facebook had 150 million active users in the U.S., and more than 500 million active users worldwide. On any given day, 50 percent of active users log on to Facebook. Twitter currently has 175 million registered users worldwide. Facebook and Twitter were founded in 2004 and 2006, respec-

J Street's success among younger American Jews is no coincidence. Rather, it is the result of J Street's ability to provide an attractive organizational response to current demographic trends in the American Jewish community. It is an organization that, in its style and political pursuits, is geared to the needs and expectations of the almost 1.5 million young Jewish adults in the United States. Young American Jews, ages 18 to 39, constitute 36 percent of America's roughly 4.1 million adult Jews and, as a study commissioned by the American Jewish Committee finds, "do appear to constitute a distinctive generation".[160] Young Jewish adults relate to their Jewishness quite unlike their predecessors, attaching greater importance to the "personal", "informal", and "episodic" nature of Jewish ties.[161] These differences are not specifically related to the Jewish community, but are in fact reflective of larger societal trends. "Jewish culture, like the culture of young people in the general community, is increasingly bottom-up, self-generated, and decentralized", the study finds, writing that "young people are creating their own identities and patterns of association (...) built around common interests and shared experiences rather than around institutions and organizations".[162] This finding is compounded by the fact that young Jewish adults are less likely to be formally affiliated with Jewish organizations than the generation of their parents. Among those ages 25 to 34, for example, only 25 percent were affiliated with at least two institutions such as a synagogue or a Jewish organization, compared to those over the age of 65, whose multiple affiliation rate was 58 percent. In another interview-based study, the Jewish respondents ages 18 to 25 were unable to decode the acronyms of major Jewish organizations such as AJC or AIPAC.[163]

---

tively. See Facebook, "Statistics", http://www.facebook.com/com/press/info.php?statistics, and Twitter, "About Twitter", http://twitter.com/about, accessed December 28, 2010.

[160] American Jewish Committee, *Young Jewish Adults in the United States Today* (New York: AJC, 2006), prepared by Ukeles Associates, 1.

[161] American Jewish Committee, *Young Jewish Adults in the United States Today* (New York: AJC, 2006), prepared by Ukeles Associates, 2.

[162] American Jewish Committee, *Young Jewish Adults in the United States Today* (New York: AJC, 2006), prepared by Ukeles Associates, 2-3.

[163] See American Jewish Committee, *Young Jewish Adults in the United States Today* (New York: AJC, 2006), prepared by Ukeles Associates, 29.

The values and attitudes of young Jewish Americans also have important policy implications for Jewish organizations. "Jewish organizations and institutions need to recognize the need to change", AJC notes, concluding that "Jewish organizations are going to need to be focused more on projects fostering greater participation and less on process, more built on interest and affinity groups than on committees and hierarchical structures".[164] This is exactly what J Street's recipe for success has been so far – attracting supporters through easy-to-access and easy-to-leave "affinity groups" on Facebook and Twitter, virtual connections that have increasingly come to replace more traditional forms of political participation. J Street has thus come to embody, quite effortlessly and convincingly, the image of "the sexy Jewish organization" today – a title once bestowed upon AIPAC, its foremost rival.[165]

While young American Jews are essentially no different from the previous generation in terms of their religiosity and the significance they attach to Holocaust memory, they however score substantially lower on aspects of Jewish peoplehood.[166] In particular, young Jewish adults evince an overall tenuous, and at best secondary, attachment to Israel. "There is a consensus among several studies that Israel is not central to young people's Jewish identity", AJC writes, pointing to research on the topic which found "a growing impatience with Israel and a growing emotional connection with the Palestinian cause, especially among Jewish graduate students". Citing further research, the AJC report concludes that, with the notable exception of young Orthodox adults, "Israel does not occupy a central emotional place in the lives of young Jews".[167] For instance, in a study of Jews ages 22 to 52 in the New York area, only 33

---

[164] American Jewish Committee, *Young Jewish Adults in the United States Today* (New York: AJC, 2006), prepared by Ukeles Associates, 92.

[165] Wolf Blitzer, "The AIPAC Formula: Why the American Israel Public Affairs Committee Is Washington's Most Effective Lobby – and American Jewry's Newest Glamour Organization", *Moment Magazine*, November 1981, 22.

[166] See American Jewish Committee, *Young Jewish Adults in the United States Today* (New York: AJC, 2006), prepared by Ukeles Associates, 32-34.

[167] American Jewish Committee, *Young Jewish Adults in the United States Today* (New York: AJC, 2006), prepared by Ukeles Associates, 34, 36, 37. A survey among young Orthodox respondents ages 18 to 39 found that 69 percent of those polled felt "very emotionally attached to Israel", see ibid., 79.

percent said that "supporting Israel" was related "a lot" to what being Jewish meant for them. In fact, on a list of 15 items of import to Jewish identity, support for Israel was ranked eleventh in significance. The same demographic skew was evidenced in AJC's 2000 Annual Survey of American Jewish Opinion, which indicated that 65 percent of Jewish Americans under the age of 40 felt "very" or "fairly" close to Israel, as opposed to 75 percent of the 40-to-59-year-olds, and 79 percent of the respondents age 60 and over.[168]

The decline in attachment to Israel among young American Jews explains why J Street has had little difficulty in establishing itself as a decidedly left-wing policy advocacy organization. Advertising the catchy slogan "pro-Israel, pro-peace", J Street attracts primarily young Jewish Americans who find little fault with its stated agenda to "redefine and expand the very concept of what it means to be pro-Israel".[169] In contrast to AIPAC, which generally supports the positions of the elected government of Israel, J Street advocates for specific policies it regards as conducive to resolving the Israeli-Palestinian conflict. "This is a group of people that loves Israel, but not unconditionally", J Street founder Jeremy Ben-Ami puts it pithily.[170] For example, in its support for the two-state solution, J Street opposes the occupation as well as the continued expansion of settlements in the West Bank. It also supports loosening the blockade of Gaza and a negotiated final status agreement which includes East Jerusalem as the capital of a future Palestinian state.[171] "We reserve the right to criticize the policies of the government of Israel. (...) We have good relationships and contacts but there is also tension", Ben-Ami says. "It truly is a relationship in progress".[172]

---

[168] See American Jewish Committee, *Young Jewish Adults in the United States Today* (New York: AJC, 2006), prepared by Ukeles Associates, 34-35.

[169] J Street, "Pro-Israel, Pro-Peace", http://www.jstreet.org/page/pro-israel-pro-peace, accessed December 28, 2010.

[170] Quoted in Michele Kelemen, "New Lobby Pushes Pro-Israel, Pro-Peace Mission", *NPR* (online), October 27, 2009.

[171] See J Street, "Boycott, Divestment, & Sanctions Movement", http://www.jstreet.org/page/boycott-divestment-sanctions-movement, accessed December 28, 2010. Being "greatly concerned" about the BDS movement, J Street says it "will not participate in targeted boycott or divestment activities".

[172] Quoted in Charley J. Levine, "Interview: Jeremy Ben-Ami", *Hadassah Magazine* (online), December 2010.

Its willingness to publicly disagree with Israeli policy has exposed J Street, perhaps unsurprisingly, to a flurry of anti-Israel accusations. Most conspicuous was the refusal of Michael Oren, the Israeli ambassador to the United States, to attend J Street's first annual conference in 2009 on the argument that, as a spokesman for the Israeli embassy explained, the organization advocates "certain policies that could impair Israel's interests".[173] Yiddish scholar Ruth R. Wisse pointedly described J Street as "anti-Israel", "a forgery", and "essentially a pro-Arab organization".[174] Malcolm Hoenlein, the executive vice chairman of the Presidents Conference, expressed similar reservations. "It's very questionable if they are in fact pro-Israel and what they are", Hoenlein said, arguing that, while "[a]nybody can purport to be pro-Israel", J Street had "not evidenced it yet".[175] Meanwhile, Harvard law professor Alan Dershowitz seemingly had sufficient evidence at hand, but only to conclude that J Street had "gone over to the dark side".[176]

However, and perhaps also unsurprisingly, various prominent Israeli officials have spoken out forcefully in J Street's defense. When the lobby hosted its annual conference in 2009, though boycotted by the Israeli embassy in Washington, it received letters of support from the leader of Kadima and former foreign minister, Tzipi Livni, as well as from the president of Israel, Shimon Peres.[177] "We can't afford to lose those who see themselves as our friends", Livni said, a stance also voiced in the liberal *Haaretz*.[178] Moreover, in 2008, a large number of Israelis with backgrounds from politics to academia were "pleased to learn of the creation of J Street. (...) Being a friend and ally – being "pro-Israel" – (...)

---

[173] Quoted in Hilary Leila Krieger, ""J Street could hurt Israel's interests"", *The Jerusalem Post*, October 11, 2009.

[174] Interview with Ruth R. Wisse, Martin Peretz Professor of Yiddish Literature and Professor of Comparative Literature, Center for Jewish Studies, Harvard University, December 11, 2008, Cambridge, MA.

[175] Hoenlein (2009 Interview).

[176] Alan Dershowitz, "J Street Can No Longer Claim to Be Pro Israel", *The Huffington Post*, April 21, 2010.

[177] See J Street, *J Street 2009 Driving Change, Securing Peace* (Washington, D.C.: J Street, 2009), 3.

[178] Quoted in Barak Ravid, "J Street: Criticism of Israel does not make us the enemy", *Haaretz*, February 19, 2010. See also Yehuda Ben Meir, "Israel can't afford to reject J Street", *Haaretz*, February 22, 2010.

does not require rigid agreement with every decision ever made or every policy pursued by the government of Israel or of the United States", a joint statement said.[179] In the same vein, David Kimche, former deputy director of the Mossad and former director-general of Israel's ministry of foreign affairs said the new lobby "may think differently from its critics on the right but it's as pro-Israel as they are".[180] Kimche was also quoted as saying that J Street was, in effect, "pursuing the ultimate pro-Israel agenda".[181]

Though it purports to be speaking for a hitherto "silent" but largely liberal "majority",[182] J Street can hardly be considered to be representative of large segments of the American Jewish community. While it is true that American Jews are overwhelmingly liberal in terms of their political orientation,[183] it is also true that J Street has been at odds in crucial instances with mainstream Jewish opinion. Its stance on the Gaza War of December 2008 and January 2009, or Operation Cast Lead, is a case in point. A press release issued by J Street on the first day of fighting stated that "there is no military solution to what is fundamentally a political conflict" and called for "immediate, strong diplomatic intervention" to negotiate a ceasefire. The next day, J Street wrote in a message to supporters that "while there is nothing 'right' in raining rockets on Israeli families or dispatching suicide bombers, there is nothing 'right' in

---

[179] Reprinted in J Street, *J Street 2008 Blazing A New Path* (Washington, D.C.: J Street, 2008), 8. The statement was signed by Shlomo Ben-Ami, former minister of foreign affairs; Avrum Burg, former speaker of the Knesset and chairman of the Jewish Agency; and Avi Primor, former Israeli ambassador to Germany and the EU, among others.

[180] David Kimche, "Don't brand "J Street" as anti-Zionist", *The Jerusalem Post*, May 2, 2008.

[181] J Street, *J Street 2008 Blazing A New Path* (Washington, D.C.: J Street, 2008), 9.

[182] J Street, *J Street 2008 Blazing A New Path* (Washington, D.C.: J Street, 2008), 1.

[183] This holds especially true for Jewish students, who represent a key target group for J Street. Research has shown that political orientation was one of the variables that maximally distinguished between Jewish and non-Jewish students: 51 percent of Jewish students identify themselves as "liberal", compared to 25 percent of non-Jews, see American Jewish Committee, *Young Jewish Adults in the United States Today* (New York: AJC, 2006), prepared by Ukeles Associates, 41.

punishing a million and a half already-suffering Gazans for the actions of the extremists among them".[184] Most American Jews were however less ambivalent about the Israeli intervention. Ironically, even J Street's own National Survey of American Jews, conducted in February/March 2009, found that 75 percent of those polled supported "the recent military action that Israel took in Gaza".[185] These attitudes, in turn, clearly resonated with Israeli public opinion. The War and Peace Index survey conducted by Tel Aviv University about a week and a half after the launching of Operation Cast Lead found that 94 percent of the Israeli Jewish public said they "support or strongly support" the operation, while another 90 percent said it should be continued "until it achieves all its objectives".[186]

The previous example is instructive in two respects. First, it contradicts J Street's fundamental claim to speak for what it regards as the "silent majority" of American Jews; the data presented here rather suggest that the organization is still struggling to find its path into the representative mainstream of American Jewish opinion. It also suggests that J Street, contrary to its stated aspiration, represents a fairly limited section of the Jewish left. Second, it hints at the practical difficulties associated with policy advocacy. Because it is a partisan lobby, J Street is furthermore constrained in its ability to win broad-based political support during elections and in the U.S. Congress, as the following comparison with AIPAC shows.

---

[184] Quoted in James Traub, "The New Israel Lobby", *The New York Times*, September 9, 2009. The press release in question was not available in the section "Press Releases" on J Street's website, as of December 2010.

[185] See J Street, *National Survey of American Jews* (Washington, D.C.: J Street, 2009), 11.

[186] At the same time 85 percent of Israeli Arab citizens opposed the operation, see Tel Aviv University, The Tami Steinmetz Center for Peace Research, "War and Peace Index – December 2008", http://www.tau.ac.il/peace/, accessed December 29, 2010.

Vertical Politics

Ever since its creation J Street has been viewed as an "alternative" or as a "counterpoint" to AIPAC, its foremost competitor on Capitol Hill.[187] Despite the obvious rivalry between both lobbies, J Street is careful to emphasize that it does not seek an oppositional relationship with AIPAC. "I'm very consciously not interested in portraying our organization as anti-Aipac", Jeremy Ben-Ami is quoted as saying.[188] Instead, J Street has cast itself as a start-up alternative to existing pro-Israel organizations. As *Haaretz* correspondent Shmuel Rosner phrases it, the group attempts to be "the un-Aipac".[189] This is why J Street's emergence does not necessarily signal a split in America's pro-Israel lobby: that two separate organizations now vie for influencing U.S.-Israeli relations must ultimately be seen as "a long-delayed reaction to the fact that Israeli society became divided over what should happen with the [occupied] territories", Israeli scholar Peter Medding says, suggesting the post-1967 split eventually translated into the creation of J Street.[190]

J Street shares many similarities with AIPAC. To begin with, both groups engage in lobbying the U.S. Congress, a task which J Street achieves mainly through J-NET, its political action network. J-NET members "serve as primary points of contact for J Street with Members of the House and Senate on policy and legislation related to Israel and the Middle East".[191] Since 2010, J Street has sponsored congressional missions to the Middle East as a way of educating members of Congress on issues of concern. These study missions are funded by the J Street Education Fund, the organizational counterpart to AIPAC's American

---

[187] Shmuel Rosner, "New Jewish-American lobby wants to be alternative to AIPAC", *Haaretz*, April 16, 2008; Michael Abramowitz, "Jewish Liberals to Launch A Counterpoint to AIPAC", *The Washington Post*, April 15, 2008.

[188] Quoted in James Traub, "The New Israel Lobby", *The New York Times*, September 9, 2009.

[189] Quoted in Neil A. Lewis, "U.S. Jews Create New Lobby to Temper Israel Policy", *The New York Times*, April 25, 2008.

[190] Quoted in Ilene R. Prusher, "Does J Street arrival signal a split in America's Israel lobby?", *The Christian Science Monitor*, October 28, 2009.

[191] J Street, *J Street 2009 Driving Change, Securing Peace* (Washington, D.C.: J Street, 2009), 16.

Israel Education Fund, which similarly finances such trips.[192] Akin to AIPAC, J Street also hosts an annual conference, both for networking purposes and in order to enhance the group's visibility in Washington. Its first conference in 2009 drew over 1,500 guests, including 148 members of Congress and U.S. National Security Adviser James Jones, one of the most senior American officials to address the audience.[193] But measured against the formidable public attention AIPAC receives for its annual meeting, J Street's conference still is less widely noticed and limited in its outreach to politically diverse policy makers. Due to its decidedly partisan character, it was dubbed by the *Forward* as "the Woodstock of the Jewish left".[194]

Important differences between J Street and AIPAC can be noted in their approach to influencing U.S. elections. Whereas AIPAC, which is not a political action committee, does not endorse or contribute to candidates, J Street does precisely that through JStreetPAC, a legally independent PAC and one of the three entities that comprise the J Street family of organizations. The affiliation with JStreetPAC is what one would expect from a policy advocacy organization like J Street; that AIPAC operates no similar structure is not quite surprising either, given the lobby's stated commitment to bipartisanship. In the 2008 congressional elections, J StreetPAC raised nearly $600,000[195] and, as the *Washington Post* reports, was ranked the largest pro-Israel PAC in the electoral cycle.[196] According to a ranking published by J Street, the organization's PAC surpassed the funds contributed by hitherto leading pro-Israel political action committees such as NACPAC, World Alliance for Israel PAC, Washington PAC, NATPAC and NORPAC, The Desert Caucus, Citizens Organized PAC, Northern Californians for Good Government,

---

[192] See Jewish Telegraphic Agency, "J Street sends first Mideast congressional mission", February 15, 2010.

[193] See Natasha Mozgovaya, "J Street "thrilled" by turnout at first national conference", *Haaretz*, October 27, 2009.

[194] Noam Neusner, "What J Street Can Learn From The Tea Party", *Forward*, September 29, 2010.

[195] See J Street, *J Street Media Kit 2-2010* (Washington, D.C.: J Street, 2010), http://www.jstreet.org/files/J%20Street%20Media%20Kit%202-2010.pdf, accessed December 28, 2010.

[196] See Dan Egen, "Groups say time is now for public financing push", *The Washington Post*, July 8, 2010.

SunPAC, and JACPAC.[197] It is in the field of campaign contributions that the rivalry between J Street and AIPAC is most visible, as candidates who receive funding from JStreetPAC often find themselves unable to raise money from other sources. For instance, the head of Washington PAC and former executive director of AIPAC, Morris Amitay, made it clear to candidates that his PAC viewed unfavorably those who had received funds from J Street. Accordingly, Representative Robert Wexler (D-FL) lost funding from Washington PAC when his endorsement by JStreetPAC became known. J Street's Amy Spitalnick attested to this potential trade-off, saying that, in some cases, a J Street endorsement would effectively preclude a candidate from obtaining financial support from other pro-Israel PACs.[198]

It is important to note that having a political action committee does not give J Street a competitive edge over AIPAC. In fact, J Street itself predominantly makes use of the AIPAC-style "conduit method" to raise funds for its endorsees. Akin to AIPAC, it acts as a relationship broker, connecting potential donors and candidates that seek financial support for their campaigns. The conduit method allows J Street to raise unlimited amounts of money for a particular candidate, whereas PACs using the traditional method, according to which donations are distributed directly by the PAC to a candidate, are limited to giving $5,000 per election, or $10,000 per election cycle, to a candidate.[199] Using this technique, JStreetPAC managed to raise over $93,000 for the Senate campaign of Jeff Merkley (D-OR) in 2008.[200] JStreetPAC however also counts checks made out directly to candidates by donors, whereas other PACs only include those contributions that were given to the PAC and then distributed to candidates. Washington PAC founder and former AIPAC executive director Morris Amitay was therefore led to charge that J Street had "not become a major player" in the fund-raising business and

---

[197] PACs ranked in order of funds contributed, highest first, see J Street, *J Street 2008 Blazing A New Path* (Washington, D.C.: J Street, 2008), 3.
[198] See Spitalnick (2009 Interview).
[199] See Michael Luo and Stephanie Strom, "Donor Names Remain Secret As Rules Shift", *The New York Times*, September 21, 2010.
[200] See J Street, *J Street 2008 Blazing A New Path* (Washington, D.C.: J Street, 2008), 3.

that its work was "no more than a drop in the bucket".[201] In the same vein, critics noted that the funds raised by J Street only represented a small fraction of the total raised by all other pro-Israel PACs. It is estimated that single-issue pro-Israel PACs disbursed more than $2.5 million for the 2008 cycle, a figure that does not include the additional millions of dollars that pro-Israel individuals donated and raised for candidates without the backing of an organization.[202]

The question of how much influence JStreetPAC can bring to bear on congressional elections has likewise been the subject of some dispute. A look at the 2008 congressional elections shows there is no clear pattern as to why candidates backed by J Street won or lost their races. For instance, Jeff Merkley (D-OR) and Gary Peters (D-MI) received over $93,000 and $42,000 from JStreetPAC, respectively, and both went on to defeat their incumbent Republican opponents. At the same time, candidates such as Ethan Berkowitz (D-AL) and Darcy Burner (D-WA) lost their races despite having received $28,000 and $57,000, respectively.[203] J Street had endorsed a total of 42 candidates, 34 of whom won their races.[204] Another curious example is that of Representative Joe Sestak (D-PA), because it shows that a candidate with a track record of supporting AIPAC-backed legislation can turn to J Street for funds *and* win the Jewish vote *and* lose the election.[205] In sum, the evidence presented here appears to be consistent with the findings of A.F.K. Organski, who cautions against overstating the impact of Jewish votes and money in

---

[201] Quoted in Nathan Guttman, "J Street Shows Its Strength in Numbers", *Forward*, November 21, 2008.

[202] See Eric Fingerhut, "Will J Street money translate into influence?", *JTA*, November 10, 2008.

[203] Again, these figures imply that J Street made use of the AIPAC-style conduit method to raise funds for its endorsees. See J Street, *J Street 2008 Blazing A New Path* (Washington, D.C.: J Street, 2008), 3.

[204] See J Street, *J Street Media Kit 2-2010* (Washington, D.C.: J Street, 2010), http://www.jstreet.org/files/J%20Street%20Media%20Kit%202-2010.pdf, accessed December 28, 2010.

[205] See Hilary Leila Krieger, ""I have a '100% voting record' on AIPAC backed legislation"", *The Jerusalem Post*, November 2, 2010; Nathan Guttman, "J Street and Republican Jewish Coalition Clash Over Their Own Influence on the Elections", *Forward*, November 8, 2010.

U.S. elections.[206] Instead of a direct pushback at the polls, candidates endorsed by JStreetPAC rather face retribution from AIPAC and from other pro-Israel PACs, as the latter would not support such candidates.

What most significantly sets J Street apart from AIPAC is its involvement in policy advocacy, which translates into strong partisan support for the policies of the Obama administration. The organization's favoritism toward Barack Obama was on prominent display after the 2008 election, when J Street took out a full-page ad in the *New York Times*, congratulating the president-elect and pledging support for the new administration's Middle East agenda. "We share the same mentality as the Obama campaign. (...) It's a very similar idea", J Street press secretary Amy Spitalnick confirms. While stressing that J Street was "not a yes-man for Obama", Spitalnick also said that the president's policy on Israel effectively "corresponds with our values and what we believe in".[207] A corollary of this partisan closeness is the J Street project "Obama-SmearBusters", a website aimed at countering "smears on President Obama's sensible approach to the Middle East with the facts".[208] Consistent with J Street's distinctive political style, the project is based on the concept of online advocacy: activists can report smears on the website or sign up for a list of regular updates, which they are then supposed to forward to friends and family members.[209]

The election of Barack Obama thus came at a highly propitious moment for J Street and quickly propelled the lobby to a position of prominence among America's Jewish organizations. J Street's invitation to the first official White House meeting with Jewish leaders for groups such as AIPAC and the Presidents Conference, which President Obama hosted in July 2009, not only boosted its visibility but also gave it the status of a legitimately pro-Israel organization.[210] J Street's ties to the Obama administration may also have been helped by the various government positions previously held by its executive director, Jeremy Ben-Ami.

---

[206] See section 6.1.2 ("AIPAC and U.S. Elections") above.

[207] Spitalnick (2009 Interview).

[208] J Street ObamaSmearBusters, "Who We Are", http://www.obamasmearbusters.com/about, accessed January 2, 2011.

[209] See J Street ObamaSmearBusters, "Become a Smear Buster", http://action.jstreet.org/t/4826/petition.jsp?petition_KEY=632, accessed January 2, 2011.

[210] See Mandy Katz, "The Man on J Street: The Story of Jeremy Ben-Ami", *Moment Magazine* (online), March/April 2010.

Before coming to J Street, Ben-Ami served as policy director on the presidential campaign of Howard Dean, the former chairman of the Democratic Party, and as deputy domestic policy adviser to President Bill Clinton.[211]

In turn, having J Street's backing has also proven to be politically expedient for the Obama administration. J Street for instance shares President Obama's unequivocal disapproval of Israeli settlement expansion, as stated in his Cairo speech of 2009, thereby giving the administration a valuable political cover against anti-Israel accusations. In a row with Israeli Prime Minister Benjamin Netanyahu, J Street recently backed Obama in his opposition to continued building in East Jerusalem, whereas AIPAC squarely sided with Netanyahu in the squabble. Whereas AIPAC called for the White House to defuse the battle with Netanyahu,[212] J Street instead delivered a petition asking the president to take "even stronger action" in the negotiations between Israel and the Palestinians.[213] Given its conspicuous and reliable support for Barack Obama's Middle East agenda, J Street has not fallen short of earning the sobriquet of being the "Obama Lobby".[214]

There is however scarce evidence to substantiate the view that J Street has had a lasting impact on U.S. Middle East policy. Despite its appeal with the younger generation of American Jews, J Street's achievements have mostly been confined to the virtual world. Here lies the fundamental difficulty associated with online advocacy: while supporters may be easily won, their affiliations may still often be superficial and fluid. Indeed, absent the current administration in office, it is questionable whether the lobby would have made a similarly rapid ascent. Considering its recent founding date, J Street nonetheless has been a remarkable accomplishment. It may be too early to assess its long-term relevance, but it is fair to say that, in addition to stirring a vivid debate on the future of pro-Israel advocacy, J Street has been a vanguard in offering a timely organizational response to the demographic shifts that

---

[211] See J Street, "Staff", http://jstreet.org/about/staff, accessed January 2, 2011.
[212] See Jay Solomon, "J Street Backs Obama in Row With Israel", *The Wall Street Journal*, March 15, 2010.
[213] Quoted in Jewish Telegraphic Agency, "J Street delivers petition to White House", March 15, 2008.
[214] James Kirchick, "The Obama Lobby", *Forward*, July 22, 2009.

will shape the outlook of the American Jewish community in the years to come.

6.3   Summary

Illustrative of what has been termed the "new" Jewish politics, both AIPAC and J Street insert themselves directly and permanently in the electoral and legislative process. Set up as single-issue and grassroots organizations, they however represent different models of pro-Israel advocacy. While AIPAC supports the policies of the Israeli government irrespective of the latter's political outlook, J Street by contrast operates as a policy advocacy organization wedded to a more narrowly defined partisan agenda. J Street has therefore predictably been at odds with some of the policies of the current Israeli government. AIPAC's recipe for success in turn has been its political flexibility and nonpartisanship, owed to the organization's long-standing tenet of not endorsing or contributing to congressional candidates.

Both lobbies also differ in terms of their political operations. While fostering its image as a liberal alternative to AIPAC, J Street has been particularly successful in appealing to the younger generation of American Jews and, in the same vein, has been a forerunner in the field of online advocacy. But even though it has an affiliated political action committee, J Street is far from rivaling AIPAC's political clout: in addition to the limitations imposed by being a policy advocacy organization, J Street has yet to find its way into the representative mainstream of the American Jewish community.

Finally, it is important to note that AIPAC has been met with considerable predisposed sympathy in the U.S. Congress: it may occasionally be able to garner the vaunted "signatures of 70 senators" on a given issue, but it can do so by building on a substantial degree of existing pro-Israel sentiment as opposed to generating or forcing it through the exercise of hard-nosed political pressure.

Table 5: Comparison of AIPAC and J Street, Main Features

	AIPAC	J Street
Type	Israel advocacy	policy advocacy
Founder	Isaiah L. Kenen	Jeremy Ben-Ami
Founding year	1959	2008
Legal status	501(c)(4)	501(c)(4)
Membership (in 2010)	100,000	140,000 (online)
Offices	19	1
Headquarters	Washington, D.C.	Washington, D.C.
Staff (in 2009)	382	16 (core staff)
PAC	none	JStreetPAC
Budget (in 2009)	$50 million	$4 million
Facebook fans	17,250	11,000
Twitter followers/Tweets	2,500/1,100	3,500/3,100

Note: Facebook/Twitter figures as of December 2010.

7 Summary

The previous chapters have provided a decidedly disaggregated view of American Jewish political organizations. Our initial distinction between modern and new Jewish politics has elucidated the basic differences in terms of the political roles that Jewish organizations seek to play. Within the category of modern Jewish politics, we have analyzed the leading Jewish umbrellas as well as the "big three" Jewish defense organizations. Within the category of new Jewish politics, we have further differentiated between the contrasting models of Israel and policy advocacy and discussed the politics of AIPAC and J Street as their respective representative examples.

As we have amply seen in the previous chapters, all Jewish organizations in question operate from their specific organizational niche: they craft and cultivate distinct political styles and identities to prevail in an environment characterized by intense peer competition. While the American Jewish Committee is known for its rather quiet and diplomatic approach to politics, the Anti-Defamation League has honed its image as a "tough" Jewish organization, with the American Jewish Congress still struggling to carve a viable niche of activity next to its rivals. While the JCPA is associated with predominantly domestic affairs, a bent for liberal politics, and a strongly participatory decision-making process, the Presidents Conference by contrast represents an internationally oriented, less liberal, and more discretionary organization. Moreover, as the example of the Claims Conference has shown, the official backing from the U.S. government can be critical for an organization's international standing and long-term political success.

True, all American Jewish organizations here under review are "pro-Israel" by some objective standard; but as we have seen, they also frame their advocacy efforts according to their own views and interests and clearly do not act as a single political force. While there is an "Israel lobby" in the sense of Jewish organizations adopting, quite unsurprisingly, positions that are friendly toward and supportive of Israel, this alleged "lobby" is all but a unified political actor – in fact, it is not a political actor at all. Considering the overall fragmentation of the interest group system and the rivalries among the Jewish organizations discussed in the previous chapters, the notion of an "Israel lobby" as an actor in its own right is neither intuitively plausible nor sustained by the empirical evidence.

Finally, at the theoretical level, we can make a general statement on the importance of structure and agency in interest group politics. Although individual agency still matters, and helps account for the differences in status and success, the institutional constraints of the polity are hard to overlook. In this sense, we have found the politics of American Jewish organizations to be highly consistent with the larger pattern of competitive and society-centered interest group politics in the United States.

Part Three: The Central Council of Jews in Germany

The third part of this dissertation provides a detailed empirical analysis of the politics of the Central Council of Jews in Germany. It argues that the Central Council often finds itself in an uneasy position toward the state, torn between the pledge of partnership on one hand and the need for critical distance on the other. The case of the Central Council can therefore be regarded as an example of state-centered politics. With the state as its foremost ally, the Central Council has to grapple with a situation in which it depends considerably, both politically and financially, on its powerful sponsor. The political style of the Central Council reflects these institutional constraints and, as we shall see, involves a politics guided by the notion of modesty and even of self-restraint.

This line of argument is organized in various chapters. The first chapter gives an overview of the current social structure of the German Jewish community, with a focus of attention on the major trends since 1945 and 1989 in particular. Chapter 2 examines both the institutional and non-institutional factors that account for the intertwined relationship between the Central Council and the state. Chapter 3 in turn takes a critical look at the oft-invoked yet imperfect "special relationship" between the German state and the Jewish community. With this background established, the fourth chapter deals at length with the characteristics of the political style of the Central Council. Specifically, it offers concise political portraits of the umbrella's past chairmen and presidents. The fifth chapter, which includes a case study of the hitherto neglected role of the Central Council during German unification, addresses the issue of partnership and dependency from yet another angle, discussing the risk of instrumentalization and alibi politics that the umbrella is exposed to due to its close relationship with the state. Finally, chapter 6 concludes with a summary of the main empirical findings.

1 Postwar Trends in German Jewry

The following chapter gives an overview of the social structure of the German Jewish community today. It discusses the impact of recent immigration after 1989 and offers a brief comparison with German Jewry after 1945.

1.1 Overview of German Jewry Today

When considered against the backdrop of Germany's historical past, it may seem unlikely that Jewish life should have taken root again in the country of former persecution.[1] Indeed widely held after the war was the assumption made by Rabbi Leo Baeck according to which the Holocaust had effectively terminated the thousand-year history of German Jewry and that Jews would never again settle on the "blood-soaked German soil" (as the World Jewish Congress had put it in 1948).[2] While some argued that resettlement in Germany was a morally reprehensible act, others believed that the remnants of the German Jewish community would vanish quickly due to their unfavorable age structure, the pull of Israel, and the lack of sustained Jewish immigration. In 1964, a study published by Germania Judaica, a major research library on German Jewry based in Cologne, concluded that the "disappearance" of the Jew-

---

[1] See Jeffrey M. Peck, *Being Jewish in the New Germany* (New Brunswick, NJ: Rutgers University Press, 2006); Leslie Morris and Jack Zipes (eds.), *Unlikely History: The Changing German-Jewish Symbiosis, 1945-2000* (New York: Palgrave, 2002); and Susan Stern (ed.), *Speaking Out: Jewish Voices from United Germany* (Chicago: Edition Q, 1995).

[2] See Michael Brenner, *After the Holocaust: Rebuilding Jewish Lives in Postwar Germany* (Princeton: Princeton University Press, 1997), translated by Barbara Harshav, 66; Chaim Yahil, "Germany", in: Berenbaum/Skolnik (eds.) (2007), vol. 7, 537.

ish population in Germany as an independent group was, "within little more than one generation, a certainty".[3]

None of these forecasts however proved accurate. More than six decades later, Germany is not only home to the fastest growing Jewish community in the world, but also represents the third largest Jewish community in Europe.[4] About 105,000 Jews are currently affiliated within 108 Jewish communities and organized in a total of 23 regional associations under the umbrella of the Central Council of Jews in Germany, the religious and political body representing German Jewry.[5] It is estimated that the overall Jewish population in Germany, affiliated and unaffiliated, ranges roughly between 100,000 and 200,000. The American Jewish Committee assessed the core Jewish population in Germany in 2007 at 120,000 and the enlarged Jewish population, inclusive of the non-Jewish relatives of Jewish immigrants, at above 206,000.[6] Federalism, a fundamental characteristic of the German political system – harking back to the tribalistic origins of the German nation and nowadays constitutionally anchored in Article 20 I of the German Basic Law – also made itself felt in the geographical distribution of the Jewish population. Each of the 16 German states today has a sizable Jewish population, as the following table shows:

---

[3] Quoted in Gertrude Samuels, "The Jews in Germany Today", *Harper's Magazine*, May 1964, 49.

[4] See Josef Joffe, "A Boom, if not a Renaissance, in Modern-Day Germany", *Forward*, July 25, 2003; Peter Laufer, *Exodus to Berlin: The Return of the Jews to Germany* (Chicago: Ivan R. Dee, 2003).

[5] See Zentralrat der Juden in Deutschland, "Mitglieder", http://www.zentralrat djuden.de/de/topic/5.html, accessed January 24, 2011.

[6] See DellaPergola (2007), 587.

Table 6: Geographical Distribution of Jews in Germany, Affiliated Members

State	Jewish population	Percentage of larger population
Baden-Württemberg	8,200	0,08
Bavaria	19,200	0,15
Berlin	10,800	0,32
Brandenburg	1,300	0,05
Bremen	1,100	0,17
Hamburg	2,900	0,17
Hesse	12,100	0,20
Mecklenburg-Vorpommern	1,700	0,10
Lower Saxony	7,300	0,10
North Rhine-Westphalia	29,000	0,16
Rhineland-Palatinate	3,300	0,08
Saarland	1,100	0,11
Saxony	2,600	0,06
Saxony-Anhalt	1,700	0,07
Schleswig-Holstein	1,300	0,05
Thuringia	800	0,04
Total	104,400*	0,13

Note: Calculated on the basis of statistics provided by the welfare agency ZWST, *Mitgliederstatistik der jüdischen Gemeinden und Landesverbände in Deutschland für das Jahr 2008* (Frankfurt am Main: ZWST, 2009), 2, and Destatis, "Die Bundesländer – Strukturen und Entwicklungen – Ausgabe 2008", April 2008. Numbers rounded to 100. *Does not include liberal communities. With the exceptions of Lower Saxony and Schleswig-Holstein, where separate liberal regional associations exist, the latter are not represented in regional associations, as they are not organized within the Central Council of Jews in Germany. They represent about 4,500 members.

Between 1989 and 2008, the German Jewish community grew by a factor of 3.8, a spectacular increase owed to Jewish immigration from countries of the former Soviet Union (FSU). After the fall of the Berlin

Wall, Jewish refugees from FSU countries have flocked to Germany in large numbers: allowed in on humanitarian grounds as so-called "quota refugees", over 53,000 immigrants joined the Jewish communities between 1990 and 1998.[7] All in all, about 220,000 "quota refugees" arrived in Germany from 1989 onwards, and over half of them have eventually become members of the Jewish communities.[8] As a result of this influx the majority of today's communities are made up of immigrants from the former Soviet Union. Mainly in East Germany, but also in other places, communities have been established which are exclusively or almost exclusively comprised of immigrants, as for example is the case in Rostock or Schwerin.[9]

1.2 Jewish Immigration to Germany After 1989

At the same time, recent immigrants often have only a tenuous connection with Judaism and face the challenge of rediscovering and, concomitantly, embracing their buried Jewish heritage. Raised in an atheist state that discouraged religious practice, many Jews from the FSU have lost their connection to Judaism and to Jewish culture. This is why the Central Council of Jews in Germany has made the integration of newcomers a "key task" and seeks to establish the necessary preconditions for integration by offering language courses and by acquainting immigrants with Jewish rites and customs and a basic knowledge of Judaism. "Helping Jewish immigrants from countries of the former Soviet Union to find their feet in German society has become one of the biggest challenges for the Central Council of Jews in Germany since it was founded in 1950 and since the end of the Cold War and the fall of the Berlin Wall", the umbrella's website reads.[10] A particularly pressing problem is the widespread dependence on public welfare: more than 60 percent of

---

[7] See Michael Brenner, "Germany", in: Berenbaum/Skolnik (eds.) (2007), vol. 7, 540.
[8] See Zentralrat der Juden in Deutschland, "Migration to Germany", http://www.zentralratdjuden.de/en/topic/154.html, accessed January 25, 2011.
[9] See Michael Brenner, "Germany", in: Berenbaum/Skolnik (eds.) (2007), vol. 7, 540.
[10] Zentralrat der Juden in Deutschland, "Integrating newcomers", http://www.zentralratdjuden.de/en/topic/108.html, accessed January 25, 2011.

immigrant households have to rely on such payments, often in spite of solid educational backgrounds as well as professional experience.[11] A look at the numbers also clearly bears out the problem of integrating recent immigrants into the existing community structures. Out of the 220,000 immigrants allowed in under the *Kontingentflüchtlingsgesetz*, a special immigration and quota law governing Jewish immigration to Germany until 2004, only about 110,000 were absorbed into the Jewish communities. It is quite revealing of these difficulties that the law was replaced by the more restrictive *Zuwanderungsgesetz* (or "Immigration Act") on January 1, 2005, which required aspiring immigrants to prove that a Jewish community would accept them as a member. Prior knowledge of the German language also became mandatory; applicants furthermore had to give evidence that they were willing to enter the German labor market and would not rely on public welfare.[12] Commenting upon the seemingly "rudimentary" nature of immigrants' connection with Jewish religion, culture, and history, a polemic editorial in the *Frankfurter Allgemeine Zeitung* made the contention that Russian Jews lacked authenticity and thus needed to be turned into "real Jews" first.[13] Since the German Jewish communities under the auspices of the Central Council adhere to the Halakhic definition of Judaism, it is impossible for new immigrants to gain membership if they do not fulfil, as is frequently the case, the strict religious requirements posited by Halakhic law.

---

[11] See Uri R. Kaufmann, "Vom Hinterhof zum Stadtplatz", *Aufbau*, September 2009, 12. Immigrants often face the difficulty of having their degrees and qualifications recognized as equivalent in Germany.

[12] In July 2006, new rules for Jewish immigration made in adjustment of the previous law came into force. They reaffirmed the principle of "preferred admission" as well as the ambition to attract those who seek to play an active part in Jewish life. Under the new rules, the ZWST will issue an "integration forecast" for each applicant to determine whether the aspiring immigrant is Jewish. The ZWST is also responsible for confirming admission to a local Jewish community, which is needed before an application can be accepted. For further details, see Zentralrat der Juden in Deutschland, "Migration to Germany", http://www.zentralratdjuden.de/en/topic/154.html, accessed January 25, 2011.

[13] Hans Riebsamen, "Kleine jüdische Wunder", *Frankfurter Allgemeine Zeitung*, November 11, 2006.

The fast pace at which the German Jewish communities have grown is primarily the result of the massive influx of immigrants from the former Soviet Union. New births, by contrast, played only a marginal role. Membership statistics published by the *Zentralwohlfahrtsstelle der Juden in Deutschland* (ZWST), a non-statutory and non-political welfare agency that represents the Jewish communities alongside the Central Council, illustrate these trends. Consider the influx to the Jewish community between 1990 and 2008, when of a total of about 131,000 new members more than 101,000 were refugees from the FSU, whereas Jewish births accounted for a modest increase of 2,600 over the same period.[14] Accordingly, the present communities are shaped to a large extent by recent immigrants and their respective cultures. In addition to an actual or perceived lack of "authenticity" or of some notion of "Jewishness", the new community members may therefore also appear less "German" than their long-established peers.

As it has depended rather on the influx of Jews from abroad than on high domestic fertility rates, the present German Jewish renaissance does not significantly increase the world Jewish population. Despite the recent dynamism of Jewish life in Germany, the world Jewish population grew by a modest 0.5 percent in 2006, and even diminished on aggregate by 0.2 percent when Israel was taken out of the equation.[15]

That the numerical growth of German Jewry is essentially driven by immigration is also visible in the age composition of the overall community, which is largely skewed to older ages. Worth noting is the continued discrepancy between low birth rates and high mortality rates: in 2008, for example, 171 Jewish births were matched by 1,038 deaths.[16] Data supplied by the ZWST likewise show that middle-aged and senior adults still account for a sizable part of the German Jewish community today. In 2008, 54 percent of all affiliated members were over the age of 51, of whom 15 percent were between the ages 71 and 80 and another 7

---

[14] See ZWST, *Mitgliederstatistik der jüdischen Gemeinden und Landesverbände in Deutschland für das Jahr 2008* (Frankfurt am Main: ZWST, 2009), 3.
[15] See DellaPergola (2007), 551.
[16] See ZWST, *Mitgliederstatistik der jüdischen Gemeinden und Landesverbände in Deutschland für das Jahr 2008* (Frankfurt am Main: ZWST, 2009), 3.

percent over the age of 80. At the same time, only 24 percent of German Jews were under the age of 30.[17]

It is important to bear in mind that, despite the remarkable increase in numbers, the percentage of Jews in the general German population stands between a tiny 0.1 and 0.2 percent. It would thus be premature and indeed inaccurate to extol the rebirth of Jewish life in Germany as an indication of a return to the prewar demographics. Even accepting the optimistic estimate of a current Jewish population of about 200,000, the present community would still fall short in size when compared to the community of 1939, which included 234,000 Jews, as defined by the Nuremberg laws. The present community also is considerably smaller than the communities that existed during the German Empire and during the Weimar Republic. Back in 1871, the Jewish population in Germany had amounted to over 512,000 and reached a peak of more than 615,000 in 1910. In 1933, more than 503,000 German Jews witnessed the appointment of Adolf Hitler as chancellor and the democratic election of the Nazi government. Also striking is the fact that even when the Nazis declared Germany *judenrein* in 1943, there were more Jews living in the country than at the time of German unification (see Table 7).[18]

It is not surprising, then, that Germany's Jewish communities are still fairly modest in size. As of December 2008, the Jewish community of Berlin, the largest in the country, reported a membership of 10,800, ahead of other major centers of Jewish life such as Munich, with 9,600 affiliated members; Frankfurt am Main, with a community of 6,900; Cologne, with a community of 4,600; and Hamburg with 2,900 affiliated members.[19] Jewish communities that were altogether inexistent or lacked active membership before 1989 have also sprung up in many

---

[17] Own calculations based on ZWST, *Mitgliederstatistik der jüdischen Gemeinden und Landesverbände in Deutschland für das Jahr 2008* (Frankfurt am Main: ZWST, 2009), 4. Women outnumbered men by a margin of 6,900, as of December 2008.

[18] Nearly 32,000 in 1943 as opposed to about 29,000 in 1990, see Samuel Miklos Stern, "Germany", in: Berenbaum/Skolnik (eds.) (2007), vol. 7, 528; ZWST, *Mitgliederstatistik der jüdischen Gemeinden und Landesverbände in Deutschland für das Jahr 2008* (Frankfurt am Main: ZWST, 2009), 1.

[19] Numbers rounded to 100, see ZWST, *Mitgliederstatistik der jüdischen Gemeinden und Landesverbände in Deutschland für das Jahr 2008* (Frankfurt am Main: ZWST, 2009), 2.

places across the country, as for instance in Schleswig-Holstein as well as in cities like Erlangen, Göttingen, Oldenburg, Celle, and Wolfsburg. The Bavarian communities of Bayreuth and Straubing, akin to those of Schwerin and Rostock in Mecklenburg-Vorpommern and those in Braunschweig and Hannover in Lower Saxony, are among those that have grown more than tenfold over the same period.

Table 7: Jewish Population in Germany, 1871-1989

Year	Jewish population
1871	512,000
1880	563,000
1890	568,000
1900	587,000
1910	615,000
1925	564,000
1933	503,000 (defined by religion)
1939	234,000 (defined by Nuremberg laws)
1941	164,000
1942	51,000
1943	32,000
1944	15,000
1946*	157,000
1948*	153,000
1949*	55,000
1952	23,000
1957-1989	29,000-31,000

Source: Samuel Miklos Stern, "Germany", in: Berenbaum/Skolnik (eds.) (2007), vol. 7, 528. Numbers rounded to 1,000. * Estimated number includes displaced persons (DPs).

Table 8: Growth of Jewish Communities in Germany From 1990 to 2008, Affiliated Members

Year	Members
1990	29,000
1991	34,000
1992	37,000
1993	41,000
1994	46,000
1995	54,000
1996	61,000
1997	67,000
1998	74,000
1999	82,000
2000	88,000
2001	93,000
2002	98,000
2003	102,000
2004	106,000
2005	108,000
2006	108,000
2007	107,000
2008	106,000

Source: ZWST, *Mitgliederstatistik der jüdischen Gemeinden und Landesverbände in Deutschland für das Jahr 2008* (Frankfurt am Main: ZWST, 2009), 1. Numbers rounded to 1,000.

1.3 Comparison with German Jewry After 1945

The present situation is reminiscent of the first decades after the Holocaust, when immigrants and refugees similarly played a key role in shaping and rebuilding Jewish life in Germany. Postwar Jewry was represented through the Central Council of Jews in Germany and consisted of three main and highly heterogeneous groups. There were the remnants of German Jewry who had survived the war in Germany; the displaced persons (DPs) from Eastern Europe who had taken temporary refuge in Germany; and the Jews who had returned to Germany or settled there after the war. Old cleavages between *Ostjuden* and the established German Jews[20] – based on traditional conflicts over religious practice and nurtured by the idiosyncrasies of the largely autonomous Jewish world of Eastern Europe with its own culture and language – again came to the forefront and led to tension between both groups. Both however were able to overcome their differences and eventually reached common ground for cooperation. Several waves of Jewish immigration to West Germany followed throughout the 1960s and 1970s and brought about a consolidation of the Jewish communities. Immigrants from Hungary arrived in 1956, followed by Jews from Poland in 1968 and from the former Soviet Union a few years later. Other groups of immigrants include Jews from Iran as well as refugees from Israel of Sephardic and Ashkenazic descent. Long before the influx of Soviet Jews in the 1990s, therefore, Germany had already been home to an ethnically varied and culturally diverse community.

What sets immigrants from the Soviet Union apart from the early refugees of the postwar era is their willingness to permanently stay in the Federal Republic. For the DPs who found themselves back in the land of the perpetrators, the Jewish community was but a community "in liquidation",[21] a transitory shelter prior to emigration. They had no intention of staying on what they regarded as the accursed German soil. The founding of the state of Israel in 1948 ushered in the dissolution of DP camps in Germany, most of which were located in the American Zone, and emigration ensued at a rapid pace. Whereas in April 1948 there were still approximately 165,000 Jewish DPs in Germany, that same number had decreased to a mere 30,000 five months later.[22] In the early 1950s, after the great stream of emigration had taken place, only 12,000 were

---

[20] See, for example, Jack Wertheimer, *Unwelcome Strangers: East European Jews in Imperial Germany* (New York: Oxford University Press, 1987).

[21] Zentralrat der Juden in Deutschland, "Foundation", http://www.zentralratjuden.de/en/topic/133.html, accessed February 21, 2011 (quotation marks in original, "communities in liquidation").

[22] See Michael Brenner, "Epilog oder Neuanfang?", in: Otto R. Romberg and Susanne Urban-Fahr (eds.), *Juden in Deutschland nach 1945* (Bonn: Bundeszentrale für politische Bildung, 2000), 36.

left of the more than 200,000 Jewish DPs who at some point of time had lived in postwar Germany. However, about 6,000 former DPs were members of the Jewish communities by 1960 and constituted a sizable portion of the overall membership in cities like Munich and Frankfurt, where they represented 80 percent and 40 percent of the Jewish communities, respectively.[23]

Those who remained in Germany after the war did so for various reasons. Most of them had not adjusted well in the countries to which they had emigrated, including Israel, which had absorbed most Jewish DPs and was struggling with economic hardship and the aftermath of the 1948 war of independence. Others hoped that their presence in the Federal Republic would help speed up their claims for restitution of property and for indemnification payments. Still others were impelled by material considerations, especially during the boom of the late 1950s. Of course this generalization does not apply to all returnees; individual circumstances such as family, health, language, and profession also often played a decisive role.[24]

However varied the reasons for remigration may have been, the returnees all shared a common denominator in that they were looked askance upon by Israel.[25] It was precisely this stance that prompted the first Israeli Consul in Munich, Chaim Yahil, to brand the Jews who had remained in Germany as a "source of danger for the entire Jewish people. (...) Those who are tempted by the fleshpots of Germany must not expect that Israel or the Jewish people should provide them with services for their convenience", Yahil declared. His opinion was shared by most emigrating German Jews, who "found it incomprehensible that Jews could feel comfortable in Germany after the horrors of the Nazi period".[26] Yahil further put the "blame" for the continued existence of a Jewish community on the German-Jewish "functionaries", though he believed that the tiny and aging postwar community was headed for natural "liquidation" and that it was only a matter of time until it would eventually dissolve itself. It was against this background that the Israeli Consulate in Munich, established for the paramount purpose of facilitating

---

[23] See Chaim Yahil, "Germany", in: Berenbaum/Skolnik (eds.) (2007), vol. 7, 537.
[24] See Brenner (1997), 138.
[25] See Brenner (1997), 139.
[26] Brenner (1997), 66.

emigration to Israel, closed its doors in 1953.[27] Similar reactions were observable in Israel in response to the sharp rise in Jewish immigration to Germany after 1989. The restrictions imposed by the Immigration Act of 2005 drew praise from Israeli authorities, who had long been concerned about the mass migration of Russian Jews to a country other than Israel. As the *Forward* reports, the Jewish Agency for Israel, a quasi-government agency responsible for immigration, had "aggressively" lobbied the German government for the new law. The Central Council of Jews in Germany, by contrast, was highly critical of the changes in immigration law and called the new rules "worthy of discussion in a few areas, and in others fully unacceptable".[28]

The most important point of the previous analysis is that Jews in Germany today still constitute a minuscule minority in an essentially non-Jewish country. In the same vein, a very large majority of Germans have never made personal contact (let alone have become acquainted) with Jews during their lifetimes. It is also doubtful whether German federalism and the concomitant dispersion of German Jewry across the country has helped facilitate the interaction and understanding between Jewish and non-Jewish Germans.[29] In addition, Jewish immigrants from the former Soviet Union, influenced by Russian culture and often alienated from Judaism, contend with the challenge of reconciling their German and Jewish identities. But the influx of Russian Jews has also brought about thriving immigrant communities – and it is in no small part because of their commitment to settle in Germany that Leo Baeck's gloomy prediction for the future of postwar German Jewry has further receded into the realm of the improbable. Instead of writing an epilogue to a once glorious past, Germany has witnessed a forceful comeback of Jewish life over the last two decades, an unforeseen development that has opened a new chapter in both Jewish and German history.

---

[27] See Brenner (2000), 37.
[28] Quoted in Nathaniel Popper, "Germany Is Moving To End Mass Migration of Jews From Russia", *Forward*, December 24, 2004.
[29] For a discussion of the image and self-perception of the Jewish minority in Germany, and its implications for the politics of the Central Council, see chapter 4.3 below.

2 State-Centered Politics in Germany: Partnership and Dependency

In order to understand the politics of the Central Council it is necessary to look at the political environment it operates within. In Germany, interest group politics follows a "state-centered" pattern, that is, both the institutional framework of the political system as well as other non-institutional factors enable the state to play an important role in interest group politics. The following analysis examines various factors associated with this model of state-centered politics and furthermore discusses their political implications for the Central Council. As we shall see, the relationship between the state and the Central Council can be characterized as an unequal partnership, in which the Central Council depends heavily on its powerful sponsor.[1]

2.1 Institutional Factors: Neo-Corporatism and *Einheitsgemeinden*

First, the German practice of interest group mediation encourages neo-corporatist arrangements between the state and interest groups. In such arrangements, there typically is a close functional relationship and a high degree of coordination between a particular group and the government. Moreover, each societal interest is normally represented by "peak associations", which hold a representational monopoly in a given policy domain, are densely and centrally organized, and often have a compulsory and nearly universal membership.

Most importantly, in neo-corporatist systems, interest groups are systematically involved in the process of making and implementing policies. Interest groups thus "regularly and legitimately work with the government agencies and, usually, with political party organizations as partners

---

[1] This approach is consistent with our initial distinction between a horizontal and a vertical level of analysis: in the case of the Central Council, both levels collapse into one.

in negotiating solutions to policy problems".[2] The Central Council of Jews in Germany, which acts as the representative of the interests of German Jewry, is such a peak association. It is recognized as the official interlocutor of the government and therefore maintains close relations with the state.[3]

The pattern of corporatism is also clearly visible in the way Jewish communities in Germany have traditionally been organized. Unlike in countries such as the United States, where various local congregations have existed independently from one another, the model of the *Einheitsgemeinde*, or "unified community", has been the norm in Germany. In *Einheitsgemeinden*, all the Jews of one locality are members of the same community; as there usually is only one synagogue in town, a certain amount of compromise among the community members is required. External unity notwithstanding, these communities have at the same time displayed "internal diversity in worldview and religion".[4] The German model of the *Einheitsgemeinde* was challenged in the late nineteenth century in several places by the Neo-Orthodox, who, unwilling to remain affiliated with their Reform brethren, founded separate communities. The separatist Orthodox communities henceforth became known as the *Austrittsgemeinden* – a term referring to the *Austrittsgesetz* ("Law on Withdrawal from the Jewish Community") adopted by Prussia in 1876 under which Jews were permitted to leave the Jewish community for religious reasons without losing their status as Jews. Prior to the adoption of the law, membership in the community had been compulsory.[5]

The composition of the German Jewish community today follows a reverse pattern: the majority of Jews are what is often termed "non-practicing Orthodox", which means they do not attend synagogue services on a regular basis but go to Orthodox synagogues during the High Holidays or family celebrations,[6] whereas the liberal communities have now assumed the role of the secessionists straying away from the religious mainstream. Although the liberal communities are not affiliated with the

---

[2] Almond/Powell/Dalton/Strøm (2010), 69.
[3] See section 2.2 below.
[4] Brenner (1997), 137.
[5] See Samuel Miklos Stern, "Germany", in: Berenbaum/Skolnik (eds.) (2007), vol. 7, 527.
[6] See Michael Brenner, "Germany", in: Berenbaum/Skolnik (eds.) (2007), vol. 7, 541.

Central Council, the latter is considered the spokesman of German Jewry as a whole due to its status as the umbrella of the country's *Einheitsgemeinden*.

Second, the relationship with the state is especially close because the Central Council is also a religious group.[7] It represents the religious interests of 108 Jewish communities and spans a wide range of religious denominations, from Orthodox to Conservative and from Reform to Progressive. Akin to the Catholic and Protestant churches in Germany, the Central Council benefits from a special legal status. It is recognized since 1963 as a corporation under public law (*Körperschaft des öffentlichen Rechts, K.d.ö.R.*), a status which grants an organization the right to levy taxes on its members, calculated as a percentage of the income tax, which is then collected by the state as part of the overall taxes. Thus, the churches and the Central Council are more than just private religious groups: they are institutionalized partners, endowed with special rights.[8]

Though the principle of religious neutrality is enshrined in Articles 4 and 140 of the German Basic Law, there is no strict separation of church and state in Germany. On the one hand, the framework governing the relationship between the churches and the state in Germany today is identical with the Weimar Constitution (WRV), which in theory ended the control of the churches by the state and, vice versa, the demands upon the state by the churches. But it was obvious when the new regulations were adopted in 1919 that the churches would not simply be reduced to the status of private associations. In this sense Article 137 I WRV, designed to emancipate both the state and the churches from one another, in good part signaled more a declaration of intent rather than a real

---

[7] The influence of the state in religious affairs is no exception. A similar arrangement can be found in the realm of media supervision and in public broadcasting services, where state intervention occurs through the involvement of political parties, see Reinhard Müller, "Staatsnah", *Frankfurter Allgemeine Zeitung*, January 6, 2011.

[8] There furthermore is a clear distinction between insiders and outsiders in religious affairs in Germany. Not all religious groups have equally institutionalized ties with the state. This is especially true for Muslim groups, who are not on an equal footing with the churches and the Central Council since they lack state recognition as corporations under public law. Muslims represent about 5 percent of German society.

change of policy.⁹ Also in the Federal Republic the term "neutrality" is interpreted in a fairly flexible manner that makes it possible to define the present situation as compatible with the stated purpose of the law. Consider the explanation given by Udo Di Fabio, a professor of constitutional law and a judge on Germany's Supreme Court. According to Di Fabio, "the Basic Law has justifiably been interpreted in a way that is very friendly towards religion" and does not preclude, but in fact stipulates, "benevolent neutrality" and "neutrality receptive to cooperation" on the part of the state towards religious groups and the churches.¹⁰

In short, institutional factors such as the practice of neo-corporatism and the official recognition of the Central Council as a corporation under public law involve a close and cooperative relationship between the Central Council and the state.

2.2   Non-Institutional Factors: Issues and Financial Support

While this model of partnership implies the idea of interdependent relations between the state and the Central Council, the umbrella's position is however more adequately described in terms of its dependency on the state. This dependency is owed to several non-institutional factors:

First, the issues the Central Council is primarily concerned with require special attention and support from the state as they cannot be dealt with by the Central Council alone or by working privately in coalition with other groups. For instance, the work of the Central Council is in large measure devoted to the fight against anti-Semitism and right-wing extremism; another key priority is the support for Israel and for Israel's right to exist. Both issues require a certain degree of backing by the German government if the policy work of the Central Council is to have a lasting impact in these areas.

Second, the Central Council and its affiliated Jewish communities are heavily dependent on public funds on the federal, state, and local levels. The Jewish population in Germany has grown almost fourfold since the fall of the Berlin Wall and, as we have previously seen, contin-

---

[9]   As Article 137 I WRV states, "There is no state church".
[10] The underlying assumption, Di Fabio says, is that churches do not constitute a "danger", but instead serve as the "pillars" of the free constitutional state, see Udo Di Fabio, "Gemeinschaftsschutz und Glaubensfreiheit", *Frankfurter Allgemeine Zeitung*, April 8, 2010.

ues to struggle with the task of integrating recent immigrants from the former Soviet Union into the existing communal structures. This has proved to be a particularly challenging task as many immigrants do not speak German as a native language and more than 60 percent of immigrant households rely on public welfare. State influence furthermore reaches into the heart of the Jewish community through the sponsorship of community leaders: for example, the chairmen of the Jewish communities in Berlin and Munich are civil servants and are eligible to receive a salary from the state.[11]

Financial aid for the Central Council was institutionalized in 2003, when former Chancellor Gerhard Schröder and then President of the Central Council Paul Spiegel signed the *Staatsvertrag*, or "National Agreement". Under the terms of this agreement, the Federal Republic provides the Central Council with 3 million euros annually, a sum that was increased to 5 million in 2008. Article 1 of the *Staatsvertrag* also spells out the desired nature of the relationship between the umbrella and the German government, which is supposed to be one of "continuous cooperation based on partnership in areas of common interest and in which the federal government holds the jurisdiction".[12] For this purpose, the federal government pledges to contribute to the maintenance and preservation of the German-Jewish cultural heritage as well as to the building of a Jewish community and to the tasks relating to integration and social work of the Central Council.[13] At the state level, a number of *Länder* agreements provide the local Jewish communities with additional financial support. In 2004, a total of 28 million euros was expended on the basis of such agreements.[14] In the words of the Israeli historian

---

[11] See Uri R. Kaufmann, "Vom Hinterhof zum Stadtplatz", *Aufbau*, September 2009, 12.

[12] Zentralrat der Juden in Deutschland, "Der Staatsvertrag im Wortlaut", http://www.zentralratdjuden.de/de/article/1.html, accessed January 27, 2011. Article 8 furthermore contains a "friendship clause", a provision under which both parties agree to resolve any future differences of opinion concerning the interpretation of the *Staatsvertrag* in an amicable way.

[13] Cooperative efforts however cannot exceed the financial framework set in the *Staatsvertrag*. Article 6 obligates the Central Council to not make further financial claims on the Federal Republic outside of the agreed payments.

[14] See Martin Dommer and Sebastian Knauer, "Viele Zimmer unterm Dach", *Der Spiegel*, 19/2004, 66.

Uri R. Kaufmann, "Such a closeness to the state would be inconceivable in all other European countries".[15]

Finally, the close ties with the state furthermore stem from the fact that, early in its history, the Central Council was stigmatized by Jewish public opinion abroad and faced enormous pressure to legitimize its existence as a Jewish organization in post-Holocaust Germany. As historian Jay Howard Geller writes, "German Jews were literally unwelcome or ostracized" at many international gatherings of Jewish organizations and "were simply not invited to these assemblies, or when they were, other delegates refrained from contact with [them]". On some occasions, they were invited but not granted voting rights.[16] Faced with isolation, the Central Council hence was pushed closer to the state in its struggle to win allies and recognition. Outright international hostility and a general lack of understanding appear to have continued for at least two decades after the Holocaust: tellingly, still in 1968, the Central Council felt the need to defiantly state in its annual report that it "insists on existing" ("*Wir bestehen darauf, zu bestehen*").[17]

The activities of the Central Council, as well as Jewish life in Germany more generally, are thus largely dependent on financial support from the state. As we will see, the dependency on the state poses numerous challenges for the Central Council as it shapes the umbrella's political style – in particular because the Central Council has at times been at odds with the German government on a number of sensitive issues.

---

[15] Uri R. Kaufmann, "Vom Hinterhof zum Stadtplatz", *Aufbau*, September 2009, 12.

[16] Jay Howard Geller, *Jews in Post-Holocaust Germany, 1945-1953* (Cambridge: Cambridge University Press, 2005), 62-63.

[17] This play on words is the motto displayed on the cover of the organization's annual report of 1968, see Zentralrat der Juden in Deutschland, *Jüdische Gemeinschaft in Deutschland. Ergänzungsbericht bei der Ratsversammlung des Zentralrats der Juden in Deutschland am 23. Mai 1968 von Generalsekretär Dr. H. G. van Dam* (Düsseldorf: Zentralrat, 1968), 14. The quote is taken from a speech by the ambassador of the State of Israel, Asher Ben-Natan.

3 An Imperfect "Special Relationship"

While the official narrative on German-Jewish relations in the period after the Holocaust continues to assert the importance of the "special relationship" between the state and German Jewry, political reality has at times been marred by uncomely imperfections. Official talk on the moral legacy of the past and the implied "special responsibility" towards the Jewish community at home and abroad has in fact often contradicted the actual behavior of political and government leaders. In the same vein, an analysis of German public opinion today shows that the notion of an alleged "special relationship" has far less support than is commonly believed.

3.1 Wiedergutmachung and Re-Nazification

Beginning at the latest with the Luxembourg Agreements of 1952 and up to the present day, German political leaders have not tired to emphasize their enduring special ties to the Jewish people. Adenauer declared *Wiedergutmachung* for the victims of Nazi persecution a "debt of honor" of the German people, a stance similarly repeated by his successor Ludwig Erhard. Social-democrat Willy Brandt is remembered for his spontaneous genuflection at a memorial for the victims of the Warsaw ghetto in 1970, a symbolic gesture that showcased Germany's commitment to assume responsibility for the past. Former Federal President Horst Köhler spelled out Germany's moral obligations more explicitly in 2005, declaring in a speech before the Israeli Knesset that "the Shoah is part of German identity".[1] Chancellor Angela Merkel has likewise stressed Germany's special responsibility for Israel and the Jewish people on numerous occasions, and has done so in accordance with the long-stand-

---

[1] Quoted in Jüdische Allgemeine, ""Die Schoa ist Teil der deutschen Identität"", February 10, 2005.

265

ing government doctrine that has been routinely documented in academia and the German press.²

Yet by the time the agreements on *Wiedergutmachung* were concluded – which themselves had serious shortcomings as they excluded certain categories of Holocaust survivors – the adverse climate in which the negotiations had taken place could not have eluded any critical observer of postwar German politics. It is no secret that the goal of reeducation and denazification of German society, as it was pursued by the allied forces, was a meek exercise soon overtaken by an unashamedly overt re-nazification, which reached even into the highest levels of government. The new elites recruited themselves from a familiar pool of applicants: "Many civil servants who had faithfully served the Nazi government acquired positions of influence under Konrad Adenauer. Most of them became CDU members", Jay Howard Geller writes in a study of the Federal Republic's formative years.³

Infamous is the example of Hans Globke, the most well-known servant of the Nazi state to achieve high standing in the West German government.⁴ Chosen as chief of staff in the federal chancellery by Konrad Adenauer, Globke, though not a member of the Nazi party, had gained notoriety for writing an interpretation of the discriminatory Nuremberg Laws as an official in the Nazi-era interior ministry.⁵ A frequently cited excuse for the practice of hiring former Nazis was that a lack of qualified candidates, owing to the human losses of the war, made it inevitable to also rely upon officials with compromised pasts. But even if this argument were convincing it would be hard to see why such officials could have remained in office for such sustained periods of time: Globke, for instance, served in the chancellor's office from 1953 to 1963, the year in

---

² See Lily Gardner Feldman, *The Special Relationship Between West Germany and Israel* (Boston: Allen & Unwin, 1984); Kerstin Münstermann, "Merkel betont "immerwährende Verantwortung"", *Der Tagesspiegel*, November 9, 2008; and Günther Nonnenmacher, "Besondere Beziehungen", *Frankfurter Allgemeine Zeitung*, January 31, 2010.

³ Geller (2005), 143. Also see Ralf Beste et al., "Welle der Wahrheiten", *Der Spiegel*, 1/2012, 32-39.

⁴ For further discussion, see Heinrich August Winkler, *Der lange Weg nach Westen II: Deutsche Geschichte 1933-1990* (Bonn: Bundeszentrale für politische Bildung, 2004), 176-177.

⁵ See Geller (2005), 143.

which Adenauer retired, and Hans Filbinger, a former Nazi judge, held office as the prime minister of Baden-Württemberg from 1966 to 1978. It was only after it was revealed that he had been a member of the Nazi party and had worked as a military judge that Filbinger was forced to resign.[6] A similar kind of personal continuity after the war could be found in the *Auswärtiges Amt*, the German foreign office. As a study commissioned by former Foreign Minister Joschka Fischer suggests, German diplomats willingly overlooked their pasts to protect each other after the war.[7] They also engaged in spinning a narrative presenting the ministry as a bastion of resistance to Hitler, whereas in reality its diplomats had been dedicated agents in the service of Nazi foreign policy. After the war and up to the 1960s, the ministry's legal team helped Germans wanted for war crimes to avoid arrest in neighboring countries, all of which has shattered the public image of this distinguished institution.[8] Against this background, and given the reemployment of officials with links to the Nazi past, it may not seem all that surprising that, despite agreements on *Wiedergutmachung*, formal diplomatic relations between West Germany and Israel were not established until 1965.

3.2 Bitburg Controversy and Börneplatz Scandal

If the early years of the Federal Republic were sometimes daunting, the 1980s in particular were full of challenges for the Central Council. Most memorable are the incidents associated with Bitburg and Börneplatz,

---

[6] The Filbinger affair drew renewed interest in 2007, when Baden-Württemberg's prime minister Günther Oettinger bestowed lavish praise on the late Filbinger, see Judy Dempsey, "Merkel faces revolt over premier's praise for Nazi-era judge", *The New York Times*, April 15, 2007.

[7] See Eckart Conze, Norbert Frei, Peter Hayes and Moshe Zimmermann, *Das Amt und die Vergangenheit. Deutsche Diplomaten im Dritten Reich und in der Bundesrepublik* (München: Karl Blessing Verlag, 2010). The study further shows how resistants such as former diplomat Fritz Kolbe, who had passed classified information to the U.S. secret service from 1943 onwards, were stigmatized as traitors and denied reinstatement to the ministry after the war.

[8] See The Economist, "Germany's Nazi diplomats. The machine's accomplices", October 30, 2010.

two locations which have come to symbolize Germany's struggle to come to terms with its past. Both examples stand in stark contrast to the idea of a so-called "special relationship" that the German government seeks to maintain with Jews in Germany and abroad.

The Bitburg affair, nearly coinciding with the fortieth anniversary of the end of the Second World War, was a critical test case for the Federal Republic and its commitment to special German-Jewish relations. At the center of the affair stood the joint visit of Chancellor Helmut Kohl and U.S. President Ronald Reagan to Kolmeshöhe military cemetery, near the town of Bitburg, a town close to a U.S. Air Force Base in Rhineland-Palatinate in proximity to the city of Trier, on May 5, 1985. The historical context, as well as the events running up to the visit and the ham-handed statements made by both government leaders in defense of their plans, stirred substantial controversy in the Jewish world and exposed Germany and the United States to a fair share of international criticism. Various reasons account for the sense of outrage and disappointment that was especially strong among Jewish groups and Holocaust survivors. Not only was the timing of the event, held at the same day of a joint visit to Bergen-Belsen, where President Reagan together with Chancellor Kohl had laid a wreath and made a public statement, perceived as offensive as it suggested a parallel between Nazi victims and their persecutors. Even more insulting seemed the fact that about two thousand German soldiers of the Third Reich, including 49 Waffen-SS veterans, some of whom had served in the Second Panzer Division "Das Reich" – the battle unit infamous for the massacre of over 600 villagers in Oradour-sur-Glane in France in 1942 – laid buried at Kolmeshöhe cemetery.[9]

To make matters worse, the visit to Bitburg had been preceded by a long period of protocolary preparation and bilateral talks. Neither the warnings of public intellectuals such as Holocaust survivor and Nobel laureate Elie Wiesel nor the reservations of the U.S. Holocaust Council and the criticism of various Jewish organizations were suffice to make President Reagan and Chancellor Kohl reconsider the trip. The U.S. Congress had also felt compelled to take action and went on record against Bitburg: in April 1985, yet to no avail, 53 senators wrote in peti-

---

[9] For an overview of events, see Geoffrey H. Hartman (ed.), *Bitburg in Moral and Political Perspective* (Bloomington: Indiana University Press, 1986), xiii-xvi.

tion to President Reagan that "a visit to Bitburg by an American President would be most unfortunate" and "strongly urge[d]" that he cancel the visit. A few days later, the U.S. Senate passed a resolution endorsed by 85 senators that the president reassess his planned itinerary, while the U.S. House of Representatives passed a resolution by a margin of 390 to 26 demanding that Reagan "reconsider the inclusion of the Bitburg cemetery" in his trip. Helmut Kohl however insisted that the joint appearance be held, since Reagan had already given his word to attend the cemetery on earlier assurances from German officials that this decision would not involve any embarrassments for the United States. Prior to the visit, Chancellor Kohl in a debate in the Bundestag thanked President Reagan for his seemingly "noble gesture": "Reconciliation is when we are capable of grieving over people without caring what nationality they are", the chancellor, who is also a trained historian, said.[10] Amid protest demonstrations in both Bitburg and Bergen-Belsen, Chancellor Kohl and President Reagan however went on to complete their visit as scheduled.

What Bitburg first and foremost symbolizes is the act of forced reconciliation between Jews and Germans. In their analysis of the events in question, scholars have viewed the Bitburg visit as the attempt of the German government to bring about a return to the quiet years of the postwar Federal Republic. Indeed, the visit to Bitburg was followed by a speech by Federal President Richard von Weizsäcker before the Bundestag, marking the fortieth anniversary of the end of World War II, in which he reasserted Germany's responsibility to remember its past. For Jürgen Habermas, the Bitburg visit must be interpreted within this context: it was Chancellor Kohl who "envisaged May 8 as the date on which the long overdue return to the normality of the 1950s could be staged in a highly symbolic fashion".[11] It also is worth noting that Bitburg recalled memories of the ceremony of reconciliation at the French-German military cemetery on the Verdun battlefield, where Chancellor Kohl and French President François Mitterand had held hands in September 1984.

---

[10] Quoted in Hartman (1986) (ed.), xv. The interpretation of the German government was similarly defended by Ronald Reagan, who argued that "there is nothing wrong with visiting that cemetery where those young men are victims of Nazism also. (...) They were victims, just as surely as the victims in the concentration camps", ibid., xiv.

[11] Jürgen Habermas, "Defusing the Past: A Politico-Cultural Tract", in: Hartman (ed.) (1986), 43.

According to Holocaust scholar Raul Hilberg, Verdun and Bitburg both served the symbolic and political purpose of helping the Kohl government "to lead the German people out of the desert".[12]

Two years later, in 1987, the Börneplatz controversy politicized large parts of German society. It was the discovery of remnants of the medieval Jewish ghetto of Frankfurt, including 19 buildings and two ritual baths (or *mikva'ot*), in the course of excavation works for an administrative building at Börneplatz that sparked a public debate on how to deal with the German-Jewish cultural heritage. The debate also carried particular significance due to the history of Börneplatz itself. Named for Ludwig Börne (1786-1837), born Löw Baruch in the Jewish ghetto of Frankfurt and a noted literary figure of the Enlightenment of whom today reminds a major German literary prize, Börneplatz was once the site of an imposing synagogue. The synagogue at Börneplatz, inaugurated in the late nineteenth century and the motif of a well-known 1919 painting by Max Beckmann, was destroyed by the Nazis during the November pogroms in 1938. When remnants of the Jewish ghetto were discovered in this area in spring 1987, an acrimonious public discussion on how to proceed ensued. The Jewish community and the churches as well as academic and cultural institutions and citizens' action groups demanded that the remnants be preserved, while the municipality of Frankfurt, in accordance with previously agreed plans, insisted on the construction of a service center for the local utility services on the same site. The controversy ended in a forced compromise after the police had cleared the excavation area and the historic remains were removed; the city agreed to preserve a small part of the discoveries in the basement of the administrative building, which was supposed to be transformed into a smaller branch of the Jewish Museum.[13] In so doing, the city literally disposed of the local Jewish history by carrying out its initial construction plans. "What remains? The service center for the utilities! Of Börneplatz and the Börneplatz conflict nothing substantial will outlive the

---

[12] Raul Hilberg, "Bitburg as Symbol", in: Hartman (ed.) (1986), 16.
[13] For a detailed account of the events, see Museum Judengasse, *Stationen des Vergessens. Der Börneplatz-Konflikt* (Frankfurt am Main: Museum Judengasse, 1992).

times", Salomon Korn, now vice-president of the Central Council of Jews in Germany, wrote in a recollection of the events.[14]

Also unfortunate was the conflict's setting in Frankfurt, a major center of Jewish life in West Germany that only recently had been shaken by the controversy over Rainer Werner Fassbinder's play *Der Müll, die Stadt und der Tod* ("The Garbage, the City and Death"). The play was widely perceived as anti-Semitic, and its scheduled premiere in 1985 was abruptly cancelled after protesters had occupied the stage of the theater.

All these events occurred during a time when Germany's past increasingly came to be seen as a burden from which it was better to escape than face it. Another illustration of this trend is the case of Anna Rosmus, a native of the Bavarian town of Passau, who received death threats when she began to dig into her hometown's Nazi past as a high school student in 1980. Rosmus's story, based on her true experience, later gained international attention with the Academy Award-nominated 1990 film "The Nasty Girl", which cast further doubt on the country's sincerity in assuming responsibility for its Nazi past.[15]

3.3 Public Opinion and the "Special Relationship"

Every special relationship of course has its imperfections. What is however revealing about the shortcomings discussed above is that they were not simply owed to thoughtless or blundering political leaders; in fact, the latter's oft-criticized decisions frequently enjoyed considerable support with the German public. As noted earlier, the task of *Wiedergutmachung*, for instance, was not a particularly popular theme in the 1950s; in fact, up to the present, Jewish claims for reparations have been met with considerable scepticism among the German population. Still in 2003, an AJC study found, 54 percent of West Germans and 45 percent of East Germans "totally" or "rather" held the opinion that "the Jews today instrumentalize the memory of the Holocaust for their personal

---

[14] Salomon Korn, "Spuren des Konflikts", in: Museum Judengasse, *Stationen des Vergessens. Der Börneplatz-Konflikt* (Frankfurt am Main: Museum Judengasse, 1992), 99.

[15] See Caroline Wiedmer, *The Claims of Memory. Representations of the Holocaust in Contemporary Germany and France* (Ithaca: Cornell University Press, 1999), 87-103.

gain". A survey conducted by ADL in 2004 further revealed that a total of 56 percent of Germans said "the Jews still talk too much about what happened to them in the Holocaust".[16] If the German government has at times been reluctant to increase the level of compensation provided, it has arguably done so in accordance with large sections of German public opinion.

In its handling of the Bitburg visit in 1985 the German government, too, acted in a way consistent with popular sentiment: polls have shown that 75 percent of the German public indeed favored the visit. Moreover, the Bundestag, whose members are elected directly by and thus are immediately accountable to the German people, by a margin of 398 to 24 overwhelmingly voted against a cancellation of the planned stop at Bitburg.[17] Current surveys further indicate that the notion of a special relationship between Jews and Germans[18] – exemplified in the following by a brief analysis of contemporary German public opinion toward Israel – is increasingly falling out of favor with sizable parts of German society. Considering that Israel is a Jewish state, the perception of Israel in Germany reveals much about the alleged special dimension in German-Jewish relations.

The growing discrepancy between government support for Israel on the one hand and its backing in German public opinion on the other has been borne out in recent research on the topic. Due to its historic responsibility for Israel, the Federal Republic has been a guarantor of diplomatic and military support for Israel, even if this at times meant taking positions "diametrically opposed (...) to German public opinion", a study finds.[19] In addition, the German population is about evenly split in its attitudes about the country's duties towards Israel. According to a 2007 survey conducted by the Bertelsmann Foundation, 49 percent of Germans believe the German people "bear a special responsibility towards

---

[16] See Werner Bergmann, "Die Haltung der deutschen Bevölkerung zur Wiedergutmachung", in: Brozik/Matschke (eds.) (2004), 20, 24.
[17] See Hilberg (1986), 20, and Hartman (1986) (ed.), xv, respectively.
[18] The shorthand terms "Jews" and "Germans" refer to non-Jewish Germans and to Jews of German or other background. Of course, the terms do not suggest a dichotomy between "Jews" and "Germans", nor do they imply that "Jews" cannot be "Germans" and vice versa.
[19] Helene Bartos, *Israeli-German Relations in the Years 2000-2006: A Special Relationship Revisited*, MPhil thesis, University of Oxford, 2007, 2.

the Jewish people", while 47 percent, especially the younger generation of Germans under age 30, disagree with this statement.[20] Similar results were found in a poll conducted by Forsa in 2008, according to which 48 percent of those surveyed said they had "no special responsibility towards the Jews today", ahead of 47 percent who said they felt such a responsibility.[21]

What is more, the Bertelsmann survey found that for almost four out of five Germans (78 percent) the State of Israel is "a state like any other state".[22] Scarce popular support notwithstanding, German politicians have rarely expressed contrary opinions challenging the legitimacy of the privileged ties between Germany and Israel. One exception is former Chancellor Helmut Schmidt, who has raised doubts about a special German responsibility for the security of Israel, on the argument that this would imply "some kind of rigid obligation to solidarity". In a conversation for a memoir with the German-born American historian Fritz Stern, Schmidt proclaimed that, let alone any special bond uniting both countries, "Germany has no responsibility for Israel".[23]

How long, then, will Germany's special relationship with Israel – a long-standing tenet of government policy and, beyond pure rhetoric, often evidenced in government action – last in its current form? Though it is always hard to predict future developments, various factors suggest a perceptible reinterpretation, if not reversal, of hitherto accepted standards in terms of German-Israeli and German-Jewish relations. At the latest with the Möllemann affair,[24] public criticism of Israel by German

---

[20] See Bertelsmann Stiftung, *Germans and Jews – United by their past, divided by their present?* (Gütersloh: Bertelsmann Stiftung, 2007), 20.
[21] See Statista, "Verantwortung Deutscher gegenüber Juden", http://de.statista.com/statistik/daten/studie/537/umfrage/verantwortung-deutscher-gegenueber-juden/, accessed February 7, 2011.
[22] See Bertelsmann Stiftung, *Germans and Jews – United by their past, divided by their present?* (Gütersloh: Bertelsmann Stiftung, 2007), 24.
[23] Helmut Schmidt and Fritz Stern, *Unser Jahrhundert. Ein Gespräch* (München: Verlag C.H. Beck, 2010), 50.
[24] In the 2002 German election campaign the deputy leader of the FDP, Jürgen Möllemann, sharply criticized Israel and accused Prime Minister Ariel Sharon as well as Michel Friedman, then vice-president of the Central Council, of provoking anti-Semitism through their behavior. See Steven Erlanger,

officials is seen less frequently as a taboo and as a morally reprehensible act given Germany's history. The controversy over the Israeli intervention to violently stop the "Freedom flotilla" headed for the Gaza shores in May 2010 further elucidates the point. Almost unnoticed by public opinion, the German Bundestag shortly after the incident passed a unanimous resolution on the Middle East conflict condemning Israel for its action. In this rare overarching partisan consensus, based on a joint motion by the CDU/CSU, SPD, FDP and the Greens, the Bundestag noted there were "strong indications" that the use of force in Israel's intervention to intercept the flotilla "violated the principle of proportionality [in public international law]". The resolution, written in an unusually patronizing tone, also called the blockade of the Gaza strip "counterproductive" as it "does not serve Israel's political and security interests".[25] The statements are all the more significant as during the run-up to the 2008 Olympic Games in Beijing, for example, a consensus in the Bundestag on how China was supposed to deal with the Tibetan question remained elusive even though Germany has far less privileged relations with China than with Israel. Philipp Mißfelder, a member of the CDU/CSU parliamentary fraction, offered a pertinent explanation: "In particular against the background of our historic responsibility and our history, which today is not coined by guilt but by great responsibility, we have to focus on reaching the goals of peace together. In this regard I think our resolution is very helpful". On behalf of the SPD parliamentary fraction, Rolf Mützenich declared that it was precisely "because of our special relationship" that Germany can speak out against the blockade of the Gaza strip, in the hopes that this "problem area is finally recognized by the political actors in Israel". Not since the rule of Emperor Wilhelm II, publicist Henryk M. Broder caustically observed, has Germany achieved a similar amount of "national unity" around one singular political issue.[26]

"Specter of High-Level Anti-Semitism Taints German Campaign", *The New York Times*, May 29, 2002.

[25] Deutscher Bundestag, "Antrag der Fraktionen CDU/CSU, SPD, FDP und BÜNDNIS 90/DIE GRÜNEN", Drucksache 17/2328 (Berlin: Deutscher Bundestag, 2010), 1, 2.

[26] Mißfelder and Mützenich quoted in Henryk M. Broder, "Einigkeit und Recht und Gaza", *Spiegel Online*, July 4, 2010.

Second, generational and demographic shifts in Germany militate against sustained levels of public sympathy for Israel and against a special German-Jewish relationship in general. Approximately 20 percent of Germans today have an immigrant background, and many non-Jewish immigrants, especially Muslims, do not necessarily regard the Holocaust as part of their national identity; some immigrants moreover hail from countries where anti-Jewish sentiment is habitually fueled or at least tolerated by the respective governments. Consider for example the incident that occurred in the German city of Duisburg during the Gaza War in January 2009. In the course of a protest rally against the war, attended by about 10,000 people and organized by the Islamist group Milli Görüs, the police forcibly entered the apartment of a student who had attached an Israeli flag to the window of his apartment in support of Israel and, in a bid to forestall an escalation of violence among the irate crowd that had gathered in front of the building, simply went on to remove the flag. The Duisburg police initially defended their actions, to which the Central Council of Jews in Germany responded with sharp criticism, but later offered an apology for the officers' behavior. The symbolical damage was however hard to overlook.[27]

In light of the above shortcomings, it would of course be wildly exaggerated to ratify the sarcastic remark made two decades ago by the Israeli psychoanalyst Zvi Rex, who famously said that "[t]he Germans will never forgive the Jews for Auschwitz".[28] Still, and in the context of the following analysis of the political style of the Central Council of Jews in Germany, the previous paragraphs stand as a powerful reminder that the oft-invoked special relationship between Jews and Germans, though by and large empirically valid, has also been contradicted by substantial imperfections.

---

[27] See Yassin Musharbash, "Police Remove Israeli Flag during Islamist Protest March", *Spiegel Online*, January 31, 2009.
[28] Quoted in Benjamin Weinthal, "The hallmark of anti-Semitism", *Haaretz*, September 19, 2008.

4 The Political Style of the Central Council of Jews in Germany

This being said, the following chapters will address two key questions: How does the structural dependency on the state on the one hand, and the need for criticalness toward state policy on the other, influence the politics of the Central Council? How do these constraints translate politically and how do they shape the political style and the self-perception of the Central Council? Especially given that a monograph about the umbrella is still lacking, archival evidence and further primary sources will be evaluated in detail in order to answer these questions.

The key findings of the following section are based on a thorough analysis of the annual reports of the Central Council, drafted by its secretary general Hendrik George van Dam and published from 1960 to 1971. Before and after that period all annual reports were drawn up internally and were not made available to the public. Because the reports in question are pertinent to a specific historical period, some of the conclusions presented here may not claim to be fully representative of the Central Council's political style today. However, as interest group research has shown, organizations usually adopt a specific political style early in their histories;[1] for this reason, the insight afforded by earlier documents is particularly valuable for understanding the contemporary politics of the Central Council. The following section also benefits considerably from a 2009 author interview with then President of the Central Council Charlotte Knobloch, in which some of the most pertinent archival material could be reviewed and its relevance discussed from a contemporary perspective. For a better understanding of the material at hand, a preliminary overview of the history and internal structure of the Central Council may first be in order.

---

[1] See Thomas L. Gais and Jack L. Walker, "Pathways to influence in American Politics", in: Jack L. Walker (ed.), *Mobilizing Interest Groups in America: Patrons, Professions, and Social Movements* (Ann Arbor: University of Michigan Press, 1991), 119.

4.1 Founding History and Internal Structure

The Central Council of Jews in Germany (*Zentralrat der Juden in Deutschland*), the political and religious umbrella organization representing the country's Jewish communities, was founded in Frankfurt am Main on July 19, 1950 by a constituent assembly including Jewish delegates from all four zones of occupation. Among the organization's most important founding fathers were three Auschwitz survivors: Norbert Wollheim, who represented the interests of Jews in the British zone of occupation; Philipp Auerbach, the leading Jewish figure in the American zone; and Heinz Galinski, the chairman of the Jewish community of Berlin.[2] The founding meeting took place in January 1951.[3] Over the course of its history, the Central Council has repeatedly shifted headquarters and has also been based in Düsseldorf and in Bonn. Since April 1999 the organization has relocated its operations to Berlin, where it is domiciled at the Leo Baeck House in Tucholskystraße, formerly home to the Academy for the Sciences of Judaism, in the city's central Mitte district.[4]

The rebuilding of Jewish community life in Germany, driven by the influx of survivors from all parts of Eastern Europe, had developed at a rapid pace immediately after the war: no less than 51 Jewish communities had been re-established as early as in 1945, and another 16 were founded only one year later.[5] By 1948, more than 100 Jewish communities – almost the same number that exists today – were listed in Germany.[6] At the same time, the path leading to a single representative body of German Jewry had been paved with obstacles. As of March 1950, and to the frustration of the German government, the Jews in Germany still had no single organization.[7] While the postwar German Jewish community displayed a desire for unity, it was also riven with internal factions that made a common representation hard to achieve. The German Jews had reorganized themselves quickly after the war in state

---

[2] See Brenner (2007), 125.
[3] See Brenner (1997), 77.
[4] See Zentralrat der Juden in Deutschland, "History", http://www.zentralratjuden.de/en/topic/130.html, accessed January 16, 2011.
[5] See Brenner (2000), 37.
[6] See Brenner (1997), 45.
[7] See Geller (2005), 82.

and regional associations, but were often loath to merge with the displaced persons' communities made up of Jews from Eastern Europe, who regarded their sojourn in Germany merely as a temporary stopover prior to emigration.[8] In addition, the idea of organizing the Jewish communities within a centralized and voluntary coordinating body lacked historical precedent. Throughout the Weimar Republic and earlier, there had been a myriad of Jewish organizations with competing ideological visions and distinct constituencies in Germany, ranging from the *Centralverein deutscher Staatsbürger jüdischen Glaubens* ("Central Association of German Citizens of the Jewish Faith") to the *Verein zur Abwehr des Antisemitismus* ("Association for the Defense Against Anti-Semitism") or to the *Verband nationaldeutscher Juden* ("Union of Jews of German Nationality") and the *Zionistische Vereinigung für Deutschland* ("Zionist Organization of Germany"), to name but a few of the most prominent examples. The election of the Nazi government quickly brought about an end to the pluralism hitherto characteristic of German-Jewish political life and forced the creation of the *Reichsvertretung der deutschen Juden* ("Reich Representation of German Jews"), headed by Rabbi Leo Baeck, in September 1933. In line with the anti-Semitic government policy and the Nuremberg racial laws, the *Reichsvertretung* was renamed the *Reichsvereinigung der Juden in Deutschland* ("Reich Association of Jews in Germany") in 1939, a step which made Jews' status as a disenfranchised and persecuted minority even more obvious.[9] After the war, the newly founded Central Council of Jews in Germany deliberately rejected the self-identification as "German Jews" that its predecessors had chosen in the pre-Nazi era. It seemed an inappropriate designation given the experience of exclusion and the strong presence of Jewish DPs in postwar Germany.[10]

The difficulties associated with the establishment of a single voice speaking for all the Jews in Germany were also perceptible in the quarrel over the seat of the umbrella. Foreign Jewish organizations such as the American Jewish Joint Distribution Committee and the Jewish

---

[8] See Geller (2005), 88.
[9] See Jacob S. Levinger and Michael Berenbaum, "Germany", in: Berenbaum/Skolnik (eds.) (2007), vol. 7, 535.
[10] See Michael Brenner, "Zentralrat der Juden in Deutschland", in: Berenbaum/Skolnik (eds.) (2007), vol. 21, 510.

Agency as well as the government of Israel – all of which viewed the rebirth of Jewish life in Germany with suspicion or flatly disapproved of it – wanted the Central Council to set up its base in Munich, then home to the country's largest Jewish population and to a large number of displaced persons. This view obviously implied a role for the Central Council not so much as an interest group representing German Jewry as to serve as an instrument of Jewish emigration. Others by contrast favored Bonn as headquarters, highlighting the political nature of the organization and the importance of staying within the bounds of government circles. Frankfurt was finally chosen as the first seat of the Central Council, though the organization remained there only for a short time – its offices were moved to Düsseldorf, a major center of Jewish life and within reasonable proximity to the country's provisional capital, in the early 1950s.[11]

The decision to move operations near Bonn was indeed consistent with the Central Council's initial outlook to act as a "political pressure group", as Jay Howard Geller puts it. Needless to say, issues such as reparations for Holocaust survivors and the legal battles over property restitution were still looming large on the domestic political agenda by the time of the umbrella's founding. The Central Council, therefore, had been intensely involved in political affairs from its earliest days: by the mid-1950s, it eventually became a multi-issue organization and "chang[ed] its orientation from a mere lobbying and legal organization to one more concerned with cultural and social work".[12] The conclusion of the Luxembourg Agreements and the subsequently enacted compensation programs for victims of Nazi persecution provided temporary relief for Holocaust survivors and allowed for greater attention to the task of reconstructing Jewish communal and religious life in Germany.[13]

Meanwhile, Jews in the German Democratic Republic were also represented in the Central Council since the latter aspired to speak for all the Jews in Germany. The existence of the Jewish community in East Germany was however repeatedly threatened, prompting many East German Jews to flee to the West. For the hostile stance of the East Ger-

---

[11] See Geller (2005), 206, 216.
[12] Geller (2005), 257, 284-285, respectively.
[13] The task of *Wiedergutmachung* was henceforth gradually taken over by the Claims Conference.

man government meant not only that Jewish efforts to obtain reparations were condemned to futility; it also manifested itself in a wave of purges and arrests in 1953, in accordance with a larger pattern of anti-Semitic agitation in Eastern Europe, where show trials such as the Slánský trial of 1952 in Czechoslovakia had been expressly targeted at Jewish communists. East German Jews held official membership in the Central Council until 1963, when contacts between both groups became increasingly difficult to sustain in the tense climate of the East-West conflict.[14] The politics and history of East German Jewry – owing to the community's negligible numerical weight, but also for reasons of economy – shall not be discussed here in further detail. At the time of German unification, there were less than 500 Jews living in the former GDR, according to official statistical records; they were organized within five Jewish associations, which all became members of the Central Council.[15]

Ever since its founding, the Central Council of Jews in Germany has pursued its mission "to promote and foster religious and cultural activities within local Jewish communities and to provide advocacy for the common political interests of the Jewish community as a whole". Among the organization's foremost tasks today is to assist Jewish immigrants from the former Soviet Union to integrate into German society. Another vital priority of its work concerns the rebuilding of Jewish community life in East Germany. With regard to domestic politics the Central Council strives to play "an active role in German political and public life" with a view to promoting understanding between Jews and non-Jews. It furthermore extends "particular solidarity to Israel", not least because the Jewish state has become the home of many Holocaust survivors.[16]

The Central Council has also founded, and oversees, a number of organizations and institutions that support its work at the supraregional level. These include the aforementioned *Zentralwohlfahrtsstelle* (ZWST), responsible for social work; the Conference of Rabbis, comprising the conferences of Orthodox (ORD) and non-Orthodox rabbis

---

[14] See Geller (2005), 179, 160-184.
[15] See Zentralrat der Juden in Deutschland, "Foundation", http://www.zentralratdjuden.de/en/topic/133.html, accessed January 17, 2011.
[16] Zentralrat der Juden in Deutschland, "Functions", http://www.zentralratdjuden.de/en/topic/138.html, accessed January 17, 2011.

(ARK); the Central Archives for Research on the History of the Jews in Germany, based in Heidelberg; the College of Jewish Studies in Heidelberg, a private university dedicated to educating leadership personnel for Jewish organizations and to training rabbis for the Jewish communities in Germany; the *Bund jüdischer Frauen in Deutschland*, a women's association; the student organization *Bundesverband jüdischer Studenten*; and *MAKKABI Deutschland e.V.*, a sports' association. It moreover serves as the publisher for the *Jüdische Allgemeine*, a weekly Jewish newspaper previously known under the name of *Allgemeine jüdische Wochenzeitung*.[17] It also initiated the Leo Baeck Award in 1957, a distinction awarded annually to individuals "who have played an outstanding role in defending the Jewish community and who have derived lessons for the future from Germany's terrible Nazi history".[18]

At the international level, the Central Council has established close ties to the Jewish communities in Europe and around the world and works in partnership with various major international Jewish organizations. It is a full and active member, entitled to a seat and a vote, on the executive bodies of the World Jewish Congress, the European Jewish Congress, the World Jewish Restitution Organization, and the Conference on Jewish Material Claims Against Germany.[19]

The umbrella's governing and decision-making structure follows democratic principles and is predicated on a system of checks and balances involving three interdependent bodies: the Council Assembly, the Directorate, and the Presidium. The Council Assembly, representing the communities, and the Directorate, representing the regional associations and larger communities, perform by and large the functions commonly attributed to the legislative branch, whereas the Presidium, together with the secretary general, acts as the umbrella's executive.

First, the Council Assembly has the powers to issue policy guidelines, adopt the budget, and oversee the work of the executive. It is the umbrella's supreme decision-making body and "determines any fundamental issues concerning the Jewish community". Whether or not the af-

---

[17] See Zentralrat der Juden in Deutschland, "Functions", http://www.zentralratdjuden.de/en/topic/138.html, accessed February 17, 2011.

[18] Zentralrat der Juden in Deutschland, "Leo Baeck Award", http://www.zentralratdjuden.de/en/topic/151.html, accessed February 17, 2011.

[19] See Zentralrat der Juden in Deutschland, "Organization", http://www.zentralratdjuden.de/en/topic/143.html, accessed February 17, 2011.

filiated communities have voting powers however depends on their size: all the regional associations as well as the larger communities – those of Berlin, Frankfurt, Munich, and Cologne – have seats in the Assembly and are entitled to one delegate for every 1,000 community members. Meetings are held at least once a year. The Assembly also has a role in appointing key leadership positions, as it elects three people from its ranks to serve on the Presidium for a period of four years.

Second, the Directorate comprises members appointed by the affiliated organizations and regional associations. It is endowed with the task of overseeing the Presidium and elects the secretary general, who runs the daily operations of the Central Council. Each regional association is represented in the Directorate through one delegate for every (full or part) 5,000 members within its constituency. As a means of facilitating the oversight of the executive, six members of the Directorate are chosen to serve on the Presidium for a period of four years.

Finally, the Presidium has the responsibility for conducting the business of the Central Council. It counts a total of nine members within its ranks and elects its own board, consisting of the president and two vice-presidents, who represent the Central Council to the larger public. The secretary general, elected by the Directorate for a period of five years, is in charge of managing the day-to-day affairs and complements the work of the Presidium.[20]

Now that this background has been provided we can turn to the archival material and to the characteristics of the Central Council's political style in particular.

4.2 Modesty and Self-Restraint

An examination of the archival record suggests there is a strong sense of modesty and self-restraint exhibited on the part of the Central Council. Rather than seeking the spotlight of public attention, the umbrella subscribes to a much more cautious principle: to "keep calm (...) in a country without Jews". [21] This unusual degree of political restraint is also ev-

---

[20] See Zentralrat der Juden in Deutschland, "Organization", http://www.zentral ratdjuden.de/en/topic/143.html, accessed February 17, 2011.
[21] Zentralrat der Juden in Deutschland, *10 Jahre Zentralrat der Juden in Deutschland. Jahresbericht 1960* (Düsseldorf: Zentralrat, 1960), 17.

idenced in the self-designation of the Central Council, which considers itself a "voice of reason", "moderate in tone", and guided by "calm objectivity".[22] In the same vein, the organization goes so far as to call for maintaining a "sense of proportion", and concludes that it must "assess [its] own possibilities realistically".[23]

The choice of the umbrella's initial headquarters – Frankfurt, then Düsseldorf, but not Bonn – was already indicative of a certain reluctance to get directly involved in German politics. Faced with growing isolation within the international Jewish community, the Central Council not only drew closer to the German government for a cooperative partnership, but also felt the compulsion to justify its very existence as a Jewish organization in Germany. "The Jewish community in the Federal Republic will have to muster the courage to affirm its own existence", we read in the organization's annual report of 1964/65.[24] To be or not to be – this indeed was the paramount question that critically preoccupied the Central Council, even in the subsequent years. The preface to the annual report of 1966/67 for instance starts with an acknowledgment of the "willingness to exist of the Jewish community in Germany", before spelling out the role attributed to the Central Council: "Surely the umbrella organization of the Jewish communities is called upon to underscore their willingness to exist and to vouch for its realization. (...) The self-image of the Jewish community in Germany is (...) a serious political factor that not only is related to the physical existence of this group, but one that is its very foundation".[25] At the same time, the Central Council addresses the question of whether it should have the impetus to strive for being more than a temporary phenomenon of the postwar era. The answer to

---

[22] Zentralrat der Juden in Deutschland, *10 Jahre Zentralrat der Juden in Deutschland. Jahresbericht 1960* (Düsseldorf: Zentralrat, 1960), 18. In original: *"Stimme der Vernunft"*, *"maßvolle Töne"*, and *"ruhige Sachlichkeit"*.

[23] Zentralrat der Juden in Deutschland, *10 Jahre Zentralrat der Juden in Deutschland. Jahresbericht 1960* (Düsseldorf: Zentralrat, 1960), 32. Note: "sense of proportion" in English and in quotation marks in original.

[24] Zentralrat der Juden in Deutschland, *Die jüdische Gemeinschaft in Deutschland. Jahresbericht des Generalsekretärs Dr. H. G. van Dam für 1964/65* (Düsseldorf: Zentralrat, 1965), 37.

[25] Zentralrat der Juden in Deutschland, *Jüdische Gemeinschaft in Deutschland. Jahresbericht 1966/67 von Generalsekretär Dr. H. G. van Dam* (Düsseldorf: Zentralrat, 1967), 5.

this rather rhetorical question is straightforward: "We have no doubt, and it has always been the policy of the Central Council, to affirm this existence and to give room to the view that the Jews of Germany, whether they were born in this country or came as immigrants, have no morally or politically compelling reason to finish the job of persecution through self-liquidation", secretary general Hendrik George van Dam writes. Van Dam further notes that "[t]he construction of a Germany forbidden to Jews would be no act of normalization, but one of anormalization", indeed "the erection of an invisible wall".[26] As mentioned before, the Central Council made this conviction the motto of its annual report of 1968, where on the front cover is defiantly marked "We insist on existing". Mired in a struggle to defend its bare existence, the political ambitions of the Central Council were accordingly limited to a fairly modest political appearance.

One insightful example of this self-imposed modesty is the umbrella's dealing with the issue of compensation for Holocaust survivors. It is striking to observe that the Central Council – already in its first annual report, but also later – candidly adopts the official term used by the German government, *Wiedergutmachung*, a term it moreover uses without quotation marks. This is particularly significant because the term has been highly controversial since its introduction and is not used by any of the other parties that are involved in the negotiating process. Up to the present day, the Conference on Jewish Material Claims Against Germany has refrained from borrowing this morally charged German term, which it regards as inappropriate. Instead of *Wiedergutmachung*, it seeks "a small measure of justice".[27] The U.S. Department of State, which maintains an Office of the Special Envoy for Holocaust Issues, has taken a similar stance and speaks of "compensation" and "restitution", both rather technical and legalistic terms.[28] Finally, the Hebrew translation of *Wiedergutmachung* does not convey a specifically moral dimension either as the terms used in Israel, *shilumim* ("payments") and *pitzuim* ("severance pays"), merely designate financial transactions. Considered

---

[26] Zentralrat der Juden in Deutschland, *Jüdische Gemeinschaft in Deutschland. Jahresbericht 1966/67 von Generalsekretär Dr. H. G. van Dam* (Düsseldorf: Zentralrat, 1967), 6.
[27] As previously noted, see Kagan (2009 Interview) and section 5.2.3 ("Negotiations with the German Government") in the second part of this dissertation.
[28] Becker (2009 Interview).

against this background it may seem fairly surprising how readily the Central Council goes on in its first annual report to "recognize the accomplishments of the public service officials without whom it would be impossible to carry through the realization of such an ingrate [sic] and difficult task as is Wiedergutmachung [sic]".[29] It is difficult to imagine a statement that better represents the official position of the German government.

On the other hand, the Central Council did not relinquish its commitment to speak out forcefully against resurgent anti-Semitism and rightwing extremism in the Federal Republic. In so doing it has been faithful to the role it always aspired to play in German politics – one that neither affords the organization with preferential treatment, nor one that degrades it to secondary status. "No discrimination and no granting of privileges" is the organization's long-standing motto reiterated in the annual report of 1970/71.[30] Likewise, the Central Council made it clear in the early decades of its history that it would not run the risk of being scapegoated for arrogating the legal duties incumbent on the state: "The Central Council does not serve as a watchman over the sell-out of the constitution and over sedition [*"Volksverhetzung"*]", the umbrella states, affirming its unwillingness "to assume the tasks of the prosecution and to treat issues which claim to be of public interest and which are of import to the reputation of the Federal Republic as a Jewish private affair".[31]

Today, by contrast, the Central Council is known for its far more publicly assertive and outspoken political style. This shift of attitudes was not only the result of a changing political culture in Germany itself; as we shall see later, it was also owed to the skilled leadership of former

---

[29] Zentralrat der Juden in Deutschland, *10 Jahre Zentralrat der Juden in Deutschland. Jahresbericht 1960* (Düsseldorf: Zentralrat, 1960), 32. In original: *"Wie erkennen die Leistung von Angehörigen des öffentlichen Dienstes an, ohne die die Bewältigung einer so undankbaren und schwierigen Aufgabe wie der Wiedergutmachung undurchführbar wäre"*.

[30] Zentralrat der Juden in Deutschland, *Jüdische Gemeinschaft in Deutschland. Jahresbericht 1970/71 von Generalsekretär Dr. H. G. van Dam* (Düsseldorf: Zentralrat, 1971), 7.

[31] Zentralrat der Juden in Deutschland, *Jüdische Gemeinschaft in Deutschland. Jahresbericht 1966/67 von Generalsekretär Dr. H. G. van Dam* (Düsseldorf: Zentralrat, 1967), 14.

President Ignatz Bubis, who in the 1990s transformed the umbrella into a more visible public affairs agency.[32] As Charlotte Knobloch says in confirmation of the organization's current state of policy, "We stand up for a self-confident Judaism".[33]

The Central Council's newly discovered boldness yet also came with diverse pitfalls, and in some instances may not have served the organization's best interests. A recent example is the debate over the shortcomings in German immigration and integration policy, touched off by Thilo Sarrazin's controversial book "Germany does away with itself". The book, written in the matter-of-fact language of a social engineer-economist, and which deals in large part with the general trends and challenges in demography, education, and the labor market, also sharply criticizes Muslim immigration to Germany on the grounds that Muslim immigrants, for various reasons and unlike other immigrant groups, contributed to a lowering of the country's intellectual, cultural, and productivity standards.[34] A vivid discussion on whether or not Sarrazin was right with his thesis preoccupied the German media for weeks, and also prompted the Central Council of Jews in Germany to position itself in the debate. Stephan J. Kramer, a convert to Judaism and the organization's current secretary general, quickly excoriated Sarrazin for his allegedly "racist" remarks that "appeal to the basest human instincts".[35] What is more, Kramer went so far as to draw a parallel between Sarrazin's views and the ideology of Göring, Goebbels, and Hitler, a bold claim qualified as "totally nuts" by the German-Jewish historian Michael Wolffsohn.[36] On a different occasion, Wolffsohn again took exception to the outspokenness of the umbrella's secretary general, bestowing upon Kramer the less than honorific title of being "the permanent loudspeaker" of the Central Council.[37] While this example is not

---

[32] See section 4.5 below.
[33] Knobloch (2009 Interview).
[34] See Thilo Sarrazin, *Deutschland schafft sich ab* (München: Deutsche Verlags-Anstalt, 2010).
[35] Stephan J. Kramer, ""Sarrazins Äußerungen sind rassistisch und zielen auf niedrigste Instinkte"", *Der Tagesspiegel*, October 13, 2009.
[36] Michael Wolffsohn, "Kein Mega-Verbrecher", *Der Tagesspiegel*, October 11, 2009.
[37] Michael Wolffsohn, "Gelehrt, geachtet, ahnungslos", *Der Tagesspiegel*, November 4, 2010.

sufficient to make a definitive statement about the political style of the Central Council, it however gives a hint of the remarkable shift from modest self-restraint to a more self-consciously assertive role in German politics over the past decades.

4.3 "A Group of Exotic People"

The annual reports under review furthermore suggest that the Central Council finds itself relegated to the role of a political outsider because of the perception of Jews in Germany as "a group of exotic people"[38] and as "expatriate Israelis".[39] Akin to the assessment given by secretary general van Dam in the late 1960s and early 1970s, the subsequent leaders of the Central Council have reached similar conclusions. Ignatz Bubis, for example, the umbrella's president from 1992 to 1999, provides a fairly bleak account of how Jews are perceived in Germany: "The majority of society does not perceive Jews as such [German citizens of Jewish faith] and does not want to regard them as such. (...) We are regarded (...) as strangers, as Israelis, as foreigners, as a race, as just about anything, but are only rarely regarded as German citizens", Bubis is quoted as saying in one of his last interviews.[40] Based not least on his decades-long experience as a community leader, Bubis, who expressly called himself a "German citizen of Jewish faith",[41] concludes that "Jews are [equated with] a "foreign" culture"[42] in Germany that is struggling to win acceptance from the larger non-Jewish public. But also in the eyes of Paul Spiegel, Bubis's successor in the office of the Council president, the Jews in Germany are clearly allotted the role of a societal

---

[38] Zentralrat der Juden in Deutschland, *Jüdische Gemeinschaft in Deutschland. Jahresbericht 1970/71* (Düsseldorf: Zentralrat, 1971), 13.
[39] Zentralrat der Juden in Deutschland, *Jüdische Gemeinschaft in Deutschland. Ergänzungsbericht bei der Ratsversammlung des Zentralrats der Juden in Deutschland am 23. Mai 1968 von Generalsekretär Dr. H. G. van Dam* (Düsseldorf: Zentralrat, 1968), 12.
[40] Ignatz Bubis, "Erschütterungen sind zu überstehen", in: Romberg/Urban-Fahr (eds.) (2000), 19.
[41] Ignatz Bubis, *Ich bin ein deutscher Staatsbürger jüdischen Glaubens. Ein autobiographisches Gespräch mit Edith Kohn* (Köln: Kiepenheuer & Witsch, 1993).
[42] Bubis (2000), 19 (quotation marks in original).

fringe group sharing the same precarious fate as other minorities. Deliberately chosen expressions such as "Jews, Turks, men of color or gays" or "Jews, Turks, blacks, homeless persons, gays" speak for themselves and reveal a great deal about the Central Council's underdog self-image.[43]

The Central Council also deplores in its early annual reports the receiving of inputs pertinent to the area of competence of the Israeli Mission to Germany, which in turn received requests that should have been addressed at the Central Council.[44] It is instructive to note in this context that the perception of Jews as "expatriate Israelis" has remained a staple of public discourse throughout the past decades. Hate mail sent to the umbrella has tellingly been focused on the actions of the Israeli government, for which the Central Council is apparently held accountable.[45]

Charlotte Knobloch, president of the Central Council from 2006 to 2010, comments on these findings as follows: "Yes, it is true. The average citizen hears about the Central Council advocating for Israel in some form or another (...) and then thinks that we are Israelis, and cannot understand that Jews devote themselves to supporting the existence of a Jewish state".[46] With regard to van Dam's initially quoted statement on the perception of Jews in Germany as "a group of exotic people", Charlotte Knobloch says she does "not disagree" with this view, acknowledging that "not much has changed since that time". The same derogatory designation still has currency today: "It happens sometimes that we are called "exotic people", I get to hear that time and again, also in letters sometimes", Knobloch avows.[47] Citing the events of the Gaza War of 2008-2009, Knobloch furthermore points out that during the confrontation the Jews in Germany were "not referred to as expatriate Israelis, or diaspora Israelis, but as plain Israelis, and when people approach us [the

---

[43] Paul Spiegel, "Ansprache am 9. November 2000", in: Romberg/Urban-Fahr (eds.) (2000), 22.
[44] See Zentralrat der Juden in Deutschland, *Die jüdische Gemeinschaft in Deutschland. Jahresbericht des Generalsekretärs Dr. H. G. van Dam für 1964/65* (Frankfurt am Main: Zentralrat, 1965), 20.
[45] See the selection of letters published in the Jüdische Allgemeine, ""Wir spucken auf euch"", April 25, 2002.
[46] Interview with Charlotte Knobloch, President, Zentralrat der Juden in Deutschland, September 1, 2009, Munich.
[47] Knobloch (2009 Interview).

Central Council] they call Israel our country".[48] Though Germany may again have become a "homeland" ("*Heimat*") for Jews, there still exists "a perceived wall of detachment" ("*gefühlte Mauer*"), Knobloch concludes.[49]

Perhaps this explains why the organization up to the present has maintained the appellation "Central Council of Jews in Germany", which suggests a degree of distance and autonomy as opposed to a more assimilative name like "Central Council of German Jews". But other factors also played a role. For one thing, the umbrella does not see itself in the immediate tradition of the Jewish organizations of the pre-Nazi era, many of which proudly asserted their German identities. After the war, the Jewish community in Germany moreover comprised a large number of immigrants of different religious affiliations and national origins, many of them displaced persons from Eastern Europe. The organization thus naturally acted as the representative body of all these groups, and not only of those who had previously lived in Germany. Indeed, a survey among the Jewish minority in Germany, carried out by the sociologists Alphons Silbermann and Herbert Sallen in the mid-1990s, found that over 78 percent of those polled consider the current, non-assimilative designation most appropriate.[50] As yet there are no plans to change the organization's original name.[51]

The self-assessment given by the Central Council notwithstanding, it is however necessary to consider the previous characterizations against the backdrop of German public opinion. On the one hand, a recent survey conducted by TNS Infratest indicates that a large majority of Germans do not think that Jews differ significantly from non-Jews in terms of their lifestyle.[52] Research has also shown that Jews, similar to Italians and ethnic German repatriates, find wide acceptance in German society. Whereas Germans evince a comparatively high propensity for social ex-

---

[48] Knobloch (2009 Interview).
[49] Charlotte Knobloch, "Die Mauer im Kopf", *Jüdische Allgemeine*, September 8, 2010.
[50] See Alphons Silbermann and Herbert Sallen, "Jews in Germany today", *Society* 32:4 (May/June 1995), 59.
[51] See Knobloch (2009 Interview).
[52] See Statista, "Unterschied im Lebensstil Juden und anderen Deutschen", http://de.statista.com/statistik/diagramm/studie/40154/umfrage/unterschied-im-lebensstil-juden-und-anderen-deutschen/, accessed February 24, 2011.

clusion towards Turks and asylum seekers, a study finds, they also tend to perceive Jews and Italians as "bourgeois" and "inconspicuous" and regard their lifestyle as "far more rarely distinct from their own".[53] Instructive is furthermore an analysis of intermarriage rates between Jews and Germans. Rates of intermarriage are generally considered a useful measure of social integration because they indicate whether or not certain relationships are deemed socially acceptable. In a comprehensive qualitative study on contemporary Jewish-German relations including issues such as interethnic love and intimacy, Lynn Rapaport finds that "intermarriage does take place at a dramatic level for Jews in Germany".[54] Curiously enough, mixed marriages involving Jews and Germans were in fact a widespread phenomenon even in the immediate postwar period. From 1951 to 1958, for instance, there were more than three times as many mixed marriages than marriages in which both partners were Jewish; about 73 percent of the Jewish men and roughly 24 percent of the Jewish women who married in this period chose non-Jewish partners. By way of comparison, for the period from 1901 to 1930 the respective figures were slightly below 20 percent for men and approximately 12 percent for women.[55] All these findings tend to militate against the notion that Jews are perceived as "exotic people".

At the same time, however, a sizable section of public opinion has harbored decidedly unfavorable views towards the Jewish minority in Germany. According to recent polls, about 28 percent of West Germans and about 29 percent of East Germans have a "rather" or "very" negative view of Jews. In addition, these attitudes are "far more negative" than in other European countries, the *Frankfurter Allgemeine Zeitung* reports.[56]

---

[53] Werner Bergmann, "Antisemitismus in Deutschland", in: Wilfried Schubarth and Richard Stöss (eds.), *Rechtsextremismus in der Bundesrepublik Deutschland. Eine Bilanz* (Bonn: Bundeszentrale für politische Bildung, 2000), 145.

[54] Lynn Rapaport, *Jews in Germany after the Holocaust. Memory, identity, and Jewish-German relations* (Cambridge: Cambridge University Press, 1997), 251.

[55] See Chaim Yahil, "Germany", in: Berenbaum/Skolnik (eds.) (2007), vol. 7, 538.

[56] Frankfurter Allgemeine Zeitung, "In Deutschland besonders starke Vorbehalte gegen den Islam", December 3, 2010.

In short, the Central Council routinely finds itself in the role of the advocate for a group of "exotic" outsiders – and, as we shall now see, adapts its political style accordingly.

4.4 "Loyalty" and Patriotism

In light of the evidence discussed above, a convincing case can be made that there is substantial pressure on the Central Council to assert its loyalty to the country. The close partnership with and financial dependency on the state as well as the lasting image of Jews as outsiders and the (self-)perception as "a group of exotic people" suggest this is the case; a closer examination of the umbrella's relationship with Israel helps to establish the point at hand.

Because the Central Council has often been mistakenly equated with an informal diplomatic outpost of the State of Israel, it has found itself compelled to respond to the so-called "dual loyalty" charge. The term "dual loyalty", which invokes the old anti-Semitic canard of Jews secretly plotting to undermine the societies in which they live, is in fact used by scholars today in "a neutral and nonpejorative fashion to describe the widespread circumstance where individuals feel genuine attachments (or loyalties) to more than one country".[57] The Central Council, connected to Israel in a special way by dint of the organization's Jewish character, has taken a judicious stance on the issue. It has argued that the only form of loyalty one may object to is that of "dual disloyalty" – that is, a lack of responsibility towards both one's community and towards society in general.[58] The concept of "dual loyalty", seen as a discursive element characteristic of unfree societies, is flatly rejected as such: "The simplistic longing for a sole and unique, absolute and unshakable loyalty on the part of the citizen towards the state belongs to the categories of thinking

---

[57] As defined by Mearsheimer/Walt (2007), 147.
[58] Zentralrat der Juden in Deutschland, *Die jüdische Gemeinschaft in Deutschland. Jahresbericht des Generalsekretärs Dr. H. G. van Dam für 1964/65* (Düsseldorf: Zentralrat, 1965), 21. The Central Council does not offer a clear definition of the term, but its meaning can be inferred from the context of the quote.

of dictatorial regimes and of state absolutism", secretary general van Dam straightforwardly clarifies the issue.[59]

Its critique of the concept of state loyalty has not hindered the Central Council to also clearly emphasize its independence from the policies of the Israeli government. One reason it has done so is the fact that the organization's public perception has been invariably linked to the image of the Jewish state (*"Image-Verbindung"*).[60] While acknowledging that Israel and the Jewish community in Germany share common interests (*"Interessenverbundenheit"*), van Dam, a widely published jurist, also makes clear in his idiosyncratically stern and well-pondered language that solidarity with Israel "does not entail a complete identity of demands and a disbandment of the constitutional responsibilities".[61] Asked whether these remarks still carry weight for the political outlook of the Central Council of Jews in Germany today, President Charlotte Knobloch responds in the affirmative: "[We] do not have the possibilities, and we do not seek them, to have an influence on Israeli politics", Knobloch says in accordance with van Dam's more convoluted statement. "The Israeli government does not confer with the Central Council regarding its [Israel's] policies. We are not a branch office of the Israeli government, as it is often falsely portrayed in the public perception. Neither are we responsible for the direction of Israeli politics. And I would like to stress: fact-based criticism is perfectly legitimate".[62]

At the same time, the Central Council has been prepared to assume its share of responsibility for the common good, which it furthermore links to the expression of patriotism. The latter is here understood as a

---

[59] Zentralrat der Juden in Deutschland, *Jüdische Gemeinschaft in Deutschland. Jahresbericht 1969/70 von Generalsekretär Dr. H. G. van Dam* (Düsseldorf: Zentralrat, 1970), 10.

[60] Zentralrat der Juden in Deutschland, *Jüdische Gemeinschaft in Deutschland. Jahresbericht 1969/70 von Generalsekretär Dr. H. G. van Dam* (Düsseldorf: Zentralrat, 1970), 7. In original: *"Die Image-Verbindung, gewollt oder nichtgewollt, provoziert oder aufgezwungen, ist ein Faktum"*.

[61] Zentralrat der Juden in Deutschland, *Jüdische Gemeinschaft in Deutschland. Jahresbericht 1966/67 von Generalsekretär Dr. H. G. van Dam* (Düsseldorf: Zentralrat, 1967), 10. In original: *"Die Interessenverbundenheit zwischen Israel und den Gemeinden der Welt führt nicht zu einer völligen Identität der Ansprüche und zu einer Auflösung der staatsrechtlichen Verpflichtungen"*.

[62] Knobloch (2009 Interview).

"healthy patriotism (...) based on the values of the Christian-Jewish Occident and that includes the merits of this country (...) [, one] that adequately includes the memory of the victims of the Shoah as well as the responsibility for the future of the Jewish people", Charlotte Knobloch points out. "And a patriotism that is proud of what has been achieved in this country over the past decades. We should also cultivate such a healthy patriotism because we must not allow the love of one's country to become a domain of the extreme right".[63] In this respect the Central Council shares many similarities with one of its predecessors, the *Centralverein deutscher Staatsbürger jüdischen Glaubens* (C.V., or "Central Association of German Citizens of the Jewish Faith"), which identified not only as a Jewish but also – and decidedly so – as a German organization.

The *Centralverein* was founded in 1893 as a Jewish defense organization aimed at fighting the growing anti-Semitism in Imperial Germany.[64] Its formation harks back to a famous pamphlet of the writer and theater director Raphael Löwenfeld, entitled "*Schutzjuden oder Staatsbürger?*", which accused the Jewish leadership in Germany of receding into the passivity of the Middle Ages instead of standing up for their rights as proud and equal citizens. True, German Jews had obtained equality before the law already in 1871 (and in 1869 in the North German Confederation); but since these rights were granted by an authoritarian government and were not backed by a broad democratic majority, the status of Jews remained precarious and various forms of discrimination continued in practice. The political style of the newly founded organization insofar represented a novelty in Jewish politics as it marked the "shift from a passive, sometimes even submissive political attitude to a self-conscious Jewish activism".[65] The *Centralverein* operated as a political mass organization – a child of its times, and a counter-model of *Honoratiorenpolitik* – and had over 70,000 individual members during

---

[63] Knobloch (2009 Interview), written statement in interview memorandum made available to author.
[64] See Avraham Barkai, *"Wehr Dich!" Der Centralverein deutscher Staatsbürger jüdischen Glaubens (C.V.) 1893-1938* (München: Verlag C.H. Beck, 2002).
[65] Borut (1995), 106-107.

the 1920s. Scholars have estimated that, at its peak, the C.V. represented at least two-thirds of all German Jews.[66]

The most distinctive characteristic of the *Centralverein* was its "total rejection of Zionist ideology"[67] in conjunction with its proud assertion of loyalty and absolute belonging to the German nation. The organization accordingly defined its Jewishness in religious and not in ethnic terms, and went to great lengths to emphasize its patriotism. In so doing it first and foremost sought to epitomize the oft-acclaimed German-Jewish symbiosis and hence proudly identified as both "loyally German and truly Jewish" (*"treudeutsch und echtjüdisch"*).[68] According to President Charlotte Knobloch, it is also the policy of the Central Council of Jews in Germany today to "stand by our country"; its support for the state of Israel by contrast distinguishes the umbrella from a predecessor organization such as the *Centralverein*.[69]

In addition to fostering a healthy patriotism, the Central Council has had the ambition to live up to the ideal of being a good corporate citizen. This objective essentially includes the responsibility of speaking out on issues of both general and Jewish concern, a task that proved to be especially painful in the immediate years after the war. For instance, fearing for the credibility of democracy in the Federal Republic, the Central Council explicitly called the bleak results of denazification and the conspicuous practice of recruiting former Nazi officials or party activists to positions of government service in particular "disastrous from a pedagogical point of view".[70] Yet, it does not see itself as being responsible for the collective betterment of German society. Specifically, it is loath to assume the role commonly associated with the Renaissance German humanist and reformer Philipp Melanchthon, which it has repeatedly re-

---

[66] See Friesel (1986), 123-124.
[67] Jehuda Reinharz, "Advocacy and History: The Case of the Centralverein and the Zionists", in: LBI (ed.), *LBI Year Book Vol. 33* (London: Secker & Warburg, 1988), 117.
[68] Erik Lindner, "Treudeutsch und echtjüdisch", *Allgemeine jüdische Wochenzeitung*, 48. Jg. Nr. 12, March 25, 1993; also see Reinharz (1974).
[69] Knobloch (2009 Interview).
[70] Zentralrat der Juden in Deutschland, *Die Jüdische Gemeinschaft in Deutschland. Jahresbericht des Generalsekretärs Dr. H. G. van Dam für 1964/65* (Düsseldorf: Zentralrat, 1965), 28. In original: *"vom pädagogischen Standpunkt aus verheerend"*.

jected in resolute terms: "While the Central Council does not claim the right to act as, and even expressly rejects the function of, a Praeceptor Germaniae, as a teacher of Germany, it however does not renounce the authorization to civic criticism [*"Befugnis staatsbürgerlicher Kritik"*] to which it is obligated as the interest representation of the surviving Jews in Germany", secretary general van Dam writes on the problem of renazification.[71] In the same vein, the annual report of 1969/70 states that the umbrella was "not instituted as a "praeceptor Germaniae", as an authorized expert for political morality [*"Sachverständiger für politische Moral"*] in the Federal Republic".[72] This issue apparently preoccupied the organization for years, as the following position, already spelled out in similar fashion a decade earlier, suggests: "The Central Council however does not feel called to act as a Praeceptor Germaniae and to become a tool of the reeducation [policy] that has been pompously announced ever since 1945. Still, it has been prepared to take its modest share, according to the amount of information at its disposal and within the boundaries of civic responsibility".[73] Again, the Central Council emphasizes its modest role and duties as a good corporate citizen.

[71] Zentralrat der Juden in Deutschland, *Die Jüdische Gemeinschaft in Deutschland. Jahresbericht des Generalsekretärs Dr. H. G. van Dam für 1964/65* (Düsseldorf: Zentralrat, 1965), 28-29.
[72] Zentralrat der Juden in Deutschland, *Jüdische Gemeinschaft in Deutschland. Jahresbericht 1969/70 von Generalsekretär Dr. H. G. van Dam* (Düsseldorf: Zentralrat, 1970), 14.
[73] Zentralrat der Juden in Deutschland, *10 Jahre Zentralrat der Juden in Deutschland. Jahresbericht 1960* (Düsseldorf: Zentralrat, 1960), 14.

Table 9: Central Council of Jews in Germany, Main Features, in 2010

Founding date	July 19, 1950
Budget	5 million euros annually
Legal status	Körperschaft des öffentlichen Rechts (since 1963)
Membership structure	23 regional associations 108 Jewish communities 105,000 individual Jews
Headquarters	Berlin (since 1999)
Previous headquarters	Frankfurt am Main, Düsseldorf
Representation in umbrellas	World Jewish Congress, European Jewish Congress, World Jewish Restitution Organization, Claims Conference

4.5 Personal Politics: Portraits of the Presidents of the Central Council

A final contention of this chapter is that the politics of the Central Council is best understood as an example of personal politics. As the officially recognized interlocutor of the German government, the top leadership of the Central Council occupies a particularly prominent position in German politics. Due to the scarcity of Jewish party politicians in Germany, the organization's leadership is often called upon to give its view on a broad range of issues. Drawing on primary sources such as the *Allgemeine jüdische Wochenzeitung* and the *Jüdische Allgemeine*, the following section provides a concise overview of the political biographies and terms of office of the chairmen and presidents – as the position was renamed in 1997 – of the Central Council and attempts to portray their distinct political styles and legacy.[74]

---

[74] An excellent overview is provided by Brenner (2007), 124-133. For general biographical information, see Zentralrat der Juden in Deutschland, "Presidents", http://www.zentralratdjuden.de/en/topic/136.html, accessed March 6, 2011. Select biographies can also be found in the various volumes of the *Encyclopaedia Judaica*, Berenbaum/Skolnik (eds.) (2007), as well as in

Table 10: Chairmen/Presidents of the Central Council of Jews in Germany, Terms of Office

Heinz Galinski	1954-1963
Herbert Lewin	1963-1969
Werner Nachmann	1969-1988
Heinz Galinski	1988-1992
Ignatz Bubis	1992-1999
Paul Spiegel	2000-2006
Charlotte Knobloch	2006-2010
Dieter Graumann	since November 2010

4.5.1 Heinz Galinski

A survivor of three concentration camps, Heinz Galinski became the first chairman of the Central Council in 1954. He was born in West Prussian Marienburg in 1912 and started his career as a textile salesman in Rathenow before moving to the nearby Berlin in the 1930s. His father, a seriously disabled veteran of World War I, died shortly after the family's arrest by the Nazis in 1943. In Auschwitz his mother and his wife were murdered; he himself was taken for forced labor for IG Farben near the extermination camp, before being sent to Dora, a camp in the proximity of Buchenwald. In April 1945, after further displacement, Galinski was liberated by British troops in Bergen-Belsen. He subsequently set out to Berlin, where he helped rebuild the local Jewish community and got involved in preparing the first restitution laws. Plans to emigrate to the United States were soon abandoned. Galinski was a founding member of the Central Council of Jews in Germany, and from 1949 to his death in 1992 served as the president of the Jewish community of Berlin.[75]

Munzinger-Archiv, Internationales Biographisches Archiv, available online at http://munzinger.de.

[75] See Andreas Nachama, "Der Mann in der Fasanenstraße", in: Andreas Nachama and Julius H. Schoeps (eds.), *Aufbau nach dem Untergang. Deutschjüdische Geschichte nach 1945* (Berlin: Argon Verlag, 1992), 27-52; Klaus Schütz, *Heinz Galinski (1912-1992). Ein Berliner unter dem Davidsschild*

It was the experience of the concentration camp that instilled in Galinski the resolve to devote his life to serving the Jewish community. His drive to restore the community in Berlin was based on the conviction that Jewish life in Germany must not be a closed chapter: "I have always represented the point of view that the Wannsee Conference [at which the extermination of the Jews was planned] cannot be the last word in the life of the Jewish community in Germany. (...) I have never been one of those who considered the community here as a liquidation community".[76] Upon his initiative a new Jewish community center was opened in Berlin in 1959. He also took a firm stand against right-wing extremism and gave a high priority to Holocaust memory and the prosecution of Nazi crimes. While his first term as chairman (from 1954 to 1963) had been a relatively tranquil phase, Galinski during his second term (from 1988 to 1992) had to deal with the burdensome legacy inherited from his predecessor and rival Werner Nachmann. Nachmann was discredited when it became known shortly after his death that he had embezzled millions of marks in reparation money. To restore the tarnished image of the Central Council thus remained the paramount task for Galinski during the subsequent years in office.[77]

As a Jewish political figure Galinski acted in the belief that political activism of the Jewish community was a necessary ingredient to consolidate democracy in the Federal Republic. The Jews of Germany, he wrote, had to respect not merely the rule of law, but were in fact called upon to fulfil "the moral duties of responsible citizens" (*"die moralischen Pflichten mündiger Staatsbürger"*). Noting that "the possibilities of participation in public affairs are not limited to the casting of votes in elections", he encouraged his coreligionists to "contribute to the consolidation of the free democratic basic order through the full exercise of their democratic rights".[78] In the tradition of prewar German Jewry, Galinski saw himself as an equal German citizen and stood up forthrightly for the

---

(Teetz: Hentrich & Hentrich, 2004); and Michael Brenner, "Galinski, Heinz", in: Berenbaum/Skolnik (eds.) (2007), vol. 7, 349.

[76] Quoted in Brenner (1997), 101.
[77] See Heinz Galinski, "Zwischen Einkehr und Umkehr", *Allgemeine jüdische Wochenzeitung*, 43. Jg. Nr. 37, September 16, 1988.
[78] Heinz Galinski, "Polarisierung schadet Demokratie. Betrachtungen zur Bundestagswahl", *Allgemeine jüdische Wochenzeitung*, 31. Jg. Nr. 40, October 1, 1976.

Federal Republic; he was, at least according to the eulogy given by Chancellor Helmut Kohl in 1992, a "German patriot".[79] At the same time, Galinski was known as an outspoken and critical observer of German politics. In the aftermath of the Yom Kippur War of 1973, for example, he publicly vented his discontent over the perceived ambiguity on the part of the German government. In an article with the blunt title "Neutrality has its limits" published in the *Allgemeine jüdische Wochenzeitung*, Galinski expressed his "dismay over the peculiar interpretation of neutrality of the German government". Israel, caught by a surprise attack of the Syrian and Egyptian armies, was in the position of the defendant; for this reason, Galinski argued, the neutrality of the Federal Republic – for it maintains "special (and not normal) relations" with the Jewish state – should have been subject to "very clear limits".[80] His defense of Israel, which he wanted to be an "imperative of political morality"[81] for the Federal Republic, however almost claimed his own life – in 1975, Galinski escaped an assassination attempt carried out by the Red Army Fraction (RAF), the terrorist group that held Germany in awe throughout the 1970s.[82]

Regarding his personality Galinski has once been described as "an unrelenting man, not widely loved, but always respected".[83] In the same vein, his successor Ignatz Bubis noted in retrospect that Galinski was "an authoritarian character, who was often misunderstood. To non-Jews

---

[79] Quoted in Ignatz Bubis and Peter Sichrovsky, *"Damit bin ich noch längst nicht fertig". Die Autobiographie* (Frankfurt am Main: Campus Verlag, 1996), 127.

[80] Heinz Galinski, "Neutralität hat Grenzen", *Allgemeine jüdische Wochenzeitung*, 28. Jg. Nr. 46, November 16, 1973.

[81] Heinz Galinski, "Engagement für Israel. Ein Gebot der politischen Moral", *Allgemeine jüdische Wochenzeitung*, 28. Jg. Nr. 42, October 19, 1973.

[82] See *Allgemeine jüdische Wochenzeitung*, "Empörung und Erleichterung. Zum Attentatsversuch auf Heinz Galinski", 30. Jg. Nr. 35, August 29, 1975. The RAF accused Galinski of being "an agent of the Zionist regime that every day drops tons and tons of bombs over Palestinian camps": *"Wir, RAF, haben Galinski ein Sprengstoffpaket geschickt, weil er ein Agent des Zionistenregimes ist, das täglich tonnenweise Bomben über palästinensischen Lagern abwirft"*.

[83] Leibl Rosenberg, "Die ersten fünfzig Jahre. Ein halbes Jahrhundert Zentralrat der Juden in Deutschland", *Universitas* 55:651 (September 2000), 832.

he may partly have appeared to be embittered, though he was held in esteem by all those who knew him personally, even by his critics". It was Galinski's "partly uncompromising attitude" which, by his own accounts, later served Bubis as "a role model in many respects".[84] Galinski received various honors, among them the title of honorary citizen of Berlin in 1987. In the same year the Jewish community of Berlin established the Heinz Galinski Foundation, which annually awards the Heinz Galinski Prize to individuals who have showed special merits for the German-Jewish dialogue.

4.5.2 Herbert Lewin

Comparatively little is known about Herbert Lewin, chairman of the Central Council from 1963 to 1969. Born in the Prussian province of Posen in 1899, Lewin had fought in World War I (along with over 100,000 German Jews, 12,000 of whom fell in battle) and lived in Berlin throughout the 1930s. Like Galinski he represented the tradition of prewar German Jewry. He studied medicine and worked at the Jewish Polyclinic in Berlin and, from 1937 until his deportation, at the Jewish Hospital in Cologne. A survivor of Auschwitz,[85] Lewin played a leading role in rebuilding the Jewish community of Cologne immediately after the war, where then mayor Konrad Adenauer asked him to repatriate the

---

[84] Bubis (1996), 126.
[85] Non-academic sources such as the Bezirksamt Charlottenburg-Wilmersdorf von Berlin, "Herbert-Lewin-Platz", http://www.berlin.de/ba-charlottenburg-wilmersdorf/bezirk/herbertlewinplatz.html, accessed March 22, 2011, report Lewin worked as a prisoner doctor during his internment. To my knowledge, in the academic literature nothing has been written about Lewin's role as a prisoner doctor. Without implying any incriminating parallel whatsoever, one may however observe that Lewin shares various biographical similarities with the infamous Jewish medical collaborator Maximilian Samuel. Like Lewin, Samuel had been "a distinguished academic gynecologist in Cologne", had been a veteran of the First World War, and worked as a prisoner doctor in Auschwitz. See the authoritative study by Robert Jay Lifton, *The Nazi Doctors: Medical Killing and the Psychology of Genocide* (New York: Basic Books, 2000), 250-253. Again, and obviously, the mere biographical similarities between the two men by no means indicate, nor are meant to suggest, any sort of collaboration with Nazi doctors on Lewin's part.

city's Jews from Theresienstadt.[86] From 1950 to 1967, he served as chief of the gynecological department at the hospital of Offenbach, near Frankfurt. During his time as chairman of the Central Council, Lewin kept a low political profile; accordingly, his name recognition in the broad Jewish and non-Jewish public remained fairly weak.[87]

Lewin is perhaps most remembered for an early incident of anti-Semitism in the Federal Republic, commonly referred to as the Lewin affair. In 1949, the city council of Offenbach had appointed Lewin to serve as chief of the gynecological department at the local hospital, yet at the urging of the CDU deputy mayor his appointment was revoked. The latter had claimed that the city's women could not be entrusted to a Jewish Holocaust survivor, on the argument that after years of exposure to the anti-Semitic vituperations of *Der Stürmer* and its lurid tales of lustful Jews preying on German maidens, ordinary Germans were not ready to accept a Jewish gynecologist. The mayor of Offenbach, a member of the SPD, also joined in the objection. Lewin thereupon protested the decision, prompting SPD party leader Kurt Schumacher to declare that the SPD would not tolerate such discrimination. Though the SPD had a historically strong record on Jewish affairs and was in fact the most welcoming and progressive political party in terms of its relationship with Jews, the Lewin controversy caused it great embarrassment. Lewin finally received the post, while the mayor of Offenbach resigned from office.[88]

Lewin's term fell into the short but eventful period when the Federal Republic for the first time witnessed serious economic and political crises. Konrad Adenauer retired from politics in 1963, and his successor Ludwig Erhard, whose governing coalition fell apart over disagreements on fiscal policy, stepped down as chancellor in 1966. The ensuing grand coalition between CDU/CSU and SPD, formed as a temporary solution under Chancellor (and former NSDAP member) Kurt Georg Kiesinger, weathered a storm of extra-parliamentary opposition before being replaced by Willy Brandt's social-liberal coalition in 1969. Why the Central Council was seen as an ally of the so-called "establishment" during these crisis-shaken years will be discussed in chapter 5.1. below.

---

[86] See Brenner (2007), 128.
[87] See Rosenberg (2000), 832.
[88] See Geller (2005), 132-133.

4.5.3 Werner Nachmann

Far more publicity than Lewin earned his successor Werner Nachmann, who served as chairman of the Central Council from 1969 to 1988. Born in Karlsruhe in 1925, Nachmann fled to France with his family in 1938 and returned to his native city as an officer in the French army in 1945. An industrialist by profession, Nachmann was also the chairman of the Jewish community of Karlsruhe and of the Association of Jewish Communities in Baden. Upon his initiative the first new synagogue after World War II was built in Karlsruhe in 1971, as well as the Heidelberg College of Jewish Studies in 1979. He received various honors, among them the Theodor Heuss Prize for his efforts to improve Jewish-Christian relations.[89]

In contrast to the rather uncompromising Heinz Galinski, Werner Nachmann represented the model of the mealy-mouthed *"Leisetreter"*, as Ignatz Bubis put it, and accordingly kept a low profile as chairman of the Central Council.[90] His diffident attitude, which involved a fair amount of political ingratiation, expectedly exposed Nachmann to the charge of being too lenient toward former Nazis. This was the case in 1978, when he came to the defense of his long-time confidant Hans Filbinger, minister president of the state of Baden-Württemberg, who faced accusations (and was ultimately forced to resign) over his role as a Nazi military judge. But also in 1985 during President Reagan's controversial visit to Bitburg cemetery as well as in response to the planned premiere of Fassbinder's play *The Garbage, the City and Death*, Nachmann was out of step with the Jewish community when he chose conciliatory words over public criticism. Politically, he was known as a supporter of the conservative CDU.[91]

A tenet of his convictions was that the Jews in Germany should integrate into society by proving their loyalty to the state.[92] Nachmann thus stood in the tradition of German-Jewish patriotism. Yet unlike Galinski,

---

[89] See Michael Brenner, "Nachmann, Werner", in: Berenbaum/Skolnik (eds.) (2007), vol. 14, 720.
[90] Bubis (1996), 127.
[91] See Brenner (2007), 129.
[92] See Rosenberg (2000), 832; Werner Nachmann, "Juden – Bürger der Bundesrepublik", *Allgemeine jüdische Wochenzeitung*, 39. Jg. Nr. 6, February 10, 1984.

he advocated a much less pluralistic concept of integration and "supported every possible form of integration, partly up to the point of assimilation".[93] Nachmann, whom Henryk M. Broder once characterized as "the epitome of the German square (Jewish, by chance)",[94] for instance proposed to change the name of the Central Council of Jews in Germany to "*Zentralrat Deutscher Juden*", or "Central Council of German Jews". He also held the belief that Jewish men in Germany should be subject to compulsory military service.[95] Today his political legacy remains overshadowed by an embezzlement scandal, which seriously tarnished the image of the Central Council.

In fact, shortly after his death in 1988 it came out that Nachmann had embezzled about DM 33 million of restitution money during his tenure as chairman of the Central Council.[96] He had taken the money from the hardship fund for victims of Nazi persecution, established by the German government in 1980 and endowed with a total of DM 400 million, which the Central Council was supposed to transfer to eligible Jewish organizations. Yet instead of immediately transferring the money, Nachmann delayed the payments so as to realize interest earnings. The fraud was hard to discover, since Nachmann only embezzled the interest and the annual balance sheet thus showed no apparent irregularities. In addition, it had simply been inconceivable that the chairman of the Central Council, who was authorized to manage the payments alone, would defraud Holocaust survivors for the benefit of his own pocket. Though it is known that Nachmann partly used the money to finance his various ailing firms, the exact whereabouts of the embezzled sums were never determined conclusively.[97]

---

[93] Bubis (1996), 127.
[94] Henryk M. Broder, "Rehabilitiert Werner Nachmann", in: Nachama/Schoeps (eds.) (1992), 299.
[95] See Bubis (1996), 128.
[96] See Bubis (1996), 165-173.
[97] Nachmann was not the first board member of the Central Council involved in an embezzlement affair. A few decades earlier, Philipp Auerbach, the Bavarian state commissioner for victims of racial, religious, and political persecution, was accused of misappropriating reparations money and had to stand trial in a German court. In August 1952, the Jewish undersecretary of state was found guilty and sentenced to a fine and to two and a half years in prison. Proclaiming his innocence to the end, Auerbach committed suicide two

4.5.4 Ignatz Bubis

Arguably the most charismatic and most influential of all German Jewish leaders of the postwar era, Ignatz Bubis gained enormous popularity in Germany despite his relatively short tenure at the helm of the Central Council from 1992 to 1999. Bubis was born to Polish-Jewish parents in then German Breslau, what now is the Polish city of Wrocław, in the province of Silesia in 1927. Bubis survived the Holocaust as a forced laborer in the camps of Deblin and Częstochowa, where he was liberated by Soviet troops in January 1945; his father was murdered in Treblinka. After the war he first lived in the Soviet occupation zone before moving to West Germany. He settled in Frankfurt am Main in 1956 and became a successful businessman in the fields of jewelry and later in real estate. Bubis called himself a "Frankfurter by passion", an honor which the city reciprocated in 2000, when the Obermain bridge was renamed Ignatz-Bubis-Brücke. Since 2001, the city of Frankfurt has furthermore awarded the Ignatz Bubis Prize for Understanding, endowed with 50,000 euros.[98]

Bubis differed from his predecessors in various respects. First and foremost, his tenure marked a caesura in the political style of the Central Council. Whereas Galinski had been perceived as a predictable and stern admonisher, Bubis represented a new kind of relaxedness that appealed to large parts of the German public. In contrast to the uncritically assimilative Nachmann, he participated actively and independently in political debates, from talk shows and live events to the print media.[99] In so doing Bubis helped transform the Central Council into a more visible public affairs agency; the traditional way of "backdoor politics" was now replaced by a more assertive and publicity-oriented model of representation.[100]

---

    days after the verdict. In contrast to Nachmann's case, however, Auerbach had not acted for personal gain; also, his embezzlement was never proved. See Brenner (1997), 135-137.

[98] An excellent overview of Bubis's life and legacy is provided by Backhaus/Gross/Lenarz (eds.) (2007).

[99] See, for example, Ignatz Bubis and Wolfgang Schäuble (ed. Frank Schirrmacher), *Deutschland wohin?* (Freiburg: Herder, 1996).

[100] Brenner (2007), 131.

The very definition of a *zoón politikón*, Bubis enjoyed, and took pride in, being a part of the German *res publica*. What Galinski had been to the Jewish community of Berlin, Bubis was to the community of Frankfurt, where he was elected president in 1978. In Frankfurt he had been the target of social protests in the 1970s – during the so-called *Häuserkampf* in the city's Westend district – and was denounced by left-wing groups as a "speculator" because of his role as one of the city's leading real estate owners. In 1985, his vehement opposition to Fassbinder's controversial play *The Garbage, the City and Death* made Bubis known to a larger public. Deeply offended by the play's anti-Semitic stereotypes cloaked in the pretense of art, Bubis resolved to find a way to prevent its staging. Together with other Jewish community members and friends who had entered the theater with fake tickets, he occupied the stage to demonstrate against the premiere. After a lengthy and heated discussion with the audience, the planned performance was finally cancelled.[101] Yet in spite of his unwillingness to retreat from a skirmish, Bubis also was famed for his open-mindedness and respect for dissenting opinions. No other Jewish leader in Germany could arguably rival Bubis's commitment to religious and social outreach; in 1996, he met with Pope John Paul II in Berlin as well as with Palestinian leader Yassir Arafat. In 1997 he helped the FDP, which he had joined in 1969, make its return to the city parliament of Frankfurt and, in 1998, became president of the European Jewish Congress. One year before his death, his fierce criticism of the German writer Martin Walser, whom he accused of relativizing the Holocaust, turned into one of the most contentious public controversies of the 1990s, known as the Walser-Bubis debate.[102]

By defining Judaism primarily as a religion, Bubis stood in the tradition of prewar German Jewry and accordingly identified as "a German citizen of Jewish faith".[103] At the same time, he was often perceived as a representative of Israel and as a stranger in his own country, a fact he repeatedly laments in his memoirs. Bubis for instance recalls an encounter with then president of the Federal Agency for Civic Education (*Bundeszentrale für politische Bildung*), Günter Reichert, who, on the occasion

---

[101] See Bubis (1996), 134-153.
[102] Walser had argued that the memory of Auschwitz should not be misused as a "moral cudgel". Outraged, Bubis condemned the remarks as "intellectual arson".
[103] Bubis (1993); see also Brenner (1997), 160.

of a banquet given by Federal President Roman Herzog for the Israeli President Ezer Weizman, candidly addressed him as a representative of the Jewish state.[104] Not least due to his affable personality and his numerous public appearances, Bubis gained enormous respect and popularity with the German public during his seven years in office. He was widely regarded as a moral authority in Germany, a role usually filled by intellectuals and, in particular, by the federal president. His ability to act as a mediator in society and between different worldviews led the newly founded magazine *Die Woche* to propose Bubis as a candidate for federal president in 1993. Bubis immediately rejected the candidature on the grounds that, first, he lacked the qualifications required for the job and, second, that the country was not yet prepared to elect a Jew – with Jews still being seen as "strangers" by mainstream society – into the highest public office in Germany.[105]

Despite his many achievements, Bubis ultimately remained sceptical about the actual impact of his work. In his last interview in *Stern* magazine in July 1999, he gave a more than bleak assessment, concluding he had "accomplished nothing or nearly nothing. (...) The majority did not even get my point. We are still strangers".[106] Bubis also said that while Galinski had been "fixated on the past" he by contrast made it his ambition to "connect the past with the future" – yet to little avail. "Today I am closer to Galinski, also in terms of embitterment", Bubis remarked in hindsight.[107] Out of fear that his grave might be vandalized in Germany, it was Bubis's last wish to be buried in Israel.[108] He died in August 1999

---

[104] When Reichert lauded "the state president" for his speech, Bubis replied that Herzog indeed was an excellent public speaker, upon which Reichert made the embarrassing remark: "I mean *your* state president!". See Bubis (1996), 224 (emphasis in original).
[105] See Bubis (1996), 248-250.
[106] Quoted in Backhaus/Gross/Lenarz (eds.) (2007), 190. In original: *"Ich habe nichts oder fast nichts bewirkt. (...) Die Mehrheit hat nicht einmal kapiert, worum es mir ging. Wir sind fremd geblieben"*.
[107] Quoted in Brenner (2007), 131.
[108] See Backhaus/Gross/Lenarz (eds.) (2007), 192, 197; Brenner (2007), 131. The gravestone of Heinz Galinski had been blown to pieces in December 1998.

and was buried at Kiryat Shaul cemetery near Tel Aviv. Shortly after his burial an Israeli artist desecrated his grave with black paint.

4.5.5 Paul Spiegel

After the death of Ignatz Bubis, Paul Spiegel was elected the sixth president of the Central Council in January 2000. He, too, was a Holocaust survivor. Born in Warendorf, Westphalia, in 1937, Spiegel fled with his family to Belgium in 1939 and survived the Nazi years in hiding. In 1945 he returned to his native Warendorf. After the war he wrote as a journalist for the *Allgemeine jüdische Wochenzeitung* as well as for the *Jüdischer Presse Dienst*. In the 1970s and 1980s he directed the office of public affairs at a large regional association of savings banks. In 1986 he founded an international artists agency in Düsseldorf. The capital of North Rhine-Westphalia also was the center of his community work: since 1967 Spiegel had been active in the Jewish community of Düsseldorf and became its president in 1984.[109]

During his tenure as president of the Central Council, Paul Spiegel followed in the footsteps of his predecessor and continued on the course of public outreach and self-confident involvement in political affairs. At the beginning of his term he called upon the German political leadership to step up its efforts to combat right-wing extremism, anti-Semitism and xenophobia in the country. In this context he rejected the German term "*Leitkultur*", or "guiding national culture", as an essentially discriminatory concept.[110] Spiegel also did not mince his words during the Möllemann affair two years later. In 2001, he became the first representative of the Central Council to attend the public ceremonial oath of the Bundeswehr in Berlin. Widely unnoticed in research has however gone his unambiguous support for the war in Iraq, as well as his attitude towards war in general. In 2003 Spiegel said in an interview for the *Jüdische Allgemeine* that there was "no alternative" to the invasion of Iraq and that,

---

[109] See Paul Spiegel, *Wieder zuhause? Erinnerungen* (Berlin: Ullstein, 2001); Ruth Beloff and Jonathan Licht, "Spiegel, Paul", in: Berenbaum/Skolnik (eds.) (2007), vol. 19, 106.

[110] See Paul Spiegel, "Ansprache am 9. November 2000", in: Romberg/Urban-Fahr (eds.) (2000), 22.

in some situations, "there is no other way to peace than violent disarmament".[111]

During Spiegel's tenure the integration of Jewish immigrants from the former Soviet Union as well as the integration of the newly founded liberal communities were of paramount concern for the Central Council. While insisting on the umbrella's representational monopoly, he took a conciliatory stance towards the Union of Progressive Jews in Germany and endeavored to settle the dispute with this non-affiliated religious organization in an amicable manner. In November 2005 the Central Council, which by its self-definition is open to all streams of Judaism, accepted three liberal state associations as members.[112]

Like Bubis and before him Galinski, Spiegel considered his efforts to have been largely futile in hindsight. "From year to year it has become more difficult to represent the interests of Jews in Germany", he noted after five years in office. "Anti-Semitism has gotten worse, which I had not expected at the time. No matter what you do, you do not accomplish anything. That is exactly the point where I am right now", Spiegel said.[113] A recipient of various high honors, among them an honorary doctorate of the University of Düsseldorf, Paul Spiegel died in April 2006. Rather than in Israel, he chose to be buried in Düsseldorf.

4.5.6 Charlotte Knobloch

The first woman and the last Holocaust survivor to serve in this position, Charlotte Knobloch was elected president of the Central Council in June 2006. She was born in Munich in 1932 to the lawyer and later Bavarian Senator Fritz Neuland. She survived the Shoah with a Catholic family in rural Franconia who passed her off as their illegitimate child. After the war she returned to Munich and married Samuel Knobloch in 1951.

---

[111] Jüdische Allgemeine, "'Täter und Opfer werden verwechselt'. Gespräch mit Paul Spiegel", March 27, 2003.

[112] See Paul Spiegel, "Kein Grund zum Klagen", *Jüdische Allgemeine*, April 1, 2004; Paul Spiegel, "Einer für alle", *Jüdische Allgemeine*, April 29, 2004; Jüdische Allgemeine, "'Wir reichen der Union die Hand'. Gespräch mit Paul Spiegel", June 24, 2004; and Jüdische Allgemeine, "'Wir verbinden alle religiösen Richtungen'", November 24, 2005. Also see section 5.1 below.

[113] Quoted in Christian Böhme and Judith Hart, "'Jetzt kann ich Bubis verstehen'", *Jüdische Allgemeine*, March 24, 2005.

Since 1985 she has chaired the Jewish Community of Munich and Upper Bavaria and in 1997 was elected to the Presidium of the Central Council as a vice-president. Since 2003 she has also served as vice-president of the European Jewish Congress and since 2005 as vice-president of the World Jewish Congress. It is not least thanks to her efforts that the Jewish community center and synagogue at Jakobsplatz was opened in Munich in November 2006.[114]

During her four-year tenure Knobloch made the integration of Jewish immigrants from the former Soviet Union as well as the fight against right-wing extremism and anti-Semitism the two top priorities for the Central Council.[115] Shortly after taking office she proposed National Socialism to be introduced as a separate school subject, an initiative she however retreated from later. In 2008, Knobloch took a tough stance towards the Catholic Church amid incidents of renewed anti-Judaism and sharply criticized Pope Benedict XVI for approving the reinstatement of the Tridentine Mass and the Good Friday Prayer, which casts the Jews as yet to be illuminated unbelievers. She also reacted swiftly in 2009 when the Vatican revoked the excommunication of the British cleric Richard Williamson, a notorious Holocaust denier. As a consequence of the Williamson affair, Knobloch temporarily suspended the dialogue with the Catholic Church. Under her leadership the Central Council furthermore maintained its privileged relations with the German government. Knobloch especially lauded Chancellor Angela Merkel for her "unparalleled" solidarity with Israel, describing their personal relationship as "excellent".[116]

Regarding German-Jewish relations, Knobloch was known for her embrace of "a healthy patriotism" in Germany, on the grounds that the

---

[114] See Marlis Prinzing, *Jüdisches Vermächtnis: Portrait, Gespräche, Perspektiven* (Lahr: Kaufmann, 2010); Michael Schleicher, *Charlotte Knobloch: Ein Portrait* (München: MünchenVerlag, 2009); Knobloch (2009 Interview); and Charlotte Knobloch, Micha Brumlik and Gesa S. Ederberg (im Gespräch mit Wilfried Köpke), *Wenn nicht jetzt, wann dann? Zur Zukunft des deutschen Judentums* (Freiburg: Herder, 2007), 18-47.

[115] See Charlotte Knobloch, "Das hat Potenzial", *Jüdische Allgemeine*, September 12, 2007; Knobloch (2009 Interview).

[116] Knobloch (2009 Interview). Knobloch also pointed out that "[t]he Central Council is nonpartisan" ("*überparteilich*") and "reaches out to all democratic parties".

love of one's country must not become the domain of the extreme right. Perhaps in a more natural way than some of the umbrella's previous leaders, she proudly identifies as a Municher and as a German citizen while at the same time asserting her solidarity with Israel, the country she regards as her "spiritual home" (*"geistige Heimat"*).[117] Straightforward and cordial in person, Knobloch has remained cautiously upbeat about the future of the Jews in Germany and concluded her tenure with more optimism than her predecessors.[118]

What distinguished Knobloch's tenure from those of her predecessors was the unusually prominent role played by the umbrella's secretary general, Stephan J. Kramer, who often acted as the spokesman of the Central Council on controversial political matters. Knobloch by contrast placed greater emphasis on education and memory, and on influencing public discourse by appealing to emotion and through personal testimony. In the mainstream press, though, this informal division of labor was widely misinterpreted as a sign of weakness and as a deficiency. With his mock candidacy to become head of the Central Council, Henryk M. Broder precisely took aim at Knobloch and mocked the allegedly overburdened president.[119] Such criticism however ignores that the dual leadership model had in fact been the norm – as well as a successful pattern of organization – during the first decades of the Central Council's history. Hendrik George van Dam, secretary general until his death in 1973 and author of all annual reports of that period, was on par with the umbrella's chairmen and was widely recognized as such.[120] It is also

---

[117] Knobloch (2009 Interview); Jüdische Allgemeine, ""Geistige Heimat der Juden in aller Welt"", May 8, 2008. See also Tobias Kaufmann, "Die Schrittmacherin", *Jüdische Allgemeine*, June 8, 2006.

[118] For an account of Knobloch's stance on patriotism and German-Jewish relations, see chapter 4.4 above.

[119] See Henryk M. Broder, "Der ideale Kandidat", *Der Spiegel*, 45/2009, 160-161; Henryk M. Broder, "Meine Kippa liegt im Ring", *Der Tagesspiegel*, October 21, 2009.

[120] Born in Berlin in 1906, Hendrik George van Dam was appointed secretary general of the Central Council in 1950. He participated in negotiations with the Claims Conference and was a delegate of the German government in Den Haag in 1952. A jurist by profession, van Dam became one of the foremost experts in the fields of restitution and indemnification and published a seminal book on the Federal Indemnification Law of 1953. Van Dam sup-

worthwhile to recall that Knobloch was already aged 74 when she took office – only Heinz Galinski had been two years older upon the beginning of his second term.

As one of the only two presidents of the Central Council who did not die in office,[121] Knobloch retired from her position after the end of her term in November 2010. Among the many honors she has received are an honorary doctorate from the University of Tel Aviv and the honorary citizenship of the city of Munich.

4.5.7 Dieter Graumann

Charlotte Knobloch was succeeded by Dieter Graumann, the first leader born both after the Holocaust and outside of Germany to be elected president of the Central Council. Graumann was born as David Graumann in Ramat Gan, near Tel Aviv, in 1950 to parents who had emigrated from Germany as displaced persons after the war. His family however returned to Germany one and a half years later. He was given the first name Dieter when he was six years old, since his parents, who had survived the camps, feared he would be identified as a Jewish boy on his first day in school. After studying economics in London and Frankfurt he worked for the German Bundesbank before starting his own real estate business. He had been active in the Jewish community of Frankfurt for many years when he became a member of the Central Council's Presidium in 2001. He was elected vice-president in 2006.[122]

In a surprisingly unconventional speech given shortly before his election as president, Graumann gave a first impression of what he wanted the Central Council increasingly to be in addition to its tradition-

---

ported the idea of a strong and truly democratic Germany and sought a gradual normalization of German-Jewish relations. He also believed in the reemergence of a viable Jewish community in Germany and is famous for coining the phrase "We insist on existing". Van Dam did not regard himself as a Zionist, and instead advocated the idea of a polycentric world Jewish community. See Chaim Yahil, "Van Dam, Hendrik George", in: Berenbaum/Skolnik (eds.) (2007), vol. 20, 473.

[121] With the exception of Knobloch and Lewin, all former chairmen and presidents died in office.

[122] See Hans Riebsamen, "Nachgeboren", *Frankfurter Allgemeine Zeitung*, November 29, 2010.

al role as the guarantor of continuity of Jewish life in Germany: surprising and unconventional. Striving to give the Central Council a decidedly fresh and modern twist, Graumann in fact argues the Jewish community should "get out of the Holocaust niche" to find its way "into the midst of life":

> Under no circumstances must we define ourselves through the role of the victims. We Jews must not reduce ourselves to a lugubrious community of victims or a funereal community of mourners. (...) By defiantly playing the role of the grumbler-in-permanence one rarely makes a particularly favorable impression. This is why we do not have to indefinitely prolong by ourselves the Jewish permanent subscription to warning and admonishing and criticizing and reprehending and disapproving. More creativity, more imaginativeness – instead of rituals of indignation. A vivid source of inspiration, a highly spirited driving force – instead of a boring admonisher-in-permanence.[123]

Citing the lessons learned from Ignatz Bubis, Graumann further added the Central Council should not waiver in its commitment to stand energetically and consequently by its convictions. Also in the future, its readiness to engage in political conflicts would not be lost, Graumann said. Whether Graumann has the potential to chart an entirely new

---

[123] Dieter Graumann, "Judentum hat Zukunft – munter und bunter", Rede von Dr. Dieter Graumann, Vizepräsident des Zentralrats der Juden, anlässlich der Gedenkstunde zum 9. November 2010 in der Paulskirche in Frankfurt am Main, http://www.zentralratdjuden.de/de/article/3116.html?sstr=munter|und| bunter, accessed March 6, 2011. In original: *"Wir müssen auch heraus aus der Holocaust-Nische und mitten hinein ins Leben finden. Auf keinen Fall dürfen wir selbst uns etwa über die Opfer-Rolle definieren. Wir Juden dürfen uns selbst eben nicht reduzieren auf eine düstere Opfergemeinschaft oder auf eine trübsinnige Trauergemeinschaft. (...) Wer trotzig in der Dauer-Mecker-Ecke hockt, hat noch selten eine besonders glückliche Figur abgegeben. Das jüdische Dauer-Abonnement von Warnen und Mahnen und Tadeln und Rügen und Missbilligen müssen wir daher selbst nicht endlos verlängern. Mehr Kreativität, mehr Phantasie – statt Empörungsrituale. Munterer Impulsgeber, quicklebendiger Antreiber – statt dröger Dauer-Mahner".* That the speech was given on a symbolic day such as November 9 is all the more noteworthy.

313

course, or whether his agenda will eventually lead the path back to the Bubis era, remains a question that will have to remain open until after the end of his tenure.

5 Why the State Always Wins

In this last chapter, we turn to a brief discussion of the risks and challenges the Central Council of Jews in Germany is exposed to given its close partnership with the state. Its main contention is that the Central Council faces the risk of instrumentalization and involvement in "alibi politics": as we shall see, the umbrella has time and again served as a powerful political asset for the German government as well as for mainstream political leaders. A case study of the role of the Central Council in the process of German unification further illustrates the point and shows how the Central Council was invoked by the German government to act as an "exculpatory witness" on its behalf.

5.1 "Establishmentization"

One risk the Central Council incurs is that of "establishmentization", understood as the bias for abandoning conflictual positions towards the government in favor of a convenient if not appeasing style of politics. In other words, the close relations with political elites tend to mitigate the willingness to engage in power struggles in which the respective group is squarely pitted against the government; in such situations, the respective group will seek a low profile so as not to damage its privileged ties to political leaders and decision makers. The risk of establishmentization furthermore correlates positively with the degree of a group's dependency on the state: in the case of the Central Council of Jews in Germany it can therefore be expected to be particularly pronounced.

Consider, for example, the restrained and quiescent position of the Central Council during the late 1960s and early 1970s, a time of student uprisings and radical social and political agendas. In the annual report of 1969/70, we find the laconic note: "The Central Council is perceived to lack political activism in various respects".[1] This statement should not

---

[1] Zentralrat der Juden in Deutschland, *Jüdische Gemeinschaft in Deutschland. Jahresbericht 1969/70 von Generalsekretär Dr. H. G. van Dam* (Düsseldorf:

surprise the curious reader, who learns that "inevitably, the criticism and rejection of the establishment, in accordance with the general mood of the times, was directed against the Jewish establishment, too".[2] In 1973, former chairman Heinz Galinski proceeded to a closer examination of this worrisome trend and diagnosed a "problem of identity among the Jewish youth" as its underlying cause. While negating the existence of a very intense generational conflict, Galinski however concedes that the relationship between the youth, many of whom sympathizers of the political left, and the old-established community members was indeed "not without problems".[3] The Central Council was accordingly seen as an ally of the political establishment; as a matter of fact, it had become an identifiable part of it.

Another possible effect of what is termed here "establishmentization" is the bias for a less confrontational approach to solving political issues. The recent quarrel over public funding between the Central Council of Jews in Germany, the German government, and the Union of Progressive Jews in Germany (*Union progressiver Juden in Deutschland*, UPJ) aptly illustrates the point.[4] Founded in 1997 as a working group of liberal and conservative communities, the UPJ currently represents about 4,500 members in Germany. Its main objective, says chairman Jan Mühlstein, is to offer a "religious alternative" within the larger

---

[2] Zentralrat, 1970), 13. In original: "*Man vermißt beim Zentralrat politischen Aktivismus von verschiedenen Gesichtspunkten her*".
Zentralrat der Juden in Deutschland, *Jüdische Gemeinschaft in Deutschland. Jahresbericht 1969/70 von Generalsekretär Dr. H. G. van Dam* (Düsseldorf: Zentralrat, 1970), 13. In original: "*Es konnte nicht ausbleiben, wie wir bereits in Berichten früherer Jahre dargestellt haben, daß sich Kritik und Ablehnung des Establishments dem allgemeinen Zug der Zeit entsprechend auch gegen das jüdische Establishment richtet, ob es nun lokal, regional oder zentral in Erscheinung tritt*".

[3] Heinz Galinski, "Kritisches Engagement. Das Identitätsproblem der jüdischen Jugend", *Allgemeine jüdische Wochenzeitung*, 28. Jg. Nr. 7, February 10, 1973.

[4] Among the most prominent exponents of liberal (or Progressive or Reform or, more generally, non-Orthodox) Judaism in Germany were Moses Mendelssohn, Leopold Zunz, Abraham Geiger, and Leo Baeck. Among their noted counterparts in the U.S. was Isaac Mayer Wise of Cincinnati.

Jewish community.[5] Yet unlike the Central Council, the UPJ started out as a self-sustaining organization without public funding and without being recognized as the official interlocutor of the German government. And unlike the Central Council, it did not maintain an institutionalized partnership with the state. As a result, the Union did not hesitate to adopt a much more assertive, even aggressive political style to secure a sound financial basis for its operations. In 2004, the UPJ publicly threatened to file a constitutional complaint against the German government unless it were granted equal access to the public funds available to the Central Council on the basis of the 2003 National Agreement.[6] This step strikes one as especially significant when considering that the UPJ otherwise

[5] Interview with Jan Mühlstein, Chairman, Union progressiver Juden in Deutschland, September 14, 2009, Munich. Various factors, Mühlstein says, contributed to the revival of liberal Judaism in Germany in the 1990s: first, the need for liberal rabbis attendant upon the closing of U.S. military bases (where many religious services, open to the general Jewish public, had been performed in the non-Orthodox tradition); second, the impact of Jewish immigration from countries of the former Soviet Union; and third, the renewed interest in non-Orthodox Judaism among the younger generation and those who had rediscovered their Jewish roots.

[6] Legal scholars have argued that the unequal treatment of the UPJ does not violate the principle of equality stated in Art. 3 of the German Basic Law, which stipulates that what is essentially the same has to be treated equally, and what is essentially different, unequally (*"allgemeiner Gleichheitssatz"*). First, the Central Council is not the addressee of the *Gleichheitssatz*; second, its privileged status is justified because it assumes functions usually performed by the state, such as the integration of Jewish immigrants. Moreover, the text of the National Agreement of 2003 does not entitle the UPJ to financial aid as it cannot be qualified as a contract for the benefit of a third party, writes Kyrill-Alexander Schwarz, "Die Verteilung der Finanzmittel aus dem zwischen der Bundesrepublik Deutschland und dem Zentralrat der Juden geschlossenen Staatsvertrag", *Religion – Staat – Gesellschaft* 6:1-2 (2005), 123-164. Yet, the key argument made by Schwarz – that the unequal treatment of the UPJ is consistent with Art. 3 Basic Law – is not convincing. If taken to its logical conclusion, Schwarz's line of argument ultimately justifies inequality by inequality: the Central Council is privileged because it performs public services it is able to perform due to its privileged status; the UPJ, lacking such privileges, is unable to perform similar services, which supposedly justifies its unequal treatment. Obviously, this is a circular argument.

defines itself not as a political, but as a decidedly religious Jewish organization. Though initially reluctant to yield to the UPJ's demands, the Central Council, pressurized by Chancellor Gerhard Schröder and fearful of a lasting schism within the Jewish community in Germany, eventually agreed to provide adequate financial support.[7] It is hard to think of finding a similarly confrontational stance adopted by the Central Council towards its main political ally: the German state.

5.2 Instrumentalization and Alibi Politics

Yet another risk that the Central Council faces is the risk of instrumentalization and involvement in alibi politics. The evidence suggests that Jewish organizations such as the Central Council frequently serve the purpose of providing political alibis to legitimize the state and some of its policies. Because the state has interests of its own and pursues these interests accordingly, Jewish organizations run the risk of being instrumentalized for specific purposes if they align themselves too closely with the state.

It is widely held that Germany's relationship with its Jewish minority is an indicator of the country's democratic culture, indeed a touchstone for German democracy as such, as U.S. High Commissioner John McCloy had put it in 1949. The attitude towards Jews, as well as state-sponsored philo-Semitism, thus came to serve as a strategy of moral legitimization of domestic and, in particular, of foreign policy goals. To serve the purpose of moral and political legitimization, the Jews in Germany were reinstated in the imaginary world of postwar Germany in a romanticizing and monumentalizing fashion: "The public rejection of anti-Semitism, the affirmation of pro-Jewish attitudes, the profession of philo-Semitism", the historian Frank Stern writes, "were increasingly instrumentalized and became both a proof of the democratic character of the Republic and elements of a "normalization" of the German relationship with its own past". The officially coveted German-Jewish reconciliation therefore meant nothing different than "the continuous reconcili-

---

[7] See Mühlstein (2009 Interview).

ation of the Federal Republic with the German past".[8] A similar claim is made by sociologist Y. Michal Bodemann, who argues that the Jews in Germany were intentionally "reinvented" by mainstream German politicians after the war "for national, partisan or personal goals": by the CDU, as a sign of redemption of guilt and as a proof of the purification from Nazism; and by the SPD, as the tacit allies of social-democratic ideals and values.[9] As Bodemann convincingly shows, the Jewish New Year's greetings of government leaders – from Adenauer to Kohl, from Brandt to Schmidt – were primarily directed at the political class itself rather than at the country's Jewish community.[10] In the same vein, vice-president of the Central Council Salomon Korn in 2009 warned against an "externally-guided and "socially acceptable" Jewish culture of representation": German-Jewish culture must not be "extorted under pressure for societal legitimation" or "serve a political calculus", Korn said. The much-acclaimed phenomenon of "German-Jewish culture", he concluded, was nothing but "a phantom": a product of imagination.[11]

The Central Council has been cognizant of the danger of instrumentalization ever since it was founded in 1950, and for example opposed Adenauer's plans to establish a Department for Jewish Affairs in the Bonn government. When the interior ministry nominated Rabbi Aaron Ohrenstein to the controversial post, the Central Council by a large majority voted against the proposal on grounds that such an appointee would play the role of a "whipping boy" when things went wrong, yet would otherwise have little responsibilities of his own. In fact, the very prospect of an official bureau for Jewish affairs within the German government had indirectly led to the creation of the Central Council a

---

[8] Frank Stern, "Antisemitismus und Philosemitismus in der politischen Kultur der entstehenden Bundesrepublik Deutschland", in: Nachama/Schoeps (eds.) (1992), 157, 154, respectively.

[9] Y. Michal Bodemann, *Gedächtnistheater. Die jüdische Gemeinschaft und ihre deutsche Erfindung* (Hamburg: Rotbuch Verlag, 1996), 177.

[10] See Bodemann (1996), 148-179. For a contrasting example, see Jüdische Allgemeine, "Wie halten Sie's mit den Juden? Fragen an die Spitzenkandidaten und Parteivorsitzenden von SPD, CDU, CSU, Bündnis 90/Die Grünen, FDP und PDS", September 12, 2002.

[11] Salomon Korn, "Deutsch-jüdische Kultur? Ein Phantom!", *Frankfurter Allgemeine Zeitung*, October 1, 2009. In original: "(...) *Aufrechterhaltung einer außengeleiteten, „gesellschaftsfähigen" jüdischen Repräsentationskultur*".

few months earlier.[12] In 1985, in the wake of the Bitburg affair, an editorial in the *Allgemeine jüdische Wochenzeitung* quite bluntly stated that "Jews are not an alibi" and that "unconditional consent" could not be expected from the Jewish community in Germany.[13] When Chancellor Helmut Kohl seized the symbolic date of November 9, 1988, marking the fiftieth anniversary of the November pogroms, as an opportunity to highlight his special ties to the country's Jews in a speech at the Westend synagogue in Frankfurt, he was met with unexpected resistance from the audience: in two instances his speech was interrupted by "some young Jews", who accused the chancellor of telling "all lies" (*"alles Lüge"*), asked him about Bitburg, and refused to tolerate being called "co-citizens" (*"Mitbürger"*). Kohl's duplicitous and embarrassing appearance was only eclipsed by the even more disastrous address given one day later by Philipp Jenninger, a member of the CDU and president of the German Bundestag, in which he had failed to sufficiently distance himself from the country's Nazi past and was forced to resign as a result of his misleadingly worded and – unintentionally – offensive remarks.[14]

Furthermore, a comparison of the Council presidents Werner Nachmann and Ignatz Bubis suggests that the risk of providing political alibis can be substantially limited by an effective and uncompromising personal leadership style. "The Nachmanns made Germany kosher again", Henryk M. Broder writes, "because they served as living proof of how well the Jews were treated. Therefore, they were wooed, courted, festooned with Distinguished Service Crosses, invited to the chancellor's parties, and taken on trips abroad by ministers".[15] Yet whereas Nachmann found little fault with providing "our assistance" (*"unsere Mithilfe"*) to help re-establish the Federal Republic on par with the free nations of the world, Bubis did not lend himself to a similarly predictable and politically expedient role.[16] He was not a purveyor of political

---

[12] See Geller (2005), 87; quote ibid. (quotation marks in original).
[13] Allgemeine jüdische Wochenzeitung, "Juden sind kein Alibi", 40. Jg. Nr. 30, July 26, 1985.
[14] Quoted in Allgemeine jüdische Wochenzeitung, "Gemeinsame Besinnung. Die Gedenkfeier des Zentralrats zum 9. November in Frankfurt", 43. Jg. Nr. 46, November 18, 1988.
[15] Broder (1992), 299, translation by Brenner (1997), 138.
[16] Quoted in Hermann Lewy, "Arbeit und Aufgaben des Zentralrats. Interview mit Werner Nachmann, Vorsitzender des Direktoriums des Zentralrats", *All-*

alibis for the ruling elites; to the contrary, as Werner Konitzer concludes in his discussion of Bubis's activism of the early 1990s, he was increasingly seen as "a disagreeable witness".[17]

To be sure, the involvement in alibi politics is not an inevitable fate for the Central Council. A recent example is the umbrella's refusal to lend further legitimacy to the *Stiftung Flucht, Vertreibung, Versöhnung* (SFVV, or "Foundation Flight, Expulsion and Reconciliation"), a documentation and exhibition center established in December 2008 as a dependent foundation under public law and administered by the German Historical Museum in Berlin. Its stated purpose is "to preserve the memory of flight and expulsion in the twentieth century in the spirit of reconciliation" and in the context of the Second World War. Presented against the general background of forced migration in last century Europe, it specifically deals with the fate of ethnic German expellees, the *Vertriebene*, and thus discusses aspects of German victimhood and German suffering. The Foundation's programmatic focus is determined by a board of trustees, which also decides "on all essential matters". It comprises 21 members, 19 of whom are elected by the German Bundestag for a five-year period: four are nominated by the Bundestag, while the federal foreign office, the federal ministry of the interior, and the federal commissioner for culture and the media nominate one member each; the *Bund der Vertriebenen* (BdV, or "Federation of Expellees"), a non-governmental umbrella organization, nominates six members; finally, the E-

---

    gemeine jüdische Wochenzeitung, 29. Jg. Nr. 38, September 29, 1974; see also Cornelia Rabitz, "Der Bubis-Faktor", *Allgemeine jüdische Wochenzeitung*, 51. Jg. Nr. 15, July 25, 1996.

[17] Werner Konitzer, "Alibi oder Zeuge? Ignatz Bubis und die fremdenfeindliche Gewalt im vereinigten Deutschland", in: Backhaus/Gross/Lenarz (eds.) (2007), 147. For a similar assessment, see Ernst Benda, "Ignatz Bubis in der deutschen Politik", in: Backhaus/Gross/Lenarz (eds.) (2007), 134-137, and Raphael Gross, "Ignatz Bubis – Ein jüdisches Leben in Deutschland", in: Backhaus/Gross/Lenarz (eds.) (2007), 12. Nonetheless, in his autobiography, Bubis states that the prominent status accorded to the chairman of the Central Council "fulfills the function of a certain alibi". Bubis however uses the term in a non-pejorative fashion, understood under the aspect of gauging the state of democracy in Germany, see Bubis (1993), 107-108, 112.

vangelical Church, the Catholic Church, and the Central Council of Jews in Germany nominate two members each.[18] The Central Council had called for a new direction of the *Stiftung Flucht, Vertreibung, Versöhnung* already in early 2010, threatening to withdraw its participation should the expulsion of Germans not be presented in the context of National Socialist policies of expansion and extermination. A bitter conflict broke out a few months later over the remarks made by two representatives of the BdV who questioned the German guilt for the outbreak of World War II and relativized the Nazi system of slave and forced labor. When Erika Steinbach, chairman of the BdV, defended the controversial claims, the representatives of the Central Council, Presidium member Lala Süsskind and vice-president Salomon Korn, suspended their membership in the Foundation, saying they would not perform an "alibi function". As a result of the Central Council's withdrawal, the Foundation tellingly suffered a severe blow to its legitimacy.[19]

As a final example of alibi politics, we shall now turn to a case study of the Central Council's role at a decisive moment in German history: the fall of the Berlin Wall and the unfolding process of German unification.

5.3 "Exculpatory Witnesses" – German Unification and the Central Council

Since the postwar revival of Jewish life in Germany is widely perceived as a vote of confidence in the Federal Republic and as a living proof of a new and truly democratic Germany, the political role played by (and projected upon) the Central Council in the run-up to German unification is a particularly worthwhile subject of inquiry. In selecting an egregious, albeit hitherto understudied example of alibi politics, the following analysis of the period from the fall of the Berlin Wall to May 1991 shows how the Central Council came to serve as a powerful political asset for the German government due to its unstrained support for the process of

---

[18] See Stiftung Flucht, Vertreibung, Versöhnung, "Faltblatt der Stiftung Flucht, Vertreibung, Versöhnung", http://www.dhm.de/sfvv/docs/Faltblatt_SFVV. pdf, accessed March 14, 2011.

[19] Quoted in Christian Semler, "Von den Revisionisten vertrieben", *die tageszeitung*, September 7, 2010.

reunification. Despite its vocal backing for German unity, however, the Central Council was greeted with less gratitude than expected. As we shall see, the umbrella's central demand – an explicit reference to the country's Nazi past in the preamble of the Treaty of Unification – was not taken into account by the German government. Left with little else than empty promises, the Central Council yet again found itself in the unfortunate position of having served as an "exculpatory witness".

What is perhaps most striking to begin with is the unusual speed with which the Central Council embraced the idea of a unified Germany. In January 1990, two months after the Berlin Wall had been breached and a few weeks after Chancellor Helmut Kohl had met with GDR Minister President Hans Modrow for roundtable talks, Chairman Heinz Galinski declared he was "not afraid of" and had "no reservations" regarding the reunification of both German states.[20] These claims stood in sharp contrast to the stance of Lord Immanuel Jakobovits, the Chief Rabbi of England, who had voiced concerns about a renewed wave of anti-Semitism in the event of unification. The Israeli government, too, distanced itself from the Central Council. In a response to Yitzhak Shamir, the prime minister of Israel, Galinski declared that comparisons between Nazi Germany and the Federal Republic after a possible fusion with East Germany were "entirely beside the point" (*"völlig abwegig"*).[21]

The complacent attitude of the Central Council is all the more surprising when considered against the backdrop of the manifold negative domestic and foreign reactions to the prospect of German reunification. Influential intellectuals like Günter Grass, who in a 1990 lecture famously coined the phrase "We cannot get by Auschwitz", opposed the idea of German self-determination and unification on the grounds that the Holocaust could only have been perpetrated by a strong and united Germany.[22] In contrast to the United States, neither the British nor the French governments were particularly keen to bring about an end to the division of both Germanys. While the British prime minister, Margaret Thatcher, opted for acquiescence, the president of the French Republic,

---

[20] Quoted in Allgemeine jüdische Wochenzeitung, "Keine Vorbehalte gegen die Einheit", 45. Jg. Nr. 3, January 18, 1990.
[21] Quoted in Allgemeine jüdische Wochenzeitung, "Nazi-Vergleich "völlig abwegig"", 45. Jg. Nr. 6, February 8, 1990.
[22] Günter Grass, *Schreiben nach Auschwitz. Frankfurter Poetik-Vorlesung* (Frankfurt am Main: Luchterhand Literaturverlag, 1990), 42.

323

François Mitterand, made no secret of his intention to try and block any move that might result in German unification. Mitterand set about convincing Soviet leaders that German ambitions had to be curtailed, and even went so far as to visit the GDR in December 1989 in a show of defiance and support for its sovereignty.[23]

Not uncritical servility, as one might have expected from Galinski's predecessor Werner Nachmann, but a clear "sense of proportions" – as secretary general Hendrik George van Dam once put it – had led Galinski to support German unification.[24] In an interview with the *Allgemeine jüdische Wochenzeitung* in late February 1990, Galinski expressed his conviction that unification was "unstoppable" and that it was "only a matter of time" before unity would eventually be achieved. At the same time, however, he also gave up his unconditional support: Galinski now stated he would not act as an "alibi-Jew" and, in a clear-cut reversal of his initial position, said that "certain reservations" and "certain worries are justified".[25] The Central Council was now determined not to simply relinquish its say on how to proceed on unification; instead of providing the German government with a political free pass, it was bound to negotiate an even-handed political deal.

Specifically, it suggested the Unification Treaty between West Germany and the GDR should include a passage taking into account "the special interests of the Jewish community". Hoping that his request would be granted, Galinski reiterated his generous support for unification, though in a slightly different way: it was "a great chance" for the

---

[23] See Tony Judt, *Postwar: A History of Europe Since 1945* (London: Heinemann, 2005), 638-643.

[24] "One must not overestimate our possibilities. We are just a decimated community of about 30,000. We are not an important voter group", Galinski said. Instead, he reiterated the time-tested guiding principle that had characterized the umbrella's political style for decades: "The only way for us to be convincing is through objectivity, through prudence. (...) The worst for us is not to be taken seriously anymore, to overestimate ourselves". Quoted in Allgemeine jüdische Wochenzeitung, ""Gewisse Sorgen sind angebracht"", 45. Jg. Nr. 8, February 22, 1990.

[25] Quoted in Allgemeine jüdische Wochenzeitung, ""Gewisse Sorgen sind angebracht"", 45. Jg. Nr. 8, February 22, 1990. In original: *"Ich glaube, die Einigung ist nicht aufzuhalten. (...) Die Einigung kommt. Ob sofort oder später, das ist ja nur eine Frage der Zeit"*.

new Germany, he said, but also "a great test of character" ("*große Bewährungsprobe*"). Galinski also said there was no reason to be afraid of a unified Germany, adding the Central Council was "the best mediator" ("*der beste Mittler*") to prove this to the public. The position of the Central Council regarding the Unification Treaty – also referred to as *Einigungsvertrag* or second *Staatsvertrag*[26] – was spelled out in detail in a memorandum to Chancellor Kohl in July 1990 and comprised essentially two points highlighting the country's sustained commitment to political continuity and historical memory: first, it called for the preamble of the Unification Treaty to state in unambiguous terms that the division of Germany had been a consequence of the National Socialist dictatorship; and second, it called for united Germany to renew its special responsibility for its Jewish citizens as well as toward the State of Israel. The Central Council's proposal was quickly viewed with favor by Chancellor Kohl, who instructed the minister of the interior, Wolfgang Schäuble, to work on an appropriate draft. Indeed, Kohl had only a few days earlier expressed his sympathies for the Central Council on the occasion of the umbrella's fortieth anniversary. In addition to the accolades bestowed on the umbrella for its "reliable, good and trustful partnership", the chancellor had further declared: "The united Germany, too, will fess up to its history in all of its parts and will be aware of its special responsibility toward the Jews".[27]

In August 1990, Interior Minister Schäuble submitted to the Central Council a first proposal for the wording of the preamble in the Unification Treaty. Its key paragraph – "(...) Aware of the continuity of German history and bearing in mind the special responsibility arising from our past for a democratic development in Germany committed to respect for human rights and to peace, (...)" – however made no explicit reference

[26] The first *Staatsvertrag* was signed on May 18, 1990 and established a "monetary, economic and social union" between the two Germanys, thus providing the legal basis for the extension of the Deutsche Mark to East Germany. It came into force on July 1, 1990.

[27] All previous statements quoted in Hans-Peter Föhrding, "Sich der Geschichte stellen. Erwartungen und Wünsche des Zentralrats an den Einigungsvertrag / Treffen mit Kanzler Kohl", *Allgemeine jüdische Wochenzeitung*, 45. Jg. Nr. 30, July 26, 1990; see also ibid., ""Jede jüdische Einrichtung in der DDR mit Leben erfüllen". Interview mit Heinz Galinski über den Zusammenschluss der beiden deutschen Staaten".

to the Nazi past and thus could not but stir the opposition of the Central Council. As Heinz Galinski wrote in a letter to the chairmen of the parliamentary groups in the Bundestag and the East German Volkskammer, the wording of the proposal "does not touch the heart of the matter" and "in no way embodies our concern expressed in the memorandum". Still optimistic about resolving the differences of opinion, Galinski subsequently drafted a new proposal, intended as a "suggestion for a compromise", on the basis of the original text submitted by the interior ministry. While integrating the original text's introductory and concluding words without changes, Galinski's rephrased paragraph contains various important amendments: first, it refers to the period between 1933 and 1945 and, second, to the singularity of the crimes perpetrated during that period; third, it stresses the "obligations towards all victims", thereby alluding to possible reparation payments for the Jewish victims of Nazi persecution in East Germany and Eastern Europe.[28] In a bid to add authority to his proposals, Galinski restated his – now clearly conditional – support for unification in increasingly militant terms: "The new era cannot and must not begin without underscoring the responsibility for the past and, concomitantly, anchoring the continuity of history". In his appeal to government leaders "to seize the historic opportunity" to incorporate these claims into the treaty, Galinski concludes on a pugnacious note: "This is what we demand, unalterably" (*"Das ist unsere unumstöß-liche Forderung"*).[29]

On August 31, one week after the Volkskammer had voted to accede to the Federal Republic under the provisions of Article 23 of the German Basic Law, the Unification Treaty was eventually signed; in its final version, though, the preamble did not contain any of the suggestions made by the Central Council. The various appeals made by Heinz Galinski

---

[28] In original: "(...) im Bewußtsein der Kontinuität deutscher Geschichte und *besonders eingedenk der zwischen 1933 bis 1945 in ihrer Einmaligkeit begangenen Gewalttaten mit der sich daraus ergebenden Verpflichtung gegenüber allen Opfern und* Verantwortung für eine demokratische Entwicklung in Deutschland, die der Achtung der Menschenrechte und dem Frieden verpflichtet bleibt (...)". Amendments to the official text suggested by the Central Council are marked in italics.

[29] All previous statements quoted in Allgemeine jüdische Wochenzeitung, "Historische Chance zu klarem Bekenntnis. Appell Heinz Galinskis an Bundestag und Volkskammer", 45. Jg. Nr. 35, August 30, 1990.

had fallen on deaf ears with the country's political leaders – from the governing coalition of Helmut Kohl to the opposition SPD, whose chairman Hans-Jochen Vogel explained he had been unable to convince the party's rank and file of the respective amendments. The "chance" to mark the beginning of a new era with an unambiguous reference to the past, Galinski said, was now "irretrievably lost".[30] Moreover, the Treaty on the Final Settlement with Respect to Germany, commonly referred to in German as the *Zwei-plus-Vier Vertrag*, was signed in Moscow on September 12: it brought an end to the four-power status of Berlin, granted the Federal Republic full sovereignty over its internal and external affairs, and thus finally cleared the way for Germany's unification.

Curiously enough, however, the Central Council responded not with outraged opposition to the broken promises with which the German government had brazenly created this *fait accompli*. Defeated and disillusioned, it was instead forced into the bitter routine of government schmoozing: in a grotesque reversal of the umbrella's earlier stance, it now lavished praise on the chancellor and the involved political parties, and in its Jewish New Year's message on September 13 – merely one day after the 2+4 talks had been concluded with the eponymous treaty – complemented the federal government for having afforded the Central Council with "understanding and support" through a "constructive attitude over the course of the year". Chancellor Helmut Kohl in turn reciprocated the time-tested routine, producing once again the expedient all-purpose formula of the "special responsibility toward the Jews".[31]

The powerlessness of the Central Council was also on display in an editorial by Heinz Galinski on October 4, the day after the Unification Treaty had entered into force. In the editorial Galinski takes great pains to restate the Central Council's support for unification in emphatic terms so as "to dispel any possible misunderstandings: Our discomfort is not

---

[30] Quoted in Hans-Peter Föhrding, "Kann es das gewesen sein? Dem Einigungsvertrag fehlt ein eindeutiges Bekenntnis zu den Verbrechen der Nazizeit", *Allgemeine jüdische Wochenzeitung*, 45. Jg. Nr. 36, September 6, 1990.

[31] Zentralrat der Juden in Deutschland, "Verantwortung für die Opfer nicht vergessen. Neujahrsbotschaft des Zentralrats der Juden in Deutschland", *Allgemeine jüdische Wochenzeitung*, 45. Jg. Nr. 37, September 13, 1990; Helmut Kohl, "Grußbotschaft von Bundeskanzler Helmut Kohl zu Rosch Haschana 5751: "Das vereinte Deutschland ist sich der Verantwortung für die Juden bewusst"", ibid.

directed against unification". Regarding the discarded amendments to the preamble of the Unification Treaty, he by contrast merely laments not having been able to "convince" the political leadership of its "necessity" and "usefulness", writing cautiously that the incident "sets one thinking" ("*stimmt nachdenklich*"). The most direct form of criticism found in the editorial has no clear addressee, but calls on the political leadership in general to show a "higher degree of sensitivity" ("*ein höheres Maß an Sensibilität*"). The restraint shown by the Central Council must therefore be seen as a means of limiting further damages to its relationship with the German government, which it hoped might provide for a "generous handling" of the immigration requests of Jews from former Soviet Union countries. Small wonder, then, that the editorial concludes with an explicit endorsement of the recent political developments: "We are prepared to write a new chapter in history" ("*Wir sind bereit, ein neues Kapitel in der Geschichte aufzuschlagen*").[32]

The struggle and eventual failure to amend the preamble of the Unification Treaty represents more than a skirmish over an apparently minor symbolic concession. First, at a more general level, it contrasts the two essential and opposing conceptions of German history after unification: on the one hand, the position of the Central Council according to which Germany has to remain firmly anchored in its awareness of the past; and on the other, the ambition of the German government to restore normality and to close the chapter of the postwar period. Whereas the Central Council wanted unification to follow on the path of historical continuity, the German government saw the fusion of both Germanys as a fresh start and as the beginning of a new era. Second, it illustrates the quandaries associated with assuming the role of an "exculpatory witness" for the state. In spite of making unification "kosher" through its unstinting and dependable support, the umbrella's efforts were however not rewarded. That the German government could do so without having to fear any serious political backlash speaks to the unequal balance of power between both actors as well as to the limited possibilities of the Central Council vis-à-vis the state. Still, the silver lining found in this case study is that, in the period after unification, the Central Council will in all likelihood be less frequently exposed to the risk of instrumentali-

---

[32] Quoted in Allgemeine jüdische Wochenzeitung, "Erinnerung als Pflicht. Heinz Galinski zum 3. Oktober", 45. Jg. Nr. 40, October 4, 1990.

zation – with the solution of the German-German question in 1990, the need for political alibis has clearly diminished. But so has the attention paid to the Central Council: on May 8, 1991, the Central Council noted "[w]ith horror" (*"Mit Erschrecken"*) that "not a single politician" had "taken notice" of the first anniversary of the end of the Second World War after the propitious events that had led to German unification only a few months earlier.[33]

---

[33] Heinz Galinski quoted in Allgemeine jüdische Wochenzeitung, "Deutsche Politiker und der 8. Mai. Geschichtsbewußtsein fehlt", 46. Jg. Nr. 20, May 16, 1991.

6 Summary

The previous analysis has argued that the Central Council of Jews in Germany often finds itself in an uneasy position, struggling to find a balance between the pledge of loyalty and partnership on the one hand and the risk of instrumentalization on the other. As we have seen, the political style of the Central Council reflects these tensions. The archival record shows that the Central Council does not assume the role of a "Praeceptor Germaniae" but rather contents itself with a more modest role in politics. The biased perception of Jews in Germany further contributes to this predicament. Due to the umbrella's role as the advocate for a group of "exotic" outsiders, the politics of the Central Council is altogether less assertive than it would otherwise be.

By the same token, one may thus legitimately raise the question as to whether the Central Council actually enjoys the privilege of a so-called "special relationship" with the German state. After all, there are commitments on both sides of the "contract". In a situation characterized by asymmetric power relations, as the example of German unification illustrates, the state however enjoys a fairly comfortable position. It does not incur the risks of dependency and instrumentalization; to the contrary, the evidence presented here suggests that the state rather stands to gain from its close partnership with the Central Council.

Part Four: Conclusions and Perspectives for Research

The purpose of this dissertation has been to provide a contrastive analysis of the most important contemporary Jewish political organizations in the United States and in Germany. Its main theoretical and empirical ambition was to describe and explain how Jewish organizations operate in what we have termed a society-centered and a state-centered model of politics. At the most general level, we have argued that both institutional and non-institutional factors of the polity have a decisive impact on the politics of Jewish organizations in the countries under review. The first part of this study introduced three major axes for analysis as well as a theory of intergroup coalitions and a conceptualization of the relationship between Jewish organizations and the state; the second part provided a detailed empirical account of the politics of Jewish organizations in the United States; finally, the third part dealt extensively with the Central Council of Jews in Germany – one of the most prominent, yet least studied (and perhaps least understood) organizations in German political life today.

The findings presented here rest on a broad empirical basis. First and foremost, more than 20 semi-structured interviews were conducted with representatives of the world's major Jewish organizations in Germany and the United States, complemented by conversations with some of the leading experts in the field. In order to put the insights thus gathered into a larger context, this dissertation has made extensive use of various hitherto underexamined archival collections. In particular, the "Politics of American Jews Project" of the American Jewish Committee Oral History Collection of the New York Public Library and the "Ethnic Groups and American Foreign Policy Project" of the Columbia University Center for Oral History Collection proved a highly valuable source of information. The analysis of the complete annual reports of the Central Council of Jews in Germany as well as the articles in the *Allgemeine jüdische Wochenzeitung* and the *Jüdische Allgemeine* (both edited by the

Central Council) allowed for a comprehensive discussion of the umbrella and, hopefully, contributed to original research on the topic.

Regarding Jewish organizations in the United States, we find that the properties of the American political system create significant rivalries among Jewish organizations and shape their political styles accordingly. Because American Jewish organizations operate in a fundamentally fluid and highly competitive environment, they need to carve characteristic organizational niches and craft distinct political styles and identities in order to maintain themselves. In the same vein, and by taking a decidedly disaggregated view of Jewish organizations, we have concluded that the notion of an "Israel lobby" as a political actor in its own right is neither intuitively plausible nor supported by the empirical evidence. The initial distinction between modern and new Jewish politics has helped illustrate this point by illuminating the variegated and at times antagonistic roles that Jewish organizations have played in the American political process.

Within the category of modern Jewish politics, our analysis of the "big three" Jewish defense organizations and the leading Jewish umbrellas has shown substantial differences in terms of style and political orientation. While the American Jewish Committee is known for its rather quiet and diplomatic approach to politics, the Anti-Defamation League has honed its image as a "tough" and more outspoken organization, with the American Jewish Congress still struggling to find a viable niche of activity next to its rivals. A similar logic obtains for the Jewish Council for Public Affairs and for the Conference of Presidents of Major American Jewish Organizations. While the JCPA is associated with predominantly domestic affairs, a bent for liberal politics, and a strongly participatory decision-making process, the Presidents Conference by contrast represents an internationally oriented, less liberal, and more discretionary organization. The main challenge for these umbrellas has furthermore been to skillfully walk the line between representing their constituent organizations, on the one hand, and assuming independent powers of their own, on the other. Fearing for new competitors in their arenas of activity, the constituent organizations – among them the "big three" – have been especially wary of seeing the coordinating bodies become players in their own right. Though the JCPA's complex decision-making system strengthens internal cohesion, it also places serious limits on the organization's political effectiveness; and while the Presidents Conference has owed its weight to a flexible and fairly discretionary leadership style, it has also done so at the constant risk of alienating the very organizations it crucially depends on for its success.

Within the category termed the new Jewish politics, we have differentiated between the contrasting models of Israel and policy advocacy and discussed AIPAC and J Street as their respective representative examples. Though both organizations, unlike their above mentioned traditional counterparts, insert themselves directly and permanently in the electoral and legislative process, they however represent different models of pro-Israel advocacy: while AIPAC supports the policies of the Israeli government irrespective of the latter's political outlook, J Street in contrast operates as a policy advocacy organization wedded to a narrowly defined partisan agenda.

An important related finding is that American Jewish organizations can enhance their political relevance by fostering a decidedly bipartisan outlook. Among the main reasons for AIPAC's formidable success has been its political flexibility and nonpartisanship, owing to the organization's long-standing tenet of not endorsing or contributing to congressional candidates. The opposite is true for J Street: not only has the organization, quite predictably, been at odds with the Israeli government in various instances; given the limitations imposed by being a policy advocacy organization, it has also yet to find its way into the representative mainstream of the American Jewish community. Moreover, bipartisanship is a determining factor for the political standing of the umbrella organizations in question. Due to its clearly liberal bent, the JCPA is to be considered a comparatively weak organization. The bipartisan appeal of the Presidents Conference in turn has made the umbrella less vulnerable to changes in the administration, a fact that has clearly added to its political clout in Washington.

While this dissertation did not aim at assessing the alleged "influence" or "power" of Jewish organizations, it has nonetheless shown that AIPAC – widely viewed as the key organization within the "Israel lobby" in the United States – is often misleadingly credited as the single most decisive factor in congressional support for Israel. It is important to note that AIPAC, while actively lobbying for its goals, also benefits considerably from predisposed sympathy in Congress. True, it may occasionally be able to garner the vaunted "signatures of 70 senators" on a given issue; but it can do so by building on a substantial degree of existing pro-Israel sentiment as opposed to generating or forcing it through the exercise of hard-nosed political pressure. All this is to say that we must be careful not to overrate AIPAC's actual political impact: that it is far from holding a position of unrivaled authority over congressional policy toward Israel is perhaps best evidenced by the rapid ascent of a rival organization such as J Street, a forerunner in online advocacy with a particular appeal among the younger generation of American Jews.

Regarding the Central Council of Jews in Germany, we have analyzed the religious and political umbrella organization of German Jewry as an example of state-centered politics. With the state as its foremost ally, the Central Council often finds itself in an uneasy position, struggling to find a balance between the pledge of partnership on the one hand and the risk of dependency on the other. As we have amply seen in the previous chapters, the umbrella's political style reflects these tensions accordingly and involves a politics guided by the notion of modesty and self-restraint. The comparatively limited level of political ambition sought by the Central Council yet must also be placed in the perspective of the overall political culture. Not least due to the biased perception of the Jewish minority in Germany the umbrella does not aspire to assume the role of a "Praeceptor Germaniae": given its role as the advocate for a group of "exotic" outsiders, the politics of the Central Council is altogether less assertive than it would otherwise be. In addition, the notion of a "special relationship" between the German state and the Jewish community has far less public support than is commonly believed and has at times been contradicted by the actual behavior of political and government leaders.

At the same time, the political outlook and relevance of the Central Council depends to a large extent on the leadership skills and personality of its chairmen and presidents. While for many years after its founding the Central Council had kept a low political profile, in the 1990s, however, the deft leadership of Ignatz Bubis helped transform the umbrella into a more visible public affairs agency. The traditional way of "backdoor politics", as it had for example been practiced by the diffident and uncritically assimilative Werner Nachmann, was now replaced by a more assertive and publicity-oriented model of representation. Despite his relatively short tenure at the helm of the Central Council from 1992 to 1999, Bubis gained enormous popularity in Germany and can arguably be characterized as the most charismatic and most influential of all German Jewish leaders of the postwar era.

A further line of investigation addressed the risks and challenges the Central Council is exposed to due to its close relationship with the state. In particular we have argued that the Central Council has frequently run the risk of instrumentalization and involvement in alibi politics. Our case study of the role of the Central Council during German unification has shown how the umbrella was invoked by the German government to act as an "exculpatory witness" on its behalf: it served as a powerful political asset to counter national and international criticism that might have impeded further steps towards unification. Yet in spite of making unification "kosher" through its unstinting and dependable support, the umbrella's efforts were ultimately not rewarded. The pledge made by Chancellor Kohl to amend the preamble of the Unification Treaty according to the suggestion of the Central Council remained an empty – indeed broken – promise. The case study, therefore, speaks first and foremost to the unequal balance of power between both actors and the Central Council's limited possibilities vis-à-vis the state. But we have also seen that the involvement in alibi politics is by no means an inevitable fate for the Central Council: its recent refusal to grant further legitimacy to the *Stiftung Flucht, Vertreibung, Versöhnung* illustrates how the umbrella can skillfully leverage its ascribed moral weight – and that its support (or the lack thereof) still matters a great deal to German political elites, even in the period after German unification.

At the theoretical level, the tenets associated with the "new" institutionalism provided a useful framework to understand how Jewish political organizations operate in two largely different political systems. Interest group politics, our study suggests, cannot be separated from the institutional context in which it occurs: it reminds us that states in effect play a crucial role in shaping the mobilization and overall capabilities of interest groups. Whereas in the pluralist system of the United States minority groups are most likely to acquire political power when working through broad-based societal coalitions, their counterparts in the neocorporatist German polity depend to a large extent on the goodwill of the state: in the state-centered model of politics as found in the Federal Republic, political power is often derived from sharing state power. Curiously, however, the distinct institutional environments in both countries tend to have a similar effect on the politics of Jewish organizations:

whereas in Germany the state clearly limits Jewish organizations in their overall potential, the fragmented American system abets a degree of competition that ultimately balances their divergent ambitions.

Consistent with the epistemology of the field, the key analytical category used in this dissertation has been the concept of "power". Understood not as a thing but as a relational concept, we have examined the horizontal and vertical relationships of power that shape the political style of Jewish organizations. In this respect James Q. Wilson's autonomy-based rationale proved an excellent paradigm for explaining coalition-building behavior among interest groups in the United States. Intent on guarding their autonomy, American Jewish organizations are generally wary of aligning themselves too closely with their peers; the practice of disjointed coalitions, involving cooperative arrangements with non-Jewish allies, is of particular importance for the rivaling "big three" Jewish defense organizations. In the German case, however, Wilson's autonomy-based rationale turns out to be devoid of explanatory value. The empirical evidence stands in sharp contradiction to Wilson's theoretical premises: curiously enough, it is the German state that serves as the principal ally for the Central Council. But this is only to say that, akin to the study of interest group politics in general, coalition theories, too, must be conceived and understood within their respective institutional context.

Accordingly, we may as well be prepared to make some predictive statements on the political conduct of Jewish organizations in both countries. Though it is, of course, impossible to foretell specific behavior, it can be reasonably argued that certain political initiatives are unlikely to yield meaningful results if transposed to the opposite institutional context. Extensive involvement in the electoral and legislative process, a strategy pioneered by AIPAC and extended to the realm of online advocacy by J Street, is hardly to be adopted by the Central Council of Jews in Germany. But even more importantly, the differences in political style are not specifically "German" (let alone "Jewish") phenomena; they are not cultural phenomena, but can be explained in large measure through the respective underlying institutional logic. Consider the example of the Claims Conference, an American Jewish organization that maintains an equally trusting partnership with the German state. Despite numerous objections to German restitution and compensation policy over the almost 60 years of its existence, the Claims Conference has preferred to stand clear of confrontative political standoffs with Germany (quite in contrast to some of its member organizations) and at times has even resisted domestic pressure from Holocaust survivors, taking sides with the German government instead.

A transatlantic and more broadly comparative perspective on Jewish organizations further indicates that substantial cultural and political transfers have taken place in rather unidirectional fashion – from Europe to the United States, and not, as one might expect, the other way around. Along with the influx of Jewish immigrants, a variety of distinct cultures and political philosophies were likewise imported to the United States, translating paradigmatically in the creation of the American Jewish Committee (founded by German-Jewish elites and as a non-Zionist organization) and the American Jewish Congress (largely influenced by Eastern European Jewry and strongly Zionist in outlook). Moreover, the concept and practice of Israel advocacy has remained an essentially American phenomenon. Cultural barriers relating to the image and self-perception of the Jewish minority as well as institutional boundaries owing to contrasting conceptions of interest representation as such appear to have precluded its transplantation to European soil. While this is evident in the political style of the Central Council of Jews in Germany today, the French case, too, offers a telling example. Recent efforts undertaken by the American Jewish Congress to encourage the creation of a French equivalent to AIPAC were met with disinterest and rejection by CRIF, the political umbrella of Jewish organizations in France; and although a small French-Jewish employers' organization, the *Union des Patrons et Professionnels Juifs de France* (UPJF), eventually accepted the Congress's guidance, its new posture can hardly be said to have had any palpable influence on the outcome of the ensuing presidential elections. Both the Central Council of Jews in Germany as well as its French counterpart CRIF have traditionally been disinclined to emulate the model of groups like AIPAC and to seek a more activist role that might put into jeopardy their privileged ties with the state.[1]

---

[1] See Stern (2009 Interview); American Jewish Congress, *2006 Annual Report of Accomplishments* (New York: AJCongress, 2006), 9; American Jewish Congress, *Forward Together – The American Jewish Congress 2007 Annual Report of Accomplishments* (New York: AJCongress, 2007), 3, 12; and Hoepfner (2006).

To be sure, the findings presented here are also subject to various limitations. Space did not always permit to pursue some promising directions for further study, which is why we may not aspire to present conclusions that can claim to hold invariably true across space and time. As we have seen in the first part of this dissertation, one possible way to structure research on Jewish organizations is around the functional, historical, and differential axes of analysis. Within the framework of a differential perspective, studies undertaken with a focus specifically on non-institutional factors would yield highly valuable dividends. For example, a comparative study of Muslim political organizations in Germany and the United States would help achieve a more nuanced understanding of the special dimension in German-Jewish relations. Likewise, an analysis of Jewish organizations in Israel – the only country in the world where Jews do not constitute a religious, ethnic, or political minority – would be suited to ascertain to what extent the biased perception of Jews by non-Jews can effectively hamper and distort the political activities of Jewish organizations. More generally, a study of the settler movement in Israel might reveal parallels in how not Jews or Jewish organizations, but Judaism itself (and its religious interpretations) may come to be used by political elites as a tool of statecraft in pursuit of certain ideological ends.

Finally, we may attempt to provide an answer to the question whether the term "Jewish politics" can be a useful conceptual tool for guiding research in political and social science. For the purpose of this dissertation, we have operationalized the term according to a pragmatic working definition by Peter Y. Medding, focusing on the horizontal and vertical politics of Jewish organizations as the key analytical categories. The overarching general question that has served as the impetus for this study however remains to be answered: whether or not there is such a thing that can arguably be qualified as "Jewish politics". In line with a central argument made by scholars like Ruth R. Wisse and, on a different note, Yuri Slezkine, one may conjecture that Jewish politics does not constitute a category of its own, but is best understood as a politics of accommodation and adaptation to the specific circumstances of the surrounding polity.[2] In the same vein, the evidence presented here strongly

---

[2] See Wisse (2008 Interview); Wisse (2007), 10, 169; and Yuri Slezkine, *The Jewish Century* (Princeton: Princeton University Press, 2004), 1, 64. This,

suggests that there is nothing inherently or manifestly "Jewish" about the advocacy of Jewish organizations. To the contrary, all organizations under review evince substantial differences in terms of their mission and political style and do not operate differently from other comparable interest groups. In broad terms, this finding by analogy challenges the essentialist belief (and misconception) that almost everything can indeed be "Jewish" if only Jews are involved in some form or another – Jewish art, Jewish culture, Jewish literature, Jewish humor, and so forth.[3]

Still, if the term "Jewish politics" is to convey any useful meaning for scholarly inquiry, it can be fruitfully used in those cases where Jews do not figure as the subject but rather as the *object* of politics. Our observation that Jewish organizations may occasionally run the risk of being instrumentalized for alibi purposes was particularly instructive in this regard. At the same time we should register the caveat that, in most instances, the term can be expected to be meaningless at best or altogether misleading. Writing about Jewish politics, it should therefore be said, counsels prudence and a keen awareness to the limited suitability of the term; rather than help to produce useful knowledge about social reality, it will more often than not obscure more than it reveals. As this dissertation has attempted to demonstrate in the broadest possible sense,

[3] however, does not hold true for Hasidic Judaism, which does not seek any form of accommodation to modernity but in fact rejects modernity as such. The great Austrian-British art historian Sir Ernst H. Gombrich has argued in this context that the term "Jewish culture" was "an invention of Hitler's forerunners and afterrunners". Likewise, Gombrich rejected the term "Jewish art". Given the "artificiality of the so-called Jewish identity", the notion of the Jews as a distinct category of individuals belongs to the realm of "collectivist myths", Gombrich contends. Regarding the commonplace distinction between Jews and Gentiles, Gombrich, who grew up in an assimilated Viennese Jewish family, writes: "We lack a term to designate all individuals of Jewish ancestry and thus cannot use but basically racist terminology. In fact, I think it was precisely the diversity of language and culture among the Jews of the diaspora that left race as the only distinguishing criterion after religion had ceased to serve that purpose". Quoted in The Gombrich Archive, "The Visual Arts in Vienna c. 1900; Reflections on the Jewish Catastrophe", http://gombricharchive.files.wordpress.com/2011/04/showdoc28.pdf, accessed May 6, 2011. For the German translation, see Ernst H. Gombrich, *Jüdische Identität und jüdisches Schicksal. Eine Diskussionsbemerkung* (Wien: Passagen Verlag, 1997), 33, 46, 54, 45, respectively.

it is a Gentile label that ultimately tells us more about larger society and the political culture of its majority than it tells us about Jews themselves.

List of Author Interviews and Conversations

Interview with Ari Alexenberg, Director, Israel Action Center, Jewish Community Relations Council of Greater Boston, December 16, 2008, Boston.

Interview with John P. Becker, Property Restitution Advisor, Office of the Special Envoy for Holocaust Issues, U.S. Department of State, July 9, 2009, Washington, D.C.

Interview with Howard Beigelman, Deputy Director of Public Policy, Orthodox Union, June 22, 2009, New York.

Interview with Deidre Berger, Director of AJC Berlin, American Jewish Committee, May 19, 2009, Berlin.

Interview with Eugene DuBow, former Director of AJC Berlin, American Jewish Committee, March 23, 2009, New York.

Interview with Rabbi Moshe Edelman, Associate Director, United Synagogue of Conservative Judaism, June 29, 2009, New York.

Interview with Ethan Felson, Vice President, Jewish Council for Public Affairs, May 8, 2009, New York.

Conversation with Peter A. Hall, Krupp Foundation Professor of European Studies, Minda de Gunzburg Center for European Studies, Harvard University, December 15, 2008, Cambridge, MA.

Interview with Malcolm Hoenlein, Executive Vice Chairman, Conference of Presidents of Major American Jewish Organizations, October 29, 2009, New York.

Conversation with Onno Hückmann, Fellow (Federal Foreign Office), Weatherhead Center for International Affairs, Harvard University, October 28, 2008, Cambridge, MA.

Conversation with Onno Hückmann, Fellow (Federal Foreign Office), Weatherhead Center for International Affairs, Harvard University, November 19, 2008, Cambridge, MA.

Interview with Kenneth Jacobson, Deputy National Director, Anti-Defamation League, June 17, 2009, New York.

Interview with Saul Kagan, Secretary, Conference on Jewish Material Claims Against Germany, June 5, 2009, New York.

Conversations with Karl Kaiser, Director, Program on Transatlantic Relations, Weatherhead Center for International Affairs, Adjunct Professor of Public Policy, John F. Kennedy School of Government, Harvard University, October 2008, Cambridge, MA.

Conversation with Ira Katznelson, Ruggles Professor of Political Science and History, Department of Political Science, Columbia University, April 30, 2009, New York.

Interview with Charlotte Knobloch, President, Zentralrat der Juden in Deutschland, September 1, 2009, Munich.

Interview with Martin Kramer, Senior Fellow, Weatherhead Center for International Affairs, Harvard University, November 6, 2008, Cambridge, MA.

Interview with Arieh Lebovitz, Communications Director, Jewish Labor Committee, June 26, 2009, New York.

Interview with Lawrence D. Lowenthal, National Senior Advisor, former Director of AJC Boston, American Jewish Committee, November 3, 2008, Cambridge, MA.

Interview with Amy Mitman, Assistant Vice President, Combined Jewish Philanthropies, November 12, 2008, Boston.

Interview with Jan Mühlstein, Chairman, Union progressiver Juden in Deutschland, September 14, 2009, Munich.

Interview with Gary Ratner, National Executive Director, Zionist Organization of America, June 26, 2009, New York.

Interview with Alan S. Ronkin, Deputy Director, Jewish Community Relations Council of Greater Boston, December 8, 2008, Boston.

Conversation (by phone) with Emily Ruda, Deputy Leadership Development Director, American Israel Public Affairs Committee, June 12, 2009.

Interview with Amy Spitalnick, Press Secretary, J Street, June 9, 2009, Washington, D.C.

Interview with Stephen Steiner, Director of Public Relations, Orthodox Union, June 22, 2009, New York.

Interview with Marc D. Stern, General Counsel and Assistant Executive Director, American Jewish Congress, June 10, 2009, New York.

Interview (follow-up) with Marc D. Stern, General Counsel and Assistant Executive Director, American Jewish Congress, June 12, 2009, New York.

Interview with Stephen M. Walt, Robert and Renée Belfer Professor of International Affairs, John F. Kennedy School of Government, Harvard University, October 6, 2008, Cambridge, MA.

Conversation with Jack Wertheimer, Joseph and Martha Mendelson Professor of American Jewish History, The Jewish Theological Seminary, March 24, 2009, New York.

Interview with Ruth R. Wisse, Martin Peretz Professor of Yiddish Literature and Professor of Comparative Literature, Center for Jewish Studies, Harvard University, December 11, 2008, Cambridge, MA.

Archival Collections

American Jewish Committee Blaustein Library, New York

> AIPAC Papers On U.S.-Israel Relations, ed. American Israel Public Affairs Committee. 1982-2000. 17 vols.
>
> Conference on Jewish Material Claims Against Germany. Annual reports. 1954-2000 (incomplete).
>
> Zentralrat der Juden in Deutschland. Annual reports. 1960-1970/71. Prepared by Hendrik George van Dam.

Center for Jewish History, New York

> Leo Baeck Institute. Council of Jews from Germany Collection. 1946-1964. 7 boxes.
>
> American Jewish Historical Society. Isaiah Leo Kenen papers, undated. 1919-1985. 23 manuscript boxes.
>
> YIVO Institute for Jewish Research. Conference on Jewish Material Claims Against Germany. Annual reports. 1954-2006 (incomplete).

The New York Public Library, Dorot Jewish Division

> Politics of American Jews Project / American Jewish Committee Oral History Collection, Astor, Lenox and Tilden Foundations. 1971-1991. Transcripts.
>
> Allgemeine jüdische Wochenzeitung, ed. Zentralrat der Juden in Deutschland. 1966-1973 (incomplete). 1973-2001. Microfilms.
>
> Jüdische Allgemeine, ed. Zentralrat der Juden in Deutschland. 2002-current. Hard copies.

Columbia University

> Butler Library. Midstream, a monthly Jewish review. 1972-2009. Microfilms.

Center for Oral History Collection. Ethnic Groups and American Foreign Policy Project. 1974-1986. Conducted by Judith Goldstein. Transcripts: 2,660 leaves, 37 interviews. Restrictions: open access, 13 interviews closed. Permission to cite, quote or reproduce required.

Harvard University, Widener Library

AIPAC Papers on U.S.-Israel Relations, ed. American Israel Public Affairs Committee, 1982-2000, 17 vols. (incomplete).

Bibliography

Aberbach, Joel D. and Bert A. Rockman, "Conducting and Coding Elite Interviews", *PS: Political Science & Politics* 35:4 (December 2002), 673-676.
Ahrari, Mohammed E. (ed.), *Ethnic Groups and U.S. Foreign Policy* (New York: Greenwood Press, 1987).
Ahrari, Mohammed E., "Domestic Context of U.S. Foreign Policy Toward the Middle East", in: Ahrari (ed.) (1987), 1-22.
AJC (ed.), *American Jewish Year Book*, 108 vols. (New York: AJC, 1899-2008).
Almond, Gabriel A., G. Bingham Powell, Russell J. Dalton and Kaare Strøm (eds.), *Comparative Politics Today: A World View* (New York: Pearson Longman, 2010).
American Jewish Committee, "National Jewish Organizations", in: AJC (ed.), *American Jewish Year Book Vol. 107* (New York: AJC, 2007), 605-665.
Atkinson, Michael M. and William D. Coleman, "Strong States and Weak States: Sectoral Policy Networks in Advanced Capitalist Economies", *British Journal of Political Science* 19:1 (January 1989), 47-67.
Avenary, Hanoch, "Shtadlan", in: Berenbaum/Skolnik (eds.) (2007), vol. 18, 521-522.
Bachrach, Peter and Morton S. Baratz, "Two Faces of Power", *American Political Science Review* 56:4 (December 1962), 947-952.
Backhaus, Fritz, Raphael Gross and Michael Lenarz (eds.), *Ignatz Bubis. Ein jüdisches Leben in Deutschland* (Frankfurt am Main: Jüdischer Verlag im Suhrkamp Verlag, 2007).
Badie, Bertrand and Pierre Birnbaum, *Sociologie de l'Etat* (Paris: Grasset, 1979).
Bala, Christian, *Konservatismus, Judaismus, Zionismus. "Kulturkrieg" in der US-Diaspora* (Baden-Baden: Nomos, 2006).
Bar-Chen, Eli, "Prototyp jüdischer Solidarität – Die Alliance Israélite Universelle", *Jahrbuch des Simon-Dubnow-Instituts* 1 (2002), 277-296.
Bard, Mitchell, "AIPAC and US Middle East policy", in: Gilboa/Inbar (eds.) (2009), 76-90.
Bard, Mitchell, "Ethnic Group Influence on Middle East Policy – How and When: The Cases of the Jackson-Vanik Amendment and the Sale of AWACS to Saudi Arabia", in: Ahrari (ed.) (1987), 45-64.
Barkai, Avraham, *"Wehr Dich!" Der Centralverein deutscher Staatsbürger jüdischen Glaubens (C.V.) 1893-1938* (München: Verlag C.H. Beck, 2002).
Barkan, Elazar and Alexander Karn (eds.), *Taking Wrongs Seriously. Apologies and Reconciliation* (Stanford: Stanford University Press, 2006).
Barry, Brian (ed.), *Power and Political Theory: Some European Perspectives* (London: Wiley, 1976).

Bartos, Helene, *Israeli-German Relations in the Years 2000-2006: A Special Relationship Revisited*, MPhil thesis, University of Oxford, 2007.

Baumgartner, Frank R. and Christine Mahoney, "The Determinants and Effects of Interest-Group Coalitions", paper prepared for delivery at the Annual Meeting of the American Political Science Association, Chicago, IL, September 2-5, 2004.

Baumgartner, Frank R. and Beth L. Leech, *Basic Interests: The Importance of Groups in Politics and Political Science* (Princeton: Princeton University Press, 1998).

Bell, Roderick, David V. Edwards and R. Harrison Wagner (eds.), *Political Power. A Reader in Theory and Research* (New York: The Free Press, 1969).

Benda, Ernst, "Ignatz Bubis in der deutschen Politik", in: Backhaus/Gross/Lenarz (eds.) (2007), 134-137.

Bentley, Arthur F., *The Process of Government: A Study of Social Pressures* (Chicago: University of Chicago Press, 1908).

Berenbaum, Michael and Fred Skolnik (eds.), *Encyclopaedia Judaica*, 22 vols., 2nd ed. (Detroit: Macmillan Reference USA, 2007).

Berenbaum, Michael, "Jewish Council on Public Affairs", in: Berenbaum/Skolnik (eds.) (2007), vol. 11, 288-289.

Berenbaum, Paul (ed.), *Not Your Father's Antisemitism: Hatred of the Jews in the Twenty-First Century* (St. Paul, MN: Paragon House, 2008).

Berger, David (ed.), *History and Hate: The Dimensions of Anti-Semitism* (Philadelphia: The Jewish Publication Society, 1986).

Berger, David, "Antisemitism: An Overview", in: Berger (ed.) (1986), 3-14.

Bergmann, Werner, "Die Haltung der deutschen Bevölkerung zur Wiedergutmachung", in: Brozik/Matschke (eds.) (2004), 16-24.

Bergmann, Werner, "Antisemitismus in Deutschland", in: Schubarth/Stöss (eds.) (2000), 131-154.

Berg-Schlosser, Dirk, "Politikwissenschaft international", in: Nohlen/Schulze (eds.) (2005), vol. 2, 722-728.

Berry, Jeffrey M. and Clyde Wilcox, *The Interest Group Society* (New York: Pearson Longman, 2009).

Berry, Jeffrey M., "Validity and Reliability Issues in Elite Interviewing", *PS: Political Science & Politics* 35:4 (December 2002), 679-682.

Biale, David, *Power and Powerlessness in Jewish History* (New York: Schocken Books, 1986).

Bindenagel, J. D., "Justice, Apology, Reconciliation, and the German Foundation: "Remembrance, Responsibility, and the Future"", in: Barkan/Karn (eds.) (2006), 286-310.

Bodemann, Y. Michal, *Gedächtnistheater. Die jüdische Gemeinschaft und ihre deutsche Erfindung* (Hamburg: Rotbuch Verlag, 1996).

Boix, Carles and Susan C. Stokes (eds.), *The Oxford Handbook of Comparative Politics* (New York: Oxford University Press, 2007).

Borut, Jacob, "Jewish politics and generational change in Wilhemine Germany", in: Roseman (ed.) (1995), 105-120.

Brenner, Michael, "Von den Hintertüren der Diplomatie auf die Bühne der Öffentlichkeit: Der Wandel in der Repräsentation des Zentralrats der Juden in Deutschland", in: Backhaus/Gross/Lenarz (eds.) (2007), 124-133.

Brenner, Michael, "Galinski, Heinz", in: Berenbaum/Skolnik (eds.) (2007), vol. 7, 349.

Brenner, Michael, "Germany", in: Berenbaum/Skolnik (eds.) (2007), vol. 7, 539-542.

Brenner, Michael, "Nachmann, Werner", in: Berenbaum/Skolnik (eds.) (2007), vol. 14, 720.

Brenner, Michael, "Zentralrat der Juden in Deutschland", in: Berenbaum/Skolnik (eds.) (2007), vol. 21, 510.

Brenner, Michael, "Warum man mit Finkelstein nicht diskutieren muss. Die neue Holocaust-Debatte und die deutsche Öffentlichkeit", in: Pieper (ed.) (2001), 201-207.

Brenner, Michael, "Epilog oder Neuanfang?", in: Romberg/Urban-Fahr (eds.) (2000), 35-44.

Brenner, Michael, *After the Holocaust: Rebuilding Jewish Lives in Postwar Germany* (Princeton: Princeton University Press, 1997), translated by Barbara Harshav.

Brenner, Michael, "The Jüdische Volkspartei – National-Jewish Communal Politics during the Weimar Republic", in: LBI (ed.), *LBI Year Book Vol. 35* (London: Secker & Warburg, 1990), 219-243.

Broder, Henryk M., "Rehabilitiert Werner Nachmann", in: Nachama/Schoeps (eds.) (1992), 299-303.

Browne, William P., "Organized Interests and Their Issue Niches: A Search for Pluralism in a Policy Domain", *Journal of Politics* 52:2 (May 1990), 477-509.

Browning, Rufus, Dale Marshall and David Tabb, *Protest Is Not Enough. The Struggle of Blacks and Hispanics for Equality in Urban Politics* (Berkeley: University of California Press, 1984).

Brozik, Karl and Konrad Matschke (eds.), *Claims Conference. Luxemburger Abkommen – 50 Jahre Entschädigung für NS-Unrecht* (Frankfurt am Main: Societäts-Verlag, 2004).

Brozik, Karl, "Gegendarstellung der Jewish Claims Conference", in: Pieper (ed.) (2001), 54-56.

Bubis, Ignatz, "Erschütterungen sind zu überstehen", in: Romberg/Urban-Fahr (eds.) (2000), 10-20.

Bubis, Ignatz and Wolfgang Schäuble (ed. Frank Schirrmacher), *Deutschland wohin?* (Freiburg: Herder, 1996).

Bubis, Ignatz and Peter Sichrovsky, *"Damit bin ich noch längst nicht fertig". Die Autobiographie* (Frankfurt am Main: Campus Verlag, 1996).

Bubis, Ignatz, *Ich bin ein deutscher Staatsbürger jüdischen Glaubens. Ein autobiographisches Gespräch mit Edith Kohn* (Köln: Kiepenheuer & Witsch, 1993).

Campbell, John L. and Ove K. Pedersen, *The Rise of Neoliberalism and Institutional Analysis* (Princeton: Princeton University Press, 2001).

Carter, Jimmy, *Palestine: Peace Not Apartheid* (New York: Simon & Schuster, 2006).

Cerny, Philip G., *The Changing Architecture of Politics: Structure, Agency, and the Future of the State* (London: Sage Publications, 1990).

Chanes, Jerome, ""America Is Different!" Myths and Realities in the Study of Antisemitism in the United States", in: Berenbaum (ed.) (2008), 217-244.

Chanes, Jerome, "American Jewish Congress (AJCongress)", in: Berenbaum/Skolnik (eds.) (2007), vol. 2, 56-58.

Chanes, Jerome, "Anti-Defamation League (ADL)", in: Berenbaum/Skolnik (eds.) (2007), vol. 2, 194-195.

Chanes, Jerome, "Conference of Presidents of Major American Jewish Organizations", in: Berenbaum/Skolnik (eds.) (2007), vol. 5, 140-143.

Chomsky, Noam, *Fateful Triangle. The United States, Israel, and the Palestinians* (Cambridge, MA: South End Press, 1999).

Cigler, Allan J. and Burdett A. Loomis (eds.), *Interest Group Politics* (Washington, D.C.: CQ Press, 2002).

Cohen, Naomi W., *Not Free to Desist. The American Jewish Committee 1906-1966* (Philadelphia: The Jewish Publication Society, 1972).

Cohen, Steven M. and Leonard J. Fein, "From Integration to Survival: American Jewish Anxieties in Transition", *Annals of the American Academy of Political and Social Science* 480:1 (July 1985), 75-88.

Conway, M. Margaret, Joanne Connor Green and Marian Currinder, "Interest Group Money in Elections", in: Cigler/Loomis (eds.) (2002), 117-140.

Conze, Eckart, Norbert Frei, Peter Hayes and Moshe Zimmermann, *Das Amt und die Vergangenheit. Deutsche Diplomaten im Dritten Reich und in der Bundesrepublik* (München: Karl Blessing Verlag, 2010).

Dahl, Robert A., "The Concept of Power", *Behavioral Science* 2:3 (July 1957), 201-215.

DellaPergola, Sergio, "World Jewish Population, 2007", in: AJC (ed.), *American Jewish Year Book Vol. 107* (New York: AJC, 2007), 551-600.

Dershowitz, Alan M., *The Vanishing American Jew. In Search of Jewish Identity for the Next Century* (Boston: Little, Brown and Company, 1997).

Derthick, Martha, *The National Guard in Politics* (Cambridge, MA: Harvard University Press, 1965).

Dicke, Klaus (ed.), *Politisches Entscheiden* (Baden-Baden: Nomos, 2001).

Diner, Hasia R., *The Jews of the United States, 1654 to 2000* (Berkeley: University of California Press, 2004).

Diner, Hasia R., "Jewish Self-Governance, American Style", *American Jewish History* 81:3-4 (Spring/Summer 1994), 277-295.

Dinnerstein, Leonard, *The Leo Frank Case* (New York: Columbia University Press, 1968).

Dollinger, Marc, *Quest for Inclusion. Jews and Liberalism in Modern America* (Princeton: Princeton University Press, 2000).

Dolzer, Rudolf, "Wirtschaft und Kultur im Völkerrecht", in: Vitzthum (ed.) (2007), 491-576.

Druks, Herbert, *The Failure to Rescue* (New York: R. Speller, 1977).

Duverger, Maurice (ed.), *Les régimes semi-présidentiels* (Paris: Presses Universitaires de France, 1986).

Edinger, Lewis J. and Brigitte L. Nacos, *From Bonn to Berlin. German Politics in Transition* (New York: Columbia University Press, 1998).

Edinger, Lewis J., *West German Politics* (New York: Columbia University Press, 1986).

Edwards, George C. III, Martin P. Wattenberg and Robert L. Lineberry, *Government in America. People, Politics, and Policy* (New York: Longman, 2006).

Eizenstat, Stuart E., *Imperfect Justice. Looted Assets, Slave Labor, and the Unfinished Business of World War II* (New York: PublicAffairs, 2003), foreword by Elie Wiesel.

Elazar, Daniel J., *Community and Polity: The Organizational Dynamics of American Jewry* (Philadelphia: The Jewish Publication Society, 1995).

Elazar, Daniel J. (ed.), *Authority, Power and Leadership in the Jewish Polity: Cases and Issues* (Lanham, MD: University Press of America, 1991).

Elazar, Daniel J., "Introduction – Jewish Political Studies as a Field", in: Elazar (ed.) (1991), 1-28.

Elazar, Daniel J., "Jewish Political Studies", *Modern Judaism* 11:1 (February 1991), 67-90.

Elazar, Daniel J., "Developments in Jewish Community Organization in the Second Postwar Generation", in: Lipset (ed.) (1990), 173-192.

Elazar, Daniel J. (ed.), *The New Jewish Politics* (Lanham, MD: University Press of America, 1988).

Elazar, Daniel J., "The New Jewish Politics", in: Elazar (ed.) (1988), 1-12.

Elazar, Daniel J., "Jewish Political Studies as a Field of Inquiry", *Jewish Social Studies* 36:3-4 (July-October 1974), 220-233.

Elon, Menachem, "Dina de-Malkhuta Dina", in: Berenbaum/Skolnik (eds.) (2007), vol. 5, 663-669.

Evans, Peter B., Dietrich Rueschemeyer and Theda Skocpol, *Bringing the State Back In* (New York: Cambridge University Press, 1985).

Fearon, James D. and David D. Laitin, "Explaining Interethnic Cooperation", *American Political Science Review* 90:4 (December 1996), 715-735.

Feldman, Lily Gardner, *The Special Relationship Between West Germany and Israel* (Boston: Allen & Unwin, 1984).

Findley, Paul, *They Dare to Speak Out: People and Institutions Confront Israel's Lobby* (Chicago: Lawrence Hill, 2003).

Fink, Carole, *Defending the Rights of Others: The Great Powers, the Jews, and International Minority Protection, 1878-1938* (New York: Cambridge University Press, 2004).

Finkelstein, Norman G., *The Holocaust Industry: Reflections on the Exploitation of Jewish Suffering* (London: Verso, 2000).

Fisher, Dana R., *Activism, Inc.: How the Outsourcing of Grassroots Campaigns Is Strangling Progressive Politics in America* (Stanford: Stanford University Press, 2006).

Fishkoff, Sue, *The Rebbe's Army. Inside the World of Chabad-Lubavitch* (New York: Schocken, 2003).

Fitz, Karsten, *The American Revolution Remembered, 1830s to 1850s. Competing Images and Conflicting Narratives* (Heidelberg: Universitätsverlag Winter, 2010).

Foundation for Public Affairs, The (ed.), *Public Interest Group Profiles 2006-2007* (Washington, D.C.: CQ Press, 2006).

Foundation for Public Affairs, The (ed.), *Public Interest Group Profiles 2004-2005* (Washington, D.C.: CQ Press, 2004).

Friedman, Murray, *The Neoconservative Revolution: Jewish Intellectuals and The Shaping of Public Policy* (New York: Cambridge University Press, 2005).

Friedman, Saul S., *No Haven for the Oppressed: United States Policy Toward Jewish Refugees, 1938-1945* (Detroit: Wayne State University Press, 1973).

Friesel, Evyatar, "The Centralverein and the American Jewish Committee: A Comparative Study", in: LBI (ed.), *LBI Year Book Vol. 36* (London: Secker & Warburg, 1991), 97-125.

Friesel, Evyatar, "The Political and Ideological Development of the Centralverein before 1914", in: LBI (ed.), *LBI Year Book Vol. 31* (London: Secker & Warburg, 1986), 121-146.

Gais, Thomas L. and Jack L. Walker, "Pathways to influence in American Politics", in: Walker (ed.) (1991), 103-121.

García Bedolla, Lisa, *Latino Politics* (Cambridge, MA: Polity Press, 2009).

Geller, Jay Howard, *Jews in Post-Holocaust Germany, 1945-1953* (Cambridge: Cambridge University Press, 2005).

Gellner, Winand and Martin Kleiber, *Das Regierungssystem der USA. Eine Einführung* (Baden-Baden: Nomos, 2007).

Gellner, Winand and John D. Robertson (eds.), *The Berlin Republic: German Unification and A Decade of Changes* (London: Frank Cass, 2003).

Gellner, Winand, "Effizienz und Öffentlichkeit – Entscheiden im präsidentiellen System der USA", in: Dicke (ed.) (2001), 71-87.

Gellner, Winand, *Ideenagenturen für Politik und Öffentlichkeit: Think Tanks in den USA und in Deutschland* (Opladen: Westdeutscher Verlag, 1995).

Gerson, Louis L., "The Influence of Hyphenated Americans on U.S. Diplomacy", in: Said (ed.) (1981), 19-31.

Giddens, Anthony, *The Constitution of Society: Outline of the Theory of Structuration* (Berkeley: University of California Press, 1986).

Gide, André, "Les Juifs, Céline et Maritain", *Nouvelle Revue Française* 295 (April 1938), 630-636.

Gilboa, Eytan and Efraim Inbar (eds.), *US-Israeli Relations in a New Era: Issues and Challenges After 9/11* (London: Routledge, 2009).

Gilboa, Eytan, "The public dimension of US-Israel relations: a comparative analysis", in: Gilboa/Inbar (eds.) (2009), 53-75.

Gilboa, Eytan, *American Public Opinion toward Israel and the Arab-Israeli Conflict* (Lexington, MA: Heath and Company, 1987).

Ginsberg, Benjamin, "Identity and Politics. Dilemmas of Jewish Leadership in America", in: Maisel/Forman (eds.) (2001), 3-27.

Giugni, Marco, "Welfare States, Political Opportunities, and the Mobilization of the Unemployed: A Cross-National Analysis", *Mobilization: An International Journal* 13:3 (September 2008), 297-310.

Glazer, Nathan, *The Social Basis of American Communism* (New York: Harcourt, Brace & World, 1961).

Goldberg, David Howard, *Foreign Policy and Ethnic Interest Groups: American and Canadian Jews Lobby for Israel* (New York: Greenwood Press, 1990).

Goldberg, J. J., *Jewish Power: Inside the American Jewish Establishment* (Reading, MA: Addison-Wesley, 1996).

Goldmann, Nahum, *The Autobiography of Nahum Goldmann. Sixty Years of Jewish Life* (New York: Holt, Rinehart and Winston, 1969), translated by Helen Sebba.

Goldstein, Kenneth, "Getting in the Door: Sampling and Completing Elite Interviews", *PS: Political Science & Politics* 35:4 (December 2002), 669-672.

Gombrich, Ernst H., *Jüdische Identität und jüdisches Schicksal. Eine Diskussionsbemerkung* (Wien: Passagen Verlag, 1997).

Goren, Arthur A., *New York Jews and the Quest for Community: The Kehillah Experiment, 1908-1922* (New York: Columbia University Press, 1970).

Goschler, Constantin, *Schuld und Schulden. Die Politik der Wiedergutmachung für NS-Verfolgte seit 1945* (Göttingen: Wallstein, 2005).

Grass, Günter, *Schreiben nach Auschwitz. Frankfurter Poetik-Vorlesung* (Frankfurt am Main: Luchterhand Literaturverlag, 1990).

Greenberg, Anna and Kenneth D. Wald, "Still Liberal After All These Years? The Contemporary Political Behavior of American Jewry", in: Maisel/Forman (eds.) (2001), 161-194.

Gross, Raphael, "Ignatz Bubis – Ein jüdisches Leben in Deutschland", in: Backhaus/Gross/Lenarz (eds.) (2007), 9-13.

Habermas, Jürgen, "Defusing the Past: A Politico-Cultural Tract", in: Hartman (ed.) (1986), 43-51.

Hagee, John, *In Defense of Israel* (Lake Mary, FL: FrontLine, 2007).

Hall, Peter A. and Rosemary C. R. Taylor, "Political Science and the Three Institutionalisms", *Political Studies* 44:5 (December 1996), 936-957.

Hall, Peter A., *Governing the Economy: The Politics of State Intervention in Britain and France* (New York: Oxford University Press, 1986).

Halperin, Samuel, "Zionist Counterpropaganda: The Case of the American Council for Judaism", *Southwestern Social Science Quarterly* 41 (March 1961), 450-463.

Hansen, Niels, "Moral als Staatsräson – Zur Bewertung der Rolle Konrad Adenauers heute", in: Brozik/Matschke (eds.) (2004), 76-88.

Hartman, Geoffrey H. (ed.), *Bitburg in Moral and Political Perspective* (Bloomington: Indiana University Press, 1986).

Hay, Colin, "Structure and Agency", in: Marsh/Stoker (eds.) (1995), 189-206.

Haynie, Kerry L. and Jane Junn (eds.), *New Race Politics in America. Understanding Minority and Immigrant Politics* (New York: Cambridge University Press, 2008).

Haynie, Kerry L., "Understanding the New Race Politics: Conclusions and Challenges", in: Haynie/Junn (eds.) (2008), 166-173.

Heclo, Hugh, "Issue Networks and the Executive Establishment: Government Growth in an Age of Improvement", in: King (ed.) (1978), 87-124.

Henry, Marilyn, *Confronting the Perpetrators: A History of the Claims Conference* (London: Vallentine Mitchell, 2007).

Henry, Marilyn, "Fifty Years of Holocaust Compensation", in: AJC (ed.), *American Jewish Year Book Vol. 102* (New York: AJC, 2002), 3-84.

Hilberg, Raul, "Bitburg as Symbol", in: Hartman (ed.) (1986), 15-26.

Hoepfner, Sebastian, *Die Stellung der jüdischen Organisationen im politischen System Frankreichs*, Dipl. thesis, University of Passau, 2006.

Hojnacki, Marie, "Organized Interests' Advocacy Behavior in Alliances", *Political Research Quarterly* 51:2 (June 1998), 437-459.

Hojnacki, Marie, "Interest Groups' Decisions to Join Alliances or Work Alone", *American Journal of Political Science* 41:1 (January 1997), 61-87.

Hula, Kevin W., *Lobbying Together. Interest Group Coalitions in Legislative Politics* (Washington, D.C.: Georgetown University Press, 1999).

Huntington, Samuel P., "The Erosion of American National Interests", *Foreign Affairs* 76:5 (September/October 1997), 28-49.

Huntington, Samuel P., *The Clash of Civilizations and the Remaking of World Order* (New York: Simon & Schuster, 1996).

Immergut, Ellen M., "The Theoretical Core of the New Institutionalism", *Politics & Society* 26:1 (March 1998), 5-34.

Jacobs, Paul, *Is Curly Jewish?* (New York: Atheneum, 1965).

Jaher, Fred Cople, "The Experience of Jews in the United States and Europe Illuminates American Exceptionalism", in: Berenbaum (ed.) (2008), 201-216.

Jelinek, Yeshayahu A. (ed.), *Zwischen Moral und Realpolitik. Deutsch-israelische Beziehungen 1945-1965* (Gerlingen: Bleicher Verlag, 1997).

Judt, Tony, *Postwar: A History of Europe Since 1945* (London: Heinemann, 2005).

Kaplan, Mordecai M., *Judaism as a Civilization: Toward a Reconstruction of American-Jewish Life* (New York: Macmillan, 1934).

Kenen, I. L., *All My Causes* (Washington, D.C.: Near East Research, 1985).

Key, V. O., *Politics, Parties & Pressure Groups* (New York: Crowell, 1964).

King, Anthony (ed.), *The New American Political System* (Washington, D.C.: American Enterprise Institute, 1978).

King, David C. and Miles Pomper, "The U.S. Congress and the Contingent Influence of Diaspora Lobbies: Lessons from U.S. Policy Toward Armenia and Azerbaijan", *Journal of Armenian Studies* 8:1 (Fall-Winter 2004), 72-98.

Kingdon, John W., *Agendas, Alternatives, and Public Policies* (New York: Longman, 2003).

Kissinger, Henry, *Diplomacy* (New York: Simon & Schuster, 1994).

Klehr, Harvey, *Communist Cadre. The Social Background of the American Communist Party Elite* (Stanford, CA: Hoover Institution Press, 1978).

Knobloch, Charlotte, Micha Brumlik and Gesa S. Ederberg (im Gespräch mit Wilfried Köpke), *Wenn nicht jetzt, wann dann? Zur Zukunft des deutschen Judentums* (Freiburg: Herder, 2007).

Kollman, Ken, *Outside Lobbying: Public Opinion and Interest Group Strategies* (Princeton: Princeton University Press, 1998).

Kolsky, Thomas A., *Jews Against Zionism. The American Council for Judaism, 1942-1948* (Philadelphia: Temple University Press, 1990).

Konitzer, Werner, "Alibi oder Zeuge? Ignatz Bubis und die fremdenfeindliche Gewalt im vereinigten Deutschland", in: Backhaus/Gross/Lenarz (eds.) (2007), 141-148.

Kotzkin, Michael C., "Local Community Relations Councils and Their National Body", in: Mittleman/Sarna/Licht (eds.) (2002), 67-101.

Krasner, Stephen D., *Defending the National Interest. Raw Materials Investments and U.S. Foreign Policy* (Princeton: Princeton University Press, 1978).

Kriesi, Hanspeter, Ruud Koopmans, Jan Willem Duyvendak and Marco Giugni, *New Social Movements in Western Europe. A Comparative Analysis* (Minneapolis: University of Minnesota Press, 1995).

Kriesi, Hanspeter, Ruud Koopmans, Jan Willem Duyvendak and Marco Giugni, "New social movements and political opportunities in Western Europe", *European Journal of Political Research* 22:2 (August 1992), 219-244.

Kristol, Irving, "The Liberal Tradition of American Jews", in: Lipset (ed.) (1990), 109-116.

Kulka, Otto Dov and Esriel Hildesheimer, "The Central Organisation of German Jews in the Third Reich and its Archives (On the Completion of the Reconstruction Project)", in: LBI (ed.), *LBI Year Book Vol. 34* (London: Secker & Warburg, 1989), 187-203.

Lamberti, Marjorie, "The Jewish Defence in Germany after the National-Socialist Seizure of Power", in: LBI (ed.), *LBI Year Book Vol. 42* (London: Secker & Warburg, 1997), 135-147.

Lamberti, Marjorie, *Jewish Activism in Imperial Germany. The Struggle for Civil Equality* (New Haven: Yale University Press, 1978).

Laufer, Peter, *Exodus to Berlin: The Return of the Jews to Germany* (Chicago: Ivan R. Dee, 2003).

Lazin, Fred A., "Jews in American Politics: Past and Present", *Society* 43:2 (January/February 2006), 62-67.

LBI (ed.), *Leo Baeck Institute Year Book*, 55 vols. (London: Secker & Warburg/ Berghahn Books, 1956-2010).

Leech, Beth L., "Asking Questions: Techniques for Semistructured Interviews", *PS: Political Science & Politics* 35:4 (December 2002), 665-668.

Levey, Geoffrey Brahm, "The Liberalism of American Jews – Has It Been Explained?", *British Journal of Political Science* 26:3 (July 1996), 369-401.

Levinger, Jacob S. and Michael Berenbaum, "Germany", in: Berenbaum/Skolnik (eds.) (2007), vol. 7, 535-536.

Licht, Jonathan and Ruth Beloff, "Spiegel, Paul", in: Berenbaum/Skolnik (eds.) (2007), vol. 19, 106.

Lifton, Robert Jay, *The Nazi Doctors: Medical Killing and the Psychology of Genocide* (New York: Basic Books, 2000).

Lipset, Seymour Martin (ed.), *American Pluralism and the Jewish Community* (New Brunswick, NJ: Transaction Publishers, 1990).

Lipson, Charles, "American Support for Israel: History, Sources, Limits", in: Sheffer (ed.) (1997), 128-146.

Lösche, Peter and Hans Dietrich von Loeffelholz (eds.), *Länderbericht USA. Geschichte, Politik, Wirtschaft, Gesellschaft, Kultur* (Bonn: Bundeszentrale für politische Bildung, 2004).

Lösche, Peter, "Verbände, Gewerkschaften und das System der Arbeitsbeziehungen", in: Lösche/Loeffelholz (eds.) (2004), 353-389.

Maisel, L. Sandy and Ira N. Forman (eds.), *Jews in American Politics* (Lanham, MD: Rowman & Littlefield Publishers, 2001).

Malbin, Michael J., "Jewish PACs: A New Force in Jewish Political Action", in: Elazar (ed.) (1988), 51-55.

Marsh, David and Gerry Stoker (eds.), *Theory and Methods in Political Science* (Basingstoke: Macmillan, 1995).

Maslow, Will, "Jewish Political Power: An Assessment", *American Jewish Historical Quarterly* 66:2 (December 1976), 349-362.

Mayhew, David R., *Divided We Govern. Party Control, Lawmaking, and Investigations, 1946-2002* (New Haven: Yale University Press, 2005).

Mearsheimer, John J. and Stephen M. Walt, "Is It Love or The Lobby? Explaining America's Special Relationship with Israel", *Security Studies* 18:1 (January-March 2009), 58-78.

Mearsheimer, John J. and Stephen M. Walt, *The Israel Lobby and U.S. Foreign Policy* (New York: Farrar, Straus and Giroux, 2007).

Medding, Peter Y. (ed.), *Values, Interests and Identity. Jews and Politics in a Changing World* (New York: Oxford University Press, 1995).

Medding, Peter Y., "Preface", in: Medding (ed.) (1995), vii-viii.

Medding, Peter Y., "The New Jewish Politics in America", in: Wistrich (ed.) (1995), 86-114.

Mendelsohn, Ezra, *On Modern Jewish Politics* (New York: Oxford University Press, 1993).

Meyer, David S. and Debra C. Minkoff, "Conceptualizing Political Opportunity", *Social Forces* 82:4 (June 2004), 1457-1492.

Miller, Fred, "Aristotle's Political Theory", *Stanford Encyclopedia of Philosophy*, http://plato.stanford.edu/entries/aristotle-politics/#PolView, accessed January 22, 2010.

Mills, C. Wright, *The Power Elite* (New York: Oxford University Press, 1956).

Mishkinsky, Moshe, "Bund", in: Berenbaum/Skolnik (eds.) (2007), vol. 4, 278-284.

Mittleman, Alan, Jonathan D. Sarna and Robert Licht (eds.), *Jewish Polity and American Civil Society. Communal Agencies and Religious Movements in the American Public Sphere* (Lanham, MD: Rowman & Littlefield Publishers, 2002).

Mokken, R. J. and F. N. Stokman, "Power and Influence as Political Phenomena", in: Barry (ed.) (1976), 33-54.

Morris, Leslie and Jack Zipes (eds.), *Unlikely History: The Changing German-Jewish Symbiosis, 1945-2000* (New York: Palgrave, 2002).

Morse, Arthur D., *While Six Million Died. A Chronicle of American Apathy* (Woodstock, NY: The Overlook Press, 1983).

Museum Judengasse, *Stationen des Vergessens. Der Börneplatz-Konflikt* (Frankfurt am Main: Museum Judengasse, 1992).

Nachama, Andreas and Julius H. Schoeps (eds.), *Aufbau nach dem Untergang. Deutsch-jüdische Geschichte nach 1945* (Berlin: Argon Verlag, 1992).

Nachama, Andreas, "Der Mann in der Fasanenstraße", in: Nachama/Schoeps (eds.) (1992), 27-52.

Newhouse, John, "Diplomacy, Inc. The Influence of Lobbies on U.S. Foreign Policy", *Foreign Affairs* 88:3 (May/June 2009), 73-92.

Nohlen, Dieter and Rainer-Olaf Schulze (eds.), *Lexikon der Politikwissenschaft: Theorien, Methoden, Begriffe*, 2 vols. (München: Verlag C.H. Beck, 2005).

Nordlinger, Eric A., *On the Autonomy of the Democratic State* (Cambridge, MA: Harvard University Press, 1981).

Novick, Peter, *The Holocaust in American Life* (New York: Mariner Books, 2000).

Olson, Mancur, *The Logic of Collective Action: Public Goods and the Theory of Groups* (Cambridge, MA: Harvard University Press, 1965).

Organski, A.F.K., *The $36 Billion Bargain: Strategy and Politics in U.S. Assistance to Israel* (New York: Columbia University Press, 1990).

Osmańczyk, Edmund Jan, *The Encyclopedia of the United Nations and International Relations* (London: Taylor & Francis, 1990).

Peck, Jeffrey M., *Being Jewish in the New Germany* (New Brunswick, NJ: Rutgers University Press, 2006).

Peled, Elad, "Should States Have a Legal Right to Reputation? Applying the Rationales of Defamation Law to the International Arena", *Brooklyn International Journal of Law* 35:1 (2010), 107-153.

Pieper, Ernst (ed.), *Gibt es wirklich eine Holocaust-Industrie? Zur Auseinandersetzung um Norman Finkelstein* (Zürich: Pendo, 2001).

Polsby, Nelson W., "The Political System", in: Schuck/Wilson (eds.) (2008), 3-26.

Presner, Todd Samuel, *Muscular Judaism: the Jewish body and the politics of regeneration* (New York: Routledge, 2007).

Prinzing, Marlis, *Jüdisches Vermächtnis: Portrait, Gespräche, Perspektiven* (Lahr: Kaufmann, 2010).

Raffel, Martin J., "History of Israel Advocacy", in: Mittleman/Sarna/Licht (eds.) (2002), 103-179.

Rapaport, Lynn, *Jews in Germany after the Holocaust. Memory, identity, and Jewish-German relations* (Cambridge: Cambridge University Press, 1997).

Reinharz, Jehuda, "Advocacy and History: The Case of the Centralverein and the Zionists", in: LBI (ed.), *LBI Year Book Vol. 33* (London: Secker & Warburg, 1988), 113-122.

Reinharz, Jehuda, "*Deutschtum* and *Judentum* in the Ideology of the Centralverein Deutscher Staatsbürger jüdischen Glaubens 1893-1914", *Jewish Social Studies* 36:1 (January 1974), 19-39.

Rheins, Carl J., "The Verband nationaldeutscher Juden 1921-1933", in: LBI (ed.), *LBI Year Book Vol. 25* (London: Secker & Warburg, 1980), 243-268.

Rich, Wilbur C. (ed.), *The Politics of Minority Coalitions. Race, Ethnicity, and Shared Uncertainties* (Westport, CT: Praeger, 1996).

Richardson, Jeremy J. (ed.), *Pressure Groups* (New York: Oxford University Press, 1993).

Riker, William H., "Some Ambiguities in the Notion of Power", *American Political Science Review* 58:2 (June 1964), 341-349.

Ro'i, Yaakov, "Jackson-Vanik Amendment", *The YIVO Encyclopedia of Jews in Eastern Europe*, http://www.yivoencyclopedia.org/article.aspx/Jackson-Vanik_Amendment, accessed April 8, 2011.

Romberg, Otto R. and Susanne Urban-Fahr (eds.), *Juden in Deutschland nach 1945* (Bonn: Bundeszentrale für politische Bildung, 2000).

Roseman, Mark (ed.), *Generations in Conflict. Youth revolt and generation formation in Germany 1770-1968* (Cambridge: Cambridge University Press, 1995).

Rosenberg, Leibl, "Die ersten fünfzig Jahre. Ein halbes Jahrhundert Zentralrat der Juden in Deutschland", *Universitas* 55:651 (September 2000), 828-836.

Rubin, Lawrence, "American Israel Public Affairs Committee (AIPAC)", in: Berenbaum/Skolnik (eds.) (2007), vol. 2, 50-52.

Rubin, Lawrence, "The Emerging Jewish Public-Affairs Culture", in: Lipset (ed.) (1990), 193-202.

Safran, William (ed.), *The Secular and the Sacred: Nation, Religion, and Politics* (London: Frank Cass, 2003).

Sagi, Nana, *Wiedergutmachung für Israel. Die deutschen Zahlungen und Leistungen* (Stuttgart: Seewald Verlag, 1981).

Said, Abdul Aziz (ed.), *Ethnicity and U.S. Foreign Policy* (New York: Praeger Publishers, 1981).

Salisbury, Robert H., John P. Heinz, Edward O. Laumann and Robert L. Nelson, "Who Works with Whom? Interest Group Alliances and Opposition", *American Political Science Review* 81:4 (December 1987), 1217-1234.

Sanua, Marianne R., *Let Us Prove Strong. The American Jewish Committee, 1945-2006* (Waltham, MA: Brandeis University Press, 2007).

Sarna, Jonathan D., *American Judaism. A History* (New Haven: Yale University Press, 2004).

Sarrazin, Thilo, *Deutschland schafft sich ab* (München: Deutsche Verlags-Anstalt, 2010).

Schattschneider, E. E., *The Semisovereign People: A Realist's View of Democracy in America* (New York: Holt, Rinehart and Winston, 1960).

Schier, Steven E., *By Invitation Only: The Rise of Exclusive Politics in the United States* (Pittsburgh: University of Pittsburgh Press, 2000).

Schleicher, Michael, *Charlotte Knobloch: Ein Portrait* (München: MünchenVerlag, 2009).

Schlesinger, Arthur M., *The Disuniting of America: Reflections on a Multicultural Society* (New York: Norton, 1992).

Schlesinger, Arthur M., "America: Experiment or Destiny?", *American Historical Review* 82:3 (June 1977), 505-522.

Schmidt, Helmut and Fritz Stern, *Unser Jahrhundert. Ein Gespräch* (München: Verlag C.H. Beck, 2010).

Schoeps, Julius H., "Juden", in: Weidenfeld/Korte (eds.) (1999), 466-475.

Schubarth, Wilfried and Richard Stöss (eds.), *Rechtsextremismus in der Bundesrepublik Deutschland. Eine Bilanz* (Bonn: Bundeszentrale für politische Bildung, 2000).

Schuck, Peter H. and James Q. Wilson (eds.), *Understanding America. The Anatomy of An Exceptional Nation* (New York: PublicAffairs, 2008).

Schulze, Rainer-Olaf, "Politik/Politikbegriffe", in: Nohlen/Schulze (eds.) (2005), 697-698.

Schütz, Klaus, *Heinz Galinski (1912-1992). Ein Berliner unter dem Davidsschild* (Teetz: Hentrich & Hentrich, 2004).

Schwarz, Kyrill-Alexander, "Die Verteilung der Finanzmittel aus dem zwischen der Bundesrepublik Deutschland und dem Zentralrat der Juden geschlossenen Staatsvertrag", *Religion – Staat – Gesellschaft* 6:1-2 (2005), 123-164.

Sebaldt, Martin, *Transformation der Verbändedemokratie. Die Modernisierung des Systems organisierter Interessen in den USA* (Wiesbaden: Westdeutscher Verlag, 2001).

Sewell, William H., "A Theory of Structure: Duality, Agency, and Transformation", *American Journal of Sociology* 98:1 (July 1992), 1-29.

Shain, Yossi, *Kinship and Diasporas in International Affairs* (Ann Arbor: University of Michigan Press, 2007).

Shapiro, Edward, "Right Turn? Jews and the American Conservative Movement", in: Maisel/Forman (eds.) (2001), 195-212.

Sheffer, Gabriel, *Diaspora Politics: At Home Abroad* (New York: Cambridge University Press, 2003).

Sheffer, Gabriel (ed.), *U.S.-Israeli Relations at the Crossroads* (London: Frank Cass, 1997).

Shell, Kurt L., "Das politische System", in: Lösche/Loeffelholz (eds.) (2004), 202-245.

Sheskin, Ira M. and Arnold Dashefsky, "Jewish Population in the United States, 2007", in: AJC (ed.), *American Jewish Year Book Vol. 107* (New York: AJC, 2007), 133-205.

Silbermann, Alphons and Herbert Sallen, "Jews in Germany today", *Society* 32:4 (May/June 1995), 53-64.

Simmons, Erica, "Hadassah, The Women's Zionist Organization of America", in: Berenbaum/Skolnik (eds.) (2007), vol. 8, 185-188.

Simon, Herbert A., "Notes on the Observation and Measurement of Power", in: Bell/Edwards/Wagner (eds.) (1969), 69-78.

Skocpol, Theda, *Diminished Democracy: From Membership to Management in American Civic Life* (Norman, OK: University of Oklahoma Press, 2003).

Skocpol, Theda, Marshall Ganz and Ziad Munson, "A Nation of Organizers: The Institutional Origins of Civic Voluntarism in the United States", *American Political Science Review* 94:3 (September 2000), 527-546.

Slezkine, Yuri, *The Jewish Century* (Princeton: Princeton University Press, 2004).

Smidt, Corwin, Lyman Kellstedt, John Green and James Guth, "Religion and Politics in the United States", in: Safran (ed.) (2003), 32-53.

Smith, Grant F., *Foreign Agents: The American Israel Public Affairs Committee From the 1963 Fulbright Hearings to the 2005 Espionage Scandal* (Washington, D.C.: Institute for Research: Middle Eastern Policy, 2007).

Smith, Tony, *Foreign Attachments. The Power of Ethnic Groups in the Making of American Foreign Policy* (Cambridge, MA: Harvard University Press, 2000).

Sollors, Werner, *Theories of Ethnicity: A Classical Reader* (New York: New York University Press, 1996).

Sonenshein, Raphael J., *Politics in Black and White. Race and Power in Los Angeles* (Princeton: Princeton University Press, 1993).

Spiegel, Paul, *Wieder zuhause? Erinnerungen* (Berlin: Ullstein, 2001).

Spiegel, Steven L., "Ethnic Politics and the Formulation of U.S. Policy Toward the Arab-Israeli Dispute", in: Ahrari (ed.) (1987), 23-44.

Stein, Lana, "American Jews and Their Liberal Political Behavior", in: Rich (ed.) (1996), 193-200.

Steinmo, Sven, Kathleen Thelen and Frank Longstreth (eds.), *Structuring Politics. Historical Institutionalism in Comparative Analysis* (New York: Cambridge University Press, 1992).

Stern, Frank, "Antisemitismus und Philosemitismus in der politischen Kultur der entstehenden Bundesrepublik Deutschland", in: Nachama/Schoeps (eds.) (1992), 150-163.

Stern, Samuel Miklos, "Germany", in: Berenbaum/Skolnik (eds.) (2007), vol. 7, 524-529.

Stern, Susan (ed.), *Speaking Out: Jewish Voices from United Germany* (Chicago: Edition Q, 1995).

Suchy, Barbara, "The Verein zur Abwehr des Antisemitismus (II). From the First World War to its Dissolution in 1933", in: LBI (ed.), *LBI Year Book Vol. 30* (London: Secker & Warburg, 1985), 67-103.

Suchy, Barbara, "The Verein zur Abwehr des Antisemitismus (I). From Its Beginnings to the First World War", in: LBI (ed.), *LBI Year Book Vol. 28* (London: Secker & Warburg, 1983), 205-239.

Surmann, Rolf (ed.), *Das Finkelstein-Alibi. "Holocaust-Industrie" und Tätergesellschaft* (Köln: PapyRossa Verlag, 2001).

Svonkin, Stuart, "American Jewish Congress", *Jewish Women: A Comprehensive Historical Encyclopedia*, http://jwa.org/encyclopedia/article/american-jewish-congress, accessed May 20, 2009.

Tivnan, Edward, *The Lobby: Jewish Political Power and American Foreign Policy* (New York: Simon & Schuster, 1987).

Tocqueville, Alexis de, *Democracy in America* [1835/1840], eds. Harvey C. Mansfield and Delba Winthorp (Chicago: University of Chicago Press, 2000).

Trice, Robert H., "Domestic Interest Groups and a Behavioral Analysis", in: Said (ed.) (1981), 121-141.

Truman, David, *The Governmental Process. Political Interests and Public Opinion* (Westport, CT: Greenwood Press, 1981).

United States Code Annotated, *Title 26. Internal Revenue Code §§ 501 to 640* (St. Paul, MN: West Group, 2002).

Vitzthum, Wolfgang Graf (ed.), *Völkerrecht* (Berlin: de Gruyter, 2007).

Walker, Jack L. (ed.), *Mobilizing Interest Groups in America: Patrons, Professions, and Social Movements* (Ann Arbor: University of Michigan Press, 1991).

Watanabe, Paul Y., *Ethnic Groups, Congress, and American Foreign Policy: The Politics of the Turkish Arms Embargo* (Westport, CT: Greenwood Press, 1984).

Watts, Jerry Gafio, "Blacks and Coalition Politics: A Theoretical Reconceptualization", in: Rich (ed.) (1996), 35-51.

Waxman, Chaim I., "The Centrality of Israel in American Jewish Life: A Sociological Analysis", *Judaism* 25:2 (Spring 1976), 175-187.

Weidenfeld, Werner and Karl-Rudolf Korte (eds.), *Handbuch zur deutschen Einheit 1949 – 1989 – 1999* (Bonn: Bundeszentrale für politische Bildung, 1999).

Wertheimer, Jack, "Jewish Organizational Life in the United States Since 1945", in: AJC (ed.), *American Jewish Year Book Vol. 95* (New York: AJC, 1995), 3-98.

Wertheimer, Jack, *A People Divided. Judaism in Contemporary America* (New York: Basic Books, 1993).

Wertheimer, Jack, "Recent Trends in American Judaism", in: AJC (ed.), *American Jewish Year Book Vol. 89* (New York: AJC, 1989), 63-162.

Wertheimer, Jack, *Unwelcome Strangers: East European Jews in Imperial Germany* (New York: Oxford University Press, 1987).

Whitfield, Stephen J., "Famished for Justice. The Jew as Radical", in: Maisel/ Forman (eds.) (2001), 213-230.
Wiedmer, Caroline, *The Claims of Memory. Representations of the Holocaust in Contemporary Germany and France* (Ithaca: Cornell University Press, 1999).
Wilson, Graham K., "American Interest Groups", in: Richardson (ed.) (1993), 131-144.
Wilson, James Q., *Political Organizations* (New York: Basic Books, 1973).
Windmueller, Steven, ""Defenders": National Jewish Community Relations Agencies", in: Mittleman/Sarna/Licht (eds.) (2002), 13-66.
Winkler, Heinrich August, *Der lange Weg nach Westen II: Deutsche Geschichte 1933-1990* (Bonn: Bundeszentrale für politische Bildung, 2004).
Wisse, Ruth R., *Jews and Power* (New York: Schocken Books, 2007).
Wisse, Ruth R., *The Modern Jewish Canon. A Journey Through Language and Culture* (New York: The Free Press, 2000).
Wistrich, Robert S. (ed.), *Terms of Survival. The Jewish World Since 1945* (London: Routledge, 1995).
Wolffsohn, Michael, *Israel. Geschichte, Politik, Gesellschaft, Wirtschaft* (Wiesbaden: VS Verlag, 2007).
Wolffsohn, Michael, *Spanien, Deutschland und die "Jüdische Weltmacht". Über Moral, Realpolitik und Vergangenheitsbewältigung* (München: C. Bertelsmann Verlag, 1991).
Wood, Elisabeth Jean, "Field Research", in: Boix/Stokes (eds.) (2007), 123-146.
Wyman, David S., *The Abandonment of the Jews: America and the Holocaust, 1941-1945* (New York: Pantheon Books, 1984).
Yahil, Chaim, "Germany", in: Berenbaum/Skolnik (eds.) (2007), vol. 7, 537-539.
Yahil, Chaim, "Van Dam, Hendrik George", in: Berenbaum/Skolnik (eds.) (2007), vol. 20, 472-473.
Zuckermann, Moshe, "Finkelstein und die Instrumentalisierung der Vergangenheit. Reflexionen aus israelischer Sicht", in: Surmann (ed.) (2001), 72-85.
Zweig, Ronald W., *German Reparations and the Jewish World: A History of the Claims Conference* (London: Frank Cass, 2001).
Zysman, John, *Governments, Markets, and Growth: Financial Systems and the Politics of Industrial Change* (Ithaca: Cornell University Press, 1983).